Pat Holtzman

CIVIL LITIGATION FOR THE PARALEGAL

OTHER TITLES IN THE DELMAR PARALEGAL SERIES:

Jonathan Lynton, Donna Masinter, Terri Mick Lyndall,
Law Office Management for Paralegals, 1992.

Ransford C. Pyle, *Foundations of Law for Paralegals: Cases,
Commentary, and Ethics*, 1992.

Daniel Hall, *Criminal Law and Procedure*, 1992.

CIVIL LITIGATION FOR THE PARALEGAL

Peggy N. Kerley
Paul A. Sukys
Joanne Banker Hames

LAWYERS COOPERATIVE
PUBLISHING

DELMAR
PUBLISHERS INC.

NOTICE TO THE READER

Cover design by John Orozco.
Cover photo by Mark Gallitelli.
Sections 1 & 2 photos by Susan Bliss.

Delmar Staff:

Senior Editor: Mary McGarry
Administrative Editor: Jay Whitney
Editing Supervisor: Marlene McHugh Pratt
Production Supervisor: Larry Main
Design Coordinator: Karen Kunz Kemp

For more information address Delmar Publishers Inc.
3 Columbia Circle, Box 15-015
Albany, New York 12212-5015

10 9 8 7 6 5 4 3

Library of Congress Cataloging-in-Publication Data

Kerley, Peggy N.
   Civil litigation for the paralegal/by Peggy N. Kerley, Paul A.
Sukys, Joanne Banker Hames.
     p. cm.—(Delmar paralegal series)
   Includes index.
   ISBN 0-8273-4771-5 (textbook)
   1. Civil procedure—United States. 2. Legal assistants—United
States—Handbooks, manuals, etc. I. Sukys, Paul A.. II. Hames,
Joanne Banker. III. Title. IV. Series.
KF8841.K47 1992
347.73'5—dc20
[347.3075]   91-21469
                                                          CIP

Contents

DELMAR PUBLISHERS INC.

 AND

LAWYERS COOPERATIVE PUBLISHING

ARE PLEASED TO ANNOUNCE THEIR PARTNERSHIP
TO CO-PUBLISH COLLEGE TEXTBOOKS FOR
PARALEGAL EDUCATION.

DELMAR, WITH OFFICES AT ALBANY, NEW YORK, IS A PROFESSIONAL EDUCATION PUBLISHER. DELMAR PUBLISHES QUALITY EDUCATIONAL TEXTBOOKS TO PREPARE AND SUPPORT INDIVIDUALS FOR LIFE SKILLS AND SPECIFIC OCCUPATIONS.

LAWYERS COOPERATIVE PUBLISHING (LCP), WITH OFFICES AT ROCHESTER, NEW YORK, HAS BEEN THE LEADING PUBLISHER OF ANALYTICAL LEGAL INFORMATION FOR OVER 100 YEARS. IT IS THE PUBLISHER OF SUCH REKNOWNED LEGAL ENCYCLOPEDIAS AS **AMERICAN LAW REPORTS, AMERICAN JURISPRUDENCE, UNITED STATES CODE SERVICE, LAWYERS EDITION,** AS WELL AS OTHER MATERIAL, AND FEDERAL- AND STATE-SPECIFIC PUBLICATIONS. THESE PUBLICATIONS HAVE BEEN DESIGNED TO WORK TOGETHER IN THE DAY-TO-DAY PRACTICE OF LAW AS AN INTEGRATED SYSTEM IN WHAT IS CALLED THE "TOTAL CLIENT-SERVICE LIBRARY®" (TCSL®). EACH LCP PUBLICATION IS COMPLETE WITHIN ITSELF AS TO SUBJECT COVERAGE, YET ALL HAVE COMMON FEATURES AND EXTENSIVE CROSS-REFERENCING TO PROVIDE LINKAGE FOR HIGHLY EFFICIENT LEGAL RESEARCH INTO VIRTUALLY ANY MATTER AN ATTORNEY MIGHT BE CALLED UPON TO HANDLE.

INFORMATION IN ALL PUBLICATIONS IS CAREFULLY AND CONSTANTLY MONITORED TO KEEP PACE WITH AND REFLECT EVENTS IN THE LAW AND IN SOCIETY. UPDATING AND SUPPLEMENTAL INFORMATION IS TIMELY AND PROVIDED CONVENIENTLY.

FOR FURTHER REFERENCE, SEE GENERALLY:

AMERICAN JURISPRUDENCE 2D: AN ENCYCLOPEDIC TEXT COVERAGE OF THE COMPLETE BODY OF STATE AND FEDERAL LAW.

AM JUR LEGAL FORMS 2D: A COMPILATION OF BUSINESS AND LEGAL FORMS DEALING WITH A VARIETY OF SUBJECT MATTERS.

AM JUR PLEADING AND PRACTICE FORMS, REV.: MODEL PRACTICE FORMS FOR EVERY STAGE OF A LEGAL PROCEEDING.

AM JUR PROOF OF FACTS: A SERIES OF ARTICLES THAT GUIDE THE READER IN DETERMINING WHICH FACTS ARE ESSENTIAL TO A CASE AND HOW TO PROVE THEM.

AM JUR TRIALS: A SERIES OF ARTICLES DISCUSSING EVERY ASPECT OF PARTICULAR SETTLEMENTS AND TRIALS WRITTEN BY 180 CONSULTING SPECIALISTS.

UNITED STATES CODE SERVICE: A COMPLETE AND AUTHORITATIVE ANNOTATED FEDERAL CODE THAT FOLLOWS THE EXACT LANGUAGE OF THE STATUTES AT LARGE AND DIRECTS YOU TO THE COURT AND AGENCY DECISIONS CONSTRUING EACH PROVISION.

ALR AND ALR FEDERAL: SERIES OF ANNOTATIONS PROVIDING IN-DEPTH ANALYSES OF ALL THE CASE LAW ON PARTICULAR LEGAL ISSUES.

U.S. SUPREME COURT REPORTS, L ED 2D: EVERY REPORTED U.S. SUPREME COURT DECISION PLUS IN-DEPTH DISCUSSIONS OF LEADING ISSUES.

FEDERAL PROCEDURE, L ED: A COMPREHENSIVE, A–Z TREATISE ON FEDERAL PROCEDURE—CIVIL, CRIMINAL, AND ADMINISTRATIVE.

FEDERAL PROCEDURAL FORMS, L ED: STEP-BY-STEP GUIDANCE FOR DRAFTING FORMS FOR FEDERAL COURT OR FEDERAL AGENCY PROCEEDINGS.

BANKRUPTCY SERVICE, L ED: A COMPLETE SERVICE FOR PRACTICE UNDER THE CURRENT BANKRUPTCY REFORM ACT.

IMMIGRATION LAW SERVICE: A PRACTICE-ORIENTED, ANALYTIC TEXT TREATMENT OF SUBSTANTIVE AND PROCEDURAL IMMIGRATION LAW, PLUS UNIQUE "HOW TO" CHAPTERS ON REPRESENTING PARTICULAR CLIENTS.

AMERICAN LAW OF PRODUCTS LIABILITY 3D: A COMPREHENSIVE PRACTICE SET, WHICH INCLUDES ANALYSIS OF GOVERNING PRINCIPLES AND ALL STATE AND FEDERAL STATUTES, RELEVANT CASELAW, FORMS, AND CHECKLISTS.

SOCIAL SECURITY LAW AND PRACTICE: ANALYSIS, FORMS, AND SOURCE MATERIAL RELATING TO THE FIELD OF SOCIAL SECURITY.

FOREWORD

Litigation is complex and becoming more complex with the addition of such aids as computerized research and computerized document management. The role of the paralegal in litigation is a unique one that provides a service to the legal environment, which differs from services provided by attorneys and law clerks. The role is one of support to the attorney and must be clearly understood for paralegals to be effectively utilized by the attorney. To enable a clear understanding of that role, this book provides an overview of civil litigation with an emphasis on the responsibilities of the paralegal in a litigation practice.

While many textbooks attempt to clarify this role, this book succeeds by providing excellent practical information in the form of checklists, charts, practice tips, etc. It includes the technical information that is needed to understand how to accomplish a task, as well as why that task must be accomplished. The paralegal student will not only be given knowledge of the Federal Rules of Civil Procedure but will also be given an understanding of how to apply these rules during a case and why that application is important.

The computer has revolutionized the practice of law, particularly in the area of litigation. A unique concept of this text is that it provides a computerized application for each chapter. For example, in the chapter that discusses the drafting of pleadings, document generators are covered. This software enables the paralegal to quickly and accurately generate lengthy or repetitive documents. Other tasks that are performed manually are also explored with regard to how they might be handled more effectively and easily by computer, thus permitting a paralegal to more efficiently utilize his or her time and bill more hours. The end result is an increase in productivity that has a positive impact on the paralegal's compensation.

This practical textbook is designed to serve as a reference manual in the litigation section of a law firm or corporation once the student has completed the course, making the book even more valuable. The impetus for this style of material comes from the practical experience and educational background of the authors. The authors bring extensive litigation practice experience from the two attorneys' perspectives. Both have practiced as well as taught in paralegal programs. The paralegal author has a wealth of knowledge as well that is derived from over thirty years of legal experience combined with teaching experience in a variety of paralegal programs.

Susan K. Stoner, Dean
Southeastern Paralegal Institute
(Approved by the American Bar Association)

PREFACE

The paralegal profession is one of the fastest growing professions in the United States today. In fact, the United States Department of Labor as recently as 1991 reported that the need for paralegals will skyrocket within the next ten years. One reason for the phenomenal growth of this relatively young profession is the unique role that the paralegal plays within the legal system. The paralegal bridges the gap between the attorney and the legal secretary by bringing to the law office a body of knowledge and a set of skills developed specifically for the day-to-day practical realities of the practice of law.

The paralegal educator is keenly aware of the need to skillfully blend the principles of the law with its practical application. Nowhere in the law is that skillful blend of theory and practice more imperative than in the study of litigation. The litigation paralegal meets new and different challenges each day on the job. These daily challenges mean that, from the very first hour on the job, the paralegal must be prepared to understand not only *what* must be done in a specific situation but also *why* it must be done. The paralegal must also know the most efficient, the most effective, and the most economical way to accomplish the task at hand. *Civil Litigation for the Paralegal* was planned and written with these specific goals in mind.

To successfully acquaint the fledgling paralegal student with this intricate blend of legal theory and practical legal skills, we have remained attuned to the fact that, for many students, civil litigation will be their first legal studies course. Consequently, we have been careful to present the study of litigation in a straightforward, yet lively fashion that should not only inform but also challenge both the student and the instructor. To provide this challenge we began each chapter with a hypothetical case that is fully developed as the chapter unfolds. Our objective in doing this was to show students that the law deals not only with books and documents but also with people—usually people in trouble, often people who have been hurt or unfairly treated and who have turned to the law and to them for help. It is our belief that this approach will give a realistic and energetic flavor to the study of litigation.

THE PLAN BEHIND CIVIL LITIGATION FOR THE PARALEGAL

For clarity and ease of understanding, we have chosen to use chronological order throughout the test. The book has been divided into four sections representing the four major stages in the litigation process. In Section 1 we introduce the student to the role of the paralegal in the litigation process. The two chapters in this section also provide an overview of the court system and the litigation process, along with a discussion of the concepts of jurisdiction and venue.

In Section 2 we begin the study of litigation in earnest by walking the student through the opening stages of a lawsuit. Naturally, this means concentrating on the preliminary legal and practical concerns that must be taken into consideration at the onset of a lawsuit. Consequently, these early chapters focus on such things as interviewing and investigation skills, the writing and filing of initial and responsive pleadings, and an understanding of motion practice. In order to accomplish our objective of making the text a practical guide for students, we have explained the requirements for pleadings and motions found in the Federal Rules of Civil Procedure and have included many examples and sample documents. We have also provided detailed explanations and guidelines for the drafting of various legal documents.

Following our chronological plan, Section 3 explores the discovery process. Since the paralegal has an extensive role in discovery, we have devoted one of the six chapters in this section to an overview of the process; the remaining five chapters discuss specific discovery techniques. Separate chapters cover depositions, interrogatories, requests for physical and mental examinations, requests for the production of documents, and requests for admissions. Again in keeping with our objective of providing students with a practical guide, we have explained in great detail the day-to-day role of the paralegal during each stage of the discovery process. These chapters also combine theory with practice, covering the discovery rules in the Federal Rules of Civil Procedure. We have also included an extensive array of sample documents, including requests for physical and mental examinations, requests for the production of documents, and requests for admissions. As a supplement to Section 3, Appendix A provides a sample deposition based on the case scenario that serves as the basis for the examples and samples in chapter 9.

Section 4 provides the student with an in-depth view of the final stages in the litigation process. We have devoted one chapter to pretrial settlements and dismissals, one to the trial itself, and one to post-trial procedures. Again in keeping with our goal of making *Civil Litigation for the Paralegal* a practical guide, we have provided students with a wide variety of suggestions for making the trial process run as smoothly as possible. Some of these tips include how to prepare a trial notebook, how to arrange for accommodations, how to contact court personnel, how to prepare a jury profile, how to use shadow juries, and how to prepare a trial box, among many others. We have also been careful to include a wide variety of practical illustrations and sample documents, including releases and dismissals, a settlement summary, a settlement letter, a detailed settlement agreement, a notice of appeal, and a motion for enlargement of time, among others. Sample letters, charts, and diagrams are also included, as are appropriate references to the Federal Rules of Civil Procedure and the Federal Rules of Appellate Procedure. As a supplement to Section 4, Appendix C provides a detailed look at the actual steps in the process of a civil trial.

TEACHING AND LEARNING RESOURCES

The practical nature of *Civil Litigation for the Paralegal* makes it an ideal text for use beyond the classroom. Because of its many forms, letters, memos, charts, and diagrams, it can easily serve as a reference manual for the paralegal in the litigation section of a law firm. Nevertheless, the primary objective of the book is to serve as a textbook for a basic civil litigation course for paralegal students. Consequently, we have included several important features to enhance this objective and to make the book the best in its market. As mentioned previously, one feature is the **commentaries** at the beginning of the chapters. The case commentaries demonstrate the practical application of the matters contained within the chapters and give a realistic color to the study of litigation.

In addition, each chapter begins with an **outline** that points out the major topics to be covered in the chapter. We have provided these topical outlines to give both the students and the instructor an overview of the chapter's content. In this way, they are armed with a sense of direction and an understanding of what we have promised to deliver in each chapter. In order to provide students with a sense of continuity both within and between chapters, the main topics within each chapter and the summaries at the end of each chapter use the same numbering system as the outline. Similarly, each chapter begins with a set of **learning objectives** and ends with a set of **questions for review and discussion**. The list of objectives parallels the list of final questions. Again, the goal here is to provide students with a sense of direction and continuity as well as with an understanding of the material itself.

Every attorney, paralegal, and paralegal instructor realizes the law has its own, highly specialized language. For this reason we have made a great effort to emphasize the importance of legal terminology and to provide accurate and clearly written definitions for these terms. All important **legal terms** appear in **boldface** within each chapter. These terms and their definitions are also compiled in a running glossary and a full glossary at the end of the book. In addition, within each chapter, whenever possible, we have included synonyms for terms that may differ from state to state. Moreover, at the end of each chapter, all bold-faced terms appearing in that chapter are listed under the heading **key terms**.

The review questions and the key terms at the end of each chapter are supplemented by two very practical exercises. These are the **activities** exercises and the **chapter project**. The activities exercises require students to investigate specific state statutes and apply them to the topics covered in the chapter. This approach provides the instructor with an opportunity to incorporate local and state rules into the course material. The chapter project offers a chance for the student to use a major paralegal task outlined in the chapter. Chapter projects include such activities as writing letters and memos, drafting pleadings, motions, and affidavits, and preparing discovery devices. For example, in the chapter project at the end of chapter 5, the student is required to draft a copy of a complaint, and at the end of chapter 10, the student must prepare a set of interrogatories.

In an effort to make *Civil Litigation for the Paralegal* as up to date as possible, we have also included as much information on computerized work as possible. A key part of this effort has been **the computerized law firm** feature, which appears within each chapter in the text. The computerized law firm shows how the paralegal can use the law firm's computer system to simplify one or more of the practical skills discussed within each chapter. For example, in chapter 6, the computerized law firm feature introduces the paralegal to the usefulness of word processing in the drafting of an amended answer. Similarly, in chapter 15, the paralegal is acquainted with the use of the computer in legal research. To supplement the computerized law firm, Appendix B includes an extensive list of computer software and services for the paralegal.

STATE-SPECIFIC POCKET-PART SUPPLEMENTS

One of the features that makes *Civil Litigation for the Paralegal* the most innovative and unique textbook of its kind on the market today is the availability of **state-specific pocket-part supplements**. For uniformity and consistency, we wrote *Civil Litigation for the Paralegal* with the Federal Rules of Civil Procedure and the Federal Rules of Appellate Procedure in mind. Whenever possible, we make appropriate references to possible differences in state and local procedures. Moreover, as noted above, we provided the activities exercises at the end of each chapter to encourage instructors to include state and local procedural variations. Often, however, this is not enough. Many instructors, ourselves included, would like a textbook written specifically with our home states in mind. We believe that our state-specific pocket-part supplements provide the next best alternative. We chose several key states, including California, New York, Ohio, and Texas, and developed pocket parts that present the procedural variations in the courts of each of these states. The pocket-part supplements are intended to familiarize the students with the rules of procedure in each of these states. Instructors may wish to use the pocket part of their own state, if that is possible, or in the alternative, choose the pocket-part supplement of the state whose rules are similar to the rules in their home state. These pocket parts may be attached to the inside back cover of the text for easy reference.

THE TEST BANK

Naturally, no textbook would be complete without a **test bank**, and *Civil Litigation for the Paralegal* is no exception. We developed the test bank with the same blend of theory and practicality that characterizes the rest of the text. Each chapter test consists of twenty-five questions. Of these twenty-five questions, ten are of the multiple choice variety. The remaining fifteen are true–false questions; of these fifteen, ten involve concepts and procedures that are explained in the chapter. In keeping with our attempt to make the textbook as practical as possible, the final five true–false questions are based on a fact pattern provided in the test. These questions require the student to analyze the facts and apply what he or she has learned in the chapter to determine the correct answers.

THE INSTRUCTOR'S GUIDE

Since each of us has been deeply involved in legal education for many years, we recognize the crucial need for a well-written and highly accurate **instructor's guide**. The guide that we have developed for *Civil Litigation for the Paralegal* provides the instructor with an excellent supplement for the text. The guide provides a key to all end-of-chapter questions, activities, and projects found in the book. Whenever possible, we have provided the complete text for any memos, letters, pleadings, and the like that are called for by the chapter projects. If, because of the individualized nature of the project, we could not provide the complete text, then we have included guidelines to show the instructor what to look for in the evaluation of each student's work. The guide may be attached to the inside back cover of the book for quick reference.

ACKNOWLEDGMENTS

Civil Litigation for the Paralegal is the result of the planning and input of many individuals and entities. With grateful appreciation, we would like to acknowledge and give our thanks to the editors of Delmar; to Bob Nirkind, who supported the authors in the original ideas for the book; to Akin, Gump, Strauss, Hauer & Field, the law firm in Dallas, which graciously granted a leave of absence to co-author Peggy Kerley for the first draft process; to the Southeastern Paralegal Institute, which initially introduced Peggy Kerley to the exciting field of paralegal textbook publishing; to DeAnza Community College and Santa Clara University Paralegal Institute, which did the same for Joanne Hames; to Mark Hames for too many things to mention; to Addie Tackett, director of the Radiologic Technology Department of North Central Technical College, and Dale Maurer, a registered radiologic technologist, who provided the medical details for the sample deposition; to Jane Skaluba, staff attorney for the Richland County Legal Services Department in Mansfield, Ohio, for her help in ensuring the accuracy of the text; to L. Dan Richards, John Falls, and Diane Hipsher of North Central Technical College for their support of the paralegal program at the college; to the spring quarter 1991 advanced business law students at North Central Technical College for their enthusiastic willingness to pilot test several of the cases in the text; to John and Louise Sukys, Jennifer Ann Sukys, and Grace Stewart for their patient understanding and loyal encouragement; and to the many paralegal students whose enthusiasm and intelligence continually motivate us. The authors gratefully acknowledge the encouragement and support and extend their sincere appreciation to these individuals and entities.

In addition, we acknowledge the contributions of the following reviewers, whose suggestions and insights have helped us enormously: Terri Bingham, Utah Valley Community College, Orem,

Utah; Steven Nelson, College of Great Falls, Great Falls, Montana; Joy O'Donnell, Pima Community College, Tucson, Arizona; and Ralph Seep, Lawyers Cooperative Publishing.

Peggy Kerley
Paul Sukys
Joanne Hames

ABOUT THE AUTHORS

Peggy N. Kerley is a paralegal instructor at Southeastern Paralegal Institute and an adjunct paralegal instructor at Southern Methodist University, in Dallas, Texas. She has more than thirty years of legal experience and is currently a freelance paralegal and owner of a computerized deposition summary business. She is the author of *Computers and the Law* and coauthor of the legal research module for *Texas Legal Assistant Educational Series*. Ms. Kerley received her undergraduate degree in political economy from the University of Texas at Dallas, and her paralegal certificate from the University of Oklahoma. She is a member of the Dallas Association of Legal Assistants.

Paul A. Sukys is a professor of law and legal studies at North Central Technical College in Mansfield, Ohio. He is coauthor of *Understanding Business and Personal Law*, and was a contributing author to the seventh edition of *Business Law with UCC Applications*. Mr. Sukys is also a charter member of the advisory committee for the paralegal program at North Central Technical College, and was instrumental in designing the curriculum for that program. He received his bachelor's and master's degrees from John Carroll University in Cleveland. Mr. Sukys received his law degree from Cleveland State University. In the past he has served as an adjunct professor at Cuyahoga Community College in Cleveland. He is a member of the Ohio Bar.

Joanne Banker Hames is currently an instructor for and the coordinator of the paralegal program at DeAnza Community College located in Cupertino, California. She earned her J.D. degree from Santa Clara University School of Law and was admitted to the California Bar in January 1972. She has been an active member since that time. For several years Ms. Hames was employed as an attorney in a busy litigation law firm. During that time she was involved in all aspects of civil litigation, including pre-trial preparation, jury trials, and appeals. For the past fourteen years, she has been involved primarily in paralegal education, teaching at DeAnza Community College and previously at Santa Clara University Paralegal Institute. Civil litigation is among the classes she has taught.

Introduction to Civil Litigation for the Paralegal

CHAPTER 1
Litigation and the Paralegal

COMMENTARY—YOUR FIRST JOB AS A PARALEGAL

You have recently completed your paralegal studies and have started looking for employment in a law office. Of the various job opportunities available, you are most interested in one in a litigation law firm. You have applied for a position of litigation paralegal and have been granted a job interview with an attorney from the law firm. It is very important for you to make a good impression during this interview. To do so you must demonstrate some familiarity with what a litigation law firm does as well as what a litigation paralegal does in such a law firm. During the interview you also wish to emphasize that you possess those skills that are important to a litigation paralegal.

OBJECTIVES

In this chapter we will see, in general, what civil litigation is, what it isn't, and the role of the paralegal in the civil litigation process. Subsequent chapters will analyze each step in the process, explaining the role of the paralegal in each. After reading this chapter, you will be able to:

1. Differentiate between civil and criminal procedure.
2. Outline the basic litigation process.
3. Explain why the basic litigation process is similar for all cases.
4. List alternatives to litigation.
5. Explain the relationship of substantive law to procedural rules.
6. Know where to find the laws relating to litigation.
7. List tasks performed by litigation paralegals.
8. Identify skills required of litigation paralegals.

1-1 WHAT CIVIL LITIGATION IS

Civil litigation is the process of resolving private disputes through the court system. Unless the parties are able to resolve their dispute, the litigation process usually results in a **trial**, or hearing, where the parties present their evidence to a judge or jury. The judge or jury then decides the dispute. Before this happens, however, a great deal of investigation, research, and preparation takes place. Although most of this occurs outside of the courtroom, it is an important part of the litigation process. Litigation attorneys and their assistants often spend considerable time gathering and analyzing the facts as well as researching the law. Formal legal documents must be prepared and filed with the court, witnesses must be interviewed, and other evidence must be identified and located.

civil litigation
The process of resolving private disputes through the court system.

trial
A court hearing where the parties present their evidence to a judge or jury, who decide the case.

Civil Law v. Criminal Law

Not all disputes that end in litigation are civil in nature, for our court system handles both civil and criminal cases. However, the litigation procedures for civil cases vary considerably from the litigation procedures employed in a criminal case. Being able to distinguish a civil case from a criminal one is therefore very important.

The rules of civil litigation, sometimes referred to as **civil procedure**, apply only if a civil law is involved. **Civil laws** are those that deal with private disputes between parties. If a lawsuit results, it is between the disputing parties. The parties may be individuals, organizations, or governmental entities. Civil law includes such areas as contracts, real estate, commercial and business transactions, and torts (civil wrongs or injuries not stemming from a contract). A typical civil case is illustrated by the following situation. While shopping at Dave's Department Store, Kirkland trips on torn carpeting, seriously injuring himself. The carpeting had been torn for several weeks, but the store had ignored the condition. Kirkland requests that the department store pay for his injuries, but the store refuses. Kirkland could sue the department store, asking the court to force the store to pay for his medical bills, for his lost wages, and for any pain and suffering he may have experienced. The basis for such a lawsuit is found in the law of torts, in particular, negligence. The procedures and rules that would govern that lawsuit are known as the rules of civil procedure or civil litigation.

Criminal law, on the other hand, deals with acts that are offenses against society as a whole, and includes such acts as murder, robbery, and drunk driving. If a criminal action results, it is usually between the government and the accused. The procedures and rules that apply when an individual is accused of committing a crime are known as the rules of **criminal procedure**. To a large extent, the Bill of Rights found in the U.S. Constitution governs the rules of criminal procedure. In a criminal case the defendant enjoys various rights, such as the right not to testify against himself. The defendant also has the right to a court-appointed counsel if he or she is indigent and is entitled to a speedy trial, all rights found in the Constitution. None of these rights exist in civil cases.

Sometimes the same act results in both a civil dispute and a criminal action. For example, suppose that Rader drives his car while under the influence of alcohol. As a result he crashes into another vehicle and injures the driver of that car, Horowitz. Rader would be arrested for the crime of drunk driving, but Horowitz might also sue civilly. The civil case (*Horowitz v. Rader*) will proceed according to the rules of civil procedure. The criminal case

(*People v. Rader*) will proceed according to the rules of criminal procedure. In the criminal case the government (in this case the state) would file an action against Rader for the crime of drunk driving. If he is found guilty the court could sentence him to jail or impose a fine, payable to the state. In the civil case, Horowitz would sue Rader for money to compensate him for his medical bills, his lost wages, and his pain and suffering. Where the same act results in both a civil action and a criminal case, the two legal cases are always kept separate. They will never be tried together. In part, this is because a different standard or burden of proof is required in the criminal case. The standard of evidence used to judge the criminal case is higher than the standard applied in civil cases.

Considerable differences between civil and criminal cases also exist in the documents that are filed in court, the proceedings that occur before trial, the hearings that take place in court, and the kinds of relief or remedies that the court can order. The documents, proceedings, and kinds of remedies that are discussed in this and subsequent chapters apply only in civil cases.

An Overview of Civil Litigation

The rules and procedures followed in the litigation process vary, depending on the court in which the action is filed. Rules or procedures applicable in one state may not apply in another state, nor may they apply if the action is in federal court. However, the general litigation process is similar from one court to another. The process of civil litigation formally begins when one party, the **plaintiff**, files a written document in court. This document is generally called a **complaint**, although in some states it is referred to as a **petition**. In the complaint, or petition, the plaintiff alleges or claims that the party who is being sued, the **defendant**, has done something, or has failed to do something, which entitles the plaintiff to some sort of relief. As noted above, the relief is frequently money, but may involve non-monetary matters, such as determining the validity of a will, issuing an injunction (an order requiring the defendant to do something or to stop doing something), or ordering specific performance of contracts (an order requiring the defendant to comply with the terms of an agreement). For example, suppose that two individuals, Ford and Fraser, enter into a contract in which Fraser agrees to sell Ford her house. Before the transfer is completed Fraser changes her mind about selling and refuses to comply with the terms of the contract. Ford might sue for any money she has lost. On the other hand, she could sue for

civil procedure
The area of law that regulates the method of resolving civil disputes in the courts.

civil laws
Laws dealing with private disputes between parties.

criminal law
The laws dealing with acts that are offenses against society as a whole; includes such acts as murder, robbery, and drunk driving.

criminal procedure
The procedures and rules that apply when an individual is accused of committing a crime.

plaintiff
The party who files a lawsuit.

complaint
The initial document filed in a lawsuit; states the factual basis for the claim.

petition
An initial document or pleading filed in court requesting some relief; in some jurisdictions the term is used instead of complaint.

defendant
The party in a lawsuit who is being sued.

specific performance of the contract. This means she is asking the court to force Fraser to fulfill the terms of their agreement.

After the complaint or petition is filed, the defendant is served with a copy of the complaint and is given the opportunity to contest the lawsuit. This is done by filing in court a document called an **answer**. In an answer, the defendant states why the plaintiff is not entitled to any relief. A defendant can also challenge a lawsuit by raising certain legal issues. This method of responding to a complaint is discussed in detail in chapter 6. At this point, the defendant also has the option of doing nothing and ignoring the complaint. However, if this is done, the defendant is said to **default**. In most cases the plaintiff will then obtain a **judgment**, an award of money damages, or other relief. If both the plaintiff and defendant have filed appropriate documents with the court, litigation proceeds with the parties trying to find out as much as they can about the other side's case. This is known as **discovery**. Sometimes, prior to the time for trial, the parties request various orders from the court dealing with the case. These requests range from very simple procedural issues, such as requests for more time in which to file a pleading, to more complicated legal issues, such as a request to dismiss the case. These requests are known as **motions**. There are some motions that, if granted, dispose of the case before any trial takes place. For example, if one party makes a motion to dismiss the case and that motion is granted, there is no trial. The matter was decided without any need for a trial (however, an appeal from this kind of order may occur). Motions can also occur during or after a trial.

If the parties are unable to settle their dispute, and the case is not disposed of by a motion, then normally the parties will eventually go to court and present evidence to support their claims. This occurs at a trial, where a judge or jury will decide the case. The litigation process does not necessarily end at trial because in a civil case both sides have the right to appeal the decision to a higher court if they feel that a substantial legal error has been committed. Even if no appeal is filed, if the plaintiff wins the case, collecting or enforcing the judgment sometimes requires further court action. At times, the plaintiff needs to obtain a **writ of execution**, a document that allows the plaintiff to seize and sell the defendant's property and use the proceeds to satisfy the judgment.

1–2 DIFFERENT TYPES OF CIVIL LAWSUITS

A civil lawsuit can vary, from a very simple procedure to a very complex court proceeding. Consider the following. Lombardi loans McNair $1,000.00. McNair signs a promissory note for that amount, promising to pay the money back in three months. At the end of four months McNair has still not paid back the money. Lombardi asks for the money, but McNair refuses to pay. The dispute between Lombardi and McNair is obviously very simple, as are the legal issues involved in the case. Nonetheless, if McNair refuses to pay, Lombardi could file a lawsuit against McNair. In such a lawsuit, there will be one plaintiff, Lombardi, and one defendant, McNair. The complaint itself will be short and straightforward.

On the other hand, some cases are more complex. This is illustrated by the following factual situation. Woo buys a new automobile. While driving the car home from the dealership, the brakes fail, the car crashes, and Woo is seriously injured. While this seems to be a simple case, it may become quite complex. In such a case, the plaintiff (or her attorney) would have to decide whom to sue. Is the dealership the only potential defendant, or does she also name the car manufacturer as a defendant? Was the car manufacturer negligent in making the brakes, or did it buy a defective part from some other business? If so, from whom was it purchased? If Woo plans to sue parties other than the dealership, and they are out of state, where can they be sued? If Woo brings all these parties into the lawsuit as defendants, they will probably try to sue one another. Complex cases like this present many practical problems. Many legal and procedural questions also arise, as does the need for extensive pretrial preparation. Often voluminous documents must be organized, analyzed, and indexed. However, whether Lombardi is suing McNair for $1,000 or whether Woo is suing the car dealership and manufacturer for $1,000,000, the basic litigation procedures outlined in this section apply.

1–3 ALTERNATIVES TO LITIGATION

Not all civil disputes are resolved through litigation. In fact, most disputes are not litigated. Several other methods of resolving disputes exist.

Settlement

Probably the most common method of resolving disputes is settlement. In a **settlement** the disputing parties discuss their problems with one another and reach an agreement. Attorneys and the legal system may never enter the picture. However, settlement can occur after a complaint and an answer have been filed in a case, but before it ever gets to court. This type of settlement presents certain legal problems that are discussed in subsequent chapters.

answer
Pleading filed by a defendant in a lawsuit that challenges the contentions or allegations in the complaint.

default
The failure of a party, usually a defendant, to appear in an action.

judgment
The relief awarded by a court after a final determination of the rights and obligations of the parties before the court.

discovery
The legal process by which the parties to a lawsuit search for facts relevant to a particular case.

motion
A request for an order from the court, usually dealing with a pending case.

writ of execution
A document issued by a court that allows a party to seize and sell property and use the proceeds to satisfy the judgment.

settlement
An agreement or contract between disputing parties in which differences are resolved.

Mediation

Another method of resolving disputes is the process of mediation. **Mediation** is a form of settlement that uses a third person, known as a **mediator**. The mediator helps the parties come to an agreement to settle their differences. Mediation has become a popular practice in family law matters. If the parties fail to come to an agreement, they are then free to pursue their case in court.

Arbitration

A third alternative to litigation is arbitration. The process of **arbitration** is similar to that of litigation. The main difference is that none of the proceedings take place in court. As a result arbitration is usually more efficient and less expensive than litigation. Arbitration often begins with one of the disputing parties requesting in writing that the dispute be arbitrated. Such a writing may loosely resemble a complaint. The parties then select an arbitrator or panel of arbitrators. **Arbitrators** are neutral third parties who hear the facts of the dispute and decide how it is to be resolved. They are often attorneys or retired judges, although in some cases they may be experts in the area that is the subject of the dispute.

Eventually each party will present his or her side of the case to the arbitrator at a hearing. An arbitration hearing is similar to a trial, with each side presenting evidence and the arbitrator deciding in favor of one of the parties. However, it does not take place in court. Because of the complexities involved in arbitration, attorneys often represent all the parties.

Arbitration can be either binding or non-binding. Binding arbitration occurs when the parties have agreed to abide by the decision of the arbitrator. This agreement often takes place prior to the dispute, and is often found in a written contract in a term which provides that "in the event of a dispute, the parties agree that it shall be resolved through arbitration." Such provisions are becoming more common in business and commercial transactions. Arbitration clauses are also commonly found in automobile insurance policies under the uninsured motorists provisions. In a non-binding arbitration proceeding, the parties are not obligated to accept the decision of the arbitrator. If either party is not satisfied with the decision, that party can usually proceed with litigation.

Administrative Agency Hearings

Some civil disputes cannot be resolved through litigation because the law does not allow it. For example, if an individual has a dispute with the government over his social security payments, that dispute must first be presented to a special board or agency that has been established to handle such disputes. Often whether or not a case can be resolved through the courts is a question of state law. In some states, for example, absent special circumstances, employees cannot sue their employers if they are injured on the job. However, employees are entitled to compensation for their injuries. If disputes arise regarding the extent of the compensation, they are resolved by a special board or agency that exists separate from the court system.

1–4 PROCEDURAL v. SUBSTANTIVE LAW

As we have discussed, the law of civil litigation deals primarily with how a civil case is handled in the court system. It consists of rules of procedure, known as procedural law. **Procedural law** tells us the method to use to enforce our rights or to obtain redress for the violation of our rights. For example, recall the dispute between Lombardi and McNair described earlier in this chapter. In that situation, Lombardi has the right to recover the money that McNair owes. The rules of procedural law dictate how Lombardi must proceed to recover the money. Lombardi would normally begin by filing a complaint in court. The rules of procedural law would govern such matters as how long Lombardi has to file the complaint, in which court it should be filed, as well as the form and content of the complaint.

However, litigation is not an area of law that can be practiced by itself. Before attorneys litigate a case, they must determine that there is a case to be litigated. This is a question of substantive law. **Substantive law** is the area of law that creates, defines, or explains what our rights are. For example, suppose that Ortiz promises to marry Hanley but then later changes her mind. Hanley has no right to sue Ortiz for breaking that promise because there is no substantive law that gives Hanley the right to sue for that kind of promise. Thus there is no basis for a civil lawsuit. On the other hand, if McNair borrows money from Lombardi with the promise to repay it by a certain date, and fails to do so, the substantive law of contracts does give Lombardi the right to enforce McNair's promise. The methods Lombardi would use to enforce that right would be determined by the rules of civil procedure.

Areas of substantive law that frequently form the basis of civil lawsuits include torts, contracts, real estate, and commercial and business transactions. This book concentrates on familiarizing you with the basics of procedural law. As your paralegal education continues, you will take specific courses in the various areas of substantive law.

mediation
A form of settlement that uses a third person to help the parties resolve their differences.

mediator
The individual in mediation who helps the parties come to an agreement regarding their differences.

arbitration
An out-of-court process for resolving disputes between individuals in which a neutral party hears both sides of the dispute and then makes a decision.

arbitrator
A neutral, third party who acts as a judge in an arbitration hearing.

procedural law
Laws containing the methods used to enforce our rights or to obtain redress for the violation of our rights.

substantive law
The area of law that creates, defines, or explains our rights.

1–5 SOURCES OF THE LAW

statutes
laws

Answers to legal questions concerning civil litigation can be found in either **primary sources** (books that contain the actual law itself) or **secondary sources** (books that explain or describe the law). Form books are an important secondary source of the law.

Primary Sources

In the American legal system, laws are found in three sources: constitutions, statutes (laws adopted by legislative action), and cases (laws created by the courts). A primary source of the law is the place in which we find the law itself. Therefore, the primary sources of the law would be found in the constitutions, code books (books containing statutes), and in case reporters (books containing opinions from the various courts). These three primary sources exist for both the federal legal system and for the various state legal systems.

The law of civil litigation is found in the same sources as are all our laws: constitutions, statutes, and case law. If a case is litigated in federal court, then the U.S. Constitution, United States Codes, the Federal Rules of Civil Procedure, and cases from the federal courts would usually control. If a case is brought in state court, then, of course, the state constitution, state codes, and state case law would be the primary sources of the law.

Constitutions provide some general guidelines that pertain to civil litigation. For example, the Seventh Amendment to the U.S. Constitution provides for the right to juries in common law cases exceeding $20.00. The U.S. Constitution also mandates that due process be followed in civil cases. Very briefly, this means that procedures that are followed in a civil case must be fair to all parties, especially to the defendant. The authority and power of the various courts in the litigation process are also often found in constitutions.

More specific litigation matters are controlled by codes or statutes. The Federal Rules of Civil Procedure cover such matters as the content and filing of pleadings, descriptions of various motions, and types of discovery permitted. State codes contain comparable provisions.

Case law, law that results from court decisions, is also a major source of rules regarding civil litigation. The courts have the power and the duty to interpret the constitutions and statutes. The Supreme Court has done that frequently with the constitutional phrase "due process." Moreover, even when a statute seems to be clear and explicit, case law cannot be ignored. For instance, California has the following statute relating to default judgments:

The court may . . . relieve a party . . . from a judgment . . . taken against him . . . through his . . . mistake, inadvertence, surprise of excusable neglect . . . . Application for such relief . . . must be made within a reasonable time, in no case exceeding six months, after such judgment, order or proceeding was taken.

The phrase, "in no case more than six months" would seem to be clear and without need of further interpretation. Nonetheless, the courts of the state have repeatedly decided that if fraud exists, a party may apply for relief after six months. Case law tells us that "in no case" does not mean never. It is therefore imperative that when you rely on a statute, you also check any case law that may relate to that statute.

In addition to the traditional sources of laws, rules relating to civil litigation are often adopted by individual courts. These are known as **local rules of court**. In the federal system, these rules can vary from district to district. In state systems, they can vary from one local area to another. In other words, within one state some rules of procedure may be different from one court to another. Local rules of a court should always be checked before initiating any litigation within that court.

Secondary Sources

When questions arise relating to litigation, the primary sources of the law are not the only reference materials that can be used. It is often quicker and easier to use a secondary source. A secondary source is a book in which an author explains or describes the primary sources of the law. Many secondary sources exist for both state and federal procedure. Secondary sources include legal encyclopedias, practice manuals, and textbooks. They also include various legal periodicals.

A secondary source that is heavily relied upon in the area of litigation is the **form book**. As the name suggests, form books contain sample forms for all aspects of litigation, from complaints to judgments. Better form books also contain explanations of the laws that relate to the various forms, and as such are valuable research tools. One example is the *American Jurisprudence Pleading and Practice Forms Annotated*, published by The Lawyer's Co-operative Publishing Co. and Bancroft Whitney Co. Figure 1–1 illustrates this.

1–6 THE ROLE OF THE LITIGATION PARALEGAL

When you become a paralegal employed to help in litigation you will have numerous tasks and responsibilities. However, the

primary source
Books that contain the actual law, i.e., case reporters, codes, constitution.

secondary source
Books that explain or describe the law.

local rules of court
Rules that are adopted by individual courts and apply only in those courts.

form books
Books containing sample forms for legal professionals to follow in preparing pleadings and other documents.

Form 1   11 Am Jur Pl & Pr Forms (Rev)

Governing Principles

The procedure in the United States District Courts in civil cases is, in
general, governed by the Federal Rules of Civil Procedure, adopted and
promulgated by the Supreme Court of the United States pursuant to the Rules
Enabling Act. The Federal Rules of Civil Procedure are applicable only to the
United States District Courts and do not affect the jurisdiction of, or deal with
the power of, appellate courts. The rules do not apply to the United States
Claims Court, the Customs Court, or the Court of Customs and Patent
Appeals. Additionally, the Rules of Civil Procedure are not applicable to
executive agencies or to military courts. (32 Am Jur 2d *Federal Practice and
Procedure* §§ 502, 505.)

Rule 10(a) provides that every pleading shall contain a caption setting forth
the name of the court, the title of the action, the file number and a designation of the character of the pleading as in Rule 7(a), which provides that there
shall be a complaint and an answer; a reply to a counterclaim denominated as
such; an answer to a cross-claim, if the answer contains a cross-claim; a third-
party complaint, if a person who was not an original party is summoned under
Rule 14; and a third-party answer, if a third-party complaint is served. In the
complaint, the title of the action shall include the names of all the parties, but
in other pleadings it is sufficient to state the name of the first party on each
side with an appropriate indication of other parties. (FRCP 10(a).)

Rule 11 provides that every pleading of a party represented by an attorney
shall be signed by at least one attorney of record in his or her individual
name, whose address shall be stated. A party who is not represented by an
attorney shall sign his or her pleading and state his or her address. Except
when otherwise specifically provided by rule or statute, pleadings need not be
verified. (FRCP 11.)

For additional forms that may be adapted for use in federal practice, see
Administrative Law; Captions, Prayers, and Formal Parts; Parties; Pleading.

ANNOTATIONS

Imputing falsity of verification as libel or slander. 38 ALR2d 181.

Construction and effect of statute as to doing business under an assumed or fictitious name or
designation not showing the names of the persons interested. 42 ALR2d 516.

Application of doctrine of idem sonans or the like to substitute or constructive service of
process. 45 ALR2d 1090.

Sufficiency of designation of court or place of appearance in original civil process. 93 ALR2d
376.

Mistake or error in middle initial or middle name of party as vitiating or invalidating civil
process, summons, or the like. 6 ALR3d 1179.

Disqualification of attorney, otherwise qualified, to take oath or acknowledgement from client.
21 ALR3d 483.

Propriety and effect of use of fictitious name of party in complaint in Federal District Court. 8
ALR Fed 675.

Pleading and verification requirements in stockholders' derivative suits in federal courts. 15 L
Ed 2d 1120.

FIGURE 1–1
Sample Pages
from *Am. Jur.*,
formally known as
*American
Jurisprudence
Pleading and
Practice Forms
Annotated.*
Reprinted with
permission by The
Lawyers
Co-operative
Publishing Co.

job of the litigation paralegal does vary from firm to firm and from
case to case. In a complex litigation case, you may be part of a litigation team along with attorneys, other paralegals, and legal secretaries. Your responsibilities may be limited to one aspect of the
case. For example, you might be responsible for organizing and indexing documentary evidence in a case (i.e., contracts, purchase
orders, letters between parties), while another paralegal in your
firm is responsible for researching legal issues that arise. In
smaller, less complex cases, on the other hand, you may be involved in all aspects of the case.

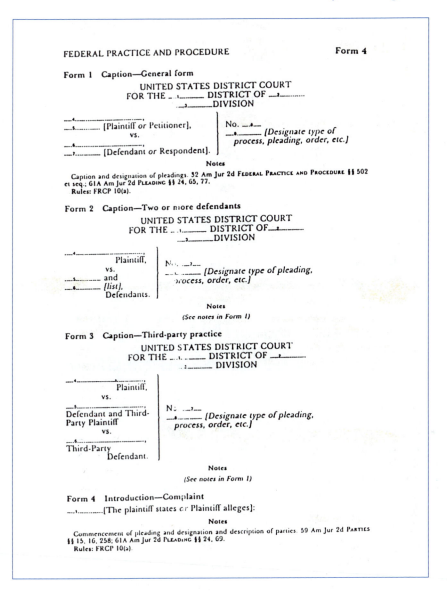

FEDERAL PRACTICE AND PROCEDURE   Form 4

Form 1 Caption—General form
UNITED STATES DISTRICT COURT
FOR THE ___.____ DISTRICT OF ___._____
___._____DIVISION

___._____,
___._____ [Plaintiff or Petitioner],   No. __.___
vs.   __.___ [Designate type of
___._____,   process, pleading, order, etc.]
___._____ [Defendant or Respondent].

Notes
Caption and designation of pleadings. 32 Am Jur 2d FEDERAL PRACTICE AND PROCEDURE §§ 502
et seq.; 61A Am Jur 2d PLEADING §§ 24, 65, 77.
Rules: FRCP 10(a).

Form 2 Caption—Two or more defendants
UNITED STATES DISTRICT COURT
FOR THE ___.____ DISTRICT OF___._____
___._____DIVISION

___._____,
___.___ Plaintiff,   No. __.___
vs.   __._____ [Designate type of pleading,
___.___ and   process, order, etc.]
___.___ [list],
Defendants.

Notes
(See notes in Form 1)

Form 3 Caption—Third-party practice
UNITED STATES DISTRICT COURT
FOR THE ___.____ DISTRICT OF ___._____
___._____ DIVISION

___._____,
___.___ Plaintiff,
vs.
___._____,   No. __.___
Defendant and Third-   __._____ [Designate type of pleading,
Party Plaintiff   process, order, etc.]
vs.
___._____,
Third-Party
Defendant.

Notes
(See notes in Form 1)

Form 4 Introduction—Complaint
___._____.[The plaintiff states or Plaintiff alleges]:

Notes
Commencement of pleading and designation and description of parties. 59 Am Jur 2d PARTIES
§§ 15, 16, 258; 61A Am Jur 2d PLEADING §§ 24, 69.
Rules: FRCP 10(a).

FIGURE 1–1
(continued)

Litigation Paralegal Job Description

The following is a list of some of the more common tasks that may be included in the job description of a litigation paralegal.

Pre-Litigation Facts Investigation

1. Interviewing clients
2. Interviewing witnesses
3. Obtaining statements from witnesses

4. Gathering evidence (police reports, photographs, etc.)
5. Organizing and indexing documentary evidence
6. Researching factual and legal issues

Commencing Litigation

1. Researching the substantive law of case
2. Drafting pleadings
3. Coordinating service of process
4. Reviewing pleadings from opposing party
5. Drafting motions including memoranda of points and authorities
6. Preparing orders after motions

Discovery

1. Drafting written forms of discovery (interrogatories, requests to produce, requests for admissions)
2. Assisting client in complying with discovery requests
3. Reviewing discovery obtained from opposing parties
4. Preparing client for deposition
5. Setting up, reviewing, and summarizing depositions

Trial

1. Organizing file and evidence for trial
2. Serving witnesses with subpoenas
3. Interviewing witnesses
4. Preparing the client
5. Drafting jury instructions
6. Drafting proposed judgments
7. Assisting with research and preparation of trial brief
8. Preparing and organizing trial exhibits
9. Assisting the attorney during trial

Post-Trial

1. Researching possible post-trial motions
2. Drafting possible post-trial motions
3. Drafting notice of appeal and requests for transcripts
4. Assisting with research and writing of appellate briefs

Miscellaneous

1. Maintaining firm's calendaring system
2. Organizing client files

3. Assisting with computerization of litigation
4. Preparing documents associated with enforcing judgments

What a Litigation Paralegal Cannot Do

Obviously, as a litigation paralegal, you can perform many tasks in the course of a lawsuit and can play an important role in the litigation law firm. However, the litigation paralegal is not an attorney and therefore cannot practice law. In a litigation law firm some important functions cannot be performed by the paralegal. With very limited exceptions, the paralegal cannot appear in court, cannot ask questions at a deposition, and cannot give legal advice to a client.

THE COMPUTERIZED LAW FIRM—The Language of Computers

SCENARIO

Congratulations! You have been hired as a paralegal by a prestigious litigation law firm, and it's your first day on the job. You have your own parking space, your own office, and your own computer. A senior paralegal who will be conducting your orientation and in-house training proudly tells you that the firm utilizes sophisticated hardware and the latest technology in "automated litigation support." Your training will include instruction in various "software applications" that will make your job easier. The firm has programs that handle document generation, screening and indexing, case management, billing and calendaring, and full text retrieval for depositions and trial. Furthermore, through the use of a modem you will be able to access legal and nonlegal databases. You have no idea what she's talking about.

PROBLEM

Your success as a litigation paralegal in a computerized litigation law firm depends on your ability to adapt your knowledge of litigation rules and procedures to the computer. You are willing and even eager to do this. You have some very basic knowledge of computers but you are overwhelmed by the whole concept of computerized litigation support. Where do you start?

SOLUTION

Adapting to a computerized litigation law firm requires that you know how the computer system in the office is set up, that you have a basic understanding of computers and common computer vocabulary, and that you become familiar with the various software programs that are available.

The computerized law firm is usually set up in one of two ways. In a smaller law firm each worker has a computer. Larger law firms, on the other hand, are often set up on a network. One main computer stores all the information needed, and each worker has a terminal (known as a dumb terminal) that can access this information.

Fortunately, you do not have to know exactly how computers work. However, some knowledge of computers is essential, and, without understanding some basic computer language, you will never learn how to effectively utilize the computer in litigation practice.

Some basic computer terms that you should know include the following:

hardware: the machinery that makes up the computer system; includes the computer itself and items such as a printer or modem

hard disk: place within the computer where information is stored

floppy disk: magnetic disk, separate from the computer, that holds information; when information is needed the floppy disk is inserted into the computer in the slot known as the disk drive

modem: an item of hardware that enables the computer to talk to other computers over a phone line

software: programmed information that allows you to perform various tasks on the computer

word processing: the most common software program, which allows you to prepare documents

database: large amounts of stored information

litigation support: refers to software packages designed to assist the litigation law firm.

Numerous software packages exist that facilitate litigation practice. As you read each chapter in this book you will see some of the ways these programs affect litigation practice. A detailed list of available programs is located in Appendix B.

1–7 SKILLS REQUIRED OF THE LITIGATION PARALEGAL

As a litigation paralegal, you will need some very definite skills. You must be able to communicate both orally and in writing. You cannot conduct intelligent interviews with clients or prospective witnesses without the ability to communicate orally. Nor can you help draft witness statements or pleadings without the ability to communicate in writing. As a litigation paralegal you also must possess organizational and analytical skills. Reviewing and analyzing documentary evidence and pleadings is often a task given to paralegals. Likewise, as a paralegal you will sometimes be asked to organize documents, discovery, and pleadings. The ability to do legal research, including familiarity with form books, is also important. Drafting court documents and preparing memoranda of points and authorities (discussion or analysis of legal questions) require this skill. In today's law office as a litigation paralegal you should be computer literate, possessing general knowledge of the computer, word processing, and database programs. This is particularly important if you become a paralegal in a firm that handles complex litigation.

Continuing Legal Education

As a litigation paralegal you keep current on changes that constantly occur in the area of litigation. Our laws are always subject to change. Codes and rules are often amended. New cases are frequently decided. In addition to changes in the law, technical advances, especially in computers and software packages, often affect the way litigation is practiced.

Local legal newspapers generally report national and state judicial and legislative developments. They also contain information related to practices adopted by the local courts. You should develop the habit of reading your local legal newspaper regularly. Local and state bar associations and paralegal associations often sponsor seminars on selected areas of law. Paralegal schools may also offer courses or seminars that would benefit the working paralegals. If you want to be a conscientious paralegal, you will take advantage of opportunities to attend these seminars.

Professional Organizations

As a paralegal you should continuously strive for professional improvement. One source for growth in the profession is affiliation with local, state, and national paralegal organizations. A partial list of national organizations includes:

National Association of Legal Assistants, Inc. (NALA)
    1601 South Main Street, Suite 300
    Tulsa, OK 74119
    (918) 587-6828

National Federation of Paralegal Associations
104 Wilmot Rd., Suite 201
Dearfield, IL 60015-5195
(708) 940-8800

American Bar Association
Standing Committee on Legal Assistants
ABA Center
750 North Lake Shore Drive
Chicago, IL 60611
(312) 988-5000

Legal Assistant Management Association
P.O. Box 40129
Overland Park, KS 66204
(913) 381-4458

1–8 PRACTICAL TIPS FOR SUCCESS IN THE LAW FIRM

Forms File—Invaluable Aid

As mentioned above, litigation paralegals often find the need to use form books. However, finding the proper form and adapting it to your particular needs is sometimes a time-consuming task. To find a proper form, a paralegal generally must go through an extensive index of the form books, looking up several topics, and then review several possible forms. Revising or adapting sample forms to fit a particular need is often required. Not only is all of this a time-consuming task, but it is also a task that repeats itself. A litigation firm will often find itself dealing in similar kinds of cases and facing similar problems in different cases. Thus, a form needed for one case can be easily followed for another. One way to ease the task of finding proper forms is for the law firm, or for you as a litigation paralegal, to maintain your own forms file. When you start employment as a paralegal in a litigation law firm you should always check to see if the firm maintains its own form files. Many do. Even if one is maintained for the firm, as an individual litigation paralegal you would be wise to keep your own form file, with an index, retaining copies of forms that you have prepared as well as copies of forms prepared by others, which might be useful in the future. Forms that should be kept include pleadings, motions, memoranda of points, and authorities and briefs.

How to Build a Litigation Training Manual

Another invaluable aid to litigation paralegals is a litigation training manual, in which the various tasks performed by the paralegals are described and step-by-step directions given. In such a training manual, consideration should be given to two distinct procedures. In describing any paralegal task, for example, preparing and filing a complaint, all of the legal requirements must be set out. Additionally, a training manual should detail office policy. A training manual might also include detailed instructions on preparing various legal forms. If a law firm has its own training manual, the new litigation paralegals should consult it. Experienced paralegals will also find it helpful when they are involved in new tasks or engaged in tasks that are infrequently performed. If a training manual does not exist the litigation paralegals can work together to assemble one. An easy way to accomplish this is for you and the other paralegals in your firm to keep a checklist or step-by-step directions for each task that you and the others perform. These can be collated into a complete training manual. As a paralegal student you can also begin keeping your own reference manual, by making checklists for each matter covered in class. See Figure 1–2 for a sample.

SUMMARY

1–1 Civil litigation is the process through which parties resolve their civil disputes in court. Civil cases deal with private disputes between individuals or parties. Civil litigation does not include the pursuit of any criminal case. Civil litigation usually begins with the plaintiff filing a complaint in court and having it served on the defendant. The defendant then responds by filing an answer or other appropriate pleading. While the parties are waiting to get to court for a trial, they try to find out as much about the other's case as possible by going through discovery. If problems with the case arise, they are often referred to the court in a proceeding known as a motion. After the trial has ended, either of the parties can appeal. Once the case is over, the prevailing party may use the court process to collect a judgment.

1–2 Some civil lawsuits are very simple proceedings, while others are very complex. Regardless of the nature of the case, the basic litigation process remains the same. However, more complex cases can involve multiple parties, multiple pleadings, and voluminous documents. They might also require extensive legal research.

PREPARING AND FILING A COMPLAINT
(Personal Injury—Auto Accident)

1. Review office file.
    a. Check client interview sheet.
    b. Review police reports.
    c. Review investigator's report.
    d. Verify statute of limitations.
2. Gather information for complaint.
    a. Plaintiffs.
        1) Names.
        2) Are all plaintiffs competent adults?
    b. Defendants.
        1) Names.
        2) Addresses for service.
    c. Location of accident.
    d. Description of injuries and expenses.
3. Were any preliminary notices or actions required?
    a. Is defendant a government entity?
    b. Is plaintiff a minor?
4. Determine which court complaint is to be filed in.
    a. Check local rules of court for any special requirements.
5. Prepare complaint.
    a. Check office forms file.
    b. Check form books if needed.
6. Prepare summons (see Training Manual—Instructions for preparing summons).
7. Have attorney review complaint.
8. Check court for proper filing fee.
9. Obtain filing fee from bookkeeper.
10. Take check, complaint, and summons (original and three copies) to court for filing.
11. Return copies to office.
12. Give copies of complaint and summons to process server for serving.
    a. Calendar for 10 days to check on service.

FIGURE 1–2 A Sample of a Litigation Training Manual.

1–3 Not all civil disputes are litigated. Other methods exist for resolving disputes. These include settlement, mediation, arbitration, and submission to special agencies or boards. Settlement occurs when the parties agree to resolve their differences. Mediation resembles settlement except that a third, neutral party (the mediator) is brought in to help the parties settle their differences. Arbitration involves the parties submitting their dispute to a third, neutral party (the arbitrator). The arbitrator decides the case. Where required by law, as in workers' compensation cases, parties are required to submit their disputes to special agencies or boards that have the power to decide disputes.

1–4 The substantive law of the case controls whether or not the parties have the right to sue. Procedural rules dictate how that case is to be handled in the court system. One cannot exist without the other. However, civil litigation deals primarily with the procedural rules.

1–5 The laws of civil litigation are found primarily in the constitutions, statutes, and cases. Cases brought in federal court are governed by the U.S. Constitution, federal statutes, and federal cases. Cases brought in state courts are controlled by state constitutions, statutes, and cases. In both federal and state courts, attention must also be paid to local rules of the various courts. In researching a question of civil litigation the paralegal may use primary sources or secondary sources. Primary sources are constitutions, code books, or case reporters. Secondary sources include textbooks, legal encyclopedias, legal periodicals, and form books. It is important for the litigation paralegal to be aware of changes that occur in the law. Reading local legal newspapers and joining professional associations can help.

1–6 Paralegals can perform a number of duties or jobs in the area of litigation. These include gathering evidence, interviewing clients and witnesses, preparing pleadings and motions, assisting with all aspects of discovery, and conducting factual and legal research.

1–7 Litigation paralegals need to have various skills. They must be able to communicate orally and in writing. They must possess organizational and analytical skills. They must be able to do legal research. Familiarity with computers is also recommended.

1–8 Litigation paralegals will find their jobs somewhat easier if personal form files and training manuals are available to them.

KEY TERMS

Know These

answer	default	petition
arbitration	defendant	plaintiff
arbitrator	discovery	primary source
civil laws	form books	procedural law
civil litigation	judgment	secondary source
civil procedure	local rules of court	settlement
complaint	mediation	substantive law
criminal laws	mediator	trial
criminal procedure	motions	writ of execution

QUESTIONS FOR REVIEW AND DISCUSSION

1. What is the difference between civil procedure and criminal procedure?
2. What are the steps in the litigation process?
3. How are a simple case and a complex case alike? How do they differ?
4. What are some of the alternatives to litigating a case?
5. What is the importance of substantive laws to civil litigation?
6. What are the primary sources for finding the law of civil litigation?
7. What are secondary sources for finding the law of civil litigation?
8. What are five tasks performed by litigation paralegals?
9. Why is it important for all litigation paralegals to know how to do legal research?
10. What skills must a litigation paralegal have? Why are these skills needed?

ACTIVITIES

1. Check the classified sections of local newspapers and legal newspapers. Are there any ads for litigation paralegals? If so, what are the job requirements? Are any particular skills described?
2. Contact your local courts and find out if they have their own rules of court. If so, how do you get a copy of them?
3. Find out if there any local paralegal associations. If so, how do you join? Do they ever sponsor seminars in the area of litigation?
4. Get a three-ring, loose-leaf binder and start your own training manual. As you go through each chapter in this book, prepare step-by-step directions or a checklist for each task described therein. As part of your training manual, include a glossary of terms and their definitions. Take these terms from those listed at the end of each chapter. Begin with chapter 1.

CHAPTER 1 PROJECT—STARTING A FORMS FILE

Get a three-ring, loose-leaf binder and start your own forms file. From the table of contents of this book set up a general index to the file. As you proceed through the course on Civil Litigation add copies of all forms that you see or prepare.

CHAPTER 2
The Courts and Jurisdiction

COMMENTARY—THE "WEIGH TO GO" CASE

You have just been hired as a litigation paralegal by a law firm, and one of the attorneys you work for has given you your first assignment. The law firm has recently been retained by "Weigh To Go," a corporation that operates a chain of low-calorie, fast-food restaurants. The corporation was formed ten years ago under the laws of the state of Texas and met with such success that it now has restaurants in Texas, Nevada, and Oregon. It plans to open restaurants in California. However, they have just learned that a few months ago another company started a similar business. This company calls itself "Go A Weigh" and does business solely within the state of California. Your attorney tells you that the firm will be filing a lawsuit based on trade name infringement and asks you to research the following questions. Should the complaint be filed in federal or state court, or does it matter? If the complaint is to be filed in federal court, which district is the proper one? If the complaint is to be filed in state court, which state or states could hear the case?

OBJECTIVES

In chapter 1 you were introduced to the general litigation process. Choosing the proper court in which to initiate a lawsuit is an important step in that process. After reading this chapter, you will be able to:

1. Describe the functions of the various courts in the civil litigation process.
2. Describe the various courts within the federal court system.
3. Describe the various courts in state court systems.
4. Define subject matter jurisdiction.
5. List the types of cases that must be brought in federal court.
6. Distinguish exclusive jurisdiction from concurrent jurisdiction.
7. Determine if a court can obtain personal jurisdiction.
8. Explain the relevance of long-arm statutes.
9. Contrast personal jurisdiction with in rem jurisdiction.
10. Identify how venue affects the location of the trial court.

2–1   THE COURTS AND LITIGATION

Since civil litigation revolves around the courts, one of the first considerations in the litigation process is the selection of the proper court in which to proceed. Numerous courts exist within the United States. Different court systems exist for each of the states and for the federal government. Furthermore, each court system contains many different courts. Although these court systems differ from one another in many ways, they do have some characteristics in common. All court systems have trial courts and courts of appeal or review. Many court systems have two levels of review courts, intermediate courts of appeal, and highest courts of appeal or courts of last resort, sometimes referred to as supreme courts. Furthermore, the function of all trial courts is similar, as are the functions of courts of appeal and courts of last resort.

Trial Courts

The civil litigation process usually begins in a **trial court**. This is where the parties to a lawsuit file their pleadings and present evidence to a judge or jury. Trial courts are also called **lower courts**. The primary function of any trial court in civil cases is to resolve disputes between parties by first determining the true facts and then applying appropriate legal principles. For instance, in a civil action, Stevens might sue Jackson for injuries he received in an automobile accident, claiming Jackson was at fault by failing to stop at a stop sign. Jackson might claim he owes Stevens nothing because it was Stevens who ran the stop sign. At the trial court, the judge or jury must decide what the facts are (that is, who did run the stop sign).

Once a factual dispute has been resolved, appropriate legal principles are applied to those facts—principles that for the most part have been established by the legislature and by higher courts. In the factual situation described above, once a trial court judge or jury has determined that Jackson did in fact run a stop sign, causing injuries to Stevens, they would then apply the legal principles of negligence and could award Stevens money damages. Because litigation usually begins in a trial court, this court is referred to as a court of original jurisdiction. **Jurisdiction** refers to the power or authority of a court to hear a particular case. A court of **original jurisdiction** is a court where the case begins and is tried.

Courts of Appeal

Courts of appeal are primarily courts of review. These courts examine what happened in the trial court to guarantee that the parties received a fair trial. A case is not retried in an appellate court. The appellate courts review the trial court's actions by reviewing a written, verbatim transcript or record of the lower court proceedings. Along with this transcript, the attorneys for the parties (or the parties themselves if they have no attorney) submit **briefs**, written documents in which the attorneys discuss and

trial court
A court where the parties to a lawsuit file their pleadings and present evidence to a judge or jury.

lower court
Another term for a trial court.

jurisdiction
The power or authority of a court to hear a particular case.

original jurisdiction
The authority of a court to first hear or try the case.

courts of appeal
Intermediate courts that primarily review the actions of lower courts.

brief
A written document in which an attorney discusses and analyzes legal issues in relationship to the facts of a case; can be prepared or filed in connection with a trial or an appeal.

analyze possible legal errors committed at trial, giving references to legal authorities in support of their claims. Attorneys (or, again, the parties themselves, if they are not represented) are also normally allowed to argue orally.

The appellate court's role is to determine if any legal errors occurred in the trial court. A **legal error** is an error in the way the law is interpreted or applied to a situation. Examples of legal errors include a judge's misstating the law when instructing the jury, or allowing attorneys to introduce evidence that is not relevant to the case or that has been improperly obtained. The appellate court is not allowed to substitute its judgment for that of the trial court when it comes to factual questions. If there is any reasonable basis for the trier of fact to have found as it did the appellate court is not empowered to reverse the decision simply because it does not believe the evidence. In the case of *Stevens v. Jackson*, described above, suppose the evidence in the case consisted of the following: Stevens, a 19-year-old college student, testified that Jackson ran the stop sign. Jackson, a police officer who was off-duty at the time of the accident, testified that Stevens ran the stop sign. There are no other witnesses. If the trial court found in favor of Stevens, an appellate court could not reverse just because an off-duty policeman is more credible to them than a 19-year-old college student. The trial court already resolved this factual question, and the appellate court is bound by it.

The appellate review is usually conducted by a three-judge panel. In order to prevail, a party must have a majority (two of the three) on his side. Since the authority of the courts of appeal is to review a trial court's actions rather than to resolve factual disputes, courts of appeal are sometimes called courts of **appellate jurisdiction**. They may also be referred to as **higher courts**.

Courts of Last Resort

Many court systems have two levels of courts with appellate jurisdiction, intermediate courts of appeal and one court of last resort. The court of last resort is often referred to as a **supreme court**. Intermediate courts of appeal and the court of last resort are primarily courts of appellate jurisdiction. They review the proceedings at the trial level. However, one basic difference exists between intermediate courts of appeal and a court of last resort. Generally, intermediate courts of appeal must review cases in which the parties request a review. On the other hand, in most civil cases a court of last resort has a discretionary right to review the cases. In other words, this court hears only those appeals that

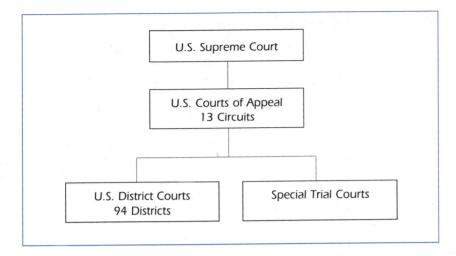

FIGURE 2–1
Federal Courts.

it wants to hear. The parties do not have the right to have their appeal heard in that court.

2–2 FEDERAL COURT SYSTEM

The federal court system was established in the United States Constitution, Article III, which created the Supreme Court and such inferior courts as Congress may establish. Today those inferior courts include trial courts and appellate courts. The trial courts are most commonly known as the United States district courts (or federal district courts), but also include various specialized courts such as U. S. Claims Court, U.S. Court of International Trade, and the U.S. Tax Court. The appellate courts are known as United States courts of appeals (or federal courts of appeals). See Figure 2–1.

United States District Courts

The United States and its territories are divided into ninety-four different districts, each one having a federal district court. Some larger districts are further subdivided into different divisions. Each state has at least one federal district court in its boundaries and, depending on population, a state may have more. The number of judges assigned to each district varies according to need. District courts are trial courts. Thus, in the *Weigh To Go* case mentioned in the commentary, if a lawsuit were pursued in the federal court system, it would be started in a district court. The complaint and answer would be filed in this court, and any trial would take place here.

legal error
An error in the way the law is interpreted or applied to a situation.

appellate jurisdiction
The power or authority of a court to review a trial court's action.

higher courts
Courts of appeal.

supreme court
A court of last resort.

Miscellaneous Federal Trial Courts

In addition to the U.S. district courts, the federal court system contains various specialized trial courts, including bankruptcy courts, the United States Court of International Trade, the United States Claims Court, and the United States Tax Court. The bankruptcy courts are an "adjunct" to each district court. All bankruptcy proceedings originate here. The U.S. Court of International Trade deals with cases involving international trade and custom duties. The U.S. Claims Court handles suits against the federal government for money damages in numerous civil matters (except for tort claims, which must be brought in district court). The U.S. Tax Court handles controversies between taxpayers and the I.R.S.

United States Courts of Appeal

The United States is divided into twelve appellate districts, each one having jurisdiction over three or more states. These courts hear appeals from district courts within their boundaries. The United States Courts of Appeal are primarily courts of review, having appellate jurisdiction. These courts review the proceedings that took place in a district court and determine if any substantial legal error was committed. In addition to the courts of appeal for each of the twelve appellate districts, a thirteenth federal court of appeals with national jurisdiction has recently been established. This court hears appeal in patent, copyright, and trademark cases from any district court and all appeals from the U.S. Claims Court and U.S. Court of International Trade. Generally, when any of the courts of appeal reviews a lower court decision, that decision is reviewed by a three-judge panel, and the majority decision prevails. However, like the district courts, the total number of justices in each appellate court varies according to need.

United States Supreme Court

The United States has only one Supreme Court, consisting of nine justices. The court is located in Washington, D.C., and holds its sessions from October through June. Primarily, the Supreme Court is a court that exercises appellate jurisdiction. In most cases, the exercise of that appellate jurisdiction is discretionary. With limited exceptions, the U.S. Supreme Court is not required to hear all cases in which a party requests a review. In other words, the Supreme Court hears only those appeals that it wants to hear. In determining whether or not to grant a hearing in a case, the Court obviously considers the importance of the decision not only to the aggrieved parties but to society as a whole.

To request a hearing in the Supreme Court a party files with the Court a document called a **petition for a writ of certiorari**. In this petition the party explains to the court why the case is important enough for the Supreme Court to consider. The justices then consider each petition and vote on whether or not to grant the petition for writ of certiorari. In order for a petition to be granted four of the nine justices must agree. If the petition for the writ of certiorari is not granted, then the decision of the court of appeals stands. If a petition for writ of certiorari is granted, however, it does not mean that the party has won the case. The party has only managed to get a full hearing (review) by the Supreme Court. After the petition has been granted and the writ has been issued, the case proceeds much like an appeal in the appellate courts. The justices consider the lower court tran- scripts. The attorneys submit legal briefs and are allowed to orally argue the case in front of the Court. Oral arguments before the Supreme Court, however, are very limited. By the time a case has reached the oral argument stage, the justices know the legal arguments for both sides. Thus, the oral argument stage often serves as a chance for the justices to ask questions about any legal arguments they want clarified. In order to prevail before the Supreme Court a party must have the vote of five out of the nine justices, or a simple majority. (In the event that fewer than nine justices are hearing the case, it takes a majority to win. Should there be a tie vote, the decision of the court of appeals stands.)

The power of review by the Supreme Court differs from that of the federal courts of appeal in another way. Normally the federal courts of appeal hear appeals from cases tried in federal district courts. The U.S. Supreme Court, however, can and does review cases originally tried in state courts as long as some federal or constitutional issue exists. Again there is usually no right to have such cases heard by the Supreme Court. As with appeals from federal court, the Supreme Court generally only hears those cases from state courts that it wishes to review.

While the Supreme Court is primarily a court of review, in certain cases it does have original jurisdiction, that is, the case is actually tried in the Supreme Court. Article III, Section 2 of the U.S. Constitution provides:

> In all cases affecting ambassadors, other public ministers and consuls, and those in which a state shall be a party, the Supreme Court shall have original jurisdiction. In all other cases before mentioned (Art. III, § 2.1) the Supreme Court shall have appellate jurisdiction, both as to law and fact, with such exception, and under such regulations as the Congress shall make.

petition for writ of certiorari
A document filed in the Supreme Court requesting that the court grant a hearing in the case.

2–3 STATE COURT SYSTEMS

Each state has its own court system, established pursuant to the laws of the state. For the most part, however, the individual states have patterned their court structures after the federal system. All states have some sort of trial courts and some sort of appellate, or review, courts. Most states also have a state supreme court or a court of last resort. The role of each of these courts is also comparable to their equivalents in the federal system. The names, however, differ from state to state. For example, general trial courts in California are called superior courts. In New York, trial courts are called supreme courts. In other states, trial courts are known as circuit courts, city courts, county courts, surrogate courts, and courts of common pleas. And many states have additional specialty trial courts such as probate court, juvenile court, and family court. In some states trial courts are broken down into different levels. For example, in California trial courts consist of superior and municipal courts. In civil cases in California, if the plaintiff were suing for more than $25,000, the action would be brought in superior court. If the lawsuit were for less than that amount, the case would be brought in the municipal court.

In addition, many state court systems today have something referred to as a small claims court (the people's court). In these courts, parties who are suing for small amounts of money go through a simplified litigation process. Attorneys are usually not involved, and all pleadings are extremely simple. These courts are intended to afford speedy legal relief in small cases where normal litigation costs would preclude other actions.

2–4 JURISDICTION

Before filing any lawsuit, an attorney must decide which of the many courts is the proper one for that lawsuit. This is a question of jurisdiction. Jurisdiction is the power or authority that a court has to hear a particular case. In determining whether a court has jurisdiction, two different issues arise. First, the case must be the kind of case that the court has to power to hear. This is known as **subject matter jurisdiction**. Second, the court usually must have power or authority over the parties, and in particular the defendant. This is usually known as **personal jurisdiction** (sometimes called in personam jurisdiction). At times, a court can hear a case if it lacks personal jurisdiction as long as it has in rem jurisdiction or quasi in rem jurisdiction. **In rem jurisdiction** means that property that is the subject of a lawsuit is located within the state. **Quasi in rem jurisdiction** sometimes exists when the defendant owns any property that is located within the state, even though that property is not the subject of the lawsuit.

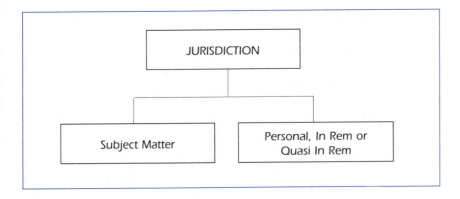

FIGURE 2–2
Jurisdiction.

However, any judgment must be satisfied or collected from that property. In order to decide a case, a court must have subject matter and either personal jurisdiction, in rem jurisdiction, or quasi in rem jurisdiction. See Figure 2–2.

Subject Matter Jurisdiction

Subject matter jurisdiction determines whether a court has the power to hear a particular type of case. For example, consider the *Weigh To Go* case. The plaintiff must file this lawsuit in a court that has the power to try this kind of case. This lawsuit could not be filed in a court that was authorized to hear only juvenile matters. Nor could it be filed in an appellate court, which does not have the power to try any cases. If a court does not have proper subject matter jurisdiction, that court does not have the power to resolve the dispute, and any judgment rendered by the court is void. A void judgment is not enforceable and can be challenged at any time.

Since different court systems exist (federal and state), an individual initiating a lawsuit must first choose the proper court system. This is not a matter within the sole discretion of the plaintiff. Various laws dictate the kinds of cases that can be brought in federal courts and the kinds that can be brought in state courts.

Subject Matter Jurisdiction of the Federal Courts. The federal courts have subject matter jurisdiction only when the Constitution, treaties, or some federal law specifically confers jurisdiction on the court. Generally, in criminal cases, the federal courts have jurisdiction where the offense is a crime under federal law. In civil cases the federal courts have subject matter jurisdiction if the lawsuit revolves around some constitutional issue, a treaty, or some federal law, or if there is diversity of citizenship, that is, the plaintiff and the defendant in the lawsuit are citizens of different states.

subject matter jurisdiction
The authority that a court has to hear a particular type of case.

personal jurisdiction
The power or authority of the court to make a ruling affecting the parties before the court.

in rem jurisdiction
The authority of a court to hear a case based on the fact that property that is the subject of a lawsuit is located within the state in which that court is situated.

quasi in rem jurisdiction
Authority of a court to hear a case based on the fact that the defendant owns property that is located within the state, even though that property is not the subject of the lawsuit, but is willing to satisfy a judgment from that property.

The United States Constitution and various federal laws provide that certain kinds of cases can be brought in federal court. Some of the more common cases in which federal jurisdiction exist include bankruptcy, patent and copyright disputes, discrimination cases, and maritime actions. Federal subject matter jurisdiction also exists where the plaintiff is the United States government or where the defendant is the United States government or a foreign consul or vice-consul.

Federal courts also have subject matter jurisdiction if diversity of citizenship exists. **Diversity of citizenship** means that the plaintiffs and the defendants are not citizens of the same state. Furthermore, complete diversity must exist before the federal court can exercise jurisdiction. This means that no plaintiff and no defendant can be citizens of the same state. For jurisdiction to be based on diversity of citizenship, there is an additional requirement. If the lawsuit is for money damages, the amount in controversy must exceed $50,000. Recall the case of *Stevens v. Jackson* described earlier in the chapter. Assume that Stevens was a citizen of Oklahoma and that Jackson was a resident of Alabama but was visiting a friend in Oklahoma at the time of the accident. As long as Stevens was claiming damages in excess of $50,000 this action could be maintained in federal court. However, suppose that at the time of the accident Jackson was driving a car owned by his friend Pearlman who lived in Oklahoma. If Stevens were to sue both Jackson and Pearlman he could not do so in federal court, because the plaintiff and one defendant were citizens of the same state. Complete diversity does not exist. Also, if Stevens were claiming damages under $50,000, the action would have to be filed in a state court.

Where plaintiffs and defendants in a case are individuals, state citizenship is normally determined by the individual's primary residence. On the other hand, corporate parties are considered citizens of both the state in which they are incorporated and the state in which they maintain their principal place of business. Corporations may thus be citizens of more than one state.

When a federal court exercises jurisdiction based on diversity of citizenship, the substantive law controlling the dispute is not found in federal law. If it were, subject matter jurisdiction would be based on that federal law rather than on the diversity of citizenship. When hearing a diversity case, therefore, the federal court must apply some state law to the substantive issues in the case. Usually the federal court applies the substantive law of the state in which the federal court is situated.

Exclusive v. Concurrent Jurisdiction. Even if the federal courts have subject matter jurisdiction, this does not always mean that the case must be brought in that court. Subject matter jurisdiction of the federal courts can be either exclusive or concurrent. **Exclusive jurisdiction** means that the action must be brought in federal court. **Concurrent jurisdiction** means that it can be brought either in federal court or in state court. Under federal law, certain subject matters must be handled in federal court. Examples of federal court exclusive jurisdiction include maritime cases, patent cases, and bankruptcy cases. On the other hand, other subject matters can be litigated in either federal or state court. Furthermore, where federal jurisdiction is based on diversity of citizenship, jurisdiction is almost always concurrent with a state. For example, consider the *Weigh To Go* case described in the commentary. The state of California has substantive laws regulating trade names. The plaintiff in our case could therefore file a lawsuit based on those laws. In such a case, the state of California would have subject matter jurisdiction. Furthermore, because the defendant is a citizen of that state, the California courts also have a basis for personal jurisdiction. Thus the action could be filed in the proper state court. On the other hand, because the plaintiff is not a citizen of California, diversity of citizenship exists, giving the federal court concurrent jurisdiction. The plaintiff therefore has the option of filing in either state or federal court. In cases where concurrent jurisdiction exists, the plaintiff makes the initial determination regarding the court. However, if the plaintiff chooses to file in a state court, in most cases the defendant has the right to have the case transferred to a federal court. The defendant accomplishes this by filing a **notice of removal**, a document presented to the court requesting that the case be removed from the state court and transferred to the federal district court. See Figure 2–3 for an example of a notice of removal.

Concurrent jurisdiction can also exist between two or more states. That is, where a case belongs in a state court system, more than one state may have subject matter jurisdiction. This would be determined by the facts of the case and the appropriate state laws.

Pendent Jurisdiction. Even if a matter is not normally within the subject matter jurisdiction of the federal courts it may still be heard in federal court if it is in conjunction with a case that is within the subject matter jurisdiction of the court. This is known as **pendent jurisdiction**. For instance, Wilson works for Chipp Inc. as an electrical engineer. In the course of his employment Wilson designs certain products, which are patented. Pursuant to a written agreement, the patent belongs to Chipp Inc. because it was developed as part of Wilson's job. Wilson leaves Chipp Inc. and starts his own company, manufacturing products

diversity of citizenship A basis for federal court jurisdiction; occurs when plaintiffs and defendants are not citizens of the same state.

exclusive jurisdiction The sole authority of *one* type of court to hear a case; often refers to the sole authority of federal courts to hear certain kinds of cases.

concurrent jurisdiction The type of jurisdiction existing when more than one court has the authority to hear a type of case; can exist between federal and state courts or between two or more different state courts.

notice of removal A document presented to the court in a case where concurrent jurisdiction exists between state and federal court, stating that the defendant is exercising his right to transfer the case from the state court to a federal district court.

pendent jurisdiction Authority of the federal courts to hear a matter normally within the jurisdiction of state courts; exists where that matter is combined with a claim that is within the authority of the federal courts.

To the Honorable Judges of the United States District Court for the Northern District of California:

Defendants, Go A Weigh, a corporation, through its attorney, respectfully shows the court:

 1. The above-entitled action was commenced in the Superior Court of the State of California, County of San Francisco, on January 10, 19___, and is now pending in that court.

 2. The above-mentioned action is a civil action for damages and injunctive relief based on alleged infringement of the trade name laws of the state of California.

 3. All defendants that are required to join in this notice have joined.

 4. The action is one of which the United States District Courts are given original jurisdiction under 28 USC § 1332 by reason of the diversity of citizenship of the parties.

 5. The amount in controversy in the action, exclusive of interest and costs, exceeds $50,000.

 6. A copy of the complaint was served on defendant at San Francisco, County of San Francisco, State of California, on January 3, 19___.

 7. Thirty days have not yet expired since the action thereby became removable to this court.

 8. At the time of the commencement of this action, plaintiff was and now is a citizen of the state of Texas; at the time of the commencement of this action, defendants and each of them were and now are citizens and residents of the State of California.

 9. Copies of all pleadings, process, and orders, served on petitioner in this action are attached and marked Exhibit A.

10. Defendants present and file with this notice a bond with a good and sufficient surety, as required by law, conditioned that defendants will pay all costs and disbursements incurred by reason of these removal proceedings, should it be determined that this action was not removable or was improperly removed.

Wherefore, defendants request that the above-entitled action be removed from the Superior Court of the State of California to the United States District Court for the Northern District of California.

Date: January 10, 199___   Respectfully Submitted,

                                                    _____
                                                    Roberta Rios,
                                                    Attorney for Defendant

FIGURE 2–3
Notice of Removal.

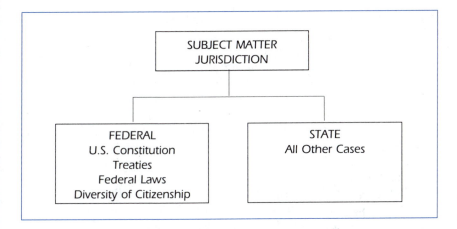

FIGURE 2–4
Subject Matter
Jurisdiction.

that he designed at Chipp and for which Chipp holds the patent. This action on Wilson's part violates his written contract with Chipp as well as Chipp's patents on the products. Chipp Inc. wishes to sue Wilson for breach of contract as well as patent infringement. A lawsuit for breach of an employment contract would not normally be within federal court subject matter unless the case involved diversity of citizenship. However, in this case, if a breach of contract action was brought along with an action based on the patent infringement, the federal court could hear the matter because of pendent jurisdiction. Since the federal court has jurisdiction over the patent case it can also exercise jurisdiction over the accompanying action based on breach of contract.

Subject Matter Jurisdiction in the State Courts.   Except for those cases that must be brought in federal court, each state has the right to determine the jurisdictional limits of the courts within that state. States usually have at least one trial court that has **general jurisdiction** in civil cases, that is, the power to hear any kind of case except those that must be brought in federal court. These are often known as county courts, circuit courts, superior courts, and courts of common pleas. However, unlike the federal system, where there is one level of trial courts, many states have created special trial courts that have limited subject matter jurisdiction. A court of **limited jurisdiction** has authority to hear only certain kinds of cases. For example, some courts have authority to hear limited types of cases, such as juvenile proceedings or family law matters. And some courts with limited jurisdiction are only empowered to hear cases where the amount of money in dispute is a limited amount. These courts are often known as municipal courts, district courts, or justice courts. See Figure 2–4.

general jurisdiction
Authority to hear any kind of case except those brought in federal court.

limited jurisdiction
Authority to hear only certain kinds of cases.

Original Jurisdiction. Determining whether or not a case belongs in federal court or state court is only one part of subject matter jurisdiction. After deciding which court system, federal or state, has subject matter jurisdiction, a party must file his lawsuit in the proper court within that system. All cases must be filed in a court that has original jurisdiction. Original jurisdiction is the power to first hear and resolve the dispute. In most civil cases, the court of original jurisdiction is the trial court (the federal district court or its state counterpart).

affirm
Action by an appellate court upholding a lower court decision.

reverse
Action by appellate court overturning a lower court decision.

reverse and remand
Action by appellate court overturning a lower court decision and sending it back to the trial court for retrial.

Appellate Jurisdiction. Appellate jurisdiction is the power of a court to review the decision of a court of original jurisdiction. In exercising appellate jurisdiction a reviewing court has the power to **affirm** the decision (uphold the lower court), **reverse** the decision (change the lower courts decision), or **reverse and remand** the case (change the lower court's decision and send it back to the trial court to be retried). Appellate jurisdiction does not give a reviewing court power to retry a case. Generally the courts of appeal do not listen to witnesses nor do they consider evidence that was not introduced in the trial court. Appellate jurisdiction lies in the federal and state courts of appeal, state supreme courts (sometimes referred to as courts of last resort), and the U.S. Supreme Court.

THE COMPUTERIZED LAW FIRM—Legal Research

SCENARIO

Your attorney, whose office is located in Texas, is anxious to file suit against Go A Weigh and has already determined that because of personal jurisdiction requirements the action must be maintained in California. Your attorney is also fairly certain that this case could be brought in federal court, under federal trademark laws. However, the attorney thinks that the case could also be brought in the state court of California under the laws of that state. While your attorney is generally familiar with practice in the federal court, he knows nothing about practice within the state of California. He would like to be able to compare the substantive law and the procedures of the two jurisdictions before making any final decisions. The attorney has a meeting with the client tomorrow morning and would like to discuss the options with the client.

PROBLEM

Your attorney asks you to research the California substantive law regarding infringement of trade names, along with the rules of procedure for that state. It's late in the afternoon, and the attorney needs the information by tomorrow morning. Your law office has numerous resource materials for practice in the federal courts and for practice in your state, but has nothing for the substantive laws or rules of procedure for the courts of other states. Your local law library does have out-of-state materials, but is located several miles away, has very limited parking, and closes at 6 p.m. How can you research this case within your time frame?

SOLUTION

One of the basic advantages of a computerized law firm is the availability of computerized legal research, which gives the law firm access to extensive legal source material. Most law firms maintain law libraries containing statutory and case materials from their own state. However, generally there is little need for out-of-state references. Whatever need does exist is usually outweighed by cost and space limitations. In recent years various companies have gathered legal source material from all states and have created a computerized database of that information. Included in this database is the case law from all of the states and statutory law from many of them, as well as federal statutory and case law. A law firm located anywhere can access this data bank with a phone call. All one needs is a computer, communication software, a modem, and a phone line. Through the phone line and the modem, the researcher's computer is in contact with the computer storing the database. Using the keyboard attached to his computer the researcher uses key words to describe the issues he is researching. The computer holding the database receives this information over the phone line and is able to search the database and locate relevant source material. That material can then be transferred to the researcher's computer and can be read on the computer monitor or screen. The researcher can also obtain a printed copy of the material by using a printer connected to his computer. Research conducted this way is usually more thorough and is accomplished much faster than by going to the library, searching various indexes and secondary sources, locating the proper books, and making photocopies. Another advantage is that the research can be done in the attorney's office at any time. The two main legal research databases are known as Westlaw and Lexis.

Challenging Subject Matter Jurisdiction. A court that lacks subject matter jurisdiction has no power to decide a case. If it attempts to do so, that judgment is void and can be challenged at any time. Subject matter jurisdiction can be challenged in different ways, depending on where the lawsuit is filed. One common way to attack subject matter jurisdiction is by filing a motion to dismiss the case.

Personal Jurisdiction

In addition to having jurisdiction over the subject matter of the case, a court must also have jurisdiction over the parties. This is known as personal jurisdiction. Personal jurisdiction means that the court has the power to render a judgment that affects the rights of the parties before the court. See Figure 2–5.

Jurisdiction over Plaintiff. Personal jurisdiction over the plaintiff seldom, if ever, presents any legal problems. The plaintiffs always file the lawsuit and select the trial court. Therefore they cannot complain that the court has no power over them. Having asked the court to make a decision concerning their rights, plaintiffs have no basis to challenge the court's right to do so.

Jurisdiction over Defendant. Personal jurisdiction over the defendant exists when a court has the power to render a judgment that affects the rights of the defendant and when the defendant has been given proper notice of the lawsuit (that is, proper service of process). Since the defendant does not normally choose to be sued in a particular court, jurisdiction over the person of the defendant must be determined by other factors. Assuming that proper notice of the lawsuit is given, all state courts have personal jurisdiction over those who reside within the territorial limits of the court. According to Rule 4 of the Federal Rules of Civil Procedure, the federal courts have personal jurisdiction over residents of the state in which the federal district court is located. Rule 4 also sets out various circumstances under which a federal district court may acquire personal jurisdiction over a defendant who does not reside within the state in which the court is located. Primarily, the rule provides that if the state court is authorized to exercise personal jurisdiction over a nonresident, then the federal court is likewise authorized.

No court has unlimited rights to exercise personal jurisdiction over nonresidents. Such a result would be basically unfair. For example, consider the *Weigh To Go* case described in the Commentary. Weigh To Go wishes to sue Go A Weigh for using a name deceptively similar to theirs. Go A Weigh is incorporated in the state of California and does all of its business in that state. The plaintiff, however, is incorporated in the state of Texas. Should the plaintiff be allowed to file this action in a court in Texas, thus requiring that the California corporation appear in a Texas court to defend itself? Does a Texas court have power to render a judgment against a defendant that is incorporated in and does business solely in California?

Whether a court has jurisdiction over a nonresident defendant depends on two factors. First, the exercise of jurisdiction must be in accordance with the Fourteenth Amendment to the U.S. Constitution. Second, the exercise of jurisdiction must be in accordance with state law.

Constitutional Limitations. The Fourteenth Amendment to the U.S. Constitution requires that "due process of law" must be followed in civil as well as criminal cases. The United States Supreme Court has stated that this means that the exercise of jurisdiction must be in accordance with "traditional notions of fair play and substantial justice." This has come to mean that a court can exercise jurisdiction over nonresident defendants only when the defendant has some substantial connection or association with the state. For instance, the defendant does business in the state or owns property in the state. Thus, in the example above, the California corporation probably could not be sued in Texas since it has no connection with the state.

State Long-Arm Statutes.   Even though the exercise of jurisdiction may be constitutionally permissible, it must also be allowed by the laws of the state in question. State laws that describe the circumstances under which the state may exercise jurisdiction over nonresident defendants are known as **long-arm statutes**. The following is an example of a such a long-arm statute:

> Any person . . . whether or not a citizen or resident of this state, who in person or through an agent does any of the following enumerated acts, submits himself, and if an individual, his personal representative, to the jurisdiction of the courts of this state as to any claim arising from:
>
> (1) the transaction of any business within this state;
>
> (2) contracting to supply services or goods in this state;
>
> (3) the causing of any injury within this state whether tortious or by breach of warranty;
>
> (4) the ownership, use, or possession of any real estate situated in this state;

long-arm statute
A statute allowing states to exercise jurisdiction over nonresident defendants.

(5) contracting to insure any person, property, or risk located within this state at the time of contracting

Utah Code Ann. § 78-27-24 (1987).

Waiver by Appearance.   As mentioned above, if a court lacks subject matter jurisdiction, any judgment rendered by the court is void. To an extent, the same is true of personal jurisdiction. However, while the parties to a lawsuit cannot waive, or give up, the requirement of subject matter jurisdiction, a defendant can waive, or give up, the requirement of personal jurisdiction. A waiver of jurisdiction means that an individual voluntarily allows a court to hear a case against him even though the court does not have the power to do so. Furthermore, in some courts if the defendant makes a general appearance in court and does not properly object to personal jurisdiction he has automatically waived any defect in personal jurisdiction. A defendant makes a **general appearance** whenever he files a pleading or takes part in the proceedings by doing anything other than objecting to jurisdiction.

Notice.   Fairness demands that before a court can decide the rights of a defendant in a lawsuit the defendant should be given proper notice of the action. This is known as service of process. How service can be accomplished is a matter determined by the laws of the jurisdiction in which the lawsuit is pending. The different methods of service of process are described in chapter 5.

Challenging Personal Jurisdiction.   A defendant must exercise care in challenging personal jurisdiction, because doing so in an improper manner may inadvertently confer personal jurisdiction on the court. Although federal courts allow defendants to challenge personal jurisdiction in the answer to the complaint, in some courts personal jurisdiction must be attacked by a **special**

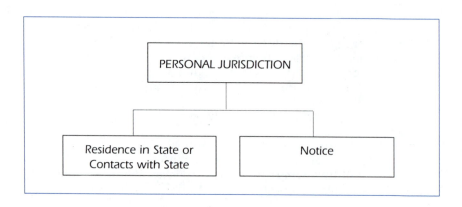

FIGURE 2–5
Personal
Jurisdiction.

appearance (an appearance for the sole purpose of questioning the court's jurisdiction). This is normally done by filing a motion known as a motion to quash service of summons. A **motion** is simply a request of the court for a written order. A **motion to quash service of summons** is a request that the court not allow the complaint to be served, thereby preventing the plaintiff from pursuing his lawsuit. In federal court, a motion to quash service of summons is also an alternative way of challenging personal jurisdiction.

In Rem Jurisdiction

Sometimes, even though personal jurisdiction may be questionable or even nonexistent, the court can still hear a case if it has jurisdiction over property that is the subject of a dispute. This is known as in rem jurisdiction and is a substitute in some cases for personal jurisdiction. See Figure 2–6. For example, Ryan Flynn, a resident of Pennsylvania, dies and leaves an estate consisting of real and personal property, all of which is located in Pennsylvania. He is survived by two sons, Martin, a Pennsylvania resident, and Michael, a resident of Georgia. In his will, Flynn leaves all of his property to Michael. Martin wishes to challenge this. Even though Michael may have no connection to the state of Pennsylvania, because the property that is the subject of this dispute is located in Pennsylvania the courts in Pennsylvania have jurisdiction to hear the matter. They have the right to determine ownership of property located within the state boundaries. This is known as in rem jurisdiction.

In exercising in rem jurisdiction, a court is limited to rendering judgments that affect only the property. The court cannot render personal judgments against the defendant that do not concern that property. For example, in the case described above, suppose that Martin Flynn claimed that he was disinherited because of slanderous remarks that had been made to his father by his brother. In addition to challenging the will, he might also wish to sue his brother for slander in the same action. In order for a court to hear this action, the Pennsylvania court would need to have personal jurisdiction over Michael.

Quasi In Rem Jurisdiction

Another substitute for personal jurisdiction is quasi in rem jurisdiction. For quasi in rem jurisdiction to exist various requirements must be met. First, a defendant must own some property within the state, although the property is not the subject of the lawsuit. Second, the plaintiff can use only that property that the

general appearance
Taking part in a court proceeding by filing a pleading or motion, except for the limited purpose of objecting to the jurisdiction of the court.

special appearance
An appearance in a lawsuit for a limited purpose, often for the sole purpose of questioning the court's jurisdiction.

motion
A request for an order from the court, usually dealing with a pending case.

motion to quash service of summons
A request that the court declare that the service of the complaint and summons is invalid, either because the court lacks jurisdiction over the defendant or because of some procedural problem with the service itself.

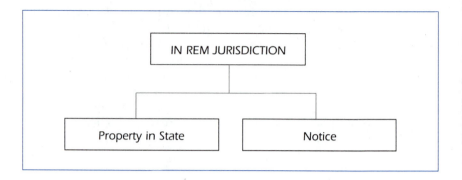

FIGURE 2-6
In Rem
Jurisdiction.

court awards to satisfy a judgment. Third, that property is usually brought before the court at the beginning of the lawsuit through an attachment proceeding. In an **attachment proceeding** the court usually orders that the property be seized and remain under the control of the court until the case is resolved.

If a court hears a case based on in rem or quasi in rem jurisdiction, due process still requires that the exercise of jurisdiction be fair and that the defendant be notified of the lawsuit. Notice is accomplished through service of process under the laws of the state in which the action is pending.

2-5 VENUE

An analysis of jurisdiction will tell a party whether to file an action in federal court or state court. If a case belongs in a state court, jurisdiction also determines in which state or states the action can be filed. However, within the federal court system and within each state court system there are a number of trial courts located in different geographical areas. Choosing the court in the proper geographical area is a question of **venue.**

Lawsuits should be filed and heard in a court that has proper venue. However, unlike jurisdiction, a court's lack of proper venue does not render a judgment void. If a defendant does not object to improper venue, he waives the right to object to the judgment rendered by the court.

Federal Court Venue

Venue in federal cases is governed by statute (28 U.S.C. § 1391). The code provides that the proper geographical location for federal actions is the district in which the defendant resides or where the cause of action arose. If jurisdiction is based on diversity of citizenship, venue is also proper where the plaintiff resides.

State Court Venue

Venue in state court actions is, of course, determined by state law. As a general rule, however, actions usually can be maintained in the county in which the defendant resides or where the cause of action arises. In different types of cases other counties might also have proper venue. For example in contract cases actions can often be heard in the county in which the contract was made, was to be performed, or was breached. And in lawsuits affecting title to real estate, the action is normally heard wherever the real estate is located.

Changing Venue

Because venue does not relate to the basic power that a court has to hear a case, under proper circumstances it can be changed. However, the place of trial can only be changed to another court that has jurisdiction. To change venue, a party makes a formal written request of the court where the lawsuit was filed. This is done by making a **motion for change of venue**. Of course, there must be a good reason before a court will consider transferring the case to another location. Some of the more common reasons include the fact that in the original location the parties cannot get a fair trial or the case was not filed in the proper court to begin with. The case might also be transferred to make the place of trial more convenient for the witnesses.

SUMMARY

2–1 The litigation process revolves around the courts. Since many different courts exist in the United States, plaintiffs must choose the proper court in which to pursue their case. The court chosen must have jurisdiction, or authority, to hear the case. In general, court systems are made up of trial courts, courts of appeal, and a court of last resort. In the litigation process the function of trial courts is to determine the facts of the dispute and apply appropriate legal principles. The primary purpose of the courts of appeal is to review the proceedings in the trial court. A court of last resort, often called a supreme court, generally has discretionary right to review lower court proceedings.

2–2 The federal court system consists of three levels of courts, U.S. district courts, U.S. courts of appeal, and the U.S. Supreme Court. The U.S. district court is primarily a trial

attachment
A court order that property be seized and remain under the control of the court until the case is resolved; usually required if the court is exercising quasi in rem jurisdiction.

venue
The proper geographical area in which to maintain an action.

motion for change of venue
A request from a party that the court transfer the case to a proper court.

court. This is where a case is originally heard. The U.S. courts of appeal and the U.S. Supreme Court are primarily courts of review. They examine the proceedings that occurred in the trial court.

2–3 The structure of any state court system is determined by the laws of that state. While some differences do exist from state to state, most state court systems are similar to the federal court system. All state court systems have some sort of trial courts and courts of appeal. Most states also have a state supreme court. The functions of the various state courts are similar to their counterparts in the federal court system.

2–4 Jurisdiction is the power or authority that a court has to hear a case. Proper jurisdiction requires that a court have the power to hear the kind of case before it (subject matter jurisdiction) and also power to make a decision binding the parties to the lawsuit (personal jurisdiction). The federal courts have subject matter jurisdiction in a case if the dispute arises under the Constitution, treaties, or federal laws. A federal court also has subject matter jurisdiction where there is diversity of citizenship and the amount in controversy exceeds $50,000. State law determines what kinds of cases can be brought in the state courts. If a court lacks subject matter jurisdiction, a judgment rendered is void. In addition to subject matter jurisdiction a court must also have personal jurisdiction over the parties. A court (federal or state) has personal jurisdiction over those who voluntarily agree to submit to the court's jurisdiction or those who reside within the state where the court is located. If a defendant resides outside of the state, then a court has personal jurisdiction only if the defendant has some substantial contacts with the state, and state law authorizes the exercise of that jurisdiction. State laws that deal with the exercise of personal jurisdiction to nonresident defendants are known as long-arm statutes. Personal jurisdiction also requires that the defendant receive proper notice of the lawsuit. In rem jurisdiction and quasi in rem jurisdiction can sometimes substitute for personal jurisdiction. In rem jurisdiction exists when the subject matter of the lawsuit involves property that is located in a state. Quasi in rem jurisdiction can exist when the defendant owns any property within the state, but the plaintiff must satisfy any judgment from property. In rem and quasi in rem jurisdiction also require that the exercise of jurisdiction be basically fair and that the defendant receive proper notice of the lawsuit.

2–5 In choosing the proper court in which to initiate a lawsuit an attorney must consider not only the question of jurisdiction, but also the question of venue. Venue relates to the selection of the proper geographical area of the court. In the federal courts venue is proper where the cause of action arose, in the district in which the defendant resides, and where jurisdiction is based on diversity, also where the plaintiff resides. In the interest of justice, venue can be changed to another court of proper jurisdiction.

KEY TERMS

affirm

appellate jurisdiction

attachment

brief

concurrent jurisdiction

courts of appeal

diversity of citizenship

exclusive jurisdiction

general appearance

general jurisdiction

higher courts

in rem jurisdiction

jurisdiction

legal error

limited jurisdiction

long-arm statute

lower court

motion

motion for change of venue

motion to quash service of
    summons

notice of removal

original jurisdiction

pendent jurisdiction

personal jurisdiction

petitition for writ of certiorari

quasi in rem jurisdiction

reverse

reverse and remand

special appearance

subject matter jurisdiction

supreme court

trial court

venue

QUESTIONS FOR REVIEW AND DISCUSSION

1. What are the functions of trial courts and courts of appeal in the litigation process?
2. How is the federal court system structured?
3. What are some of the different courts in state court systems?
4. What is subject matter jurisdiction?
5. What are three types of cases that can be brought in federal court?
6. What is the difference between exclusive jurisdiction and concurrent jurisdiction?
7. When does a court have personal jurisdiction over a party to a lawsuit?
8. Why do states have long-arm statutes?
9. What is the difference between personal jurisdiction and in rem jurisdiction?
10. What is venue?

ACTIVITIES

1. Find out about the court structure in your state. List the various courts and the functions of each.
2. Check the laws of your state to see if a long-arm statute exists. If it does, what does it provide?
3. Check the laws of your state to see how to do the following:
    (a) Challenge subject matter jurisdiction.
    (b) Challenge personal jurisdiction.
    (c) Change venue from one court to another.

    Also check form books for your state to find proper forms to accomplish (a), (b), and (c).

4. Review the factual situation in the Commentary in this chapter. Assume that Go A Weigh is operating within your state instead of California. In which court or courts could an action by Weigh To Go against Go A Weigh be filed? Check the United States Codes and the laws of your state, and give some authority for your answer.

CHAPTER 2 PROJECT—SELECTING THE PROPER COURT

Review the case of *Stevens v. Jackson* found in section 2–1 of this chapter. Assume that the facts described occurred in your city and that both Stevens and Jackson are residents of your state. Determine which court has original jurisdiction over the matter. Give the address of that court as well as a reference to your state laws that determine jurisdiction and venue. If the case were to be appealed, which court in your state would hear the matter? Again, give the address of the court as well as a reference to controlling state law.

Initiating Litigation

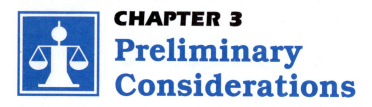

CHAPTER 3
Preliminary Considerations

COMMENTARY—THE KELSEY CASE

Seven months ago Janet Kelsey was injured in an automobile-bus collision. The accident occurred when the brakes on the bus failed, resulting in the driver's inability to stop for a red light. The bus, in which Kelsey was a passenger, was hit broadside by a car entering the intersection at the green light. The bus was owned and operated by the city. However, all maintenance on the bus was performed by Allied Auto Repair, a private company under contract with the city to maintain and repair all city buses. Kelsey has requested that your firm represent her in a personal injury lawsuit for the injuries she sustained in the accident. Your attorney has requested that you do some preliminary research to determine whether this lawsuit should be accepted and, if so, whether any immediate action must be undertaken.

OBJECTIVES

Chapter 2 covered the factors that determine the appropriate court for filing any lawsuit. However, before any action is filed in court, certain preliminary aspects of litigation must be considered and reviewed. After reading this chapter, you will be able to:

1. Explain the importance of a cause of action to the litigation process.
2. List the reasons that a paralegal must be familiar with the elements of a cause of action.
3. Define the various types of time limitations on filing a lawsuit.
4. Explain the importance of tickler systems.
5. List the practical considerations that affect the decision to accept a case.
6. Explain the procedure for turning down a case.
7. Identify the ethical standards an attorney must consider before accepting a case.
8. Describe the responsibilities of a litigation paralegal in seeing that ethical standards are followed.
9. Identify the ethical requirements for an attorney during the course of litigation.
10. Describe the special ethical problems that affect litigation paralegals.

3–1 DETERMINING THE EXISTENCE OF A CAUSE OF ACTION

Not all damages suffered by individuals are recoverable through the litigation process. The mere fact that a party has been injured or has sustained some monetary loss does not in itself give that person the right to sue. A legal right to recover damages must exist. This legally recognized right to relief is known as a **cause of action**. For example, suppose that Bricker drives his motorcycle negligently and fails to stop at a stop sign. He is hit by Steinman, who is driving in accordance with all traffic laws, in a careful and prudent manner. Bricker is the only one injured in the accident. Can Bricker recover his damages from Steinman? Obviously not. In this kind of case, where the defendant has done nothing wrong, there is no cause of action, or right to sue.

In determining whether a cause of action exists, you, as a paralegal, must examine both the law and the facts in the case. First, you must determine what general area of substantive law applies to the case. For example, is it a contract case or a tort case? Or is it both? Second, the general substantive area of law must be narrowed and a more specific topic identified. Then you can examine that specific area and determine what factors or elements must be present before a cause of action is created. For example, the *Kelsey* case described in the commentary is controlled by the substantive law of torts. More specifically, it is covered by the tort of negligence. A review of the law of negligence reveals that for Kelsey to have a cause of action the following elements must be shown:

1. The defendant must have a duty of due care toward the victim;
2. That duty must have been breached (a careless act);
3. The defendant's careless act must be the actual cause of the damages;
4. The defendant's careless act must be the proximate cause of the damages (i.e., the damages must be foreseeable);
5. Damages must have been sustained.

Once the elements of a cause of action have been ascertained, the final step in determining whether a cause of action exists in a particular case is to review the case itself to see if facts exist that support each of the elements. In determining whether or not Kelsey has a cause of action in negligence against Allied Auto Repair, the analysis might go as follows:

1. An auto repair company owes a duty of care to all users of vehicles that it maintains or repairs. Since Kelsey was a passenger on the bus, Allied owed her a duty of due care.
2. If the bus were properly maintained the brakes would not fail. Thus, there is some evidence of a breach of the duty owed to the users of that bus.
3. If the brakes had not failed, the accident would not have happened. Allied's failure to properly maintain the brakes is, therefore, the actual cause of Kelsey's injuries.

4. Kelsey's injuries were a foreseeable consequence of Allied's actions. This establishes proximate or legal causation.
5. Kelsey has sustained injuries and incurred expenses, thus establishing damages.

Since each of the elements of the cause of action is supported by facts, the conclusion, then, is that Kelsey does have a cause of action against Allied Auto Repair for negligence. See Table 3–1 for examples of the elements of some common causes of action.

Identifying the elements of a cause of action is important in the litigation process for various reasons. Probably most important is that each of the elements must be proven at trial for the plaintiff to prevail. In other words, to win the case the attorney must present evidence that supports each element of the cause of action. Also, in some state jurisdictions, the initial pleading must allege facts that support each element of the cause of action.

cause of action
Facts supporting a legally recognized right to relief from a court.

Knowing the elements of the cause of action in a particular case is essential to any litigation paralegal assisting the attorney

TABLE 3-1

ELEMENTS OF A CAUSE OF ACTION

Fraud

1. The defendant misrepresented, concealed, or failed to disclose a fact.
2. The defendant knew of the falsity of the statement.
3. The defendant intended to defraud.
4. The plaintiff justifiably relied on the statement.
5. Damages resulted.

Breach of Contract

1. Existence of a contract.
2. Plaintiff's performance or excuse of performance of his duties under the contract.
3. Defendant's breach or failure to perform.
4. Resulting damages.

Strict Liability—Products Liability

1. Defendant manufactured or distributed a product.
2. The product was defective.
3. The product was used in a foreseeable manner.
4. The defective product caused an injury.
5. Damages resulted.

in pretrial preparation. Understanding what the attorney must prove at trial enables you to gather appropriate evidence and conduct relevant discovery. It also equips you to prepare pleadings that comply with legal requirements and to review opposing pleadings for legal deficiencies.

Identifying the elements of a cause of action in a particular case may take some research. Case law and statutes might need to be reviewed. Secondary source books, such as encyclopedias and practice manuals, are valuable references. Form books, which often contain explanations and legal analysis of the forms, are also helpful.

3–2 TIME LIMITATIONS

Even though all of the elements of a cause of action exist in a particular case, parties have time limits in which to initiate their lawsuits. As a paralegal, you must be aware of these time limits in every case.

Statute of Limitations

The basic time limit is known as a **statute of limitations**. Unless a case is filed within the appropriate statute of limitations it will be dismissed regardless of the merits of the case. Statutes of limitations are found in state and federal codes and may vary from one jurisdiction to another. See Tables 3–2 and 3–3. These time limitations also differ depending on the type of case.

Commonly, statutes of limitations set definite and exact times for filing suit, and are easily determined and calculated. For example, a plaintiff might have one year from the date of an accident in which to file an action for personal injuries. Since the date of the accident is easily determined from police reports and witnesses, the statute of limitations is calculated with no difficulty.

In some cases, however, time limitations are not as easily determined. For example, in professional malpractice cases or in fraud cases, the statute of limitations might start to run not from the date of the malpractice or fraudulent act, but from the date that the plaintiff discovers or should have discovered the malpractice or fraud. Sometimes this is years after the defendant's wrongdoing. This kind of statute of limitations often presents numerous legal and factual questions, and proving the date that the plaintiff discovered or should have discovered the wrongdoing becomes an important part of the trial process.

TABLE 3–2

STATUTES OF LIMITATIONS

(Federal Statute—Actions Against the United States)

Except as provided by the Contract Disputes Act of 1978, every civil action commenced against the United States shall be barred unless the complaint is filed within six years after the right of action first accrues. The action of any person under legal disability or beyond the seas at the time the claim accrues may be commenced within three years after the disability ceases.
28 U.S.C. § 2401(a)

(State of California Statute—Contract Action)

The periods prescribed for the commencement of actions other than for the recovery of real property are as follows:

Two Years—Oral Contracts . . .

Within two years: 1. An action upon a contract obligation or liability not founded upon an instrument of writing . . .
Cal. Code of Civ. Proc. §§ 335 & 339

TABLE 3–3

STATUTES OF LIMITATIONS

(Date of Discovery)

(State of California Statute—Legal Malpractice)

. . . An action against an attorney for a wrongful act or omission, other than for actual fraud, arising in the performance of professional services, shall be commenced within one year after the plaintiff discovers, or through the use of reasonable diligence should have discovered, the facts constituting the wrongful act or omission, or four years from the date of the wrongful act or omission, whichever occurs first. . . .
Cal. Code of Civ. Proc. § 340.6

statute of limitations
A time limit in which to initiate a lawsuit or be barred from doing so.

claim statute
A type of law that requires that a written notice describing a claim be presented to the defendant before a lawsuit can be filed.

Claim Statutes

In lieu of statutes of limitations, some types of cases are governed by special statutes known as **claim statutes**. This kind of statute requires that a written claim be presented to the defendant before a lawsuit can be filed. These statutes are common when a governmental entity is being sued or where the defendant is deceased, and a probate is pending. Naturally, there are time limits for presenting the claim, time limits that are often shorter than the statute of limitations for similar cases. See the following examples of claim statutes.

The written claims that must be presented are usually much less formal than a complaint or petition. Basically, they require that the prospective defendant be notified that a claim is pending, who is making the claim, what the claim is for, and the amount of the claim. The party then has the opportunity to pay the claim before any lawsuit is filed. See Figure 3–1 for an example.

In some cases, failure to comply with the claim requirements can prevent a party from pursuing a lawsuit.

Laches

In addition to the statute of limitations, equitable cases (cases in which the plaintiff is asking for something other than money damages) are governed by another time limitation known as **laches**. See Table 3–4. Laches is an equitable principle that prevents lawsuits from being filed where, in fairness to the defendant, too much time has elapsed, even though the statute of limitations may not have expired. For example, suppose Jensen and Wilson sign a written contract in which Wilson agrees to sell his house to

laches
An equitable principle, similar to a statute of limitations, that prevents lawsuits from being maintained after a delay of time, where the defendant would be unfairly prejudiced because of the delay.

TABLE 3–4

CLAIM STATUTES

(Federal Statutes—Claims Against United States)

... An action shall not be instituted upon a claim against the United States for money damages for injury or loss of property or personal injury or death caused by the negligent or wrongful act or omission of any employee of the Government while acting within the scope of his office or employment, unless the claimant shall have first presented the claim to the appropriate Federal agency and his claim shall have been finally denied by the agency in writing and sent by certified or registered mail. The failure of an agency to make final disposition of a claim within six months after it is filed shall, at the option of the claimant any time thereafter, be deemed a final denial of the claim for purposes of this section. . . .
28 U.S.C. § 2675(a)

A tort claim against the United States shall be forever barred unless it is presented in writing to the appropriate Federal agency within two years after such claim accrues or unless action is begun within six months after the date of mailing, by certified or registered mail, of notice of final denial of the claim by the agency to which it was presented.
28 U.S.C. § 2401(b)

CLAIM FOR DAMAGE, INJURY, OR DEATH

INSTRUCTIONS: Please read carefully the instructions on the reverse side and supply information requested on both sides of this form. Use additional sheet(s) if necessary. See reverse side for additional instructions.

FORM APPROVED OMB NO. 1105-0008 EXPIRES 4-30-88

1. Submit To Appropriate Federal Agency:

2. Name, Address of claimant and claimant's personal representative, if any. (See instructions on reverse.) (Number, street, city, State and Zip Code)

3. TYPE OF EMPLOYMENT ☐ MILITARY ☐ CIVILIAN	4. DATE OF BIRTH	5. MARITAL STATUS	6. DATE AND DAY OF ACCIDENT	7. TIME (A.M. OR P.M.)

8. Basis of Claim (State in detail the known facts and circumstances attending the damage, injury, or death, identifying persons and property involved, the place of occurence and the cause thereof) (Use additional pages if necessary.)

PROPERTY DAMAGE

9.

NAME AND ADDRESS OF OWNER, IF OTHER THAN CLAIMANT (Number, street, city, State, and Zip Code)

BRIEFLY DESCRIBE THE PROPERTY, NATURE AND EXTENT OF DAMAGE AND THE LOCATION WHERE PROPERTY MAY BE INSPECTED. (See instructions on reverse side.)

PERSONAL INJURY/WRONGFUL DEATH

10.

STATE NATURE AND EXTENT OF EACH INJURY OR CAUSE OF DEATH, WHICH FORMS THE BASIS OF THE CLAIM. IF OTHER THAN CLAIMANT, STATE NAME OF INJURED PERSON OR DECEDENT.

WITNESSES

11.

NAME	ADDRESS (Number, street, city, State, and Zip Code)

12. (See instructions on reverse)   **AMOUNT OF CLAIM** (in dollars)

12a. PROPERTY DAMAGE	12b. PERSONAL INJURY	12c. WRONGFUL DEATH	12d. TOTAL (Failure to specify may cause forfeiture of your rights.)

I CERTIFY THAT THE AMOUNT OF CLAIM COVERS ONLY DAMAGES AND INJURIES CAUSED BY THE ACCIDENT ABOVE AND AGREE TO ACCEPT SAID AMOUNT IN FULL SATISFACTION AND FINAL SETTLEMENT OF THIS CLAIM

13a. SIGNATURE OF CLAIMANT (See instructions on reverse side.)	13b. Phone number of signatory	14. DATE OF CLAIM

CIVIL PENALTY FOR PRESENTING FRAUDULENT CLAIM	CRIMINAL PENALTY FOR PRESENTING FRAUDULENT CLAIM OR MAKING FALSE STATEMENTS
The claimant shall forfeit and pay to the United States the sum of $2,000. plus double the amount of damages sustained by the United States. (See 31 U.S.C. 3729.)	Fine of not more than $10,000 or imprisonment for not more than 5 years or both. (See 18 U.S.C. 287, 1001.)

95-107
Previous editions not usable.

NSN 7540-00-634-4046

STANDARD FORM 95 (Rev. 7-85)
PRESCRIBED BY DEPT. OF JUSTICE
28 CFR 14.2

FIGURE 3–1(a) Claim Form (front).

PRIVACY ACT NOTICE

This Notice is provided in accordance with the Privacy Act, 5 U.S.C. 552a(e)(3), and concerns the information requested in the letter to which this Notice is attached.
A. *Authority:* The requested information is solicited pursuant to one or more of the following: 5 U.S.C. 301, 28 U.S.C. 501 et seq., 28 U.S.C. 2671 et seq., 28 C.F.R. Part 14.

B. *Principal Purpose:* The information requested is to be used in evaluating claims.
C. *Routine Use:* See the Notices of Systems of Records for the agency to whom you are submitting this form for this information.
D. *Effect of Failure to Respond:* Disclosure is voluntary. However, failure to supply the requested information or to execute the form may render your claim "invalid".

INSTRUCTIONS

Complete all items - Insert the word NONE where applicable

A CLAIM SHALL BE DEEMED TO HAVE BEEN PRESENTED WHEN A FEDERAL AGENCY
RECEIVES FROM A CLAIMANT, HIS DULY AUTHORIZED AGENT, OR LEGAL REPRESENTATIVE
AN EXECUTED STANDARD FORM 95 OR OTHER WRITTEN NOTIFICATION OF AN INCIDENT,
ACCOMPANIED BY A CLAIM FOR MONEY DAMAGES IN A **SUM CERTAIN**
FOR INJURY TO OR LOSS OF PROPERTY, PERSONAL INJURY, OR DEATH
ALLEGED TO HAVE OCCURRED BY REASON OF THE INCIDENT.
THE CLAIM MUST BE PRESENTED TO THE APPROPRIATE FEDERAL AGENCY
WITHIN **TWO YEARS** AFTER THE CLAIM ACCRUES.

Any instructions or information necessary in the preparation of your claim will be furnished, upon request, by the office indicated in item #1 on the reverse side. Complete regulations pertaining to claims asserted under the Federal Tort Claims Act can be found in Title 28, Code of Federal Regulations, Part 14. Many agencies have published supplemental regulations also. If more than one agency is involved, please state each agency.

The claim may be filed by a duly authorized agent or other legal representative, provided evidence satisfactory to the Government is submitted with said claim establishing express authority to act for the claimant. A claim presented by an agent or legal representative must be presented in the name of the claimant. If the claim is signed by the agent or legal representative, it must show the title or legal capacity of the person signing and be accompanied by evidence of his/her authority to present a claim on behalf of the claimant as agent, executor, administrator, parent, guardian or other representative.

If claimant intends to file claim for both personal injury and property damage, claim for both must be shown in item 12 of this form.

The amount claimed should be substantiated by competent evidence as follows:
(a) In support of the claim for personal injury or death, the claimant should submit a written report by the attending physician, showing the nature and extent of injury, the nature and extent of treatment, the degree of permanent disability, if any, the prognosis, and the period of hospitalization, or incapacitation, attaching itemized bills for medical, hospital, or burial expenses actually incurred.

(b) In support of claims for damage to property which has been or can be economically repaired, the claimant should submit at least two itemized signed statements or estimates by reliable, disinterested concerns, or, if payment has been made, the itemized signed receipts evidencing payment.

(c) In support of claims for damage to property which is not economically repairable, or if the property is lost or destroyed, the claimant should submit statements as to the original cost of the property, the date of purchase, and the value of the property, both before and after the accident. Such statements should be by disinterested competent persons, preferably reputable dealers or officials familiar with the type of property damaged, or by two or more competitive bidders, and should be certified as being just and correct.

(d) Failure to completely execute this form or to supply the requested material within two years from the date the allegations accrued may render your claim "invalid". A claim is deemed presented when it is received by the appropriate agency, not when it is mailed.

Failure to specify a sum certain will result in invalid presentation of your claim and may result in forfeiture of your rights.

INSURANCE COVERAGE

In order that subrogation claims may be adjudicated, it is essential that the claimant provide the following information regarding the insurance coverage of his vehicle or property.

15. Do you carry accident insurance? ☐ Yes, If yes, give name and address of insurance company (*Number, street, city, State, and Zip Code*) and policy number. ☐ No

16. Have you filed claim on your insurance carrier in this instance, and if so, is it full coverage or deductible?	17. If deductible, state amount

18. If claim has been filed with your carrier, what action has your insurer taken or proposes to take with reference to your claim? (*It is necessary that you ascertain these facts*)

19. Do you carry public liability and property damage insurance? ☐ Yes, If yes, give name and address of insurance carrier (*Number, street, city, State, and Zip Code*) ☐ No

SF 95 (Rev. 7-85) BACK
☆U.S. GOVERNMENT PRINTING OFFICE: 1988 - 201-760/80006

FIGURE 3–1(b) Claim Form (back).

Jensen for $100,000. For various reasons, Wilson changes his mind and refuses to complete the sale. Rather than sue on the contract, Jensen finds another house for the same price and takes no immediate legal action against Wilson. Three years later, however, after a surge in the real estate market, Jensen decides to do something. Wilson's house is now worth $200,000, and Jensen assumes that if he can purchase the house for the contract price of $100,000, he can immediately sell it and make a large profit. He, therefore, sues Jensen for specific performance of the contract (a lawsuit to make Wilson sell him the house according to the terms of the agreement). The statute of limitations on a written contract might be four years. Technically, the complaint would be filed in a timely fashion. However, in fairness and equity, Jensen waited too long to file his action. Thus laches could prevent him from prevailing in his action.

Remember that laches applies only in equitable cases. If Jensen sued Wilson for money damages for breach of the contract, and the appropriate statute of limitations was four years, time limitations would not be a bar. (However, under contract law, Jensen's damages would be the difference between the contract price and the fair market value of the house at the time the contract was to be performed, not the date that the action is filed.)

Tickler Systems

Missing a statute of limitations or a claim statute can result in a clear malpractice claim against the law firm. Therefore, all litigation firms have a calendar or tracking system to remind them of these and other important dates. These calendaring systems are known as **tickler systems**. Before the advent of computers in the law firm, reminders were kept by hand. A firm might use a special calendar or a small file box organized by dates. Today, numerous software packages exist that help the firms keep track of important dates.

Whether or not a firm uses a computer, certain precautions should always be followed. First, when a case is tickled for the statute of limitations, it should be calendared early enough to allow for the preparation of the complaint and for the obtaining of any necessary signatures. Second, the file should be re-calendared for a date near the statute of limitations, at which time it should be checked to verify that the complaint has in fact been filed. Third, if calendaring the case is not your responsibility as a litigation paralegal, you should still check cases assigned to you to make sure that proper calendaring has occurred. You might even wish to keep your own calendar, in addition to the firm's calendar, for cases assigned to you.

tickler system
A calendaring system.

THE COMPUTERIZED LAW FIRM—Calendar Control

SCENARIO

Your attorney has accepted the Kelsey case and has made you part of the litigation team that will be handling the case. Part of your responsibilities will be monitoring the file and keeping track of important dates, including the time requirements for filing a claim and the lawsuit itself. Furthermore, new rules adopted by your local court impose strict time limits on all aspects of litigation and severe penalties for not complying with these limits. Along with the Kelsey case, you are working on several other cases in the office and have similar responsibilities in each of them.

PROBLEM

In a busy law firm you may be working on several cases simultaneously. In each case there will be numerous time limitations on work that must be done on the case. How do you keep track of all the dates for all of the cases?

SOLUTION

Computer software can assure that reminders of filing and other deadlines are timely generated. With a computer reminder system, there is no chance that a paralegal will fail to turn a desk calendar page or neglect to pull a manual reminder from an index card file. To use a computer reminder system you type in the dates you want to remember. When the program was installed in the computer the correct date was set. The computer has a clock and always knows the date. Each day, when you access the program, it displays the reminders for that date that were previously entered. These programs can also be set up to give you an earlier reminder (perhaps a week ahead of time). Some programs also allow you to program regularly scheduled events. For example, if your litigation team meets the first Tuesday of each month, this can be automatically entered. You need not enter the date for each meeting. Numerous simple and inexpensive software programs are available. Two programs often found in a law firm are SideKick Plus and WordPerfect Office.

SideKick, now Sidekick Plus, was one of the earliest TSR (Terminate and Stay Resident) software products. This feature means that you can be in the middle of drafting a document in WordPerfect and decide to check the next day's calendar or tickler system. By touching the "hot keys" CTRL and ALT, SideKick Plus's memo appears on the screen. This program is out of sight, but always available for quick and easy access.

In WordPerfect's office program the calendar module offers a feature missing from other calendar programs. It allows you to keep memos, list appointments, and sort to-do projects. This program is preferable if a law firm is already utilizing WordPerfect word processing software because it uses similar key strokes. In addition to specialty software programs most word processing packages include some form of calendar or reminder system.

3-3 FEASIBILITY OF THE LAWSUIT

Even though an attorney may determine that a case has merit, that is, a cause of action exists, he or she may nevertheless decide that the lawsuit is not practical. Litigation takes a great deal of time and can cost a great deal of money, not only in attorney fees but in costs. For example, it may be necessary to hire expert witnesses to establish certain facts. Experts charge substantial fees for their services. Or there may be numerous witnesses who have to be questioned and deposed. This also is costly. Before an attorney accepts a case he should always review it to see if it is practical. This involves reviewing the damages suffered by the plaintiff so that the value of the case can be determined. It also might involve some preliminary research into the defendant's ability to pay a judgment. You might be asked to assist in doing this.

3-4 TURNING DOWN A CASE

If an attorney decides not to accept a case he must clearly communicate this to the concerned individual. This should be done in writing so that there is a record of the fact. Many attorneys have been sued for malpractice by individuals who claim that the attorney led them to believe that their case was being handled and only learned after the statute of limitations had expired that the attorney had not in fact accepted the case.

In turning down a case an attorney must exercise care in stating an opinion regarding the merits of the case to the prospective client. An attorney can be sued for malpractice for advising a person that he has no case if another attorney feels otherwise. It is also advisable to warn the person about any possible statute of limitations. See Figure 3–2 for a sample letter.

OKIMURA & RESNICK
ATTORNEYS AT LAW

Robert Okimura
Leslie Resnick

17 Plaza Square
Boise, Idaho 83707

Area Code 208
Telephone 555-1212

Mr. Mark Jones
20 Birch Place
Boise, ID 83707

Dear Mr. Jones,

Thank you for contacting us regarding your dispute with ABC Corporation. As I explained to you on the telephone, our law firm is presently unable to represent you in this matter. Please note that our inability to accept your case is not a reflection or comment on the merits of your case. If you wish to pursue this matter you should consult other legal advice. If you decide to do so, you should act as soon as possible. As we have previously explained to you, the statute of limitations in these kinds of cases is _____ years from the date of your injury. If you have not filed a lawsuit within that time you will be prevented from doing so.

Very truly yours,

Robert Okimura

Robert Okimura,
Attorney at Law

FIGURE 3–2
Letter Turning
Down Case.

3–5 ETHICAL CONSIDERATIONS IN ACCEPTING A CASE

All attorneys are subject to a certain code of conduct, usually defined by state law, and referred to as **Canons of Ethics** or **Rules of Professional Conduct**. Although these rules apply to attorneys rather than paralegals, you must still be aware of them. The attorney's compliance with these rules often depends on factual and legal research done by the paralegal. Moreover, if a paralegal is working under the direction or supervision of an attorney, and the paralegal violates any of the rules, the attorney may nevertheless be held responsible. Ethical considerations enter into two aspects of the litigation process. First, certain ethical standards will determine if the attorney can take a particular case. Second, other ethical standards will govern the attorney's and the paralegal's conduct during the course of litigation.

Competency to Handle the Case

Obviously, an attorney should not accept a case if he does not possess the ability, knowledge, or time to handle it. This decision is up to the attorney, and the paralegal has little, if any, input into it. However, competency means more than simply having the ability to handle a case. It also means that attorneys are prohibited from neglecting cases that they have accepted. This can concern a paralegal. When you are assigned to a case you should make sure that the case is not ignored. Some tickling or calendaring system should be established to remind the attorney or paralegal to regularly review all cases.

Frivolous Claims

Lawsuits that have no merit should not be pursued. Again, this is usually determined by the attorney, but the attorney may rely on your research in making this decision. If an attorney handles a frivolous case, he risks being sued himself by the defendant in the action in addition to subjecting himself to disciplinary proceedings by the state bar association.

Conflict of Interest

A law firm cannot accept a case if a **conflict of interest** exists. A conflict of interest usually arises when a firm is asked to sue a party whom it currently represents or previously represented in another case. Although prior representation does not always result in a conflict, the potential for a conflict exists and must be closely examined before accepting the case.

A conflict is determined by whom the firm represents, rather than by whom any particular attorney in the firm represents. For example, in the *Kelsey* case described in the commentary, your firm would have to consider suing Allied Auto Repair. Suppose, however, that one of the corporate attorneys in the firm had prepared and filed incorporation documents for the business on a previous occasion. Could a litigation attorney now sue the company? Probably not.

canons of ethics or rules of professional conduct Rules regulating ethical standards for legal professionals.

conflict of interest A law firm's loyalty to one client competing with loyalty to another client or potential client; usually arises when a firm is asked to sue a party who it currently represents or previously represented in another case.

Before accepting a case, a firm must determine that no conflict exists. The larger the law firm, the more likely that some conflict may exist. As a litigation paralegal, you may be responsible for checking for conflicts. All law firms need to keep some centralized list of all clients. Without such a list, a conflict check could only be made by questioning each attorney in the firm. This is not only time-consuming, but unreliable. Many law firms, especially larger ones, now have centralized computerized lists of all clients. This makes the conflict check simple and more accurate.

Conflict problems can also arise when an attorney or a paralegal has changed jobs, and the prior law firm represented a party who is now a potential defendant. The prior relationship might result in a conflict of interest in the current litigation. Should you find yourself in such a situation, you should immediately inform the attorney handling the case. Steps can then be taken to isolate you from the case.

Even where a conflict does exist, the firm can still handle the case if the prior client will agree in writing to waive the problem. In the event that a conflict is not waived, the firm cannot accept employment in the new case.

3–6 ETHICAL CONSIDERATIONS AFTER ACCEPTING A CASE

Communication with the Client

Lawyers owe a duty to their clients to keep them advised about the status of their cases. Failure of lawyers to do this is the basis of one of the most common complaints against attorneys. Litigation can sometimes take years, and much of the litigation process does not personally involve the client. If a lawyer fails to communicate with his client on some sort of regular basis, the client may think that the attorney is doing nothing on the case. You can be a real asset to the attorney in maintaining communication with the client. In fact, parties often feel more comfortable dealing with the paralegal. In any event, if you have been assigned to a case you should establish some procedure for regularly advising the client about the status of his action. And the most important rule to remember is to *always return phone calls promptly*.

Communication with the Opposing Party

It is unethical for an attorney or a paralegal working with an attorney to personally contact an opposing party who is represented by his own attorney. Contact must always be made with the attorney. If the opposing party is not represented by counsel, communication is allowed. If you are required to contact an opposing party, you should first verify that the opposing party is not represented. Naturally, an opposing party can be contacted to ascertain whether or not he is represented and who is representing him. However, once that information is disclosed all further communication should cease.

Confidentiality

Communication between a client and an attorney is confidential. The attorney is prohibited from disclosing any information revealed to him by his client. Even mentioning the client's name without discussing the facts of the case may be a violation of this ethical requirement. As part of the litigation team, the paralegal is bound by the same rules. Whether you are present during conferences between the client and the attorney, whether the client directly communicates with you, or whether information is relayed to you by the attorney, you must honor the confidentiality. You should not discuss the case with anyone not directly involved in the case.

Honesty

An attorney must never knowingly make a false representation about a case to a court or other tribunal. While paralegals do not usually appear in court, you may frequently assist in the preparation of documents that are filed in court. You must be careful that factual and legal information is true and accurate.

In addition to honesty with the court, attorneys and paralegals should always be honest in their dealings with other attorneys and other paralegals. Aside from basic ethical considerations, a firm's reputation will be destroyed if its attorneys and paralegals cannot be trusted by other firms.

Attorney Fees

In setting fees in a case, an attorney is concerned with at least two ethical standards. First, the fee should not be unreasonable or unconscionable. Second, the fee arrangement, including any additional expenses, should be clearly explained to the client.

A fee in a litigation case can be set in a number of different ways. At the outset of the case the attorney could simply set a **flat fee**, or fixed sum, to handle the case. For example, an attorney and client might agree that the attorney will handle the client's contract dispute for $10,000. Since the amount of time needed to

flat fee
A legal fee based on a fixed sum rather than on an hourly rate or on a percentage of a recovery.

properly litigate a case is hard to predict, it is rare to see a fee set in this manner. However, if the fee is set this way, the attorney must make a reasonable, good-faith effort to make the fee commensurate with the expected work in the case.

More commonly, the attorney and client will agree to an hourly billing. In an **hourly billing** the client is charged a fixed amount for each hour the law firm spends on the case. The hourly rate cannot be excessive, but there are substantial differences in fees charged by lawyers, often depending on the attorney's experience. It is also becoming common for firms to bill for paralegal time. For example, a firm handling some complicated business litigation might charge the client as follows: Senior Litigation Attorney—$200/hr; Junior Litigation Attorney—$125/hr; Paralegal—$90/hr. It is, of course, unethical to bill the client for time not spent on the case.

An alternative way of setting a fee in litigation is the contingent fee, a common arrangement in personal injury cases. In the **contingent fee** agreement the attorney takes a percentage of whatever recovery is obtained. If no recovery is made, the attorney receives no fee. In this type of fee arrangement, there are times when an attorney receives a large fee for little time spent. Such a result, however, does not make the arrangement unreasonable. Contingent fees have been allowed on the theory that they permit people to pursue cases they couldn't afford otherwise.

A fee is the compensation that an attorney receives for his time and efforts in a case. However, it is not the only expense incurred during the litigation process. Courts require filing fees to process documents. Investigators and experts are often needed to help prove the case, and process servers have to be paid to serve papers. Out-of-pocket expenses such as these are known as **costs**. Most attorneys expect that the client will pay the costs of suit in addition to the fee that is charged. Even if the case is handled on a contingent fee basis, the attorney may request that the client put up funds to cover expected costs. Sometimes the attorney will advance or pay for these costs himself, expecting reimbursement (in addition to his fee) when the case is settled. It is important for the attorney to make this clear to the client.

Only the attorney may set fees. The paralegal is not permitted under professional guidelines to be involved in establishing fees in a case. However, you should be aware of the fee structure in case a question arises about a billing entry during the course of litigation.

Written Fee Agreements

The fee arrangement between the client and the attorney should always be in writing and signed by the client. In some jurisdictions, this is now required by canons of ethics. However, even if not required, common sense dictates that the agreement should be clearly set forth in writing to avoid any dispute. The fee arrangement is usually included in a document referred to as a **retainer agreement**. See Figure 3–3 for a sample retainer agreement.

Fee Sharing

In addition to ethical standards regarding the amount of fee a lawyer may charge, there are also standards regarding fee sharing. Generally, an attorney cannot share a fee in a case with a non-lawyer. This includes a paralegal.

Property of Client—Trust Accounts

An attorney cannot commingle his own assets or property with property belonging to a client. To handle this kind of

hourly billing
A legal fee based on a fixed amount for each hour the law firm spends on the case.

contingent fee
An attorney's fee based on a percentage of whatever recovery is obtained.

costs
Out-of-pocket expenses incurred in pursuing a case in litigation; includes such items as filing fees and costs of service.

retainer agreement
An agreement between an attorney and client setting forth the fee arrangement.

I hereby retain the law firm of Okimura & Resnick to represent me in the following legal matter: contract dispute between undersigned and ABC Corporation.

The attorneys agree to perform all legal services called for under this agreement.

Compensation for said representation shall be as follows:

$200.00 per hour for all work performed by an attorney;

$90.00 per hour for all work performed by a paralegal: Additionally, client agrees to pay all actual out-of-pocket expenses incurred in connection with this matter. Actual expenses include, but are not limited to, such items as filing fees, service fees, long distance telephone calls, photocopying, or travel. Attorney agrees to provide client with an itemized list of all actual expenses and costs.

I hereby agree to pay to attorney the sum of $2500.00 as a retainer in this matter.

_____
Client

Date: _____

OKIMURA & RESNICK
Attorneys at Law

By: _____
Date: _____

FIGURE 3–3
Retainer Agreement.

a situation, attorneys have special bank accounts, known as **trust accounts**, into which they deposit all money belonging to their clients. It is allowable to have one trust account for many clients, as long as accurate records are kept.

In litigation, trust accounts are utilized for two main purposes—advances by the client and settlement or satisfaction of judgments. First, if the client gives the attorney money that is specifically designated for costs, then the money should be deposited in a trust account until the cost is actually incurred. The attorney should not deposit the funds into his general account. Second, when a case is settled, the attorney must exercise care regarding any money he receives. A settlement check is primarily the property of the client. However, the attorney does want to be certain that he receives his fee and costs. In fact, the attorney may have a lien against the settlement if so provided in the retainer agreement. Because of the client's interest in the check, however, the attorney cannot deposit it into his personal account. The attorney must deposit the check into the trust account. After he makes certain that the settlement check has cleared, he can make proper disbursements from the trust account, paying the client his share and reimbursing himself for his costs and fee. Where the trust account contains money for more than one client, the attorney should always make sure that the check has cleared before making any disbursements. Failure to do so could result in the property of one client being used for the benefit of another.

The importance of proper control and management of trust accounts cannot be minimized. Intentional misuse of clients' funds is theft and punishable criminally. Negligent misuse of client funds will often result in disciplinary proceedings against an attorney. This is one area where bar associations are especially strict.

Special Problems for Paralegals

During the course of litigation, you will probably have personal contact with the client. Particular care must be taken in answering client's questions. You cannot give legal advice. If a client asks a question that calls for legal advice, it must be referred to the attorney.

Also of particular concern is making certain that the client understands your status in the law firm. The client cannot be allowed to assume that the you are an attorney. You must be careful to properly identify yourself.

trust account
A special bank account maintained by attorneys into which they deposit all money belonging to their clients or other parties.

SUMMARY

3–1 Before filing any lawsuit, it must be determined that a cause of action, or legally recognized right to sue, exists. This may involve researching the law and analyzing the evidence in the case. The paralegal must understand the legal and factual basis for the cause of action to properly assist the attorney in preparing for trial.

3–2 All lawsuits must be filed in a timely manner. Time limitations for filing lawsuits are known as statutes of limitations and claim statutes. The equitable concept of laches also limits the time in which to file suit. Time limits vary depending on the type of case and the jurisdiction. All firms maintain some type of tickler system to keep track of time requirements.

3–3 In addition to reviewing the legal basis of the lawsuit and the ethical restraints in accepting a case, an attorney should consider the practicalities of the lawsuit. In particular, the damages and the ability of the defendant to pay a judgment must justify the cost of litigation.

3–4 An attorney must clearly notify a prospective client if he decides not to take a case. He should also warn the individual of time limitations in pursuing the case. The attorney must also be careful in making any representations regarding the merits of the case.

3–5 In deciding to accept a case, an attorney is bound by certain ethical standards. He cannot accept a case if he is not competent to handle it, if the case is without merit or frivolous, or if there is a conflict of interest.

3–6 After accepting a case, the members of the law firm, especially the attorney and the paralegal, are bound by other ethical standards. They should keep the client advised about the status of the case. They must never communicate personally with an opposing party once they know that party is represented by his own attorney. They must honor the confidentiality of their client and not discuss the case with third parties. They must be honest in their dealings with the court and other law firms. Attorney fees should be reasonable and clearly explained to the client. In some cases written fee agreements are necessary. Any monies belonging to the client must be kept in a trust fund and not commingled with the attorney's personal property. Paralegals must be careful not to give legal advice and to properly identify themselves to clients.

KEY TERMS

canons of ethics	hourly billing
cause of action	laches
claim statute	retainer agreement
conflict of interest	rules of professional conduct
contingent fee	statute of limitations
costs	tickler system
flat fee	trust account

QUESTIONS FOR REVIEW AND DISCUSSION

1. What is a cause of action?
2. What is the importance of a cause of action to the litigation process?
3. What are the various types of time limitations on filing a lawsuit?
4. What is a "tickler system" and why is it important in a litigation law firm?
5. What practical considerations must be reviewed prior to accepting a case?
6. What is the proper procedure for turning down a case?
7. What are the various ethical standards that control an attorney's decision to accept a case?
8. How can a litigation paralegal assist the attorney in reviewing ethical standards that are considered prior to accepting a case?
9. What are the ethical responsibilities governing law firms that handle litigation?
10. What are the special ethical problems of litigation paralegals?

ACTIVITIES

1. Review the commentary at the beginning of the chapter. Research the potential causes of action that may exist against Allied Auto Repair, the city, the bus driver, and the driver of the other vehicle involved in the collision. Prepare an interoffice memorandum explaining your conclusions.
2. Research the laws of your state. What are the statutes of limitations for the following types of cases: an action for personal injuries based on negligence; an action for personal injuries based on strict liability; an action for personal injuries based on medical malpractice; an action for legal malpractice; an action for property damage based on negligence; an action

based on a written contract; an action based on an oral contract; an action for fraud.
3. Contact your state bar association and obtain copies of any ethical standards or rules that it has adopted.

CHAPTER 3 PROJECT— PRELIMINARY DETERMINATIONS

Review the commentary at the beginning of the chapter. Research the following questions and present your findings in an interoffice memorandum:

1. What is the appropriate statute of limitations in your state for this case?
2. Do the laws of your state allow you to sue the city? If so, are there special claim statutes that apply? If there are, does Kelsey still have time to file a claim?
3. Are there other types of cases in your state that require that a claim be submitted prior to filing a lawsuit?

CHAPTER 4

Interview and Investigation Prior to Litigation

COMMENTARY—THE MORRISON CASE

Oscar Morrison has contacted your firm to represent him in a personal injury lawsuit against his former employer, Acme, Inc., for asbestosis allegedly contracted on the job. Your attorney has asked that you handle the preliminary arrangements for the interview, help determine whether the firm should accept the case, locate the necessary forms to gather information during and after the interview, and coordinate the interview. Your attorney has explained that she would like for you to participate in the interview so that the client will be comfortable communicating with you throughout the expected lengthy litigation. You are to function as a viable member of the litigation team, which may consist of senior attorney, several junior associates, and one or more paralegals.

OBJECTIVES

In chapter 3 important preliminary considerations affecting the filing of a lawsuit were discussed. Interviewing and investigation are also important steps in the beginning litigation process. After reading this chapter, you will be able to:

1. Outline the paralegal's responsibility in preparing for the client interview.
2. Describe how to set up a client interview.
3. Describe an ideal client interview questionnaire.
4. List forms or documents that might be needed during the client interview.
5. Explain the paralegal's role during the client interview.
6. Identify potential sources for locating fact witnesses or elusive defendants.
7. Discuss the techniques for interviewing fact witnesses.
8. Describe methods for locating and preserving evidence.
9. Explain the functions of an expert witness.
10. Explain the paralegal's role in procuring an expert witness.

4–1 THE CLIENT INTERVIEW

Successful litigation begins with proper preparation and investigation of both the facts and the law. This preparation and investigation often starts with the client interview. In most cases, the client is the most knowledgeable about the facts of the case. During a client interview these facts are communicated to the attorney handling the case. The attorney is then able to determine what aspects of the case need further investigation or research. Not only is the client interview an essential step in the fact-gathering process, but it also establishes the foundation for the long-term relationship between the client and the firm. The interview establishes the tone for the representation. If the interview goes smoothly, the client's impression of the firm will be favorable. However, if the paralegal and attorney are not prepared for the interview, have not researched the issues, and are not familiar with the basic facts of the potential representation, the client will have good cause to question his or her choice of counsel.

The client interview also affords the paralegal the opportunity to become an integral part of the litigation team. You may be asked to participate in various levels of responsibility for the interview, including:

1. researching potential causes of action or defenses;
2. scheduling the interview;

3. developing an interview questionnaire or form to fit the particular case;
4. gathering forms and documents the client will have to sign;
5. taking notes during the interview;
6. producing a summary of the interview.

Preparation for Initial Client Interview

Researching Potential Causes of Action or Defenses. Preparation is essential to a successful interview. Once you are assigned a case such as the Morrison case discussed in the commentary, you should take the opportunity to review all information available on the subject matter of the potential litigation and the causes of action or defenses. In the last chapter various sources for researching the elements of a cause of action were described. In addition, however, you should find out as much as you can about the factual subject matter of the lawsuit. Your firm's library or the local library will offer an abundance of magazine and newspaper articles on recent asbestos cases, including who has been sued, the outcome of jury trials, and reports on damage awards. You should also refer to medical journals covering the causes and effects of asbestosis. Only by understanding the factual basis of the lawsuit will you be able to ask relevant and pertinent questions during an interview.

Scheduling the Interview. Once it is determined that a potential cause of action exists, the initial client interview can be scheduled. Before scheduling the interview, however, remember to check the firm's client lists to rule out any conflict with any of the potential defendants. In scheduling the interview, the attorney's calendar should be checked for acceptable dates. You may contact the client by telephone to discuss available dates or suggest a tentative date by letter and request confirmation that the date is acceptable. If contact is made by telephone, a confirming letter should be sent. The date for the initial interview should be set as early as possible. When setting up the initial interview, the client should be instructed to bring with him all necessary information for preparing the case. This information will vary depending on the nature of the case. However, it may include such items as names and addresses of opposing party and all witnesses, copies of any correspondence between client and opposing party, and written verification of damages (medical bills, wage statements, etc.). Figure 4–1 is an example of an appointment-setting letter that requests the client to bring pertinent information with him to the interview.

Selecting the location for the interview is important. If the client is critically ill, has difficulty walking, or expresses reluctance to talk in the formal environment of the law firm, the interview may have to be held at the client's home, office, or hospital room. Most interviews in the law firm are conducted in either the attorney's office or a conference room. If a conference room is required, you may be asked to schedule the conference room and prepare it for the interview.

SCHNEIDER & FENTON
ATTORNEYS AT LAW
45 North Main St.
San Antonio, Texas 78265
(512) 555-1312

ALLYSON SCHNEIDER
GLEN BARDWELL

ANTHONY FENTON
K.W. POST

Oscar Morrison
189 Montalban Dr.
San Antonio, Texas 78265

Dear Mr. Morrison,

An appointment has been scheduled for you with attorney Allyson Schneider of our firm at 10 a.m. on Monday, June 15, at our offices to discuss your case. This interview should require approximately one hour. Please bring with you to the interview the following items checked on the list below:

    (X) Social Security number
    ( ) Copy of insurance policy
    (X) Information relating to the opposing party, such as insurance carrier, etc.
    (X) Accident or incident reports
    (X) Photographs and/or diagrams of injury site
    (X) Newspaper clippings relating to accident or injury
    (X) Witness statements
    ( ) Description of automobiles involved in accident, including license tags, owner, and amount of damage
    (X) Medical bills and information relating to treating physicians and hospitals
    (X) Employment information concerning time lost because of accident
    (X) Any other relative information or documents.

Producing the information requested at the time of the interview will enable us to expedite the handling of your claim. Please call me if you have any questions about the items requested.

Sincerely,

Alan Berkshire
Alan Berkshire
Paralegal

FIGURE 4-1
Letter Advising Client of Initial Interview Appointment.

Enter the location and time of the interview on the attorney's calendar and on your calendar or reminder system. A follow-up telephone call to the client the day before the interview ensures that the attorney's time is not wasted because of a last minute cancellation.

Developing Interview Questionnaires or Forms.   It is important to have some idea of the questions to be asked during a client interview. During any client interview the attorney or paralegal will first need to elicit general background information, such as address, phone number, employer, etc. The heart of the interview will, however, consist of questions specifically related to the case. Forms for client interviews containing sample questions can be found in many form books and practice manuals in the law firm's library. However, interview forms are useful only if they are tailored to the specific case. An interview form your attorney utilized in a construction contract case would be worthless in an asbestosis case. If you cannot find a form specifically tailored to your situation, you will have to develop your own. To do this, you should follow the pattern set by a form that involves a similar case. You will then need to refer to your own factual and legal research into the case. Once you understand what the attorney has to prove at trial, you should be able to formulate questions geared toward gathering that information. Figure 4–2 is an example of an interview questionnaire.

Gathering Forms and Documents for Client Signature.   Prior to the actual interview you should set up the file and locate copies of all forms that the client will need to sign. The first form to be filled out should be the **representation letter** or **retainer agreement** that establishes the ground rules of the litigation, including fees, billing rates, retainer, and work to be performed by the law firm. A sample retainer agreement was shown in chapter 3 (Figure 3–6).

In Mr. Morrison's case, the client's medical history and related expenses must be documented. Information concerning Mr. Morrison's medical treatment by a hospital, doctor, physical therapist, or laboratory can only be obtained through a written **release** or **authorization** signed by Mr. Morrison. A release or authorization is a signed statement by the client that authorizes someone (such as a doctor or employer) to give the attorney information regarding his client, information that otherwise might be treated as confidential. Figure 4–3 is a standard medical release form.

To further establish damages as a result of the alleged asbestosis, Mr. Morrison's employment records, tax returns, and/or

---

representation letter
A letter from an attorney to a new client establishing the ground rules of the litigation, including fees, billing rates, retainer, and work to be performed by the law firm.

retainer agreement
An agreement between an attorney and client setting forth the fee arrangement.

release
A signed statement authorizing someone to give confidential information to an attorney.

authorization
A signed statement authorizing someone (such as a doctor or employer) to give the attorney information that otherwise might be treated as confidential.

PERSONAL DATA:

Name:
Home Address:
Address for Billing:
Home Telephone:
Work Telephone:
Fax Number:
Date of Birth:
Social Security No.:
Driver's License No.:
Spouse's Name:
Spouse's Work Phone:
Employer:
Address:

INFORMATION RELATING TO CLAIM:

Type of claim (EEOC, med. malpractice, etc.):
Date of incident leading to claim:
Brief statement of incident (or attach statement):

Itemize damages incurred to date:

Do you anticipate additional damages? If so, describe:

Name and address of any doctors you have seen:

Identity, address, and phone of any potential witnesses:

Description and location of any documents or correspondence
pertinent to litigation:

Have you made any statements to anyone (orally or in writing)
regarding this case? If so, describe.

Do you have any insurance which covers this claim? If so, please
describe.

Have you been served with any papers relating to this case?
Have you heard from any lawyers concerning this case?

PRIOR LITIGATION:

Type of litigation:
Date and place of litigation:
Outcome of litigation:

Attorney representing you:

FIGURE 4–2
Client Interview
Form.

> I, OSCAR MORRISON, hereby authorize and permit you to furnish to the law firm of SCHNEIDER & FENTON, or its representative, orally or in writing, all documents they request pertaining to my medical treatment as a result of or related to exposure to asbestos, including, but not limited to, all x-rays, medical records, nurses' notes, medical charts, diagnostic studies, and medical opinions relating to my past, present, or future physical condition, treatment, care, or hospitalization.
>
> A copy of this authorization shall have the same effect and force as an original.
>
> *Oscar Morrison*
> OSCAR MORRISON

FIGURE 4–3
Medical
Authorization.

earnings statements must also be obtained. The social security earning's record, which offers a complete history of his employment and earnings, should be requested early in the investigative process of this case. Figure 4–4 is a release for that employment information.

These form releases should be signed but not dated until they are used, to ensure they are current. An employer or hospital might refuse to honor the releases if the date is too old.

> I, OSCAR MORRISON, hereby authorize and permit the law firm of SCHNEIDER & FENTON, or its representative, to inspect, review, and make copies of any and all employment and/or earnings records regarding myself, including, but not limited to, employment application, vacation leave, sick or medical leave, W-2 forms, termination, and any other documents relating to my employment with _____. The release of this information is to be used for litigation purposes.
>
> A copy of this authorization shall have the same effect and force as an original.
>
> *Oscar Morrison*
> OSCAR MORRISON

FIGURE 4–4
Authorization for
Release of
Information
Relating to
Employment and
Earnings.

The Paralegal's Role in the Interview

You have completed the research assignments and pre-pared all the necessary forms. The day of the interview has arrived. Your attorney should introduce you to the client and explain your role in the case. Giving the client a copy of your business card will assist him in contacting you should the need arise. This will facilitate information exchange between the firm and the client.

Your attorney may ask that you take notes during the interview and have them transcribed for the file. If you have prepared a questionnaire for the interview, you should give a copy to the attorney and keep a copy for yourself. You can then take notes on your copy of the questionnaire. This technique will make your note taking easier. If you do not understand an answer to a question, or are unsure of a name or word, ask questions. Sometimes it is necessary to ask that the client spell proper names that may appear later in pleadings filed with the court. Always make sure that you have the correct spelling of your client's name. Your notes should be complete and accurate.

During the interview, particular note should be made of the statute of limitations. As soon as the interview concludes, you should check to make sure that a reminder, or tickler, was placed in the firm's litigation tracking system.

Prior to concluding the interview, review the checklist of information the client was asked to furnish. If any information is missing, make a written list of it and give it to the client. Be sure that you calendar the file to check that you receive everything. In a personal injury case like the Morrison case, the client might also be asked to keep a **medical diary**, a document in which the client keeps track of medical treatment, daily health complaints, type and amount of medication, mileage to physicians' offices, and other related medical expenses. The client will be more receptive to keeping the journal up-to-date if he or she realizes it will be used in calculating damages and evaluating the case for settlement. As the case progresses, the paralegal might periodically review the journal. Figure 4–5 is a sample medical diary.

Interview Summary

Promptly upon completion of the interview you should have interview notes typed for the attorney's review and a copy placed in the client's file. The interview summary may reveal areas that need further development, either from a legal issue or factual standpoint. You may utilize the form to develop a "to-do" list for additional investigation.

medical diary
A document in which the client keeps track of medical treatment, daily health complaints, type and amount of medication, mileage to physicians' offices, and other related medical expenses.

DATE: _____

MEDICAL TREATMENT:

VISIT TO DR. _____ (NAME)

REASON FOR VISIT: _____

DIAGNOSIS: _____

MEDICATION PRESCRIBED: _____

VISIT TO HOSPITAL OR OTHER MEDICAL SERVICE:

NAME: _____

REASON FOR VISIT: _____

DIAGNOSIS: _____

TYPE OF TREATMENT: _____

HEALTH COMPLAINTS:

TIME OF COMPLAINT: _____

DESCRIPTION OF HEALTH COMPLAINT: _____

MEDICATION:

NAME OF MEDICATION: _____

PRESCRIBED BY:_____

CONDITION FOR WHICH PRESCRIBED: _____

_____

AMOUNT OF MEDICATION TAKEN: _____

ADDITIONAL NOTES RELATIVE TO HEALTH:

_____

_____

_____

FIGURE 4–5
Medical Diary.

4–2 LOCATING FACT WITNESSES OR ELUSIVE DEFENDANTS

Prior to filing a lawsuit, all available facts should be accumulated and organized. These facts are normally derived from the client, other witnesses, or documents. Mr. Morrison's interview may yield many of the facts necessary to pursue the filing of a lawsuit on his behalf. However, more information may be needed to substantiate his claims. For example, other employees at the tire company may have additional insight into the working conditions, chemicals to which he may have been exposed, and safety policies of the company. However, over the ten-year period of his employment many of these co-workers may no longer be employed by the tire company. Steps must be taken to locate and interview these important fact witnesses.

In addition to locating fact witnesses, the defendant should be located prior to filing suit. Sometimes, pending litigation causes potential defendants to become elusive. You may be asked to research the opposing party's address for service of process. This effort should be made early in the investigation so that it does not hamper prompt service of the complaint or petition. Refer to Table 4–1 for a checklist of potential sources for locating fact witnesses or the elusive defendant.

Steps for Locating the Agent of Corporations or Partnerships

The opposing party in the Morrison case is a corporation. Your client may know the physical address of the rubber manufacturing plant. However, additional information is needed before the lawsuit can be filed. You will need to obtain the legal name of the company and the name and address of the individual who should

TABLE 4–1

CHECKLIST OF SOURCES FOR LOCATING FACT WITNESSES OR ELUSIVE DEFENDANTS

- ✓ Client
- ✓ Client's competitors
- ✓ Accident report
- ✓ Court records of prior litigation
- ✓ Department of Motor Vehicles
- ✓ Friends and/or neighbors
- ✓ Employer and/or co-workers
- ✓ Professional organizations or unions
- ✓ Telephone book
- ✓ County assessor or recorder
- ✓ Relatives
- ✓ Hospital and medical service providers
- ✓ Physicians
- ✓ Ambulance company
- ✓ Computerized services, such as NEXIS and INFORMATION AMERICA

be served with the suit. This individual is known as the **agent for service of process** If the defendant is a corporation, this information is available from the secretary of state's office and may be obtained by telephone or use of a computer service, such as NEXIS or INFORMATION AMERICA. In some states, if a defendant is a partnership or limited partnership this information may also be available from the secretary of state's office. However, in other states if a defendant is a partnership or limited partnership this information may be filed in the county recorder's office in the county where the partnership has its principal place of business. Obtaining this information should be done early in the investigative stage of the lawsuit.

4–3 TECHNIQUES FOR INTERVIEWING FACT WITNESSES

Once you have located a potential fact witness, a telephone call should be made to determine what information the witness has and whether the witness is willing to be interviewed. You should identify yourself as a paralegal working with the attorney representing Mr. Morrison. The witness should clearly understand who the potential parties in litigation are and what claims are being made on behalf of Mr. Morrison. If the witness has information that may be relevant to the case, a personal visit should be arranged to take his or her statement.

THE COMPUTERIZED LAW FIRM—Nonlegal Database

SCENARIO

The Morrison case is set for trial in one week. One of your key witnesses is Jared Hill, who worked with your client at Acme, Inc. You have phoned Mr. Hill to advise him of the trial date and discovered that the number was disconnected. You have attempted to personally contact him at the home address you have in your file, but find that he has moved. You have made an attempt to reach him at his last known place of employment, but are told that he no longer works there.

PROBLEM

Your attorney wants you to locate this witness and subpoena him for trial. You have checked the local telephone directory and contacted the post office but have found no referral phone number or address. Your time is limited. How can you locate this witness?

SOLUTION

Various nonlegal databases can provide information concerning the location of individuals. INFORMATION AMERICA is one computer database service that can assist you with locating current information about your witnesses. One of its features is the People Finder, which contains files for 11 million individuals, 80 million households, and 60 million telephone numbers nationwide. Profile data includes current address, telephone number, date of birth, information about the type of residence, and information on family members. An additional service is the availability of a list of neighbors' names and telephone numbers. (However, no unlisted telephone numbers are found in the database.) A computerized law firm can access these databases by the use of a modem.

You may locate a witness or secure an address for service of process with any of the following information:

individual's last known address;
individual's name and state; or
individual's telephone number.

Technical assistance in the form of an 800 number can be accessed during business hours. The cost of searches and services on INFORMATION AMERICA is considerably less than that of hiring a private investigator or of manually performing the information search. The time it takes to conduct a computerized search is minimal, especially compared with the time needed to conduct a manual trace.

An interview form similar to the client interview form discussed earlier will expedite the interview and help elicit all pertinent facts from the witness. This form, a tape recorder, and a writing pad are necessary tools for the witness interview. A verbatim tape recording of the interview is preferable, but if the witness is reluctant to have his or her statement taped, you should be prepared. You will have to take written notes of the interview. In such a case, if possible, write out a statement and have the witness sign it before the interview concludes. Even if the statement is tape-recorded you should probably take written notes in case the tape player malfunctions. Once the interview has been completed, a typed witness statement should be prepared,

agent for service of process
Individual designated by a corporation who is authorized to be served with a lawsuit.

either from the recorded interview or from your written notes or statement. This typewritten statement can then be transmitted to the witness for review and signing. Never tape record a witness's statement, in person or over the phone, without the witness's knowledge and permission. In some jurisdictions this is a crime.

Selecting the location for the interview is critical. Remember that this witness's statement is voluntary. You should exercise extreme courtesy and cooperation in scheduling the interview. The witness may prefer that the interview be in the evening so that it won't interfere with a job. Perhaps the witness does not want to travel downtown to the law firm, but would rather have the interview at his home in a suburb. Flexibility is essential. You should make all arrangements for the interview to suit the witness's preferences.

The attorney may participate in the interview or request that you conduct the interview alone. Good planning will ensure that the interview goes quickly and smoothly. Preparation may include a review of the information on the interview form and facts about the witness from the earlier client interview.

Good interview techniques include listening attentively, taking detailed notes, and asking questions to clarify confusing or incomplete information. When asking questions, avoid **leading questions**. A leading question is a question that suggests the answer. For example the question, "Isn't it true that the rubber company has a reputation for not caring about the welfare of its employees?" is a leading question. The witness feels that "yes" is the anticipated answer, and will tend to respond accordingly. A better way to phrase the question would be, "Could you tell me what the rubber company's reputation is regarding the welfare of its employees?" This type of question calls for the witness's own feelings and is not suggestive. A witness should be encouraged to tell a story in his or her own words . Avoid the appearance of rushing the narrative or reacting to the story as it unfolds.

At times, more information may be derived from the client's body language than from the witness's own words. You should learn to evaluate the body language as well as the testimony of a witness and make note of any discrepancies. You should also make notes regarding the **demeanor**, or appearance, of the witness. Will he make a good witness in court? Is he articulate or does he ramble on? Is he hostile? Your evaluation of a witness can be very helpful to an attorney.

Thoroughness is critical in a witness interview. Failure to be thorough can result in a witness changing or adding to his testimony at the time of trial or deposition. You should endeavor to obtain the most complete information about the client's claim as possible. Also, keep in mind that the rules of evidence generally do not allow an attorney to introduce a written witness statement at trial unless the witness is present in court and testifies in person. If a witness is unavailable at the time of trial, there is, however, a way of presenting his testimony to the court. A formal deposition (as described in chapters 8 and 9) can be taken. At the time of the interview, therefore, you should determine if he or she would be willing to testify at trial. You should also ask if the witness plans to leave the area or might be unavailable at the time of trial for some other reason. The attorney can then take steps to legally preserve his or her testimony for trial.

4–4 METHODS FOR LOCATING AND PRESERVING EVIDENCE

Co-workers and other fact witnesses are essential to Mr. Morrison's case. However, testimony from witnesses is only one kind of evidence that can be used to prove a case. Written documents, photographs, and items of personal property are often introduced as evidence at trial to prove the facts of the case. In the situation described in the commentary, evidence such as photographs of the scene, medical records of Mr. Morrison, Environmental Protection Agency citations, time cards indicating days absent because of illness, and plant safety programs are all critical. Your attorney may ask that you take responsibility for locating and organizing all available evidence.

Documents relating to your client such as his medical bills or records, or his employment records, are usually easy to obtain. If you have an authorization for the release of this information signed by the client, you can obtain these documents by sending a copy of that release to the appropriate person or business. For other types of evidence, a telephone call or letter may suffice. If it doesn't, a subpoena and deposition may be required. Moreover, any evidence in the possession or control of a defendant will have to be obtained through the proper discovery process. These last two methods are discussed in detail in subsequent chapters.

See Table 4–2 for a checklist of types and sources of evidence in a personal injury case such as the Morrison case.

Evidence Control and Retrieval

You have assembled evidence to help substantiate Mr. Morrison's claim. This evidence includes photographs of the plant, labels from products used by workers in the plant, and copies of Mr. Morrison's x-rays. In order to avoid charges by the opposition that the evidence has been tampered with or replaced, each piece of evidence should be tracked from its receipt by your law firm

leading question
A question that suggests the answer.

demeanor
The appearance of a person; an important factor in weighing the testimony of that person.

TABLE 4–2

TYPES AND SOURCES OF EVIDENCE IN A PERSONAL INJURY CASE

Police Reports—Local, county, or state police and Department of Motor Vehicles

Automobile Ownership—Department of Motor Vehicles

Insurance Coverage—State Department of Insurance and Department of Motor Vehicles

Weather Reports—United States Weather Bureau

Fire Reports—Fire Marshal

Aviation Records (on accidents or safety standards)—Federal Aviation Administration

Property Ownership or Taxes—Local Tax Assessor's Office and State Department of Revenue

Birth and Death Records—Bureau of Vital Statistics and Local Coroner's Office

Medical Treatment—Doctor, hospital, ambulance company, x-ray firm, and physical therapist

Personal Data—Registrar of Voters, criss-cross directories, U.S. Post Office, Social Security Office, county court records (including judgments and/or liens, criminal, marriage and divorce), and computerized services such as NEXIS and INFORMATION AMERICA

Newspaper or Publicity—Local newspapers and television stations, archives of local library, and computerized services such as NEXIS and INFORMATION AMERICA

---

until its final introduction as a trial exhibit. Evidence should be marked to indicate its source, date of acquisition, and storage location. An **evidence log** will enable you to maintain an accurate record of the evidence, including any transfer of custody. Each time the evidence is removed from its storage location, the removal should be documented on the exhibit log. Figure 4–6 is a suggested form of an evidence log.

Preservation of Evidence

The method for preserving evidence varies, depending on the nature of the evidence. Photographs tend to fade or become

STYLE OF CASE: _____

EVIDENCE: _____

DATE ACQUIRED: _____ ACQUIRED BY: _____

MANNER BY WHICH ACQUIRED: _____

PARTICULAR IDENTIFYING MARKS: _____

LOCATIONS OF EVIDENCE: _____

EVIDENCE CUSTODIAN: _____

CHAIN OF EVIDENCE CUSTODY:

RELEASED TO   DATE   PURPOSE OF RELEASE

_____

_____

_____

_____

_____

FIGURE 4–6
Evidence Log.

damaged from handling. X-rays require a special folder for preservation. An original $300,000 note may be maintained in the firm's vault, with a copy of the note retained in an envelope labeled with the location of the original.

Some forms of evidence do not lend themselves to storage in the law firm during a lengthy litigation because of their size or daily use on a job site. Photographs of these exhibits may be taken and retained in the client's file for use in preparing the case for trial, at which time the original piece of evidence may be introduced.

Ensuring that evidence is preserved in its original form may be one of your responsibilities. Because of the varied nature of the evidence in Mr. Morrison's case, in-depth research on preserving the evidence could be required.

4–5 EXPERT WITNESSES

In a case involving technical or medical issues, **expert witnesses** are often necessary. Experts can perform several functions in a case. They can be hired in an advisory capacity, to explain the technical aspects of the case to the attorney. More often, they are hired to be witnesses during the trial. Before individuals are allowed to testify as experts, they must be qualified by the court to do so. In qualifying experts, the court looks at their

evidence log
A document attached to an item of physical evidence recording the chain of possession of that piece of evidence.

expert witness
An individual with special education, experience, and expertise, who is hired to explain the technical aspects of a case to a judge or jury and who is allowed to express his expert opinion.

education, skill, and experience in that field. If an individual is qualified as an expert, at trial this individual can explain and simplify complicated technical issues for the judge or jury. For example, a jury might have difficulty understanding the mechanical functions of a tire manufacturing plant or the significance of a lung x-ray. Expert witnesses may translate the technical language to easily understood language through photographs, charts, or models. Also, expert witnesses, unlike lay witnesses, are allowed to testify about their expert opinions regarding matters within their expertise. For example, in the Morrison case, a proper expert could testify that in his opinion chemicals to which Mr. Morrison was exposed at work caused the asbestosis.

The decision to hire an expert witness is made by the supervising attorney. However, you may be asked to locate an expert. Suggested sources for locating potential experts include:

- professional organizations
- published court records of experts
- other attorneys in your office
- colleges or universities
- professional journals
- attorneys who have handled similar litigation

If the expert has testified in prior cases you might wish to talk to the attorney who tried the case to get an evaluation of the expert's ability as a witness. The demeanor of an expert witness can be even more important than that of a lay witness. Although the expert's professional credentials are important, his or her ability to explain matters to a judge or jury in a simple and clear manner, without appearing condescending, is just as important.

Once you have located an expert you must keep certain practical considerations in mind. An expert's time is very valuable, and use of that time by your law firm can be expensive. Most experts charge the firm not only for the time they spend testifying in court, but also for any time spent in talking to the attorneys (or paralegals). Any interview of an expert must be carefully orchestrated to maximize the expert's time. Preparation in advance of the interview will obviate the need for a lengthy interview process. Know ahead of time what areas need to be covered and make notes. Also, if the expert is local, arranging the interview to take place at the expert's place of business can save time and therefore expense.

One pitfall to avoid in securing an expert witness is the "professional testifying expert." An excessive number of court appearances can have a negative impact on the jury, especially where that expert has always testified for the plaintiff or for the defendant. An expert whose testimony has been balanced will be more effective.

Before deciding to use a particular expert you should review the expert's resume and determine if he has testified in prior cases. If he has qualified as an expert in prior cases, he is likely to be qualified by the court in your case. You should also review all prior cases to make sure that he has not given testimony that would contradict the testimony he expects to give in your case.

Your responsibilities in the area of expert witnesses may include locating an expert, coordinating the interview of the expert witness with the attorney, taking notes during an interview, reviewing the qualifications of the expert, reviewing prior testimony of the expert, and, if the expert is located some distance away, handling hotel and air travel reservations.

SUMMARY

4–1   A client interview establishes the foundation for the relationship between the client and the law firm. The paralegal is often involved in different aspects of this procedure. Paralegal responsibilities might include researching potential causes of action or defenses prior to the interview, scheduling the interview, developing an interview questionnaire, gathering forms and documents for client signature, taking notes during the interview, and producing a summary of the interview.

4–2   Locating witnesses who have knowledge of the facts of the case is an essential part of the litigation process and is often a paralegal function. Likewise, locating the defendant in the action is a task often assigned to paralegals. Various sources exist to help the paralegal find witnesses or elusive defendants. Some of those sources include the client, an accident report, official records, and computerized services such as NEXIS and INFORMATION AMERICA.

4–3   When interviewing fact witnesses a paralegal should always be properly identified. The paralegal should always be courteous and consider the convenience of the witness. Tape-recorded interviews are preferred, but if the witness objects a written statement or notes can be used. A questionnaire should be prepared before the interview, and care should be taken during the interview itself to avoid the leading question. After the interview the paralegal should prepare a typewritten statement for signature by the witness. During the interview the paralegal should observe and make note of the witness's demeanor.

4–4 Paralegals are often involved in locating and preserving evidence in a civil case. Evidence includes documents or other items that tend to prove the facts of the case. Items of evidence relating to the client can often be obtained by a simple request accompanied by a signed release from the client. In other situations discovery methods must be utilized. After evidence is obtained proper care must be taken to control and preserve the evidence for trial. To avoid charges that evidence has been altered, the chain of possession of the evidence must be verified.

4–5 Expert witnesses are often essential in a case. They are able to explain technical matters to a judge or jury and can offer their professional opinions regarding issues in the case. Paralegals are sometimes asked to locate experts, coordinate interviews between the expert and the attorney, take notes during the interview, review the qualifications and prior testimony of the expert, and handle hotel and air travel reservations.

KEY TERMS

agent for service of process
authorization
demeanor
evidence log
expert witness

leading question
medical diary
release
representation letter
retainer agreement

QUESTIONS FOR REVIEW AND DISCUSSION

1. What is the paralegal's responsibility in preparing for the client interview?
2. What are the steps in setting up a client interview?
3. What types of questions should be included in a client interview questionnaire?
4. What forms might be needed during the client interview for client signature?
5. What is the function of a paralegal during the client interview?
6. What are some possible sources for locating fact witnesses or elusive defendants?
7. How should fact witnesses be interviewed?
8. What are the methods for locating, controlling, and preserving evidence?

9. What is the importance of the expert witness?
10. What is the paralegal's role in retaining an expert witness?

ACTIVITIES

1. Review the commentary at the opening of this chapter and draft questions for your attorney to ask at the initial interview.
2. Assume that you are to interview one of Oscar Morrison's friends and co-workers. Draft a questionnaire to be used during the interview.
3. You have been asked to assist the attorney in finding an expert witness to help establish that Morrison's work environment contributed to the asbestosis. Identify and locate places in your general area where you might find such an expert.

CHAPTER 4 PROJECT—TAKING A WITNESS STATEMENT

For this project you need to work with another student in the class. One of you should assume the role of a friend and co-worker of Oscar Morrison, while the other assumes the role of a paralegal working in the firm representing Mr. Morrison. The "paralegal" is to conduct a tape-recorded interview of the co-worker. After the interview is recorded, both students should prepare a typewritten statement of the interview.

CHAPTER 5

The Initial Pleadings

COMMENTARY—THE HENDRICKS CASE

Your attorney has just given you a file containing the preliminary investigative reports and notes concerning new clients, Margaret and Paul Hendricks. After reviewing the various documents in the file, and after discussing the matter with your attorney, you learn the following facts. While vacationing in Nevada, the Hendricks, residents of the state of California, attended a sales presentation regarding vacation property located in Idaho. During the sales presentation, which was conducted by May Forrester, a real estate agent with Hearth & Home Real Estate Co., the Hendricks were shown numerous color slides of the vacation property, all depicting large, level lots surrounding a man-made lake. The lots were owned by Paradise Found, Inc., an Idaho corporation. They were told during the presentation that the lots were ready for building. The lots were being offered for the price of $60,000. However, only two lots remained unsold, and the realtor expected these to go quickly. Swayed by the sales presentation, the Hendricks purchased a lot without personally visiting the site. They paid cash and were given a deed. Shortly thereafter they visited the property in Idaho, only to find that the lot they owned was nothing like the photos they had seen. The lake was completely dry, no lots had been built on, and in fact a great deal of preparation would have to be done before any building. There were no utilities, sewers, or roads. They immediately contacted the realtor, May Forrester, the company she works for, Hearth & Home Real Estate Co., and the seller of the property, Paradise Found, Inc. The sellers have refused to return the Hendricks' money and say that nothing can be done. Incidentally, the file also indicates that Hearth & Home Real Estate Co. is really a partnership owned by Harry and Harvey Rice. Your attorney is anxious to initiate a lawsuit in this matter and has asked you to prepare a complaint, for her review, naming all proper parties and containing all possible causes of action.

OBJECTIVES

In chapter 4 you were introduced to the methods for obtaining information necessary to pursue a lawsuit. After that information is obtained, the next step in the litigation process is the preparation and filing of the initial pleadings. After reading this chapter, you will be able to:

1. Define the term *pleadings.*
2. Describe, in general, the contents of a complaint or petition.

3. Discuss the various considerations in determining and identifying parties to the lawsuit.
4. Describe the various allegations found in a complaint.
5. Explain the types of relief that can be requested in a complaint.
6. Outline the steps in drafting a complaint.
7. Explain the process of filing the complaint.
8. Define a summons.
9. List the different methods of serving a complaint.
10. Describe the procedure for amending the complaint.

5-1 INITIAL PLEADINGS

Pleadings in General

After completing preliminary investigation, interviewing, and research, the attorney determines whether or not to pursue the case. If the decision is made to proceed, the litigation process formally begins with the preparation and filing of appropriate pleadings. **Pleadings** are the various documents filed in a court proceeding that define the nature of the dispute between the parties. Not all documents filed with the court are pleadings. The term *pleading* technically refers only to those papers that contain statements, or **allegations,** describing the contentions and defenses of the parties to the lawsuit. The pleadings set the framework for all of the steps and proceedings that follow, and, if an issue is not raised in the pleadings, the parties may be prevented from bringing it up at trial. Although pleadings relate to contentions of the parties, these documents are always prepared by the law firm representing the party. As a paralegal in a litigation firm, one of your duties might include the drafting of these documents. You might also be asked to review pleadings prepared by the opposing side.

The content and format of the various pleadings are largely controlled by the appropriate statutory law. Cases filed in federal court are governed primarily by the Federal Rules of Civil Procedure. Cases filed in a state court would be governed by the laws of the state. In addition to state rules, many county or area courts have their own individual rules, known as local rules of court. Within the federal court system, various district courts may also have their own local rules. Local rules can differ from one court to another, even if the courts are located in the same state. Before preparing or filing any pleading, therefore, you must check all local rules. In spite of the numerous technical rules that may govern pleadings, most courts take a fairly liberal attitude in reviewing or judging the sufficiency of the documents. The courts today are concerned that the parties resolve their disputes based on the merits of the case, rather than on some technical rule regarding the format of a document.

The Complaint in General

Assuming that your law firm represents the plaintiff in an action, the initial pleading that you prepare and file, and that starts the court process, is generally known as a **complaint**, or in some cases, a **petition**. The complaint is the pleading in which the plaintiff states the basis for the lawsuit. Generally the complaint does the following:

1. Identifies the plaintiffs and defendants in the lawsuit, and describes their status and capacity to sue and be sued;
2. Contains a statement showing that the court in which it is filed has proper jurisdiction and venue;
3. Describes the factual basis for the lawsuit;
4. Makes a request or demand for some relief from the court.

The complaint itself usually follows a set format, with various parts known as:

1. the **caption**—the part of the complaint that identifies the court in which the complaint is filed, the names of the plaintiffs and defendants, and the title of the document (see Figure 5–1);
2. the allegations (or cause of action)—a description of the parties, statements showing proper jurisdiction and venue, the factual basis for the lawsuit, and a description of the loss or damages incurred;
3. the **prayer**—a request for some relief or remedy from the court;
4. The **subscription** and **verification**—the signature of the attorney filing the document, the date, and the plaintiff's statement, under penalty of perjury, that the contents of the complaint are true.

5-2 PARTIES TO THE LAWSUIT

The parties to the lawsuit are known as the plaintiff, the one who files the action, and the defendant, the one who is sued. They are identified in the caption by their names, indicating whether they are named as plaintiff or defendant. For example, in the situation described in the commentary, if the Hendricks wished to sue the realtor the names of the parties would appear in the

pleadings
Documents filed in a lawsuit describing the claims and defenses of the parties.

allegations
Contentions stated in a pleading.

complaint
The initial document filed in a lawsuit; states the factual basis for the claim.

petition
An initial document or pleading filed in court requesting some relief; in some jurisdictions the term is used instead of complaint.

caption
The part of a pleading or motion identifying the court, the parties, the nature of the document, and the docket number.

prayer
The part of a complaint in which the relief is requested; sometimes known as the "wherefore" clause or demand.

subscription
The signature at the end of a pleading.

verification
A statement under penalty of perjury that the contents of a document are true to the best of the knowledge of the person verifying; sometimes attached to pleadings and responses to discovery requests.

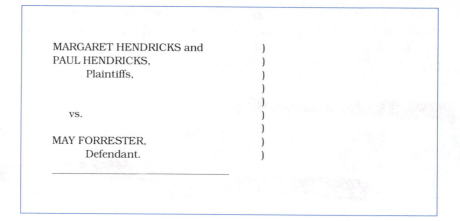

MARGARET HENDRICKS and)
PAUL HENDRICKS,)
     Plaintiffs,)
)
)
     vs.)
)
MAY FORRESTER,)
     Defendant.)

FIGURE 5–1
Designation of
Parties in Caption.

caption as shown in Figure 5–1. In the body of the complaint, the parties are then described in more detail.

Normally the question of who is named as a plaintiff and who is named as a defendant is relatively simple. At times, however, problems can arise. As a paralegal involved in preparing or drafting a complaint, you should be aware of some of these problem areas.

Real Party in Interest

The plaintiff in any lawsuit should be the one who is entitled to the relief sought in the complaint. This is known as the **real party in interest.** In most cases, parties do not file lawsuits unless they have personally suffered some loss. However, at times a special relationship exists that creates a different situation. For example, an executor may wish to sue on behalf of an estate, or a trustee may sue on behalf of a trust, or a collection agency may wish to sue on a debt assigned to it for collection. In such cases, is the plaintiff the executor or the estate, the trustee or the trust, the collection agency or the creditor? Under Rule 17a of the Federal Rules of Civil Procedure the executor, trustee, and even the collection agency could be named as plaintiffs in the lawsuit, even though they were not suing on their own behalf. However, if the action is in state court appropriate state laws should always be checked.

real party in interest
The person who is entitled to the relief sought in a complaint; usually the plaintiff, but in some cases the real party in interest is represented by another in a lawsuit.

Status

Status of a party refers to the type of entity that describes the party. Most commonly a party to a lawsuit will be an individual, a corporation, a partnership or other unincorporated business, or a governmental agency. Unless a party is simply an individual, the status of the party will usually be described both in the caption and in a separate allegation within the body of the complaint. For example, if the Hendricks were to sue the seller of the property, they would be identified in the caption as follows:

PARADISE FOUND, INC., an Idaho corporation,

Defendant

In addition, within the body of the complaint you would include a paragraph describing that status, such as the following:

Defendant, PARADISE FOUND, INC., is and was at all times herein mentioned a corporation duly organized and existing under the laws of the state of Idaho.

THE COMPUTERIZED LAW FIRM—Nonlegal Database

SCENARIO

Your attorney is ready to file suit on behalf of the Hendricks and asks you to prepare a draft of the complaint for his review. The attorney reminds you that the statute of limitations is running and that you have only a few days to file the complaint. The attorney also asks you to prepare instructions for the process server detailing who should be served with a copy of the complaint and where the documents are to be served. A review of the information in the file indicated that among the various defendants will be Hearth & Home Real Estate Co., and Paradise Found, Inc., both out of state businesses.

PROBLEM

The complaint you are drafting calls for allegations describing the status of the various defendants. You believe that one business is a corporation and the other a partnership, but you need to verify this information. You also need to know the identity of the agent for service of process for the corporation along with that individual's address. How can you get this information without wasting valuable time?

SOLUTION

Determining the corporate status of a company for purposes of filing a lawsuit against it is often difficult and time-consuming. In some cases, the company is not a legitimate corporation because it has failed to meet the state's filing or tax payment requirements. If this is the case, you may be able to sue the individuals behind the corporation. Even where the corporation is duly organized and authorized to do business as a corporation, the company name furnished by the client may not be the correct name. Sometimes the principal place of business for the company is unknown. A computerized law firm can access a nationwide database that may provide the information.

Information America, the database mentioned in the previous chapter, allows you to locate detailed information about businesses as well as individuals. As of 1991, records from the secretary of state's offices in twenty-three states were available. This means you could get specific information on corporations, including correct corporate name, agent for service of process, principal place of business, officers or directors of a corporation, whether the company is in good standing with the secretary of state, and the type of corporate structure.

A unique location resource available on Information America is the Business Finder, which includes information on over 8.5 million companies nationwide. You enter only the name of the company and the state in which it is located and determine critical corporate data.

Another important feature of Information America is the Dun & Bradstreet section, which contains extensive financial information on companies. Using this source, you can determine before a lawsuit is filed whether there is any possibility for recovery of a judgment if the litigation is successful.

Capacity

Minors and Incompetents. You also need to make certain that the parties named in the complaint have **capacity**, or the legal right, to sue or be sued. Competent, adult individuals generally have the right to sue or be sued. However, children or incompetent adults do not have the capacity to pursue their own lawsuits. Unless a general guardian or conservator has already been appointed, the court will appoint a special person, referred to as a **guardian ad litem**, to pursue the case on behalf of the minor or incompetent. Even the parents of a child cannot file a lawsuit on their child's

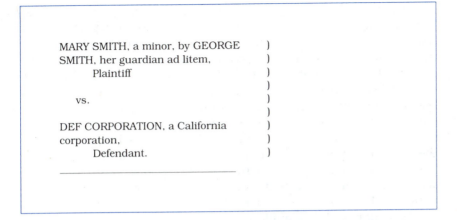

MARY SMITH, a minor, by GEORGE
SMITH, her guardian ad litem,
    Plaintiff

    vs.

DEF CORPORATION, a California
corporation,
    Defendant.

FIGURE 5–2
Designation of
Parties—Guardian
Ad Litem.

behalf unless they have been appointed as a guardian by the
court. A guardian ad litem is usually appointed at the request of
the parent or guardian. The person wishing to be appointed files a
motion or a petition with the court prior to filing any lawsuit, asking to be named as guardian ad litem. The complaint in such a
case would have the same caption as the petition or motion for the
appointment of the guardian. See Figure 5–2 for an example of
how the parties would be designated in such a case.

Although children or incompetents cannot sue in their own
names, they can generally be named as defendants in the complaint. However, after they are served with the complaint they may
be entitled to have a guardian appointed to represent their interests. Again, local law should be reviewed to determine if the appointment of a guardian ad litem for a defendant is necessary, and
if so how is it accomplished.

Corporations and Other Business Entities. A corporation is a
"person" for legal purposes, including lawsuits. As such it has
capacity to sue or be sued in the corporate name. In fact, if a
corporation is a plaintiff or a defendant in a lawsuit, it must be
identified by the corporate name, rather than the name of the
directors, officers, or shareholders. Exceptions do occur, however, in the case of corporate defendants. If the corporation fails to
act like a corporation, not keeping corporate minutes, not holding
meetings, failing to keep corporate assets separate from personal
assets, then the individuals behind the corporation can be sued
individually. This is known as "piercing the corporate veil." The
directors, officers, or shareholders of a corporation will also be
named individually as defendants if they have personally done
something wrong.

capacity
The legal right to
sue or be sued.
guardian ad litem
An individual
appointed by the
court to represent
the interests of a
minor who is a
party to a lawsuit.

Know

Business entities other than corporations may be treated differently. An unincorporated association, such as a partnership, does not have legal existence separate and apart from the partners. It is proper, therefore, for such organizations to sue and be sued in the name of its members. Whether or not such a business must be sued in the name of its members is a question of local law. For example, some jurisdictions allow a partnership to be sued in the partnership name. Before doing this, however, you should check the law regarding collection of a judgment when the individual partners have not been named. Limitations may be placed on those assets that can be seized to satisfy the judgment. When suing a partnership or other unincorporated business entity, it is common to list both the partners' names and the business name. For example:

HARRY RICE and HARVEY RICE, a partnership,
doing business as

Hearth & Home Real Estate Co., Defendants.

Governmental Agencies.   There is no question about the right of a governmental entity to sue on a claim. However, because of the common law doctrine of sovereign immunity (the king could not be sued), many jurisdictions have laws that limit and regulate the circumstances under which a governmental entity can be sued. Appropriate statutes must be checked to see if the claim is one for which the offending governmental agency can be sued. Even where a statute permits the government to be sued, many laws require that claims be filed with the governmental agency before actually filing a lawsuit. (See chapter 3.) In such a case, it may be necessary to allege in the body of the complaint that this has been done.

Special Problems with Parties

Parties Using Fictitious Names.   Many businesses do not use their true names in the operation of their businesses. Individuals, either operating alone or with others, often choose to do business under a name that has more business appeal than their real name. At times, even corporations will do business under a name other than the real corporate name. If a plaintiff uses a fictitious name in his business, a lawsuit that he files related to that business should identify the plaintiff by his proper name. If he wishes, the plaintiff may indicate that he is doing business under another name. The plaintiff would then be identified as follows:

MARTIN REDSHAW, doing business as Marty's Diner,
Plaintiff.

If the plaintiff is doing business under a fictitious name, before the lawsuit is filed you should verify that the plaintiff has complied with all local laws regarding such usage. Some states, for example, require that fictitious name statements be filed, and failure to do so can affect the right of a party to sue in some cases.

Where the defendant is doing business under a fictitious name, the true name of the party may be unknown to you when you are preparing the complaint. Your state may have various records that can be checked, but these are not always complete or accurate. It is therefore necessary to identify the defendant in the complaint by the fictitious name. In such a case, when the true name of the defendant or defendants is determined, the complaint can generally be amended.

Fictitious Defendants. Not to be confused with parties who use a fictitious name in business is a concept known as **fictitiously named defendants**, a procedure that is allowed in some jurisdictions. This term usually refers to defendants whose very identity is unknown. They are usually identified as "Does." In jurisdictions that allow their use, "Does" are commonly named as defendants in complaints to cover a situation where a new defendant is discovered after the statute of limitations has run. In such a case the attorney argues that the complaint was filed against the newly discovered defendant within the statute of limitations. He was just referred to by an incorrect name. The attorney then tries to amend the complaint to "correct" the name.

Joining Multiple Parties

Many lawsuits involve disputes with multiple plaintiffs and/or defendants. The rules concerning joinder of multiple parties can be extremely involved and confusing. However, joinder of parties usually falls into two categories, joinder that is allowed but not required, known as **permissive joinder**, and joinder that is required, or **compulsory joinder**. Before drafting any complaint with multiple parties you may need to review these rules. For example, in the *Hendricks* case described in the commentary, you may need to know whether the Hendricks can sue the realtor, the company for which she works, and the seller in the same lawsuit. This is determined by the rules of joinder, which are usually found in the appropriate state laws (or Rules 19–21 of the Federal Rules of Civil Procedure, if the case is in federal court).

fictitiously named defendants
Defendants in a lawsuit who are not identified by their correct names; usually refers to the practice in some state courts of including several "Does" as defendants to provide for discovery of additional defendants after the statute of limitations has run.

permissive joinder
A concept allowing multiple parties to be joined in one lawsuit as plaintiffs or defendants as long as there is some common question of fact or law.

compulsory joinder
The required association of multiple parties as plaintiffs or defendants in a lawsuit; occurs when the court cannot render relief without the presence of all the parties.

The rules regarding permissive joinder, joinder of parties that is allowed but not required, are usually very liberal. Parties are permitted to be joined together in a complaint as plaintiffs or defendants as long as there is some common question involving them. Of course, you would not name someone as a plaintiff in a complaint unless your law firm represented the party. Whether certain parties must be joined in the same complaint is a more difficult issue. Generally if the court cannot resolve the matter without the presence of a party, then joinder of the party is required. For example, suppose that title to a certain piece of real property is in question, and four different individuals are claiming ownership. If one of those parties files a lawsuit to determine ownership (known as a **quiet title action**) he would have to name the other three claimants as defendants. The court could not determine ownership unless all four parties were before the court. Where parties are required to be joined in the lawsuit, they are sometimes referred to as **indispensable parties**.

Even where it appears that joinder of certain parties is essential to the case, if jurisdiction over one of the parties is impossible to obtain the court may allow the matter to proceed without that party being named. These cases obviously present complicated legal issues that need to be thoroughly researched before preparing the complaint.

Class Actions

At times the number of potential plaintiffs in an action becomes too numerous to be practical. When this happens a **class action** can result. A class action occurs when one or more parties who share a claim with a multitude of others file a lawsuit in their own names and also claim to represent numerous others in a similar situation. In order to maintain a class action, the party filing the lawsuit must usually get permission from the court to proceed with the action. If the court grants permission, it will also direct that all members of the class are to get notice of the action. Generally the court also orders that all class members who can be identified should get individual notice. This can be an overwhelming and expensive task. If your firm is involved in a class action, as a litigation paralegal you may be asked to take responsibility for this part of the litigation. Included in the notice to all potential members of the class is usually an explanation that any potential class member can request in writing that he or she be excluded from the class. If a member does not request exclusion, that class member will be bound by any judgment in the case.

Class actions permit cases to be brought where the amount of damages suffered by each plaintiff is minimal but the total damages suffered by all is substantial. In such a case it is not practical for parties to maintain their own individual lawsuits. The cost of litigation would outweigh any benefit. By joining together, the class of injured parties is able to minimize expenses and justify the litigation.

Every jurisdiction has its own rules, found in statutes and cases, regarding class action lawsuits. These rules usually deal with such matters as who can file, who is entitled to notice of the action, how that notice is to be given, and who must bear the cost of notice. Rule 23 of the Federal Rules of Civil Procedure governs class actions in federal court.

Interpleader

A special type of action or complaint, known as **interpleader**, also involves questions of joinder of parties. Interpleader refers to a type of action in which several different parties claim ownership to a fund or property that is in the control of another. For example, an insurance company provides liability coverage to an airline with a policy limit of one billion dollars. A plane crashes, and the heirs of the victims file claims with the airline and the insurance company in excess of ten billion dollars. If liability is clear, the insurance company might determine at the outset that it is going to have to pay the policy limits. However, the question of how this money is to be appropriated remains. The insurance company does not want to unilaterally make this decision, since it would probably be sued if the claimants did not agree with the distribution. The appropriate action, therefore, is for the insurance company to ask the court to decide how the funds should be disbursed. This is accomplished by filing an action in interpleader with the court, naming all of the claimants as defendants. The insurance company can then deposit the policy limits with the court and withdraw from the action, leaving the claimants to fight over the money.

5–3 PLEADING JURISDICTION AND VENUE

The complaint in any action must contain some allegation showing that the lawsuit is being filed in the proper court. This involves questions of both jurisdiction and venue. In a complaint filed in federal court, these allegations are usually very specific. In showing jurisdiction, the plaintiff usually states why the action is being filed in federal court, giving a citation to the appropriate

quiet title action
A type of lawsuit in which the court is asked to determine ownership to real property.

indispensable party
A party who must be joined in a lawsuit in order for the court to be able to render a fair and complete judgment in the case.

class action
An action maintained by or against one or more individuals on their own behalf and on behalf of numerous others in the same situation.

interpleader
A type of lawsuit in which the court is requested to determine ownership to certain property that is being claimed by several parties; the action is filed by one holding the property even though that person has no ownership interest in the property and is filed to protect the holder from delivering the property to the wrong party or parties.

United States Code section. See Figure 5–3 for sample allegations regarding federal jurisdiction.

In state courts, jurisdiction is determined by state law. Normally it is not necessary to make any express statement that jurisdiction belongs in state court rather than federal court. Such a conclusion will usually follow from all of the facts alleged in the complaint. In many states, however, there are different kinds of trial courts with different kinds of jurisdiction. For example, some state trial courts are empowered to hear civil cases only where the amount in dispute is under a set amount of money. Somewhere in the complaint and in the prayer, or demand for relief, it should appear that the amount claimed is within the jurisdiction of the court in which the case is filed.

In federal or state courts, venue can be determined by a number of factors. The most common factor is the residence of either the plaintiff or the defendant. Proper venue can be shown in the complaint by an allegation that one of the parties resides in the district in which the action is filed. Venue is also proper in the place where the cause of action arose. Therefore, another common way of establishing venue is by alleging that the cause of action arose in the district in which the action is filed. However, there are many different ways to establish venue, depending on the nature of the case. See Figure 5–4 for examples of allegations showing venue.

FIGURE 5–3
Sample Allegations Regarding Federal Jurisdiction.

(Diversity of Citizenship)

Plaintiff is, and was at all times herein mentioned, domiciled in and a citizen of the State of California.

Defendant is, and was at all times herein mentioned, domiciled in and a citizen of the State of Nevada.

This is a civil action involving, exclusive of interest and costs, a sum in excess of $50,000. Every issue of law and fact in this action is wholly between citizens of different states.

(Constitutional Question)

This is a civil action for [describe claim] arising under Amendment _____ to the United States Constitution. This Court has jurisdiction by reason of Title 28, United States Code, Section 1331.

At all times herein mentioned, defendant was and now is a resident of the County of _____ , State of _____ .

or

The County of _____ is the proper county in which to bring and maintain this action by virtue of the fact that defendant ABC Corporation has its principal executive offices located therein.

or

The County of _____ is the proper county in which to bring and maintain this action by virtue of the fact that the real property which is the subject of this action is located in said county.

FIGURE 5–4
Sample Venue
Allegations.

5–4 PLEADING THE CLAIM OR CAUSE OF ACTION

Although the complaint or petition usually follows certain legal technicalities, it is primarily a document that shows the factual basis for the lawsuit. It does not contain any discussion or analysis of legal theories. However, when reviewing the facts that are alleged in the complaint, the defendant's attorney and the court should be able to tell that there is a legal basis for the lawsuit, even though the legal basis need not be expressly stated in the complaint. How detailed this factual description must be depends on the jurisdiction in which the lawsuit is filed. If you recall the discussion in chapter 3 you remember that before deciding to file any lawsuit, an attorney must determine that a party has a "cause of action." That is, a kind of dispute exists where one party is entitled to some kind of legal remedy. In some jurisdictions the complaint must contain factual allegations or statements that support each element of the cause of action. Because this method of pleading is based on a New York law known as the "Field Code," these jurisdictions are sometimes known as "code pleading" jurisdictions. Other jurisdictions, including the federal courts, have a less stringent requirement. The complaint must contain sufficient facts to put the defendant on notice as to why he is being sued, but it is not essential that each element of the cause of action be supported by factual allegations. This method of pleading is known as "notice pleading." Although these differences exist in the technical requirements between code pleading jurisdictions and notice pleading jurisdictions, any complaint that is sufficient under code pleading rules would also be sufficient under notice pleading rules. The important thing to remember is that both types of pleading require that facts, and not legal theories, be alleged. For example, in a claim resulting from injuries sustained in an automobile accident, the allegations could read as shown in Figure 5–5.

Handling Multiple Claims

Often, a plaintiff has more than one potential claim against the defendant. Again, consider the Hendricks case described in the commentary. If the plaintiffs can prove that their realtor knew that the slides of the property were forgeries and that the property was not suitable for building and lied to them about it, they have a claim for fraud or intentional misrepresentation. Such a claim, if proven, would entitle the plaintiffs to punitive damages in addition to their out-of-pocket losses. On the other hand, proving that a misrepresentation was intentional is sometimes difficult, and the plaintiff's attorney may wish to also have a claim for negligent misrepresentation, in the event that the defendant's intent cannot be adequately shown. Certainly, in the case described, the realtor should have been more certain about her facts before making representations to prospective buyers. Proving negligent misrepresentation would entitle the plaintiffs to their actual losses but would not result in punitive damages. This is an alternative claim, which can be stated in the complaint. Normally, this claim would be set out in a second cause of action, sometimes referred to as a **count**, separate from the first cause of action or first count for fraud. In the Hendricks case, other causes of action may also be possible. For example, the Hendricks might simply wish to disaffirm the contract (rescind it) and get their money back (restitution). Additionally, since the Hendricks did not have their own real

FIGURE 5–5
Allegations
Describing a
Claim (Negligence).

1. On May 1, 1990, on a public highway called Market Street in San Antonio, Texas, defendant negligently and carelessly drove a motor vehicle causing it to collide with another vehicle driven by plaintiff who was also traveling on said highway.

2. As a result plaintiff was severely injured, having had his leg broken and having suffered other bruises, contusions and muscle strain. Also as a result plaintiff was prevented from transacting his business, suffered great pain of body and mind, and incurred expenses for medical attention and hospitalization in the sum of $5,000.00.

estate agent, the facts might indicate that May Forrester was acting in a dual capacity, representing both Paradise Found, Inc. and the Hendricks. As such, May Forrester would be in a special fiduciary relationship with the Hendricks, a relationship that she abused. This could result in another claim.

A complaint may contain any number of causes of action or counts. Whenever a cause of action arises out of the same general factual situation, the rules of pleading usually allow them to be joined in the same complaint.

Determining whether the defendant's conduct toward the plaintiff results in more than one claim or cause of action can be very difficult. As a general rule, if the claims provide different remedies or are proven by different facts or evidence in the case, they should probably be separated into distinct causes of action. However, because the rules of interpreting pleadings are so liberal, if two or more claims were combined into one cause of action, the court would either allow the pleading to stand as written or allow it to be amended.

A question sometimes arises when a complaint contains two causes of action that are inconsistent. For example, consider the following situation. Bryant signs a contract with Yates to buy a house for $200,000. Before the time for the deal to close, Yates informs Bryant that he has changed his mind and will not sell. As of the date of sale, the value of the house had increased to $220,000. Bryant now has a choice. Does he want the house, or should he make Yates pay for any damages that he incurred because he did not get the house, the damages being the difference between the purchase price and the fair market value at the time and place of sale. If he gets the house at the original contract price, he will not have incurred the loss of profit in the house. Therefore asking for both the specific performance of the contract and for damages because it wasn't performed are inconsistent. The rules of pleading usually allow the plaintiff to allege causes of action that are inconsistent. However, the plaintiff will not get a judgment on both of them.

Handling Multiple Parties

We have already seen that a complaint may contain multiple plaintiffs or defendants. When this occurs questions always arise about whether the parties should be joined within the same cause of action, or whether separate causes of action are required. No absolute rules govern this situation, and the rules of pleading in most jurisdictions are liberal enough to allow almost any method of handling this situation. However, some guidelines are commonly followed.

count
In some complaints the parts stating the various causes of action; each cause of action is stated in a separate count; sometimes referred to as a cause of action instead of a count.

Multiple Plaintiffs. Multiple plaintiffs should be joined within the same cause of action if they have a joint claim or if they are suing for the same thing. For example, in the factual situation described in the commentary, both Margaret and Paul Hendricks are suing for the same thing—the damages that they sustained in buying the lot. Note that they are not each suing for one-half of the damages. They are suing together for the total damages. Therefore they should be joined in the same cause of action.

Where the plaintiffs are suing for something different, however, their claims should be in separate causes of action. For example, suppose that Herbert and Wanda Sepulveda, husband and wife, are both injured in the same automobile accident and wish to sue the driver of the other vehicle. In such a case they are suing for different things. He is suing for his injuries, and she is suing for her injuries. They would, therefore, have two separate causes of action. However, the two causes of action would be in one complaint. Where there are multiple plaintiffs and defendants it is not necessary that they all be parties to each of the causes of action. Again, where there is some common factual or legal basis among the various causes of action, they can be joined in one complaint.

5–5 DEMAND FOR RELIEF

Every complaint or petition filed in an action contains a demand for relief from the court, often called a prayer. Courts have the power to grant two different types of relief, money damages and equitable relief. Money damages usually means the award of money to the plaintiff as compensation for some loss. Equitable relief, on the other hand, involves the court ordering the defendant to do something or to stop doing something other than simply paying money damages. In some state jurisdictions, only certain courts have the power to grant equitable relief. Before preparing and filing any complaint requesting this type of relief, be sure to check jurisdictional power of the court.

Money Damages

Probably the most common relief sought in a civil lawsuit is money damages. The primary purpose of damages in a civil suit is to compensate plaintiffs for a loss that they have sustained. These damages are known as **compensatory damages**. In certain kinds of cases, compensatory damages may be referred to by other names. For example, in personal injury cases compensatory damages are categorized as either special damages or general damages. Special damages are actual out-of-pocket expenses incurred by the plaintiff, such as doctor's bills and lost earnings. General damages are not out-of-pocket expenses, but include such things as pain and suffering, loss of use of a limb, or disfigurement caused by a scar. Even though general damages do not reimburse the plaintiff for an economic expense, they do compensate the plaintiff for some loss.

Although money damages in most civil cases are compensatory in nature, sometimes a plaintiff is entitled to recover **punitive, or exemplary, damages**. These are meant to punish the defendant and are awarded only when the defendant has committed some extremely offensive act. Such damages are not favored by the courts and come under careful scrutiny by the appellate courts. Nevertheless they are allowed in some cases.

In the course of any lawsuit, the parties will inevitably incur substantial expenses, or costs. These can include such items as filing fees, process server fees, deposition fees, and expert witness fees. Costs are not included in computing the plaintiff's damages. However, if the plaintiff wins his lawsuit, he will generally be awarded certain costs in addition to the actual damages. On the other hand, should the defendant win the case, he will generally be awarded his costs from the plaintiff. Items that are included in these recoverable costs are usually determined by a specific statute. One element that is usually not included in the list of recoverable costs is the attorney fee in the case. Unless the lawsuit is based on a contract that specifically provides for the payment of attorney fees in the event of a legal dispute, or unless there is some special law governing the situation, parties are expected to pay their own attorney fees.

Equitable Relief

There are some legal disputes that cannot be settled by the award of money damages. For example, suppose Friedman sells Brockland his business. As part of the sales agreement, Friedman agrees not to open a competing business within a fifty-mile radius for a period of two years. However, two months after the sale, Friedman opens a competing business across the street from Brockland. As a result Brockland's business income substantially decreases. While money damages might compensate Brockland for his past loss, if Friedman continues in business Brockland will continue to lose money, the exact amount of which would be difficult to calculate. Brockland would therefore prefer that the court order Friedman to close down his competing business. Such an order would be a kind of relief known as **equitable relief**. (Lawsuits in which equitable relief is sought are known as actions in equity, whereas lawsuits in which money damages are sought are

compensatory damages Damages intended to compensate or reimburse a party for the actual loss sustained; most common measure of damages in a civil case.

punitive, or exemplary, damages Damages assessed to punish the defendant for some type of extremely offensive conduct.

equitable relief Remedy provided by a court other than money damages.

known as actions at law.) A complaint may combine a request for equitable relief and money damages.

The types of equitable relief that can be ordered by a court of equitable jurisdiction are varied. Some of the more common types of equitable relief are:

Specific Performance—An order requiring a party to perform a contract.

Rescission—An order rescinding or voiding a contract.

Restitution—An order to return money or property, usually paid in connection with a contract that was subsequently rescinded.

Declaratory Relief—A court order defining or explaining the rights and obligations of parties under some contract.

Quiet Title—An order clarifying ownership of real property.

Injunction—An order requiring a party to stop doing something.

Along with the award of equitable relief, the court will also probably award the prevailing party his costs of suit, just as in the case of an award of money damages.

Provisional Remedies

In most courts a substantial time elapses between the filing of a complaint and the actual trial in that case. Therefore, when injunctive relief is the primary object of a lawsuit, the plaintiff will often request some immediate provisional remedy from the court as soon as a complaint is filed. Provisional remedies usually include a temporary restraining order and a preliminary injunction. A **temporary restraining order** usually compels the defendant to stop certain conduct immediately. These are granted without any formal hearing, based primarily on affidavits or declarations (written statements under penalty of perjury) that are submitted to the court. Because the courts are hesitant to grant any orders without giving all sides the opportunity for a hearing, temporary restraining orders (T.R.O.'s) remain in effect for a very short time, usually until a hearing can be scheduled in court. As soon as possible, then, a hearing is scheduled at which both sides have the opportunity to argue for or against the restraining order remaining in effect until the time of trial. This hearing is not a full trial of all the issues. Should the court decide to keep the restraining order in effect, it will issue a **preliminary injunction**, an order that remains in effect until the trial, at which time the injunction would become permanent if the plaintiff proves his case.

5–6 DRAFTING THE COMPLAINT

Once you have identified the parties to the lawsuit, determined what causes of action the plaintiff has, and what relief is to be requested, you are prepared to start drafting the complaint for your attorney's review. Before actually writing the document, however, be sure to check any local court rules regarding technical requirements for the pleading. Is a certain kind or size of paper required? Does the size of print matter? Is there a special format that must be followed? Many courts have special rules regarding these kinds of matters. Also, in order to save a great deal of time, you should check various form books in your law library (or a form file, if one is kept in the office) for a sample complaint that deals with a similar factual situation. Even the most experienced litigation attorneys and paralegals follow forms whenever possible. If a case is to be filed in federal court, *American Jurisprudence Pleading and Practice Forms Annotated (Am. Jur.)*, published by The Lawyers Co-operative Publishing Co. and Bancroft Whitney Co., can be helpful. Additionally, some illustrative form pleadings are included in an Appendix of Forms found with the Federal Rules of Civil Procedure.

In some jurisdictions a complaint is prepared on numbered paper known as pleading paper. However, many jurisdictions have discontinued this practice. The first part of any complaint or petition is known as the caption. The caption contains the name of the court in which the action is being filed, the names of the plaintiffs and defendants, and the title of the document. In some jurisdictions it also contains the name, address, and phone number of the attorney and who the attorney represents. In other jurisdictions, the caption also contains the addresses of the plaintiff and defendant. See Figure 5–6 for an example of a caption.

Below the caption will be the body of the complaint containing various jurisdictional and factual allegations that constitute the plaintiff's cause of action. These allegations are broken down into short, numbered paragraphs. Since there is no absolute method for paragraphing, the use of form books or other sample complaints is very helpful in setting up this part of the complaint. In the absence of a form to follow, you can use normal paragraphing rules.

Even though there is no mandatory order in which paragraphing must be done, there are usual ways in which it is done:

1. In most cases you will see paragraphs on jurisdiction and venue first.
2. If any of the parties are businesses, either corporate or otherwise, allegations concerning their status or capacity will then follow.

specific performance An order requiring a party to perform a contract.

rescission An order rescinding or voiding a contract.

restitution An order to return money or property, usually paid in connection with a contract that was subsequently rescinded.

declaratory relief A court order defining or explaining the rights and obligations of parties under some contract.

quiet title An order clarifying ownership of real property.

injunction An order requiring a party to stop doing something.

temporary restraining order A court order requiring that a party take some action or refrain from certain conduct, usually issued by the court without a formal hearing at the beginning of a lawsuit upon the application of one party; it remains in effect only until a hearing can be scheduled, and at that time may be replaced with a preliminary injunction.

preliminary injunction A court order made prior to final judgment in the case, directing that a party take some action or refrain from taking some action until the trial in the case takes place.

UNITED STATES DISTRICT COURT
FOR THE NORTHERN DISTRICT OF CALIFORNIA

MARGARET HENDRICKS and)
PAUL HENDRICKS,)
    Plaintiffs,) No.
)
) COMPLAINT FOR FRAUD
    vs.)
)
MAY FORRESTER, an individual,)
HARRY RICE & HARVEY RICE,)
a partnership, doing business as)
Hearth & Home Real Estate Co.,)
PARADISE FOUND, INC., a)
corporation,)
    Defendants.)

FIGURE 5–6
Caption.

3. If there is more than one defendant in the lawsuit, it is standard to include an "agency" allegation. An agency allegation is one that claims that one or more of the defendants were agents or employees of one or more of the other defendants. Such an allegation refers to the substantive legal principle of vicarious liability or respondent superior, a concept that imposes liability of an employer for certain acts of his employees.

4. Following these standard allegations will be various allegations describing the factual basis for the lawsuit and a description of the damages that were suffered.

All statements contained in a complaint, or any pleading, should be true. However, at times a plaintiff is not certain about some facts that must be alleged in the complaint. For example, the plaintiff does not know for sure if the defendant business is a corporation or some other business entity, although the plaintiff believes that they are incorporated. In such cases, the proper way to plead the facts is "on information and belief." See Figure 5–7 for an example of the allegations for a cause of action that might be filed by the Hendricks. Paragraphs 2, 3, and 5 illustrate allegations made on information and belief.

Many complaints contain more than one cause of action. In such a case, it is important to remember that each cause of action should be sufficient in itself to constitute a legally sufficient complaint. Because of that it is often necessary to restate many of the

UNITED STATES DISTRICT COURT
FOR THE NORTHERN DISTRICT OF CALIFORNIA

MARGARET HENDRICKS and PAUL HENDRICKS, Plaintiffs,	))) No.)) COMPLAINT FOR FRAUD
vs.	))
MAY FORRESTER, an individual, HARRY RICE & HARVEY RICE, a partnership, doing business as Hearth & Home Real Estate Co., PARADISE FOUND, INC., a corporation, Defendants.	)))))))

FIRST CAUSE OF ACTION
(Fraud)

JURISDICTION

1. Plaintiffs are, and were at all times herein mentioned, domiciled in and citizens of the State of California. Defendants, MAY FORRESTER, HARRY RICE & HARVEY RICE, are and were at all times herein mentioned, domiciled in and citizens of the State of Nevada. Defendant, PARADISE FOUND, INC., was and is now a corporation duly organized and existing under the laws of the state of Idaho, with its offices and principal place of business in the state of Idaho. This is a civil action involving, exclusive of interest and costs, a sum in excess of $50,000. Every issue of law and fact in this action is wholly between citizens of different states.

2. Plaintiffs are informed and believe and thereupon allege that Defendants, HARRY RICE AND HARVEY RICE, are a partnership doing business as HEARTH & HOME REAL ESTATE CO.

3. Plaintiffs are informed and believe and thereupon allege that Defendant, PARADISE FOUND, INC., is a corporation duly organized and existing under the laws of the state of Idaho.

4. Plaintiffs are now, and at all times mentioned in this complaint have been residents of San Francisco County, California.

5. Plaintiffs are informed and believe and thereupon allege that at all times herein mentioned, each of the defendants was the agent

FIGURE 5–7
One Cause of Action.

and employee of each of the remaining defendants and in doing the things hereinafter alleged, was acting within the scope of said agency.

6. On or about June 1, 1990, in the City of Reno, State of Nevada, defendant, MAY FORRESTER, made the following false and fraudulent representations to plaintiffs: Defendant represented that certain real property was ideal vacation property, that said property had been approved for and was suitable for building, that said property abutted a man-made lake, and that said property was worth at least $60,000.

7. The representations made by the defendant were false in that said real property has not been approved nor is it suitable for building, it is not adjacent to any body of water, and was and is valued at less than $5,000.

8. Defendant, at the time she made said representations, knew them to be false and made the statements with the intent to defraud and deceive plaintiffs and to induce them to purchase that certain real property described above.

9. Plaintiffs at the time the representations were made believed them to be true and had no reasons to believe that said representations were untrue. In reliance upon said representations, plaintiffs were induced to, and did purchase the above described real property. Had plaintiffs known the true facts they would not have taken such action.

10. By reason of the facts alleged, plaintiffs have been damaged in the sum of $60,000.

FIGURE 5–7
(continued)

same allegations that were alleged in prior causes of action. It is not necessary, however, to expressly restate those allegations. If something is being repeated it can be referred to and incorporated by reference. Figure 5–8 illustrates the addition of a second cause of action. See paragraph 11 for an illustration of a paragraph incorporation of prior allegations.

Remember that not all parties to the complaint must be parties to all causes of action. However, each of those named in the caption must be a party to at least one cause of action within the complaint, and this includes "Doe" defendants where allowed.

After the allegations in the complaint you will find the prayer. The prayer is normally located at the end of all of the allegations.

UNITED STATES DISTRICT COURT
FOR THE NORTHERN DISTRICT OF CALIFORNIA

MARGARET HENDRICKS and PAUL HENDRICKS, Plaintiffs,	))) No.)
vs.	) COMPLAINT FOR FRAUD &) NEGLIGENT) MISREPRESENTATION
MAY FORRESTER, an individual, HARRY RICE & HARVEY RICE, a partnership, doing business as Hearth & Home Real Estate Co., PARADISE FOUND, INC., a corporation, Defendants.	))))))))

FIRST CAUSE OF ACTION
(Fraud)

Plaintiffs allege against each and every defendant:

Jurisdiction

1. Plaintiffs are, and were at all times herein mentioned, domiciled in and citizens of the State of California. Defendants, MAY FORRESTER, HARRY RICE & HARVEY RICE, are and were at all times herein mentioned, domiciled in and citizens of the State of Nevada. Defendant, PARADISE FOUND, INC., was and is now a corporation duly organized and existing under the laws of the state of Idaho, with its offices and principal place of business in the state of Idaho. This is a civil action involving, exclusive of interest and costs, a sum in excess of $50,000. Every issue of law and fact in this action is wholly between citizens of different states.

2. Plaintiffs are informed and believe and thereupon allege that Defendants, HARRY RICE AND HARVEY RICE, are a partnership doing business as HEARTH & HOME REAL ESTATE CO.

3. Plaintiffs are informed and believe and thereupon allege that Defendant, PARADISE FOUND, INC., is a corporation duly organized and existing under the laws of the state of Idaho.

4. Plaintiffs are now, and at all times mentioned in this complaint have been, residents of San Francisco County, California.

5. Plaintiffs are informed and believe and thereupon allege that at all times herein mentioned, each of the defendants was the agent and employee of each of the remaining defendants and in doing the things hereinafter alleged, was acting within the scope of said agency.

6. On or about June 1, 1990, in the City of Reno, State of Nevada, defendant, MAY FORRESTER, made the following false and fraudulent representations to plaintiffs: Defendant represented that certain real property was ideal vacation property, that said property

FIGURE 5–8
Adding a Second
Cause of Action.

had been approved for and was suitable for building, that said property abutted a man-made lake, and that said property was worth at least $60,000.

7. The representations made by the defendant were false in that said real property has not been approved nor is it suitable for building, it is not adjacent to any body of water, and was and is valued at less than $5,000.

8. Defendant, at the time she made said representations, knew them to be false and made the statements with the intent to defraud and deceive plaintiffs and to induce them to purchase that certain real property described above.

9. Plaintiffs at the time the representations were made believed them to be true and had no reasons to believe that said representations were untrue. In reliance upon said representations, plaintiffs were induced to, and did purchase the above described real property. Had plaintiffs known the true facts they would not have taken such action.

10. By reason of the facts alleged, plaintiffs have been damaged in the sum of $60,000.

SECOND CAUSE OF ACTION
(Negligent Misrepresentation)

11. Plaintiffs reallege and incorporate by reference the allegations of paragraphs 1 through 7 above in their entirety.

12. At the time defendant MAY FORRESTER made said representations, she had no sufficient or reasonable ground for believing said representations to be true in that she, the defendant, did not have information and data sufficient to enable her to make a determination whether the representations were true. At the time of making the representations, defendant concealed from plaintiffs her lack of information and data that prevented them from making a true evaluation of the facts.

13. At the time said representations were made plaintiffs had no knowledge of their falsity, but, in fact, believed them to be true. Because of the fiduciary and confidential relationship that existed between defendant and plaintiffs, plaintiffs justifiably relied upon said representations.

14. Plaintiffs at the time the representations were made believed them to be true and had no reasons to believe that said representations were untrue. In reliance upon said representations, plaintiffs were induced to, and did purchase the above described real property. Had plaintiffs known the true facts they would not have taken such action.

15. By reasons of the facts alleged, plaintiffs have been damaged in the sum of $60,000.

FIGURE 5–8
(continued)

At the end of the prayer are the date, signature, and address of the attorney filing the complaint. This is sometimes referred to as the subscription. Whenever an attorney signs a pleading in federal court that signature represents that the allegations in the pleadings are made in good faith. The prayer and signature are shown in Figure 5–9.

In the case described in the commentary, if the attorney for the Hendricks decided to sue all of the parties for fraud and negligent misrepresentation, and May Forrester for breach of a fiduciary duty, the entire complaint would look as shown in Figure 5–10.

In some jurisdictions, including federal court, if the plaintiff is requesting a jury trial in the case, that request is often included in the complaint. In federal courts, under Rule 38b of the Federal Rules of Civil Procedure such a demand must be made no later than ten days after service of the last pleading.

Also in some jurisdictions certain kinds of complaints, such as those seeking injunctive relief or punitive damages, often are required to be verified, or sworn to under penalty of perjury. This is usually done by the plaintiff rather than the attorney. See Figure 5–11 for a sample verification.

Along with the complaint itself, many courts have a form cover sheet that must be filled out and accompany the complaint. See Figure 5–12 for a sample cover sheet from a federal court.

5–7 FILING THE COMPLAINT

After the complaint has been prepared, reviewed by the attorney, and properly signed, it can be **filed** in the proper court. Filing of a complaint means that the original of the document is given to the court. The court, in turn, assigns a number, known as a **docket number**, to the case and starts a file that will contain all subsequent pleadings and other documents dealing with the case. All subsequent pleadings and papers filed in connection with the case must contain the docket number to assure proper filing. In order to file a complaint, the court usually requires a filing fee, which must be paid before the court will accept the document. Filing fees will be waived if the plaintiff can show financial hardship. The amount of the filing fee is usually determined by local rules. Whenever you file a complaint with the court, you should have copies of the complaint on which the docket number and date of filing can be noted.

Recently, a new method of filing documents, including complaints, has become available to attorneys. Many courts now accept fax filings, with an additional fee. Each court must be contacted for its own rules regarding fax filings.

filed
Depositing with the court a document that is related to a lawsuit.

docket number
A number assigned to a lawsuit by the court; each pleading or document filed in the action must bear this number.

WHEREFORE, plaintiffs pray for judgment against defendants as follows:

On the first cause of action:

1. For judgment in the sum of $60,000;
2. For costs of suit;
3. For such other relief as the court deems just.

On the second cause of action:

1. For judgment in the sum of $60,000;
2. For costs of suit;
3. For such other relief as the court deems just.

Dated: _____   By _____
Glenda Yee
Attorney for Plaintiffs
246 Marshall Ave.
San Francisco, CA 96730

FIGURE 5–9
Prayer and
Signature.

Regardless of how you file a complaint, always be sure that the document is filed within the statute of limitations. Not filing it on time will result in the lawsuit being dismissed.

5–8 THE SUMMONS

At the time that the complaint is filed, the court will issue a **summons**. A summons is a form that explains that the defendant has been sued and should answer the complaint by a certain date. Issuing of the summons simply involves the clerk of the court affixing his or her signature to the form. It is expected that the attorney for the plaintiff will have the form filled out and will submit it to the clerk at the time the complaint is filed. The original summons is not filed with the court at this time. The plaintiff retains it until after the defendants have been served. At that time the original summons can be returned to the court for filing, along with evidence that the defendants have been served. In some courts, if the summons is not returned to the court within a certain time, the case can be dismissed. See Figure 5–13 for a copy of a summons used in federal court.

5–9 SERVICE OF THE COMPLAINT

The defendant in any lawsuit is entitled to receive notice of the action. This is accomplished by **service of process**. A copy of the summons and a copy of the complaint must be delivered to

summons
A document issued by the court explaining that the defendant has been sued and that he has a certain time limit in which to respond; a copy of the summons is served on the defendant along with the complaint.

service of process
Delivering a copy of the summons and complaint in a lawsuit to the defendant in a method prescribed by law.

UNITED STATES DISTRICT COURT
FOR THE NORTHERN DISTRICT OF CALIFORNIA

MARGARET HENDRICKS and)
PAUL HENDRICKS,)
    Plaintiffs,) No.
)
) COMPLAINT FOR FRAUD,
  vs.) NEGLIGENT
) MISREPRESENTATION
MAY FORRESTER, an individual,) and BREACH OF
HARRY RICE & HARVEY RICE,) FIDUCIARY DUTY
a partnership, doing business as)
Hearth & Home Real Estate Co.,) JURY TRIAL DEMANDED
PARADISE FOUND, INC., a)
corporation,)
)
    Defendants.)

Plaintiffs allege against each and every defendant:

FIRST CAUSE OF ACTION
(Fraud)

Jurisdiction

1. Plaintiffs are, and were at all times herein mentioned, domiciled in and citizens of the State of California. Defendants, MAY FORRESTER, HARRY RICE & HARVEY RICE, are and were at all times herein mentioned, domiciled in and citizens of the state of Nevada. Defendant, PARADISE FOUND, INC., was and is now a corporation duly organized and existing under the laws of the State of Idaho, with its offices and principal place of business in the State of Idaho. This is a civil action involving, exclusive of interest and costs, a sum in excess of $50,000. Every issue of law and fact in this action is wholly between citizens of different states.

2. Plaintiffs are informed and believe and thereupon allege that Defendants, HARRY RICE AND HARVEY RICE, are a partnership doing business as HEARTH & HOME REAL ESTATE CO.

3. Plaintiffs are informed and believe and thereupon allege that Defendant, PARADISE FOUND, INC., is a corporation duly organized and existing under the laws of the State of Idaho.

4. Plaintiffs are now, and at all times mentioned in this complaint have been, residents of San Francisco County, California.

5. Plaintiffs are informed and believe and thereupon allege that at all times herein mentioned, each of the defendants was the agent and employee of each of the remaining defendants and, in doing the things hereinafter alleged, was acting within the scope of said agency.

FIGURE 5–10
Sample
Complaint.

6. On or about June 1, 1990, in the City of Reno, State of Nevada, defendant, MAY FORRESTER, made the following false and fraudulent representations to plaintiffs: Defendant represented that certain real property was ideal vacation property, that said property had been approved for and was suitable for building, that said property abutted a man-made lake, and that said property was worth at least $60,000.

7. The representations made by the defendant were false in that said real property has not been approved nor is it suitable for building, it is not adjacent to any body of water, and was and is valued at less than $5,000.

8. Defendant, at the time she made said representations, knew them to be false and made the statements with the intent to defraud and deceive plaintiffs and to induce them to purchase that certain real property described above.

9. Plaintiffs at the time the representations were made believed them to be true and had no reasons to believe that said representations were untrue. In reliance upon said representations, plaintiffs were induced to, and did purchase the above described real property. Had plaintiffs known the true facts they would not have taken such action.

10. By reason of the facts alleged, plaintiffs have been damaged in the sum of $60,000.

SECILINE CAUSE OF ACTION

SECOND CAUSE OF ACTION
(Negligent Misrepresentation)

11. Plaintiffs reallege and incorporate by reference the allegations of paragraphs 1 through 7 above in their entirety.

12. At the time defendant MAY FORRESTER made said representations, she had no sufficient or reasonable ground for believing said representations to be true in that she, the defendant, did not have information and data sufficient to enable her to make a determination whether the representations were true. At the time of making the representations, defendant concealed from plaintiffs her lack of information and data that prevented them from making a true evaluation of the facts.

13. At the time said representations were made plaintiffs had no knowledge of their falsity, but, in fact, believed them to be true. Because of the fiduciary and confidential relationship which existed between defendant and plaintiffs, plaintiffs justifiably relied upon said representations.

14. Plaintiffs at the time the representations were made believed them to be true and had no reasons to believe that said representations were untrue. In reliance upon said representations, plaintiffs were induced to and did purchase the above described real

FIGURE 5–10
(continued)

property. Had plaintiffs known the true facts they would not have taken such action.

15. By reasons of the facts alleged, plaintiffs have been damaged in the sum of $60,000.

THIRD CAUSE OF ACTION
(Breach of Fiduciary Duty)

Plaintiffs allege against defendant MAY FORRESTER:

16. Plaintiffs reallege and incorporate by reference the allegations of paragraphs 1 through 15 above in their entirety.

17. Defendant MAY FORRESTER owed a fiduciary duty of loyalty, honesty, and confidentiality to plaintiffs by virtue of her status as their real estate broker.

18. The acts and omissions of defendant, MAY FORRESTER, as alleged above constitute intentional breaches of her fiduciary duties to plaintiffs.

19. As a direct and proximate result of defendant's breach of her fiduciary duties, plaintiffs have been damaged in the amount of $60,000.

20. Defendant's breach of fiduciary duties were willful, malicious, oppressive, and in conscious disregard of plaintiffs' rights. Accordingly, plaintiffs request punitive damages in the amount of $100,000.

WHEREFORE, plaintiffs pray for judgment against defendants as follows:

On the first cause of action:

1. For judgment in the sum of $60,000.
2. For costs of suit.
3. For such other relief as the court deems just.

On the second cause of action:

1. For judgment in the sum of $60,000.
2. For costs of suit.
3. For such other relief as the court deems just.

On the third cause of action (against defendant, MAY FORRESTER, only):

1. For compensatory damages in the sum of $60,000.
2. For punitive damages in the sum of $100,000.
3. For costs of suit.
4. For such other relief as the court deems just.

Dated: September 1, 1990   By _____

Glenda Yee
Attorney at Law
246 Marshall Ave.
San Francisco, CA 96730

FIGURE 5–10
(continued)

I, Margaret Hendricks, am one of the plaintiffs in the above entitled action. I have read the foregoing complaint. The facts stated therein are within my knowledge and are true and correct, except those matters stated on information and belief, and, as to those, I believe them to be true and correct.

I declare under penalty of perjury under the laws of the State of California that the foregoing is true and correct.

Executed this _____ day of September, 1990, at San Francisco, California.

_____

FIGURE 5–11
Verification.

the defendant. It is the plaintiff's responsibility, rather than the court's, to see that the defendant is properly served. As a litigation paralegal one of your duties may be to arrange for service after the complaint has been filed.

All jurisdictions have rules regarding who can serve the papers, how they can be served, and time limits for service. Although there may be some differences from one jurisdiction to another, there are some similar concepts. Generally, plaintiffs cannot serve the papers themselves. Someone must do it for them. Various law enforcement agencies, such as the U.S. Marshal or a local sheriff, sometimes take responsibility for serving civil complaints. They may, however, charge the plaintiff a fee for doing this. In other instances, the complaint is served by a licensed process server, an individual licensed by the state to serve papers. In some cases, the complaint is served by any adult who is not a party to the action.

Not only must you be concerned about who serves the complaint but also with how it is served. A common method of service is **personal service**. In personal service, a copy of the summons and complaint are personally delivered to the defendant. Sometimes this is difficult, if not impossible. Some laws, such as Rule 4 of the Federal Rules of Civil Procedure, allow a copy of the summons and complaint to be left with a competent adult at the defendant's residence. Some states also allow the papers to be served by mail or in some cases by publication. When personal service cannot be accomplished, appropriate laws must be reviewed to determine alternatives.

If the defendant in the lawsuit is a corporation, service is usually accomplished by serving an officer or director of the corporation or by serving an individual whom the corporation

personal service
Notice of a lawsuit or other proceeding, which is given to a party by personally delivering a copy of the papers to that party.

JS 44
(Rev. 07/86)

CIVIL COVER SHEET

The JS-44 civil cover sheet and the information contained herein neither replace nor supplement the filing and service of pleadings or other papers as required by law, except as provided by local rules of court. This form, approved by the Judicial Conference of the United States in September 1974, is required for the use of the Clerk of Court for the purpose of initiating the civil docket sheet. (SEE INSTRUCTIONS ON THE REVERSE OF THE FORM.)

I (a) PLAINTIFFS

DEFENDANTS

(b) COUNTY OF RESIDENCE OF FIRST LISTED PLAINTIFF _____
(EXCEPT IN U.S. PLAINTIFF CASES)

COUNTY OF RESIDENCE OF FIRST LISTED DEFENDANT _____
(IN U.S. PLAINTIFF CASES ONLY)
NOTE: IN LAND CONDEMNATION CASES, USE THE LOCATION OF THE
TRACT OF LAND INVOLVED

(c) ATTORNEYS (FIRM NAME, ADDRESS, AND TELEPHONE NUMBER)

ATTORNEYS (IF KNOWN)

II. BASIS OF JURISDICTION (PLACE AN × IN ONE BOX ONLY)

☐ 1 U.S. Government
Plaintiff

☐ 2 U.S. Government
Defendant

☐ 3 Federal Question
(U.S. Government Not a Party)

☐ 4 Diversity
(Indicate Citizenship of
Parties in Item III)

III. CITIZENSHIP OF PRINCIPAL PARTIES (PLACE AN × IN ONE BOX FOR PLAINTIFF AND ONE BOX FOR DEFENDANT)
(For Diversity Cases Only)

	PTF DEF		PTF DEF
Citizen of This State	☐1 ☐1	Incorporated or Principal Place of Business in This State	☐4 ☐4
Citizen of Another State	☐2 ☐2	Incorporated and Principal Place of Business in Another State	☐5 ☐5
Citizen or Subject of a Foreign Country	☐3 ☐3	Foreign Nation	☐6 ☐6

IV. CAUSE OF ACTION (CITE THE U.S. CIVIL STATUTE UNDER WHICH YOU ARE FILING AND WRITE A BRIEF STATEMENT OF CAUSE.

DO NOT CITE JURISDICTIONAL STATUTES UNLESS DIVERSITY.)

V. NATURE OF SUIT (PLACE AN × IN ONE BOX ONLY)

CONTRACT	TORTS		FORFEITURE /PENALTY	BANKRUPTCY	OTHER STATUTES
☐ 110 Insurance	**PERSONAL INJURY**	**PERSONAL INJURY**	☐ 610 Agriculture	☐ 422 Appeal 28 USC 158	☐ 400 State Reapportionment
☐ 120 Marine	☐ 310 Airplane	☐ 362 Personal Injury—	☐ 620 Food & Drug	☐ 423 Withdrawal	☐ 410 Antitrust
☐ 130 Miller Act	☐ 315 Airplane Product	Med Malpractice	☐ 630 Liquor Laws	28 USC 157	☐ 430 Banks and Banking
☐ 140 Negotiable Instrument	Liability	☐ 365 Personal Injury—	☐ 640 R.R. & Truck		☐ 450 Commerce/ICC Rates/etc.
☐ 150 Recovery of Overpayment	☐ 320 Assault, Libel &	Product Liability	☐ 650 Airline Regs	**PROPERTY RIGHTS**	☐ 460 Deportation
& Enforcement of	Slander	☐ 368 Asbestos Personal	☐ 660 Occupational	☐ 820 Copyrights	☐ 470 Racketeer Influenced and
Judgment	☐ 330 Federal Employers'	Injury Product	Safety/Health	☐ 830 Patent	Corrupt Organizations
☐ 151 Medicare Act	Liability	Liability	☐ 690 Other	☐ 840 Trademark	☐ 810 Selective Service
☐ 152 Recovery of Defaulted	☐ 340 Marine				☐ 850 Securities/Commodities/
Student Loans	☐ 345 Marine Product	**PERSONAL PROPERTY**	**LABOR**	**SOCIAL SECURITY**	Exchange
(Excl. Veterans)	Liability	☐ 370 Other Fraud		☐ 861 HIA (1395ff)	☐ 875 Customer Challenge
☐ 153 Recovery of Overpayment	☐ 350 Motor Vehicle	☐ 371 Truth in Lending	☐ 710 Fair Labor Standards	☐ 862 Black Lung (923)	12 USC 3410
of Veteran's Benefits	☐ 355 Motor Vehicle	☐ 380 Other Personal	Act	☐ 863 DIWC (405(g))	☐ 891 Agricultural Acts
☐ 160 Stockholders' Suits	Product Liability	Property Damage	☐ 720 Labor/Mgmt.	☐ 863 DIWW (405(g))	☐ 892 Economic Stabilization
☐ 190 Other Contract	☐ 360 Other Personal	☐ 385 Property Damage	Relations	☐ 864 SSID Title XVI	Act
☐ 195 Contract Product Liability	Injury	Product Liability	☐ 730 Labor/Mgmt.	☐ 865 RSI (405(g))	☐ 893 Environmental Matters
			Reporting &		☐ 894 Energy Allocation Act
REAL PROPERTY	**CIVIL RIGHTS**	**PRISONER PETITIONS**	Disclosure Act	**FEDERAL TAX SUITS**	☐ 895 Freedom of
☐ 210 Land Condemnation	☐ 441 Voting	☐ 510 Motions to Vacate	☐ 740 Railway Labor		Information Act
☐ 220 Foreclosure	☐ 442 Employment	Sentence	Act	☐ 870 Taxes (U.S. Plaintiff	☐ 900 Appeal of Fee Determination
☐ 230 Rent Lease & Ejectment	☐ 443 Housing/	☐ 530 Habeas Corpus	☐ 790 Other Labor	or Defendant)	Under Equal Access to
☐ 240 Torts to Land	Accommodations	☐ 540 Mandamus & Other	Litigation	☐ 871 IRS—Third Party	Justice
☐ 245 Tort Product Liability	☐ 444 Welfare	☐ 550 Civil Rights	☐ 791 Empl. Ret. Inc.	26 USC 7609	☐ 950 Constitutionality of
☐ 290 All Other Real Property	☐ 440 Other Civil Rights		Security Act		State Statutes
					☐ 890 Other Statutory Actions

VI. ORIGIN (PLACE AN × IN ONE BOX ONLY)

☐ 1 Original
Proceeding

☐ 2 Removed from
State Court

☐ 3 Remanded from
Appellate Court

☐ 4 Reinstated or
Reopened

Transferred from
☐ 5 another district
(specify)

☐ 6 Multidistrict
Litigation

Appeal to District
☐ 7 Judge from
Magistrate
Judgment

VII. REQUESTED IN COMPLAINT:
CHECK IF THIS IS A **CLASS ACTION**
☐ UNDER F.R.C.P. 23

DEMAND $

Check YES only if demanded in complaint:
JURY DEMAND: ☐ YES ☐ NO

VIII. RELATED CASE(S) IF ANY (See instructions):

JUDGE _____ DOCKET NUMBER _____

DATE

SIGNATURE OF ATTORNEY OF RECORD

UNITED STATES DISTRICT COURT

FIGURE 5–12 Cover Sheet.

AO 440 (Rev. 5/85)   Summons in a Civil Action

United States District Court

——————————————— DISTRICT OF ———————————————

SUMMONS IN A CIVIL ACTION

V.

CASE NUMBER:

TO: (Name and Address of Defendant)

YOU ARE HEREBY SUMMONED and required to file with the Clerk of this Court and serve upon

PLAINTIFF'S ATTORNEY (name and address)

an answer to the complaint which is herewith served upon you, within _____ days after service of this summons upon you, exclusive of the day of service. If you fail to do so, judgment by default will be taken against you for the relief demanded in the complaint.

———————————————   ———————————————
CLERK   DATE

———————————————
BY DEPUTY CLERK

FIGURE 5–13 Summons.

has designated to accept service. This individual is known as the **agent for service of process**. The name and address of corporate officers, directors, or agents for service can usually be obtained from the secretary of state where the corporation is incorporated or does business.

In addition to the manner of service, you also need to be concerned about any time limits that may affect service. For example, in federal court the copy of the complaint and summons should be served within 120 days of the filing of the complaint. Failure to do so, without justification, can result in dismissal of the action. (See Rule 4j of the Federal Rules of Civil Procedure.) It is a good idea, therefore, to tickle or calendar the file to check for timely service. After service has been completed, the person serving the complaint must certify in writing when, where, and how service was accomplished. This is done in a document called a **proof of service**. A form for the proof of service will probably be found on the reverse side of the summons. See Figure 5–14 for a copy of the form used in a federal court.

The proof of service should then be filed with the court.

5–10 AMENDING THE COMPLAINT

Regardless of how careful you are when you draft a complaint, at times additions, deletions, or changes must be made. To do this you need to amend the complaint. Most jurisdictions view the rules of pleading very liberally. No court is interested in seeing a party lose a case because of some technical deficiency in the pleadings that could be easily corrected. As long as an amendment does not drastically alter the nature of the case, or cause any undue hardship to the defendant or delay in the case, it will probably be allowed. Rule 15 of the Federal Rules of Civil Procedure allows the plaintiff to amend the complaint once, as a matter of right, before an answer is filed. After that the plaintiff generally needs either a stipulation from the other parties agreeing to the amendment or an order from the court. A **stipulation to amend the complaint** is a written agreement among all parties (signed by their attorneys) allowing the plaintiff to make certain changes in the complaint. It would generally be filed in court along with the amended complaint. See Figure 5–15 for a sample stipulation to amend the complaint.

If the plaintiff could not obtain a stipulation he would have to make a motion in court asking the court to allow the filing of the amended complaint. When a complaint is amended the statute of limitations usually relates back to the original date of filing. In other words, a complaint can usually be amended even after the

agent for service of process
Individual designated by a corporation who is authorized to be served with a lawsuit.

proof of service
Written verification that papers have been delivered to a party, detailing when, where, and how the papers were delivered.

stipulation to amend the complaint
Written agreement among all parties allowing the plaintiff to make certain changes in the complaint.

AO 440 (Rev. 5/85) Summons in a Civil Action

RETURN OF SERVICE

Service of the Summons and Complaint was made by me[1]	DATE
NAME OF SERVER	TITLE

Check one box below to indicate appropriate method of service

☐ Served personally upon the defendant. Place where served : _____

_____

☐ Left copies thereof at the defendant's dwelling house or usual place of abode with a person of suitable age and discretion then residing therein.
Name of person with whom the summons and complaint were left: _____

☐ Returned unexecuted: _____

_____

_____

☐ Other (specify): _____

_____

_____

STATEMENT OF SERVICE FEES

TRAVEL	SERVICES	TOTAL

DECLARATION OF SERVER

I declare under penalty of perjury under the laws of the United States of America that the foregoing information contained in the Return of Service and Statement of Service Fees is true and correct.

Executed on_____   _____
_____ *Date* _____   *Signature of Server*

_____
Address of Server

1) As to who may serve a summons see Rule 4 of the Federal Rules of Civil Procedure.

FIGURE 5–14 Proof of Service.

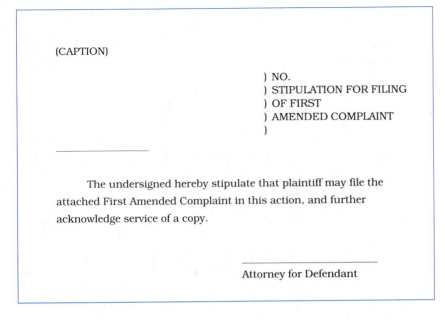

(CAPTION)

) NO.
) STIPULATION FOR FILING
) OF FIRST
) AMENDED COMPLAINT
)

_____

    The undersigned hereby stipulate that plaintiff may file the attached First Amended Complaint in this action, and further acknowledge service of a copy.

                            _____
                           Attorney for Defendant

FIGURE 5–15
Stipulation to File Amended Complaint.

statute of limitations has expired. A major exception to this rule is the case in which the amendment seeks to add a new defendant, one who was not named in the original complaint. In jurisdictions that allow their usage, the use of fictitiously named defendants, Does, avoids this problem. In such a case, when the complaint is amended, it is not to bring in a new defendant, but rather to correct his name.

    After an amended complaint is filed with the court, it must be served. However, if the defendants have obtained an attorney to represent them, service can be accomplished by mailing a copy of the amended complaint to the attorney.

SUMMARY

5–1   Pleadings are the documents filed in a court that define the nature of the dispute between the parties. The initial pleading filed in a lawsuit by the plaintiff is known as the complaint, or in some instances a petition. The complaint or petition sets out the factual basis for the lawsuit. It is made up of a caption, which identifies the parties and the court, the body, which contains the factual allegations describing the dispute, the prayer, which is a request for relief, and the subscription, which consists of the signature and address of the plaintiff's attorney, and the date. Sometimes complaints are verified, that is they contain the plaintiff's statement that the contents of the complaint are true under penalty of perjury.

5–2 Before naming the various parties to the lawsuit, you must determine that the plaintiff is the real party in interest, identify and describe the status of the plaintiff and defendant, and determine that the plaintiff and defendant have the capacity to sue and be sued. A plaintiff is the real party in interest when he or she is the one who is entitled to the relief that is requested in the complaint. Status refers to the type of entity that describes the party, i.e., individual, corporate, or other business entity, or governmental agency. Most competent adult individuals, corporations, and unincorporated associations have capacity to sue or be sued in their own names. However, minors and incompetent adults cannot sue on their own behalf, and a guardian ad litem must be appointed to represent their interests. A governmental entity can only be sued when allowed by law. Some jurisdictions allow the plaintiff to name fictitious defendants, or Doe defendants, in a lawsuit to provide for later discovered defendants. All jurisdictions allow multiple plaintiffs and defendants to be joined in one lawsuit, as long as there is some common factual or legal question among them. Where the number of potential plaintiffs in a lawsuit is too numerous to be practical, a class action may result. In a class action, certain named plaintiffs represent members of a class in a similar situation.

5–3 The complaint must contain some allegation showing that the court in which the action is pending has proper jurisdiction and venue in the case.

5–4 The body of the complaint, referred to as the cause of action or sometimes a count, contains allegations that describe the factual basis for the lawsuit. Some jurisdictions, known as code pleading jurisdictions, require that each element of the cause of action be supported by factual allegations. Other jurisdictions, known as notice pleading jurisdictions, only require that there be sufficient facts to put the defendant on notice as to why he is being sued. A complaint may contain multiple counts or causes of action, as well as multiple parties, as long as some common question exists.

5–5 Every complaint or petition contains a prayer, which is a request for relief from the court. Courts can grant either money damages or equitable relief. Money damages are usually compensatory, that is, compensating the plaintiff for a loss that he has sustained. In some cases, punitive damages are awarded. Punitive damages usually require some sort of extremely bad conduct on the part of the defendant. Equitable relief is varied, but includes such kinds of orders as specific performance, rescission, restitution, declaratory relief, and injunctions. Courts also have the power to grant provisional remedies such as a temporary restraining order or preliminary injunction pending the trial.

5–6 Before drafting a complaint, you should check form books or form files for complaints with similar factual situations. The physical appearance of the complaint is usually determined by the laws of the jurisdiction in which the complaint is filed. Local rules of courts may also control.

5–7 After the complaint has been reviewed by the attorney and signed by the appropriate parties, it is filed in court. Filing involves giving the document to the court clerk with an appropriate filing fee. The court then assigns a docket number to the case. All subsequent papers filed in the case must bear this number. A complaint must be filed within the statute of limitations.

5–8 A summons is a form that explains to the defendant that he has been sued. It is issued by the court clerk at the time the complaint is filed. After the defendant is served, the summons is returned to the court.

5–9 A copy of the complaint and a copy of the summons must be served on the defendant. Depending on the law of jurisdiction, these documents are usually served by a U.S. Marshal, local sheriff, licensed process server, or any adult who is not a party to the action. Service can be accomplished in different ways. Personal service, delivering a copy of the documents personally to the defendant, is preferred. Under some circumstances, substituted service, leaving a copy of the documents at the defendant's home or business with another adult, is allowed. Some jurisdictions also permit service by mail or by publication. After the papers are served, the individual serving the papers fills out a proof of service, and this is later filed with the court.

5–10 Additions, deletions, or changes to a complaint can be accomplished by amending the pleading. Amendments are liberally allowed, but after an answer has been filed require either a stipulation from all parties or a court order. Unless an amendment adds new parties to the complaint, the statute of limitations relates back to the original date of filing the complaint.

KEY TERMS

agent for service of process
allegations
caption
class action
compensatory damages
complaint
compulsory joinder
count
declaratory relief
docket number
equitable relief
exemplary damages
fictitiously named defendants
filed
guardian ad litem
indispensable party
injunction
interpleader

permissive joinder
personal service
petition
pleadings
prayer
preliminary injunction
proof of service
punitive damages
quiet title action
real party in interest
rescission
restitution
service of process
specific performance
subscription
summons
temporary restraining order
verification

QUESTIONS FOR REVIEW AND DISCUSSION

1. What is the purpose of pleadings?
2. What matters are generally contained in a complaint or petition?
3. What factors should be reviewed before determining who will be named as parties to a lawsuit?
4. What is the difference between notice pleading and code pleading?
5. What are the types of remedies that may be requested from a court?
6. What are the steps in drafting a complaint?
7. What is involved in filing a complaint?
8. What is a summons?
9. How is service of process accomplished?
10. What is the procedure for amending the complaint?

ACTIVITIES

1. Review the laws of your state, and find all state laws that deal with the initial pleadings in a lawsuit. Check with your local

courts to see if any local rules of court in your area regulate any aspect of the initial pleading.

2. Review the sample complaint found in this chapter. Does it meet the legal requirements in your state? If not, what would you have to change?

3. Find a set of form books in your law library that provide sample forms for use in the courts of your state. Find a form for a complaint or petition for fraud and negligent misrepresentation. How does it compare with the sample complaint in this chapter?

CHAPTER 5 PROJECT—DRAFTING A COMPLAINT

Consider the following factual situation: Lowell Orloff, while shopping in a local department store, "The Wear House," tripped and fell on a piece of torn carpeting. Lowell suffered severe injuries, including a broken leg. Lowell incurred medical bills in excess of $5,000 and was off work for three weeks, losing earnings in the amount of $6,000. Lowell is married to Barbara Orloff. "The Wear House" is a corporation incorporated under the laws of your state. The correct corporate name is A & B Corporation. Using form books from your state, prepare a complaint on behalf of Lowell Orloff against The Wear House based on their negligently maintaining their premises.

CHAPTER 6

Responses to the Initial Pleading

COMMENTARY—THE GRANGER CASE

Your supervising attorney has given you the file of a new client who has recently been named as a defendant in a lawsuit for personal injury damages. Included in the file are the attorney's notes and copies of a summons and complaint. (See Figure 6–1 for a copy of the complaint.) After reading the file and discussing the case with the attorney, you learn that the client, Linda Granger, owns a flower shop and had employed Wesley Linstrom to make deliveries. Deliveries were made in a van owned by Granger. According to your client, last year Linstrom was involved in an automobile accident that is the subject of this lawsuit. The morning of the accident Linstrom had taken the van without Granger's knowledge and driven several hundred miles to visit his girlfriend. In the past your client had allowed Linstrom to use the van for some personal errands. However, these always involved very short distances, and he always asked ahead of time. The client also stated that Linstrom told her that the accident happened when the driver of the other vehicle stopped suddenly for no reason and he, Linstrom, was unable to stop because the brakes on the van failed. The file indicates that your client was served with a copy of the summons and complaint fifteen days ago. Your attorney has requested that, after reviewing the file, you prepare responsive pleading for review.

OBJECTIVES

In chapter 5 you were introduced to the procedures for preparing, filing, and serving the initial pleading. The next step in the litigation process involves the response to a pleading. After completing this chapter, you will be able to:

1. List the possible responses to the initial pleading.
2. Describe the time limitations for these responses along with methods for changing these limitations.
3. Distinguish a general denial from a specific denial.
4. Explain the importance of pleading affirmative defenses.
5. Describe the general format of an answer.
6. Explain the procedure for serving and filing an answer.
7. Explain the process for amending responsive pleading.
8. Define a counterclaim, cross-claim, and third-party complaint.
9. Describe methods of raising legal challenges to the initial pleading.
10. Describe results of a failure to file any response to the initial pleading.

UNITED STATES DISTRICT COURT
FOR THE NORTHERN DISTRICT OF CALIFORNIA

GORDON SHEFFIELD and AMY SHEFFIELD,
     Plaintiffs,
 	
 vs.
 	
 WESLEY LINSTROM and LINDA GRANGER,
     Defendants.
	) Civil No.12345
	) COMPLAINT FOR
	) NEGLIGENCE
	)
	)
	)
	)
	)
	)
	)

Plaintiff GORDON SHEFFIELD alleges:

JURISDICTION

1. Plaintiff is, and was at all times herein mentioned, domiciled in and a citizen of the state of California. Defendants and each of them are, and were at all times herein mentioned, domiciled in and a citizen of the state of Oregon. This is a civil action involving, exclusive of interest and costs, a sum in excess of $50,000. Every issue of law and fact in this action is wholly between citizens of different states.

FIRST COUNT

2. At all times herein mentioned, plaintiff was and now is a resident of the judicial district in which this action is filed.
3. At all times herein mentioned, defendant, LINDA GRANGER, was the owner of a certain motor vehicle, Oregon license number 123 XYZ.
4. At all times herein mentioned, defendant, WESLEY LINSTROM, was operating said motor vehicle with the permission and consent of defendant, LINDA GRANGER.
5. At all times herein mentioned defendant, WESLEY LINSTROM, was the agent, employee, and servant of defendant LINDA GRANGER, and at all times was acting within the course and scope of said agency and employment.
6. On May 1, 19___, on a public highway called Market Street in San Francisco, California, defendant WESLEY LINSTROM negligently and carelessly drove the above mentioned motor vehicle,

FIGURE 6–1
Complaint.

Oregon license 123 XYZ, causing it to collide with another vehicle driven by plaintiff, who was also travelling on said highway.

7. As a result plaintiff was severely injured, having had his leg and arm broken and having suffered other bruises, contusions, and muscle strain. Also as a result plaintiff was prevented from transacting his business, suffered and continues to suffer great pain of body and mind, and incurred expenses for medical attention and hospitalization in the sum of ten thousand dollars and will continue to incur such expenses in an amount yet undetermined.

SECOND COUNT

Plaintiff, AMY SHEFFIELD, alleges against defendants and each of them as follows:

8. Plaintiff realleges and incorporates by reference the allegations of paragraphs 1 through 5 above in their entirety.

9. On May 1, 19___, plaintiff was a passenger in a vehicle being driven by co-plaintiff, Gordon Sheffield, on a public highway called Market Street in San Francisco, California. At said time and place, defendant, WESLEY LINSTROM, negligently and carelessly drove a motor vehicle, Oregon license 123 XYZ, causing it to collide with the vehicle in which plaintiff, AMY SHEFFIELD, was a passenger.

10. As a result plaintiff was severely injured, having had her back broken and having suffered other bruises, contusions, and muscle strain. Also as a result plaintiff was prevented from transacting her business, suffered and continues to suffer great pain of body and mind, and incurred expenses for medical attention and hospitalization in the sum of fifteen thousand dollars and will continue to incur such expenses in an amount yet undetermined.

Wherefore plaintiff, GORDON SHEFFIELD, demands judgment against defendants and each of them in the sum of $100,000.00 and costs.

Wherefore plaintiff, AMY SHEFFIELD, demands judgment against defendants and each of them in the sum of $150,000.00 and costs.

Dated: April 30, 19___

Terry Alvarez
_____
TERRY ALVAREZ
ALVAREZ & COE
100 Market Street
San Francisco, California 94101
Attorney for Plaintiffs

FIGURE 6–1
(continued)

6–1   RESPONDING TO THE INITIAL PLEADING

After the initial pleading has been filed and served, the next step in the litigation process is up to the defendants. At this point they have various options. The defendants can contest the lawsuit, negotiate a settlement with the plaintiff, or do nothing at all. If the defendants challenge the lawsuit they can do so on two bases. They can either contest the facts of the case or they can challenge the action on some legal basis. For example, in the factual situation described in the commentary, defendant Granger might deny that at the time of the accident Linstrom was acting as her employee or she might deny that his negligence caused the accident. In such a case she would be contesting the facts of the case. On the other hand, she might claim that she was not properly served with the complaint and summons and that therefore the action should be dismissed. This would be a legal challenge to the action.

Time Limits

If the defendants choose to contest the action, they must act within certain time limitations. This time limit is normally fixed by the statutory laws of the jurisdiction in which the action is pending and can vary from one jurisdiction to another. In federal court this time is normally twenty days, although there are some exceptions. (For example, if the defendant is located out of the state the time can be enlarged, or if the defendant is the United States government the time to answer is sixty days.)

Frequently, as in the Granger case, a substantial part of this time has elapsed before the defendant locates and retains an attorney. As a result, once an attorney is retained only a few days may remain for the attorney to evaluate the case, consider the possibility of an early settlement, or prepare a proper response to the complaint or petition. In most cases, the time in which to respond can be extended or enlarged, either by obtaining a stipulation from the plaintiff's attorney (which may have to be approved by the court, depending on the laws of the jurisdiction) or by making a motion, or formal request from the court, for such an order.

Stipulations Enlarging Time

A **stipulation enlarging time** in which to respond is an agreement between the attorneys in an action that the defendant's attorney might have additional time in which to respond. In federal court this agreement or stipulation must be approved by the court, although in some state courts it need not be. If the stipulation is subject to court approval, it should follow the same formalities required of the pleadings and bear the caption and docket number of the case. See Figure 6–2 for an example of such a stipulation.

If the stipulation does not require court approval, a letter between the attorneys confirming their agreement will suffice. The letter need not be filed in court, so it does not require a caption or docket number. Since you might be asked to write such a letter or prepare a formal stipulation for court approval, you should be aware of some possible problems which can arise. When preparing the stipulation you should not state that the agreement is for an extension of time in which to "answer." Rather, you should state that the agreement is for an extension of time in which to respond or "answer or otherwise respond." Plaintiff's attorneys have been known to complain or object when, having given a defendant an extension of time in which to "answer," they were served with a motion to dismiss or some other kind of legal challenge to the complaint. Although most courts refuse to sanction this type of narrow interpretation of the term "answer," you can avoid any problem by making the agreement clear.

Another problem arises when the attorneys agree to an **open stipulation**. Most agreements for extensions or enlargements of time are for a definite amount of time. Sometimes, however, especially if attorneys are seriously discussing settlement, the extension of time will be open-ended. In such a case, the parties stipulate that the defendant need not answer until he is given notice by the plaintiff. This is referred to as an open stipulation. If such an agreement exists in any case on which you are working, be careful to tickle or calendar the case for review so that it is not forgotten. This is particularly important if your firm represents the plaintiff.

Motions to Extend or Enlarge Time

If the defendant's attorney feels that more time is needed to prepare a response, and the plaintiff's attorney is unwilling to agree, an extension of time can be requested from the court. This is done by making a **motion** with the court. A motion is a formal request of the court for some kind of order. The details of motion practice are discussed in chapter 7, but a motion to extend or enlarge time is usually made by filing papers with the court explaining the request and the reasons for it, serving these papers on the other attorneys in the action, and then possibly appearing in court for a brief hearing on the motion.

stipulation enlarging time
An agreement between parties or their attorneys extending the time for filing or serving some document.

open stipulation
An agreement between parties or their attorneys that a defendant need not answer a complaint within the time directed by law and need not answer until specifically notified by plaintiff to do so.

motion
A request for an order from the court, usually dealing with a pending case.

UNITED STATES DISTRICT COURT
FOR THE NORTHERN DISTRICT OF CALIFORNIA

GORDON SHEFFIELD and AMY SHEFFIELD, Plaintiffs,	) Civil No. 12345) STIPULATION AND ORDER) FOR ENLARGEMENT) OF TIME))
vs.	))
WESLEY LINSTROM and LINDA GRANGER, Defendants.	)))

IT IS STIPULATED by plaintiffs and defendant, LINDA GRANGER, through their respective counsel, that the time within which defendant, LINDA GRANGER, may have to respond to the complaint shall be, subject to approval by the court, extended to and including _____ 19___ or such other date as the court may order.

There have been no previous stipulations or orders.

Dated _____ 19___   *Terry Alvarez*
                                  _____
                                  TERRY ALVAREZ
                                  100 Market Street
                                  San Francisco, California 94101
                                  Attorney for Plaintiffs

                                  Taylor Martin
                                  _____
                                  TAYLOR MARTIN
                                  15 Plaza de Oro
                                  Sacramento, California 94813
                                  Attorney for Defendant

ORDER

Pursuant to the above stipulation filed herein, and good cause appearing, IT IS SO ORDERED.

Dated _____ 19___   _____
                                  Judge, District Court

FIGURE 6–2
Stipulation and
Order Enlarging
Time to Respond.

6-2 THE ANSWER

An **answer** is a pleading that challenges the plaintiff's right to the relief requested in the initial pleading. Normally this is done by contesting all or some of the facts that have been alleged in the complaint or petition. Answers are prepared using one of three main formats, the general denial, the specific denial, or the qualified denial.

General Denial

The substance of a **general denial** is only one paragraph or allegation, in which the defendant denies all of the allegations contained in the complaint. In federal court, general denials are proper when the defendant is denying all of the factual contentions of the complaint, including the allegations of subject matter jurisdiction, personal jurisdiction, and venue. However, an alternative method of challenging jurisdiction or venue does exist. These matters, along with certain other defenses, can be raised by a motion to dismiss the action. This method is discussed in section 6–5 of this chapter.

answer
Pleading filed by a defendant in a lawsuit that challenges the contentions or allegations in the complaint.

general denial
A type of answer in which all of the allegations of the complaint are denied.

THE COMPUTERIZED LAW FIRM—Word Processing to Amend Pleadings

SCENARIO

An answer to a complaint has been filed by your law firm in the Granger case. Although your attorney intended to deny the allegations contained in Paragraph 6 of the complaint, the answer that was filed contained no reference to this paragraph. As a result it was deemed admitted. Your attorney has called the plaintiffs' attorney, and it was stipulated that an amended answer could be filed. You have been asked to prepare an amended answer for the attorney's review.

PROBLEM

You need to make a slight change to a lengthy document that has already been prepared. Is there a way to do this without retyping the entire document?

SOLUTION

Probably the most important time advantage offered in a computerized law firm is the utilization of word processing for drafting and revising documents. Word processing is the software that allows you to use a computer in lieu of a typewriter. The advantages of word processing over typing are numerous. With word processing the document being prepared is first "typed" into the computer's memory, rather than on a piece of paper. The printed words appear on a screen or monitor. Changes can be made to the document before a "hard copy" is produced (that is, printed out). Information can be inserted, deleted, or moved around without retyping the entire document. When the drafter is satisfied with the document, a copy can be printed. Another advantage is that the finished document can be saved, or stored, either on the computer's hard disk or on a floppy disk. Thus, if a document needs to be revised or amended at a later date, the original document can be "called up" or retrieved and changes made. There is no need to retype the entire document. Another advantage offered in connection with pleadings is the ability to copy from one document to another without retyping. Since all documents filed in court in the same case usually bear the same or similar caption, it is not necessary to retype this information every time a new pleading or other court document is prepared.

One word processing software that has become popular among lawyers is WordPerfect. Perhaps one reason for this is that it was designed specifically for and addressed the unique word processing needs of the legal profession. With this program you can quickly draft and revise pleadings by using "block" and "move" function keys to change the order of a sentence, paragraph, or page. Automatic paragraph numbering ensures the correct numbering of paragraphs following changes made during the draft process. When you are in doubt about a particular word, the massive thesaurus provides the appropriate word. Filing pleadings with typographical and spelling errors can be avoided by using one of the largest computer dictionaries, WordPerfect's Spell Check. For those jurisdictions still using pleading paper, WordPerfect offers automatic line numbering.

Another key advantage of WordPerfect is its interaction with other software. Many publishers of form books now offer their forms on disk. These can be used with WordPerfect software. A floppy disk containing a basic form is installed in the computer. With WordPerfect individualized changes and additions can be made to the form. A hard copy is then produced. Much of the typing is eliminated entirely.

While many state jurisdictions follow the same procedures that apply in federal court, some states do have different rules and procedures. Some state courts severely limit the use of general denials. Moreover, in some courts general denials cannot be used if the complaint has been verified. Furthermore, the use of a general denial is insufficient to raise certain legal defenses such as lack of personal jurisdiction. Such a defense must be raised by motion. In fact, filing an answer of any kind might constitute a waiver of this defense.

Specific Denial

A **specific denial** is an answer in which the defendant specifically replies to each of the contentions alleged in the complaint. The defendant replies to the various contentions by admitting them, denying them, or denying them on information and belief.

Most complaints or petitions contain some allegations that are uncontested. For example, a defendant in a lawsuit might agree that the court has jurisdiction to hear the case even though that defendant is challenging the plaintiff's right to recover any damages. Allegations or contentions to which the defendant agrees are admitted in the answer. An admission of an allegation can be explicit in the answer or it can be implied by silence. If an allegation is not specifically denied, it is deemed to be admitted. Therefore, in drafting an answer, you must always use care not to ignore any allegation, unless you want to admit it.

Occasionally, a defendant may not be absolutely certain about a certain allegation, or may not have sufficient knowledge of the facts. Just as the plaintiff is allowed to plead facts on information and belief, so also is the defendant allowed to deny allegations in the same way. Denials on information and belief should be used only when the pleader honestly does not have firsthand knowledge of the true facts. If the truth or falsity of acts is within the knowledge of the defendant, the defendant has an obligation to the court to express this knowledge. Likewise, if the information regarding the truth or falsity of an allegation can be easily obtained by the defendant, he has an obligation to do so.

specific denial
A type of answer in which the defendant specifically replies to each of the contentions alleged in the complaint.

qualified denial
A type of answer denying all of the allegations of the complaint except those that are specifically admitted.

Qualified Denial

A **qualified denial** is a combination of specific and general responses. In a qualified denial, the answering defendant expressly admits or denies certain allegations, then generally denies everything else.

Affirmative Defenses

An **affirmative defense** is a fact or circumstance that will defeat the plaintiff's claim, even if the plaintiff can prove every contention that is alleged in the complaint. For example, suppose that the plaintiff has filed a lawsuit for breach of contract, alleging that the plaintiff loaned the defendant $75,000.00, that when the loan was due the defendant refused to pay, and that the defendant continues to refuse to pay. Normally if the plaintiff could prove these allegations at trial, the plaintiff would prevail and obtain a judgment for the amount of the unpaid loan. However, if the defendant alleges and proves that he filed bankruptcy and that this debt was discharged in bankruptcy, the plaintiff will lose the case. The fact that the debt was discharged in bankruptcy is an affirmative defense and operates to defeat the plaintiff's claim.

True affirmative defenses must be alleged in the answer or they will generally be deemed waived. Thus, in the situation just described, the defendant must specifically allege in the answer that the debt was discharged in bankruptcy. If the defendant simply denies that the money is owed, this is insufficient, and the plaintiff would still get a judgment.

Whether or not a matter is an affirmative defense is a question of substantive law. Some matters, such as the expiration of the statute of limitations, operate as affirmative defenses in all kinds of cases. However, other affirmative defenses vary depending on the area of substantive law involved. In other words, what constitutes affirmative defenses in contract cases may be very different from what constitutes affirmative defenses in tort cases. Researching the substantive law of the case may be necessary to determine what affirmative defenses exist in a particular situation.

A partial list of affirmative defenses is found in Rule 8(c) of the Federal Rules of Civil Procedure. This list includes the following:

(Affirmative Defenses Applicable to Contract Disputes)
accord and satisfaction
duress
estoppel
failure of consideration
fraud
illegality
payment
release
statute of frauds
waiver

(Affirmative Defenses Applicable to Tort Cases)
assumption of the risk
contributory negligence
injury by fellow servant

(Affirmative Defenses Applicable to All Cases)
arbitration and award
discharge in bankruptcy
laches
res judicata
statute of limitations

If any of these defenses are claimed in an action in federal court they must be specifically alleged in the answer as an affirmative defense. Failure to do so could result in the defense being waived. This list, however, is not all-inclusive. Other affirmative defenses do exist under different areas of substantive laws.

6–3 DRAFTING THE ANSWER

An answer is a pleading that will be filed in court. As such it follows the same general format as the complaint or petition. It contains a caption, body or allegations, prayer, or "wherefore" clause, and signature. In some jurisdictions it is prepared on pleading paper (paper that is numbered along the left side). Before drafting an answer you might want to consult a form book, just as you do in drafting a complaint.

Caption

The caption on an answer is similar to the caption on the complaint. The names of the plaintiff and defendant are listed just as they are on the complaint. The document is titled (answer) and the docket number, which appears on the complaint, is included. The caption for an answer that would be prepared by your law firm on behalf of Granger would look as shown in Figure 6–3.

Body

The content of the body of the answer depends on whether it is a specific, general, or qualified denial. A general denial contains only one paragraph, as described above. See Figure 6–4 for an example of a general denial.

A specific denial is more detailed. However, there are only a few different paragraphs or allegations that are generally used in an answer. If the defendant is denying all of the facts alleged in a

affirmative defense
A fact or circumstance alleged by a defendant in an answer, which if proven would defeat the plaintiff's claim, even if the plaintiff proves all of the contentions of his claim.

UNITED STATES DISTRICT COURT
FOR THE NORTHERN DISTRICT OF CALIFORNIA

GORDON SHEFFIELD and AMY SHEFFIELD, Plaintiffs,	) Civil No.12345) ANSWER)))
vs.	))
WESLEY LINSTROM and LINDA GRANGER, Defendants.	)))

FIGURE 6–3
Caption.

paragraph of the complaint, the following paragraph could appear in the answer:

> Defendant denies each and every allegation of Paragraphs 1, 2, & 3 of the complaint.

UNITED STATES DISTRICT COURT
FOR THE NORTHERN DISTRICT OF CALIFORNIA

GORDON SHEFFIELD and AMY SHEFFIELD, Plaintiffs,	) Civil No.12345) ANSWER)))
vs.	))
WESLEY LINSTROM and LINDA GRANGER, Defendants.	)))

Defendant, LINDA GRANGER, answers as follows:

Defendant denies each and every allegation of plaintiffs' complaint.

Dated:_____   *Taylor Martin*

TAYLOR MARTIN
15 Plaza de Oro
Sacramento, California 94813
(916) 555-1212
Attorney for Defendant, Linda Granger

FIGURE 6–4
General Denial.

Where a defendant is denying an allegation on information or belief, the following paragraph could be used:

> Defendant denies having sufficient knowledge or information to form a belief as to the allegations contained in Paragraph 4 of the complaint.

Note that this paragraph does not contain an express denial of the allegations of the complaint. The federal rules provide that when a defendant states he lacks information and belief about an allegation this will be deemed to be a denial. Some attorneys, however, prefer to expressly deny the allegations, and some jurisdictions require it. In such a case, the following paragraph could be used:

> Defendant denies having sufficient knowledge or information to form a belief as to the allegations contained in Paragraph 4 of the complaint, and thereupon denies said allegations.

For those allegations in the complaint that the defendant admits the following paragraph applies:

> Defendant admits the allegations contained in Paragraph 5 of the complaint.

If the defendant wishes to admit part of a paragraph and deny part of it the following paragraph could be used:

> Answering Paragraph 6 of the complaint, defendant admits that an automobile collision occurred between plaintiff and defendant but denies each and every other allegation contained in said paragraph.

> In a qualified denial, the following paragraph might appear in the body of the answer:

> Defendant admits the allegations of Paragraphs 1, 2, and 3 of the complaint and denies each and every other allegation of plaintiff's complaint.

Answering a Multi-Count Complaint. In a complaint containing more than one count or cause of action, it is common to find a paragraph incorporating paragraphs from previous counts. (See Figure 6–1, Paragraph 8.) Responding to this paragraph sometimes presents difficulties, especially when some of the incorporated paragraphs have been admitted and some denied. The following is an example of a response that can be used.

> In answer to Paragraph 8 of Count Two of the complaint, wherein plaintiff incorporates by reference certain paragraphs of Count One of the complaint, defendant admits, denies, and alleges to the same effect and in the same

manner as she admitted, denied, and alleged to those specific paragraphs previously in this answer.

In answering a complaint with more than one count or cause of action, certain questions sometimes arise regarding the format of the answer. Should each cause of action or count be answered separately in the answer, or can an allegation in the answer contain replies to allegations in the various counts? It is purely a matter of preference and can be done either way. For example, in the Granger case, if Granger were to deny Paragraphs 4, 5, 6, 7, 9, and 10 of the complaint, the body of the answer could be set up in one of two ways:

Answer to Count 1

1. Defendant denies each and every allegation contained in Paragraphs 4, 5, 6, and 7 of plaintiffs' complaint.

Answer to Count 2

2. Defendant denies each and every allegation contained in Paragraphs 9 and 10 of plaintiffs' complaint.

Alternatively the denial in the answer could be as follows:

1. Defendant denies each and every allegation contained in Paragraphs 4, 5, 6, 7, 9, and 10 of plaintiffs' complaint.

Affirmative Defenses. Whether a defendant files a general denial or a specific denial, affirmative defenses might apply. In drafting an answer it is necessary to review the substantive law of the case as well as the facts to determine if an affirmative defense exists. For example, suppose that in the factual situation described in the Granger case your client's records indicate that the accident occurred on April 29 instead of May 1. Since personal injury actions of this sort have a one year statute of limitations in California, she would want to assert the expiration of the statute of limitations as an affirmative defense. The defendant might also want to assert the negligence of plaintiff, Gordon Sheffield, as an affirmative defense. In drafting the answer, affirmative defenses appear in the body, following the paragraphs denying or admitting the allegations in the complaint.

Prayer and Signature

The body of the answer is followed by a simple prayer, or "wherefore" clause, the date, and the signature of the attorney. In some courts, including federal court, the signature of the attorney is followed by the attorney's address. The prayer usually requests that the plaintiffs be allowed no recovery. The date, signature, and address follow the same format as the complaint.

In its entirety, an answer prepared on behalf of Linda Granger to the complaint described in the commentary would look as shown in Figure 6–5.

Verification

In federal court, complaints are not generally verified. In some state jurisdictions, however, plaintiffs are permitted to verify a complaint at any time. If the complaint has been verified, usually the defendant cannot use a general denial and, furthermore, must verify the answer.

Service and Filing

After the answer is prepared it must be served on the plaintiff or the plaintiff's attorney, and it must be filed in court. The procedures for serving an answer are usually very simple. If a party is represented by an attorney, service can be made on the attorney rather than the party. While the answer can be personally served on the plaintiff's attorney, it does not have to be. Mailing a copy of the answer to the attorney will suffice.

In addition to serving a copy of the answer on the plaintiff or the attorney, the pleading must also be filed in court. This is done in the same way as a complaint. Courts may also require that a filing fee accompany the answer.

Amending

Most courts have liberal rules regarding the amending of any pleading, including an answer. Under federal rules, as long as the case has not been placed on the trial calendar, a party may amend an answer any time within twenty days after it is served. If more than twenty days has elapsed, or if the case has been placed on the trial calendar, then the answer can be amended only with permission of the court or by written consent of the adverse party.

6–4 COUNTERCLAIMS, CROSS-CLAIMS, AND THIRD-PARTY COMPLAINTS

At times, defendants themselves have a claim and are entitled to some relief from the court. They may be asserting this claim against the plaintiff, a co-defendant, or a third party (someone who is not a party to the original action). In federal court when

UNITED STATES DISTRICT COURT
FOR THE NORTHERN DISTRICT OF CALIFORNIA

GORDON SHEFFIELD and AMY SHEFFIELD,
    Plaintiffs,

    vs.

WESLEY LINSTROM and LINDA GRANGER,
    Defendants.

) Civil No.12345
) ANSWER
)
)
)
)
)
)
)
)

Answer to First Count

Defendant, LINDA GRANGER, answers as follows:

1. Defendant admits the allegations of Paragraphs 1, 2, and 3 of the complaint.

2. Defendant denies each and every allegation of Paragraphs 4, 5, 6, and 7 of the complaint.

Answer to Second Count

3. In answer to Paragraph 8 of Count Two of the complaint, wherein plaintiff incorporates by reference certain paragraphs of Count One of the complaint, defendant admits, denies, and alleges to the same effect and in the same manner as she admitted, denied, and alleged to those specific paragraphs previously in this answer.

4. In answer to Paragraph 9 of Count Two of the complaint, defendant admits that plaintiff, AMY SHEFFIELD, was a passenger in a vehicle being driven by co-plaintiff, GORDON SHEFFIELD, but denies each and every other allegation contained in said paragraph.

5. Defendant denies each and every allegation contained in Paragraph 10 of the complaint.

First Affirmative Defense

As and for an affirmative defense, defendant alleges that plaintiffs' right to maintain this action is barred by the statute of limitations in that more than one year has now elapsed between the date plaintiffs' alleged cause of action arose and the date plaintiffs filed their complaint.

FIGURE 6–5
Answer.

Second Affirmative Defense

As and for a separate affirmative defense, defendant alleges that plaintiffs were themselves negligent in that plaintiff Gordon Sheffield failed to use ordinary care in the operation of his motor vehicle and failed to keep a proper lookout for other vehicles, and that both plaintiffs Gordon Sheffield and Amy Sheffield failed to exercise ordinary care in that neither wore a seat belt. Defendant further alleges that said negligence contributed in whole or in part to any injuries which may have resulted.

Wherefore defendant prays:

1. That the court enter judgment dismissing the complaint;
2. That defendant be awarded costs incurred herein; and
3. That defendant be awarded such other and further relief as the court may deem just.

Dated: _____ 19 ___   *Taylor Martin*

TAYLOR MARTIN
15 Plaza de Oro
Sacramento, California 94813
(916) 555-1212
Attorney for Defendant, Linda Granger

FIGURE 6–5
(continued)

defendants assert a claim against a plaintiff, it is known as a **counterclaim**. When the claim is asserted against a co-defendant, it is known as a **cross-claim**. Finally, when the claim is against a new party, it is known as a **third-party complaint**. Counterclaims and cross-claims are included with the answer. Third-party complaints are pleadings that are separate from the answer. Regardless of which form the defendant's claim takes, the content of the claim is the same. The content of the defendant's claim for relief is similar to the content of the plaintiff's claim in a complaint. Usually the defendant states the jurisdictional basis for the court's hearing the matter, unless the basis for the court's jurisdiction is the same as in the complaint. This is followed by numbered paragraphs describing the factual basis for the claim.

In some state jurisdictions, although defendants have the same rights to assert claims, the format and the names of the pleading differ. For example, in some states if defendants assert a claim they do so in a pleading entitled a cross complaint. This pleading, which is separate from the answer, is used against a plaintiff, co-defendant, or third party.

counterclaim
In federal practice, a claim asserted by a defendant against the plaintiff; part of the answer.

cross-claim
In federal practice, a claim for relief made by one defendant against another defendant.

third-party complaint
In federal practice, a claim asserted by a defendant in a lawsuit against a party not named in the original complaint; the claim must be related to the circumstances described in the original complaint.

Counterclaims

In most instances if a defendant has a claim against the plaintiff that arises out of the same transaction as the claim described in the complaint, that claim must be asserted in a counterclaim or the right to make a claim is lost. Moreover, since such a claim must be asserted or is deemed waived, it is not necessary that the counterclaim satisfy the court's jurisdictional requirements. The fact that the court has jurisdiction over the plaintiff's claim is sufficient. Counterclaims that must be asserted or lost are known as **compulsory counterclaims**. A compulsory counterclaim that is not included as part of the answer is thereafter barred. Exceptions occur when the assertion of the claim involves bringing in third parties over whom the court cannot acquire jurisdiction, or when the defendant's claim has already been asserted in another action. Of course, if a defendant fails to assert a compulsory counterclaim in the answer, under proper circumstances the responsive pleading can be amended to add the counterclaim. (Amendment of answers is discussed in section 6–6 of this chapter.)

Because it saves a great deal of court time, the courts encourage the parties to resolve all of their disputes in one action. Consequently, if a defendant has a claim against the plaintiff that did not arise out of the factual situation described in the complaint, he can still assert that claim in the answer as a counterclaim. Such a counterclaim is a **permissive counterclaim**. Unlike compulsory counterclaims, permissive counterclaims must satisfy the court's jurisdictional requirements. As a rule, claims forming the basis for a permissive counterclaim are not lost if they are not made as part of the answer.

In the Granger case, if Sheffield was negligent in operating his vehicle and that negligence was a cause of the accident, Granger could file a counterclaim against him for the damage to her vehicle. The factual situation might also provide the basis for a counterclaim for **contribution**. Contribution is a claim for partial reimbursement from a person whose wrongdoing contributed to the injuries claimed in the complaint. In this instance, if Linstrom and Gordon Sheffield were both negligent, they both contributed to Amy Sheffield's injuries. If Granger is found liable to Amy Sheffield (either as Linstrom's employer or as the owner of the van) she might be entitled to contribution from Gordon Sheffield. Although claims for contribution do relate to the claim of the complaint, they do not always have to be asserted with the answer. They can be raised after the liability of the defendant has been established. Figure 6–6 is an example of an answer and counterclaim.

Since all counterclaims are part of the answer they are served in the same manner as the answer.

Cross-claims

A cross-claim, a claim by one defendant against another, is allowed whenever the claim arises out of the same transaction or occurrence that is the subject matter of the complaint. For example, again in the factual situation described in the Commentary, if Granger believes that the accident was Linstrom's fault she could file a cross-claim against him. Her claim might be twofold, just as the counterclaim was against Gordon Sheffield. First, she might be claiming damages for any destruction to her van caused by his negligence. Second, she might be claiming total reimbursement or indemnification for any judgment against her in the complaint. (Under the substantive law of torts an employer is liable to third parties for injuries caused by the negligence of their employees while they are in the course and scope of their employment. However, the employer has a claim against the employee for reimbursement or indemnification.) Cross-claims often involve claims for indemnification. If Linda were to file such a cross-claim, it would look as shown in Figure 6–7.

Since cross-claims are part of the answer, they are served in the same manner as the answer.

Third-Party Complaints

A defendant in a lawsuit may feel that some third party, i.e. someone not named in the original complaint, is responsible, in whole or in part, for the damages claimed in the complaint. In the Granger case, facts suggest that the accident occurred because the brakes failed and Linstrom was unable to stop. Suppose that Granger had taken the car in to have the brakes checked two days before the accident and was told that the brakes were in perfect condition. Under such circumstances she might feel that the auto repair service should be responsible for any damages. She could, therefore, bring the auto repair service into the action by filing and serving them with a third-party complaint.

A third-party complaint, unlike the cross-claim and counterclaim, is a separate pleading. Because it is a claim for relief, it resembles the complaint. The main difference is in the caption, which changes to reflect the fact that a third-party complaint is being filed. The defendant filing the third-party complaint is now known as the defendant and third-party plaintiff. The person against whom the claim is asserted is known as the third-party defendant. A third-party complaint against the auto repair service would look as shown in Figure 6–8.

Under the Federal Rules of Civil Procedure, a defendant has the right to file a third-party complaint within ten days of filing the answer. If the third-party complaint is filed within this time, no

compulsory counterclaim
In federal practice, a claim by a defendant against the plaintiff arising out of facts alleged in a complaint; it must be asserted by the defendant or is barred.

permissive counterclaim
A claim by a defendant against a plaintiff that is allowed, but not required, to be asserted in a lawsuit; it need not arise out of the same circumstances described in the complaint.

contribution
Concept that requires joint defendants to reimburse one another, in an equitable manner, for any judgment assessed against them, even though each defendant might be liable to the plaintiff for the entire amount of the judgment.

indemnification
A concept allowing one defendant, who has paid a judgment, to seek reimbursement from another defendant.

UNITED STATES DISTRICT COURT
FOR THE NORTHERN DISTRICT OF CALIFORNIA

GORDON SHEFFIELD and AMY SHEFFIELD, 　　　Plaintiffs,	) Civil No. 12345) ANSWER AND) COUNTERCLAIM))
vs.	))
WESLEY LINSTROM and LINDA GRANGER, 　　　Defendants.	)))

Answer to First Count

Defendant, LINDA GRANGER, answers as follows:

1. Defendant admits the allegations of Paragraphs 1, 2, and 3 of the complaint.

2. Defendant denies each and every allegation of Paragraphs 4, 5, 6, and 7 of the complaint.

Answer to Second Count

3. In answer to Paragraph 8 of Count Two of the complaint, wherein plaintiff incorporates by reference certain paragraphs of Count One of the complaint, defendant admits, denies, and alleges to the same effect and in the same manner as she admitted, denied, and alleged to those specific paragraphs previously in this answer.

4. In answer to Paragraph 9 of Count Two of the complaint, defendant admits that plaintiff, AMY SHEFFIELD, was a passenger in a vehicle being driven by co-plaintiff, GORDON SHEFFIELD, but denies each and every other allegation contained in said paragraph.

5. Defendant denies each and every allegation contained in Paragraph 10 of the complaint.

First Affirmative Defense

As and for an affirmative defense, defendant alleges that plaintiffs' right to maintain this action is barred by the statute of limitations in that more than one year has now elapsed between the date plaintiff's alleged cause of action arose and the date plaintiffs filed their complaint.

FIGURE 6–6
Answer and
Counterclaim.

Second Affirmative Defense

As and for a separate affirmative defense, defendant alleges that plaintiffs were themselves negligent in that plaintiff Gordon Sheffield failed to use ordinary care in the operation of his motor vehicle, and failed to keep a proper lookout for other vehicles, and that both plaintiffs Gordon Sheffield and Amy Sheffield failed to exercise ordinary care in that neither wore a seat belt. Defendant further alleges that said negligence contributed in whole or in part to any injuries which may have resulted.

Counterclaim

As a counterclaim against plaintiff, Gordon Sheffield, defendant alleges:

1. On or about April 29, _____, in a public highway called Market Street in San Francisco, California, plaintiff, Gordon Sheffield, negligently drove a motor vehicle, causing it to collide with another motor vehicle, owned by defendant Linda Granger.

2. That the motor vehicle driven by Gordon Sheffield was owned jointly by plaintiffs Gordon Sheffield and Amy Sheffield and that at all times herein mentioned was driven and operated by Gordon Sheffield with the knowledge and consent of plaintiff Amy Sheffield.

3. As a result of plaintiff's negligence, defendant's motor vehicle was damaged, and defendant has incurred expenses in the amount of $5,000 to repair said vehicle.

4. Also as a result of said motor vehicle collision, co-plaintiff, AMY SHEFFIELD, has commenced a tort action against defendant for the recovery of $150,000.00, her alleged damages resulting from the collision. Defendant alleges that should judgment be assessed against defendant in favor of plaintiff Amy Sheffield, that defendant Linda Granger is entitled to recover from plaintiff Gordon Sheffield all or part of said judgment.

Wherefore defendant prays:

1. That the court enter judgment dismissing the complaint;
2. That defendant have judgment against plaintiff Gordon Sheffield in the amount of $5,000.00;
3. That defendant have judgment against plaintiff Gordon Sheffield in an amount equal to any judgment in favor of plaintiff Amy Sheffield;

FIGURE 6–6
(continued)

4. That defendant be awarded costs incurred herein;

5. That defendant be awarded such other and further relief as the court may deem just.

Dated: _____ 19___

Taylor Martin
_____

TAYLOR MARTIN
15 Plaza de Oro
Sacramento, California 94813
(916) 555-1212
Attorney for Defendant, Linda Granger

FIGURE 6–6
(continued)

UNITED STATES DISTRICT COURT
FOR THE NORTHERN DISTRICT OF CALIFORNIA

GORDON SHEFFIELD and AMY SHEFFIELD, Plaintiffs,	) Civil No.12345) ANSWER AND CROSS-CLAIM)))
vs.	))
WESLEY LINSTROM and LINDA GRANGER, Defendants.	)))

Answer to First Count

Defendant, LINDA GRANGER, answers as follows:

1. Defendant admits the allegations of Paragraphs 1, 2, and 3 of the complaint.

2. Defendant denies each and every allegation of Paragraphs 4, 5, 6, and 7 of the complaint.

Answer to Second Count

3. In answer to Paragraph 8 of Count Two of the complaint, wherein plaintiff incorporates by reference certain paragraphs of Count One of the complaint, defendant admits, denies, and alleges to the same effect and in the same manner as she admitted, denied, and alleged to those specific paragraphs previously in this answer.

FIGURE 6–7
Answer and
Cross-claim.

4. In answer to Paragraph 9 of Count Two of the complaint, defendant admits that plaintiff, AMY SHEFFIELD, was a passenger in a vehicle being driven by co-plaintiff, GORDON SHEFFIELD, but denies each and every other allegation contained in said paragraph.

5. Defendant denies each and every allegation contained in Paragraph 10 of the complaint.

First Affirmative Defense

As and for an affirmative defense, defendant alleges that plaintiffs' right to maintain this action is barred by the statute of limitations in that more than one year has now elapsed between the date of plaintiffs' alleged cause of action arose and the date plaintiffs filed their complaint.

Second Affirmative Defense

As and for a separate affirmative defense, defendant alleges that plaintiffs were themselves negligent in that plaintiff Gordon Sheffield failed to use ordinary care in the operation of his motor vehicle, and failed to keep a proper lookout for other vehicles, and that both plaintiff Gordon Sheffield and Amy Sheffield failed to exercise ordinary care in that neither wore a seat belt. Defendant further alleges that said negligence contributed in whole or in part to any injuries that may have resulted.

Cross-Claim

As a cross-claim against defendant, Wesley Linstrom, hereinafter referred to as cross-defendant, defendant and cross-claimant, hereinafter referred to as cross-claimant, alleges:

1. On or about April 29, 19___, on a public highway called Market Street in San Francisco, California, cross-defendant, Wesley Linstrom, without the knowledge or permission of cross-claimant, Linda Granger, negligently drove a motor vehicle, owned by cross-claimant Linda Granger, causing it to collide with another motor vehicle.

2. As a result of cross-defendant's negligence, cross-claimant's motor vehicle was damaged, and defendant has incurred expenses in the amount of $5,000 to repair said vehicle.

FIGURE 6–7
(continued)

3. Also as a result of said motor vehicle collision, plaintiffs, GORDON SHEFFIELD and AMY SHEFFIELD, have commenced a tort action against cross-claimant for the recovery of $250,000.00, their alleged damages resulting from the collision. Cross-claimant alleges that should judgment be assessed against her in favor of plaintiff Amy Sheffield, that cross-claimant Linda Granger is entitled to recover from cross-defendant the amount of said judgment.

Wherefore defendant and cross-claimant prays:

1. That the court enter judgment dismissing the complaint;

2. That cross-claimant have judgment against cross-defendant Wesley Linstrom in the amount of $5,000.00;

3. That defendant have judgment against cross-defendant in an amount equal to any judgment in favor of plaintiff Amy Sheffield;

4. That defendant be awarded costs incurred herein;

5. That defendant be awarded such other and further relief as the court may deem just.

Dated: _____ 19___

Taylor Martin

TAYLOR MARTIN
15 Plaza de Oro
Sacramento, California 94813
(916) 555-1212
Attorney for Defendant, Linda Granger

FIGURE 6–7
(continued)

permission of the court is required. If a defendant decides to file a third-party action after that time, permission from the court is required. This would be obtained by making a motion in court. At the time that the third-party complaint is filed, it will be necessary to have a new summons issued, directed to the third-party defendant. See Figure 6–9 for a sample of such a summons.

A third-party complaint and summons must be served in the same way as a complaint is served.

Replies and Answers

Responses must be made to allegations contained in counter-claims, cross-claims, and third-party complaints. The response to

UNITED STATES DISTRICT COURT
FOR THE NORTHERN DISTRICT OF CALIFORNIA

GORDON SHEFFIELD and AMY
SHEFFIELD,
    Plaintiffs,

    v.

WESLEY LINSTROM,
    Defendant
LINDA GRANGER,
    Defendant and
    Third-Party Plaintiff,

    v.

BRAKEFAST, Inc.,
    Third-Party Defendant.

) Civil No. 12345
)
) Third-Party Complaint

Linda Granger, Third-Party Plaintiff, alleges:

1. Plaintiffs, GORDON SHEFFIELD and AMY SHEFFIELD, have filed against defendant LINDA GRANGER a complaint, a copy of which is hereto attached as "Exhibit A."

2. At all times herein mentioned, third-party defendant is an automotive garage engaged in the business of servicing and repairing automobiles including brake systems.

3. On or about April 25, 19___, third-party plaintiff took her automobile, Oregon license XYZ 123, to third-party defendant's automotive garage for the specific purpose of having the brakes checked and serviced.

4. On or about April 25, 19___, third-party defendant negligently and carelessly checked, serviced, and inspected said brakes and negligently and carelessly advised third-party plaintiff that said brakes were in good condition.

5. On or about April 29, 19___, the brakes on said automobile failed, causing the vehicle to collide with another motor vehicle driven by plaintiff, Gordon Sheffield.

6. As a result of said collision, plaintiffs have filed the complaint attached as Exhibit A, claiming damages from third-party plaintiff.

7. Any damages claimed by plaintiff are a direct and proximate result of the negligence of third-party defendant, and should any

FIGURE 6–8
Third-Party
Complaint.

damages be assessed against third-party plaintiff, she is entitled to judgment against third-party defendant in the same amount.

Wherefore third-party plaintiff demands judgment against third-party defendant for all sums that may be adjudged against defendant, LINDA GRANGER, in favor of plaintiffs Gordon Sheffield and Amy Sheffield.

Dated: _____   *Taylor Martin*
                            _____

TAYLOR MARTIN
15 Plaza de Oro
Sacramento, California 94813
(916) 555-1212
Attorney for Defendant and
   Third-Party Plaintiff,
Linda Granger

FIGURE 6–8
(continued)

a counterclaim is entitled a **reply**. Except for the title of the document, it resembles an answer in all respects. The responses to cross-claims and third-party complaints are entitled answers, and do not differ from an answer to the complaint. Under the Federal Rules of Civil Procedure, all responses are due twenty days after service of the pleading containing the claim.

Amending

Counterclaims, cross-claims, and third-party complaints can be amended one time as long as a response to them has not been filed and served. Otherwise, court permission or the agreement of adverse parties is needed.

6–5 LEGAL CHALLENGES TO THE COMPLAINT

The primary purpose of an answer is to challenge the factual basis for the plaintiff's claim. However, not all defenses or challenges to a complaint deal with the truth or falsity of the factual allegations. Sometimes defendants wish to challenge the action on a more technical, legal basis. For example, the defendant might be challenging the court's authority to hear the case (jurisdiction), or the defendant might be claiming that he was not properly served with the complaint. Some jurisdictions, including federal court, allow this type of defense to be raised either in the answer or in a

---

UNITED STATES DISTRICT COURT
FOR THE NORTHERN DISTRICT OF CALIFORNIA

GORDON SHEFFIELD and AMY SHEFFIELD, Plaintiffs,	) Civil No.12345)) Summons
v.	
WESLEY LINSTROM, Defendant. LINDA GRANGER, Defendant and Third-Party Plaintiff,	
v.	
BRAKEFAST, Inc., Third-Party Defendant.	

To the above-named Third-Party Defendant:

You are hereby summoned and required to serve upon TERRY ALVAREZ, plaintiff's attorney, whose address is 100 Market St., San Francisco, California, and upon TAYLOR MARTIN, who is attorney for LINDA GRANGER, defendant and third-party plaintiff, and whose address is 15 Plaza de Oro, Sacramento, California, an answer to the third-party complaint which is herewith served upon you within 20 days after the service of this summons upon you exclusive of the day of service. If you fail to do so, judgment by default will be taken against you for the relief demanded in the third-party complaint. There is also served upon you herewith a copy of the complaint of the plaintiff which you may but are not required to answer.

_____
Clerk of Court

[Seal of District Court]
Dated _____

FIGURE 6–9
Summons on Third-Party Complaint.

---

motion. Other jurisdictions require that certain defenses be raised in a special pleading, sometimes known as a demurrer.

In federal court many legal challenges to the action are raised by the defendant in a **motion to dismiss** the case. A motion to dismiss is a request that the court immediately terminate the action without granting the plaintiff any of the relief that was requested in the complaint. Legal challenges or defenses that can be raised in a motion to dismiss under Rule 12 of the Federal Rules of Civil Procedure include:

reply
In federal practice, the written response to a counterclaim.

motion to dismiss
A request that the court dismiss or strike the case.

1. lack of jurisdiction over the subject matter;
2. lack of jurisdiction over the person;
3. improper venue;
4. insufficiency of process;
5. insufficiency of service of process;
6. failure to state a claim upon which relief can be granted;
7. failure to join a party under Rule 19 (an indispensable party).

The defenses of lack of subject matter jurisdiction, failure to state a claim, or failure to join a party can be brought up by the defendant at any time, even after all the pleadings have been filed. The other defenses must be raised in an answer or motion or they are waived.

If the defendant makes a motion to dismiss, he must do so before filing an answer and within the time permitted to answer (twenty days after service of the complaint). Whether these defenses are raised by motion or by the answer, if a party so requests the court will usually hold a hearing prior to trial to determine the validity of the defense. If the motion to dismiss is denied, the court will generally require that the defendant file his answer within ten days. An alternative method of challenging service of the complaint or personal jurisdiction is the **motion to quash service of summons**.

Another response to a complaint that is allowed in federal court is the **motion for a more definite statement**. If the complaint (or cross-claim, counterclaim, or third-party complaint) is so vague or ambiguous that the opposing party cannot reasonably be required to frame a responsive pleading, that party may petition the court to order the claimant to revise his pleading. In some state jurisdictions another type of pleading, known as a **demurrer**, is used to challenge the legal sufficiency of the complaint. The grounds for a demurrer are similar to those for a motion to dismiss the case. When a demurrer is filed, the court usually holds a hearing to determine the issues that have been raised. If the demurrer is sustained, either the case is dismissed or the plaintiff is given the opportunity to amend it. If the demurrer is overruled, the defendant is given a short time in which to file his answer.

6–6 FAILURE TO ANSWER

If a party fails to answer a pleading to which a response is required (that is, the defendant fails to answer the complaint, or the plaintiff fails to reply to a counterclaim), then a judgment by default may follow. In most jurisdictions, including federal court, obtaining a judgment is a two-step process. First, the plaintiff or the plaintiff's attorney files with the court an **affidavit**—a statement under penalty of perjury, sworn to before a notary—verifying that the opposing party has defaulted (not responded) and requesting that the clerk enter that party's default. Entry of default is not the same as a default judgment. **Entry of default** means that the failure to respond had been noted in the court's file. See Figure 6–10 for an example of the request to enter default and accompanying affidavit. After the default has been entered, then the claimant can apply for a default judgment.

To obtain a default judgment, the plaintiff must prove the claim. This can be done at a brief court hearing where evidence is presented to a judge. In lieu of a court hearing, many jurisdictions allow the plaintiff to submit affidavits to substantiate the claim. The laws of the jurisdiction determine the exact procedure that is followed, although generally a default judgment cannot be obtained if the defendant is a minor, incompetent, or in the military service. In federal court, the plaintiff may also request a hearing before a jury to determine the amount of damages.

Setting Aside Defaults

Courts usually permit parties against whom a default judgment was entered to petition the court to set it aside by making a motion to set aside the default judgment. The most common grounds for making and granting such a motion are that the judgment was entered through mistake, inadvertence, surprise, or excusable neglect. This type of motion must usually be made within certain time limits after the judgment was obtained. For example, Rule 60 of the Federal Rules of Civil Procedure provides that the motion must be made within a reasonable time of the judgment having been rendered (but not to exceed one year). Default judgments can also be set aside, without a motion, if the plaintiff will stipulate or agree to do so.

SUMMARY

6–1. Defendants must respond to the initial pleading within certain time limitations. These time limitations are controlled by the laws of the jurisdiction in which the matter is pending. In federal court, the defendant has twenty days from the date of service of the complaint in which to respond. Time limitations in which to respond can be enlarged or extended, either by stipulation or agreement of the parties or by obtaining a court order. In some jurisdictions a stipulation to extend the time must be approved by the court.

motion to quash service of summons
A request that the court declare that the service of the complaint and summons is invalid, either because the court lacks jurisdiction over the defendant or because of some procedural problem with the service itself.

motion for a more definite statement
A motion made in response to a complaint in which the defendant challenges the clarity or specificity of the complaint.

demurrer
A pleading used in some state jurisdictions that challenges the legal sufficiency of the complaint.

affidavit
A written statement that certain facts are true or are believed to be true, made under oath.

entry of default
Action by a court clerk noting that the defendant has failed to file a proper response to the complaint.

UNITED STATES DISTRICT COURT
FOR THE NORTHERN DISTRICT OF CALIFORNIA

GORDON SHEFFIELD and AMY SHEFFIELD, Plaintiffs,	) No.12345)) AFFIDAVIT AND REQUEST)) TO ENTER DEFAULT)
vs.	))
WESLEY LINSTROM and LINDA GRANGER, Defendants.	)))

State of California
County of San Francisco

I, Terry Alvarez, being duly sworn say:

1. I am the attorney for plaintiffs in the above action.
2. A copy of the summons and complaint was served on defendant on May 15, 19___, and the return of service of John Smith, United States Marshal, is on file in this action.
3. Defendant, Wesley Linstrom, has not answered or otherwise appeared in this action, and the time within which defendant may appear has expired.

Terry Alvarez

TERRY ALVAREZ
ALVAREZ & COE
100 Market Street
San Francisco, California 94101
(415) 555-1212
Attorney for Plaintiffs

Subscribed and sworn to before me on June 20, 19___

Request to Clerk to Enter Default

To: Clerk

Defendant, Wesley Linstrom, having failed to answer or otherwise appear in the above-entitled action, and the time for appearance having expired, you are requested to enter his default pursuant to Rule 55(a) of the Federal Rules of Civil Procedure.

Dated June 20, 19___   *Terry Alvarez*

TERRY ALVAREZ
Attorney for Plaintiffs
100 Market Street
San Francisco, California 94101

FIGURE 6–10
Affidavit in Support of Entry of Default.

6-2 An answer is a pleading that challenges the plaintiff's claim for relief. An answer can consist of either a general denial, a qualified denial, or a specific denial. A general denial contests all of the allegations contained in the complaint. In some jurisdictions a general denial cannot be used if the complaint has been verified. A qualified denial specifically admits or denies certain allegations, then denies everything else. A specific denial contains specific responses to each allegation contained in the complaint. An answer might also contain affirmative defenses. Affirmative defenses are facts or circumstances that operate to defeat the plaintiff's claim, even if all of the contentions of the complaint are proven. Affirmative defenses are often matters of substantive law and therefore vary according to the nature of the case.

6-3 An answer is a pleading and as such follows the same general format as the complaint or petition in the case. It contains a caption that states the name and address of the attorney for the defendant, the title of the court and the case, the docket number, and the title of the document (answer). The body of the answer contains numbered paragraphs in which the defendant responds to the allegations of the complaint followed by affirmative defenses, if they exist. The answer concludes with a prayer and the signature and address of the attorney filing the document. The answer is served on the plaintiff or his attorney and filed in court. Service can be accomplished by mailing a copy of the answer to the attorney or the plaintiff if unrepresented. An answer can usually be amended. In federal court a party may amend an answer any time within twenty days after it is served, as long as the case has not been placed on the trial calendar. After twenty days (or if the case is set for trial) court permission or a stipulation is required.

6-4 The defendant in any action has the right to make a claim for relief. In general he may make any claim that he has against the plaintiff whether it is related to the claim stated in the complaint or not. He may make a claim against a co-defendant or a third person (not a party to the original action) if the claim stems from the circumstance or transaction described in the complaint. The names of the documents in which defendants assert their claim may differ from one jurisdiction to another. In federal court, a claim against the plaintiff is known as a counterclaim. A claim against a co-defendant is known as a cross-claim, and a claim against a third person is known as a third-party complaint.

6-5 In addition to being contested on the factual allegations, lawsuits can be challenged on technical legal grounds (such as lack of jurisdiction, expiration of the statute of limitations, insufficiency of service of process). Legal challenges are often raised in some manner other than the answer. In federal court, even though legal challenges can be asserted in an answer, a motion to dismiss the action or a motion to quash service of summons can be an alternative. A motion for a more definite statement is also a possible response where the complaint is so vague or ambiguous that the opposing party cannot reasonably respond. Some jurisdictions have a pleading known as a demurrer that also operates to challenge the complaint on technical legal grounds.

6–6 If a party fails to answer the complaint, the plaintiff can request that the defendant's default be entered in the court record and that a default judgment be granted in plaintiff's favor. A court hearing may be required before the court will grant a judgment.

KEY TERMS

affidavit
affirmative defense
answer
compulsory counterclaim
contribution
counterclaim
cross-claim
demurrer
entry of default
general denial
indemnification
motion

motion for a more definite statement
motion to dismiss
motion to quash service of summons
open stipulation
permissive counterclaim
qualified denial
reply
specific denial
stipulation enlarging time
third-party complaint

QUESTIONS FOR REVIEW AND DISCUSSION

1. What kinds of responses can the defendant make to the initial pleading?
2. What time limitations apply to these responses? Can these time limitations be changed? If so, how?
3. What is the difference between a general denial, a qualified denial, and a specific denial?
4. What is an affirmative defense, and why is it important?
5. What is the general format of an answer?
6. What is the procedure for serving and filing an answer?
7. How are responsive pleadings amended?

8. What are counterclaims, cross-claims, and third-party complaints?
9. What are the different ways in which a defendant can challenge legal deficiencies with the initial pleading or process?
10. What happens if the defendant fails to file a timely response to the initial pleading?

ACTIVITIES

1. Review the laws of your state. How much time does a defendant have to respond to the initial pleading? Must a stipulation to enlarge or extend that time be approved by the court?
2. Review the laws of your state that deal with responses to the initial pleading. What responsive pleadings are allowed? What responsive motions are permitted?
3. Review the Commentary at the beginning of this chapter. If the action were filed in your state court, and Granger were to file a claim against Linstrom, the Sheffields, and Brakefast, Inc., how would she do so?

CHAPTER 6 PROJECT—DRAFTING AN ANSWER AND CROSS-CLAIM

Review the complaint found in chapter 5 (Figure 5–10). Assume that your law firm represents May Forrester and that you have been requested to draft an answer and cross-claim on her behalf. You have been given the following facts: May Forrester was indeed a real estate agent working for Hearth & Home and did make a sales presentation to the Hendricks. Prior to the sales presentation, she was given facts and photos regarding the property by one of her employers, Harry Rice. Rice told her that he had visited the property and had taken the photographs himself. During the sales presentation, she only repeated what she had been told. Furthermore, she had worked for Home & Hearth Real Estate for three years and had no reason to doubt her employer. Draft an appropriate answer and cross-claim.

CHAPTER 7
Motion Practice

COMMENTARY—THE OVERLAND CASE

Your firm has just been retained by Overland Corporation, a farm machinery manufacturer, to represent it in a lawsuit. A complaint, naming it as defendant, was filed in federal court in the state of Nebraska. The complaint bases federal court jurisdiction on diversity of citizenship, alleging that plaintiff is a citizen of Nebraska and that defendant, Overland Corporation, is a resident of Delaware. The president of Overland Corporation, however, states that while Overland is incorporated in Delaware, it has its headquarters and conducts most of its business in Nebraska. Your supervising attorney has told you that since a corporation is a citizen both of the state of incorporation and the state where the principal place of business is located, she believes that diversity does not exist and that, therefore, the federal court does not have subject matter jurisdiction. She has asked you to draft a motion to dismiss the action on that basis.

OBJECTIVES

In chapter 6 you were introduced to the various responses to the initial pleadings. Some of those responses are presented to the court in the form of a motion. After completing this chapter, you will be able to:

1. Define a motion.
2. Explain the procedure for making a motion.
3. Explain the procedure for opposing a motion.
4. Define the term *affidavit*.
5. Explain the role of the paralegal in setting motions for hearing.
6. Explain the method for obtaining orders after hearings on the motion.
7. Define the term *sanctions* and explain their use in motion practice.
8. Identify some common pretrial motions.
9. Explain the procedure for making motions during trial.
10. Identify some common post-trial motions.

7–1 MOTIONS GENERALLY

During the course of litigation questions or problems regarding the case inevitably arise. Sometimes these questions or problems involve practical, procedural issues. For example, in the case mentioned in the commentary, the attorney representing Overland might not be able to adequately research the law and prepare responsive documents within twenty days of serving the client. As explained in chapter 6, this problem is easy to solve. The attorney asks for and usually receives more time than the law normally allows. Other times these problems involve more complicated and substantial legal issues. For example, in the Overland case, the defense attorney believes that diversity of jurisdiction is lacking and that, therefore, the federal court is not the proper forum for the case. This issue is more complicated, and the parties may have a substantial disagreement regarding the facts and the law. Consequently, the defense attorney is less likely to get the plaintiff's attorney's agreement to dismiss the case. If the attorneys cannot resolve the problems by themselves, a court order is required to settle the issue. The application for such a court order is a **motion**.

Except for motions made during the trial, motions are required to be written, filed in court, and served on the opposing attorneys (or parties, if not represented). If the motion is contested, the opposing attorneys will also file papers opposing the motion. Often the written documents are followed by a brief court hearing before the judge rules on the motion. Although they are not considered to be pleadings, in appearance motions do resemble pleadings. The documents filed in a motion follow the same formalities required of pleadings, all containing the same caption as the pleadings. As a paralegal you might be asked to research the law governing the particular motion involved or prepare the written documents that are filed in court. You might also be requested to contact the court to set the motion for a hearing.

7–2 PREPARING, SERVING, AND RESPONDING

Many different types of motions are possible. Some motions are individually described by statute. These statutes explain the specific procedures and time limits for making such motions. On the other hand, other motions may be only briefly, if at all, described. Regardless of any special procedures that may apply to some motions, certain procedures are common to all motions.

Preparation of the Written Papers

The party making the motion, known as the **moving party**, begins by preparing written papers for service and filing. These papers all follow the same general format as pleadings. The written papers filed in making a motion usually include different documents: the motion, the notice of hearing on the motion, affidavits in support of the motion, and a memorandum of points and authorities in support of the motion. In motion practice, the term motion is used in two different contexts. On one hand, it refers to the whole process of making a request for an order from the court. On the other hand, it is used to refer to one of the documents filed in support of that request.

The document entitled "motion" describes the nature of the motion, the grounds for the motion, and the relief requested. The content of the motion will obviously depend on the type of motion being made and will be specifically drafted for that purpose. A motion made on behalf of Overland Corporation to dismiss the complaint filed against it might look as shown in Figure 7–1.

motion
A request for an order from the court, usually dealing with a pending case.

moving party
The party making a motion.

notice of hearing on motion
The part of a written motion that describes the nature of the motion being made and tells when and where a hearing on the motion will occur.

affidavit
A written statement that certain facts are true or are believed to be true, made under oath.

UNITED STATES DISTRICT COURT
DISTRICT OF NEBRASKA

JOHN JONES, Plaintiff,	))) Civil No. 123456)) Motion to Dismiss))
vs.	
OVERLAND CORPORATION, Defendant.	)))

      OVERLAND CORPORATION, by PAT RIVAS, its attorney, moves the court to dismiss the complaint on file on the following grounds: the complaint in this action alleges that this action is filed in federal court because it involves a dispute between citizens of different states; however, the court lacks subject matter jurisdiction as alleged in the complaint in that plaintiff and defendant are citizens of the same state as is more clearly stated in the affidavit of Owen Young, hereto annexed as Exhibit A.

A Memorandum of Points and Authorities in support of this motion is served and filed with this motion.

Dated August 1 19___

                Pat Rivas
                PAT RIVAS
                Attorney for Defendant
                769 Maine Street
                Omaha, Nebraska 68101
                (402) 555-1212

FIGURE 7–1
Motion to Dismiss.

    The **notice of hearing on the motion** is a simple paper stating when and where the court hearing on the motion will take place. It might look as shown in Figure 7–2.

    In many courts the motion and the notice of hearing on the motion can be combined into one document.

    Although not always required, motions are commonly supported by affidavits. An **affidavit** is a statement, under penalty of perjury, sworn to before a notary or other person authorized to administer an oath. An affidavit usually describes the factual basis for making the motion and is made by the person having personal knowledge of those facts. It can be the statement of the attorney, a party, or a third person. Even though it may be the statement of a party or a witness, the attorney or paralegal will normally prepare the document based on what the individual has told them. An affidavit serves the same purpose as testimony from a party or witness and is used in lieu of that testimony. As such, an affidavit should be written in the first person and should contain detailed facts. An affidavit in support of the motion described in the commentary might look as shown in Figure 7–3.

UNITED STATES DISTRICT COURT
DISTRICT OF NEBRASKA

JOHN JONES, Plaintiff,	))) Civil No. 123456)
vs.	) Notice of Motion))
OVERLAND CORPORATION, Defendant.	)))

To: Lane Borman, Attorney for Plaintiff,
Please take notice, that the undersigned will bring the above motion on for hearing before this Court at Room _____, United States Court House, _____, City of Omaha on the _____ day of _____ 19___, at 10 o'clock a.m. of that day or as soon thereafter as counsel can be heard.

Pat Rivas
PAT RIVAS
Attorney for Defendant
769 Maine Street
Omaha, Nebraska 68101
(402) 555-1212

FIGURE 7–2
Notice of Motion.

UNITED STATES DISTRICT COURT
DISTRICT OF NEBRASKA

JOHN JONES,	
Plaintiff,	)
	)
	) Civil No. 123456
	)
vs.	) Affidavit of Owen
	) Young in Support of
	) Motion to Dismiss
	)
OVERLAND CORPORATION,	)
Defendant.	)
	)

I, Owen Young, being first duly sworn, depose and say:

1. I am the president of OVERLAND CORPORATION, the defendant in this action, and am acquainted with the facts in this case, and have personal knowledge of the matter set forth in this affidavit.

2. I make this affidavit in support of the motion to dismiss the action.

3. I held the office of president of OVERLAND CORPORATION at all times mentioned in the complaint filed in this action.

4. At all times mentioned in the complaint, OVERLAND CORPORATION has been incorporated under the laws of the state of New York.

5. At all times mentioned in the complaint, OVERLAND CORPORATION has had its principal place of business in the state of Nebraska. The corporation maintains four sales offices throughout the state of Nebraska, maintains its primary bank account in the state of Nebraska, and keeps copies of all corporate records within the state of Nebraska. Business conducted within the state of Nebraska accounts for over 75% of the total income of said corporation.

_____
Owen Young

Subscribed and sworn to before me on _____ 19____

_____

FIGURE 7–3
Affidavit in
Support of Motion.

In some courts a **declaration** is used in lieu of an affidavit. Like the affidavit, a declaration is a statement under penalty of perjury but it is not sworn to before a notary.

Along with a supporting affidavit, most attorneys also support a motion with a **memorandum of points and authorities**. In some courts this is required. A memorandum of points and authorities is a legal argument in the form of a discussion or analysis of the law (statutes, cases, or constitutional provisions) that applies to the case. If you are asked to help prepare a

declaration
A statement under penalty of perjury that certain facts are true or believed to be true.

memorandum of points and authorities
A legal argument in the form of a discussion or analysis of the law that applies to the case.

memorandum of points and authorities you will have to research the law that governs the case.

Although the general requirements for motion practice are found in the Federal Rules of Civil Procedure or appropriate state laws, motion practice is an area that is often the subject of local rules of court, both in the federal and state courts. Before preparing any motion it is imperative that you review all of the laws that regulate motion practice in the particular court in which the action is filed.

Service and Filing

The motion and supporting papers must be filed with the court and copies served on the other parties to the action. All jurisdictions impose some time limitations on the service of motions. Under the Federal Rules of Civil Procedure, unless changed by a specific statute or court order, the written motion and notice of hearing must be served not later than five days before the time set for the hearing. This time period can be changed by court order. You must be careful to check local rules of court, however, regarding this time limit. State courts may have different time requirements, and even some federal courts have local rules that have changed this notice requirement.

Should a situation arise making it impossible or impractical to comply with the time requirement imposed by statute or local rule, the courts allow the moving party to request that the time be shortened. In a sense, this request is in itself a motion. Courts generally treat this as an **ex parte** motion, meaning that no prior notice need be given nor any court hearing scheduled. If the court grants this request, it is often referred to as an **order shortening time**. The order shortening time is then served on the opposing party with the notice of hearing on the motion and the other moving papers. Service of a motion is usually accomplished by mailing copies of the moving papers to the opposing attorneys. Proof of service of the moving papers is in the form of an affidavit or declaration by the person mailing the papers and is sometimes known as a **proof of service by mail** or **certificate of mailing**.

Responding to Motions

To oppose a motion, an attorney commonly serves and files papers in opposition. These usually consist of affidavits in opposition to the motion and a memorandum of points and authorities in opposition to the motion. These affidavits and the memorandum have the same technical requirements as do the moving papers. For most motions in federal court, opposing affidavits must be

---

ex parte
Refers to motions or hearings where the moving party is not required to give prior formal notice to opposing parties.

order shortening time
A ruling from the court, often in connection with motions, allowing a moving party to give less notice of a hearing on a motion than is required by statute.

proof of service by mail or **certificate of mailing**
Verification that a pleading, motion, or other document has been served by mailing a copy of the document to another party or attorney.

THE COMPUTERIZED LAW FIRM—Word Processing to Draft Motions

SCENARIO

You are in the process of preparing a draft of a motion to dismiss in the Overland case as requested by your attorney. In talking to another paralegal in the firm, you are told that she prepared and filed a similar motion in another case just recently. She shows you a copy of the papers filed in that case, and you note that except for the names, case number, and dates, your motion will be identical.

PROBLEM

The documents you must draft are substantially similar to documents previously drafted in connection with other cases. How can you minimize needless repetition now and in the future?

SOLUTION

Motions often are little more than repetitive forms. WordPerfect, the word processing program described in the previous chapter, is an excellent form creation and management tool. With this program you can create a form for a new case from an existing form, without having to retype everything. For example, suppose your office filed a motion to dismiss in the case of *Nolan v. Ybarra*. Except for the names, dates, and case number the information contained in the motion is identical to the one you are preparing in the case of *Jones v. Overland Corporation*. If the motion in the Nolan case is saved on disk, it can be called up and revised. By using the "search" and "replace" function keys necessary changes can be easily made. You simply tell the computer to search the document for each place where the name Ybarra appears and replace it with the name Overland Corporation. You do this for each item that needs to be changed, and you have the new document you need.

With WordPerfect you can also create forms for specific motions for pretrial, trial, or post-trial and store these motions as forms, identified by the type of motion: "pretrial.mtn," "trial.mtn," or "ptrial.mtn." After retrieving the motion form, the changes can be made and the new form saved under a separate title to connect it with the case in which the motion is to be filed: "Smith.mtn," or by the date of the particular motion: "010591.mtn."

WordPerfect also provides directories and subdirectories to help in locating forms that have been prepared and stored. This avoids the necessity of manually searching for copies of similar motions.

served not later than one day before the hearing. Again, this time limit will vary depending on the state or local rules. As a litigation paralegal you might be involved in drafting these documents for the attorney's review.

7–3 COURT PROCEDURES INVOLVING MOTIONS

In addition to the written documents, motions often involve court hearings. The attorneys for the moving and responding parties appear before a judge and present oral arguments in support of or in opposition to the motion. The judge considers the written documents and the oral arguments and then makes a decision. After the judge rules on the motion, a written order, reflecting that ruling, must be submitted to the judge for signature.

Hearings

Since a hearing on the motion is a court appearance, it must be handled by the attorney. However, as a litigation paralegal, you might have some responsibilities in scheduling the hearing. Different courts have different methods of scheduling motion hearings. In some courts motions are heard at set times and in set departments (sometimes referred to as "law and motion"). In other courts you might have to specifically arrange a time with the judge hearing the motion. This is done through the judge's clerk. In any event, scheduling the motion will probably require that you call the court, talk to the clerk handling the motion calendar, and arrange for a convenient date. Be sure to check your attorney's calendar for conflicts. It is also advisable to call the opposing attorneys prior to doing this to schedule the hearing at a time that is convenient for all parties. This eliminates the need for continuing the hearing date. When setting a motion for hearing, be sure that you allow sufficient time for service of the moving papers. In state courts you may have to give more than five days notice. Be sure you have checked this. Also be sure to check state rules regarding service by mail. State rules may require that additional time be added if the papers are served by mail.

In lieu of court hearings on motions, some courts today are using telephone conference calls between the judge and the various attorneys. This can save substantial time. Local rules of court would probably control this procedure.

Orders After Motions

After the motion is heard, the judge will make a ruling, which is called an **order**. Most courts require that the prevailing party prepare the written order for the judge's signature. As a litigation paralegal you might be asked to do this. Some courts have local rules that require that the moving party submit a proposed order with the moving papers. Sometimes a judge's ruling on a case is not a simple granting or denying of the motion. At times orders become very involved. If you are asked to prepare an order after a hearing be sure that you know exactly what must be included in the order. The attorney may give you his notes from the hearing or simply tell you what to include in the order. In either case be sure that you understand the notes or directions before drafting the order. Figure 7–4 is an example of an order.

Sanctions

All courts expect that motions will be made or opposed in good faith. In order to prevent unnecessary or frivolous motions, courts generally have the power to punish an attorney who files such a motion. Courts also have the power to punish attorneys whose improper or unreasonable conduct causes the other side to make a motion. This punishment usually is in the form of an award of attorney fees to the opposing side. In some cases, where the court finds the behavior particularly unreasonable or unjustified, the court may find a party or attorney in contempt of court. Furthermore, if a party fails to comply with an order issued after a motion, the court may impose additional sanctions. In some extreme cases the court may even strike the pleadings of one who fails to comply with a court order, making it possible for the other side to win without trial. Should the court grant an order finally disposing of the case, that order would be immediately appealable.

7–4 SPECIFIC MOTIONS

As mentioned above, there are many different kinds of motions, some of which will be described in code sections, some of which are not. Some of the more common motions that are mentioned in the Federal Rules of Civil Procedure and that are seen in many state jurisdictions are described below.

Pretrial Motions

Motions can be made at any time during the litigation process. Consequently, they deal with all aspects of litigation. Pretrial motions deal with issues or problems that arise before the trial occurs. Most often, these motions deal with requests that are ancillary to the primary relief requested in the complaint. These requests or motions often relate to the pleadings, the jurisdiction

order
A ruling from the court, usually after a motion.

UNITED STATES DISTRICT COURT
DISTRICT OF NEBRASKA

JOHN JONES,
      Plaintiff,

            vs.

OVERLAND CORPORATION,
      Defendant.

) Civil No. 123456

) Order

      This action was heard on _____ 19___, on the motion of defendant, OVERLAND CORPORATION, for an order dismissing this action. Pat Rivas appeared as counsel for defendant, in support of the motion, and Lane Borman appeared as counsel for plaintiff in opposition thereto. It appears to the court that defendant is a citizen of the same state as plaintiff and that therefore this court lacks subject matter jurisdiction. Therefore,

      IT IS ORDERED that the complaint filed herein on _____ 19___ be and it is hereby dismissed.

Dated _____

_____
Judge, District Court

FIGURE 7–4
Order After
Motion.

and venue of the court, and the discovery process. However, some pretrial motions deal with substantive issues that may affect the very right to trial.

Motion to Dismiss. A **motion to dismiss** the action is a request that the court terminate the lawsuit immediately, without a hearing on the merits of plaintiff's claim. A motion to dismiss is often made in lieu of an answer, and if granted eliminates the need for one. Such a motion can be made for several reasons. In federal proceedings a motion to dismiss the case is proper when the court lacks subject matter or personal jurisdiction, when venue is improper, when process (the summons) or service of process is insufficient, where the complaint fails to state a claim upon which relief can be granted, or where a necessary party has not been joined.

Motion for a More Definite Statement. If a complaint (or other claim for relief) is so vague and ambiguous that it cannot be understood and responded to, the party required to respond may make a **motion for a more definite statement.** Such a motion is intended to require the claimant to clarify his allegations and make them more intelligible. The moving party is expected to point out the defects in the complaint and explain what details need to be added to the claim.

Motion to Strike. A **motion to strike** is a request that the court delete portions of a pleading that are insufficient, redundant, immaterial, or scandalous.

Motion to Amend. As discussed in previous chapters, all pleadings can be amended. Under some circumstances pleadings can be amended as a matter of right without the necessity of a court order. If a court order is required, the party wishing to amend a pleading must make a **motion to amend**. The courts are very liberal in allowing parties to amend pleadings and would probably grant such a motion unless the amended pleading would unfairly prejudice the other party.

Motion for Judgment on the Pleadings. After all pleadings have been filed in an action, any party may make a **motion for judgment on the pleadings**. The moving party in such a motion claims that the allegations in the pleadings are such that no controverted issues remain and judgment can be entered for only one party. For example, if the defendant were to admit all of the allegations in the complaint, no disputed issue would remain. The pleadings themselves indicate that plaintiff is entitled to judgment.

Motion for Change of Venue. If an action is commenced in the wrong judicial district, a party can request that the court transfer the case to a proper court by making a **motion for change of venue**. Furthermore, in cases where venue is proper in more than one district, a party can request a change of venue to another

motion to dismiss
A request that the court dismiss or strike the case.

motion for a more definite statement
A motion made in response to a complaint in which the defendant challenges the clarity or specificity of the complaint.

motion to strike
A request made to the court to delete part or all of a pleading; can also refer to a request made during trial to delete testimony.

motion to amend
A request by one party to the court to allow a change in the content of a pleading.

motion for judgment on the pleadings
A motion claiming that the allegations in the pleadings are such that no controversial issues remain and that judgment can be entered for only one party.

motion for change of venue
A request from a party that the court transfer the case to a proper court.

proper district for the convenience of parties and witnesses or in the interest of justice.

Motion to Quash Return of Service. Where the defendant claims that he was improperly served with the summons and complaint he can make a **motion to quash the return of the service** (or motion to quash service of summons). A defendant is improperly served if the manner of service is not in accordance with the appropriate statute or if the defendant is not subject to the personal jurisdiction of the court. When such a motion is granted service is negated. If the defect in service was in the manner of service, the defendant can be served again. However, if the court does not have personal jurisdiction over the defendant, the action cannot proceed in that court. If the plaintiff wants to pursue the case, he or she will have to begin the process again, this time in a court that does have personal jurisdiction over the defendant.

Discovery Motions. An essential part of the litigation process is **discovery**. Discovery is a legal process by which parties of the lawsuit are able to discover facts that are relevant to the case. Much of discovery involves requiring the opposing side to reveal those facts or provide pertinent documents. Problems often arise regarding exactly what has to be revealed or provided. If one party refuses to provide information to another, the party requesting the information can make a **motion to compel** the requested discovery. If the motion is granted the court will order the party to comply with the discovery request and impose some sort of penalty or sanctions if the party refuses. If the court finds that the initial refusal to comply with discovery request was unreasonable, it can also impose sanctions for that initial refusal. (Sanctions are usually in the form of attorney fees awarded to the moving party.) Likewise if the court finds that the motion to compel was not made in good faith it can impose sanctions on the moving party. A second type of discovery motion is a **motion for a protective order**. A motion for a protective order is a request that the court limit the other party's right to discovery.

Motion for Summary Judgment. Prior to the time of trial, it may appear that there really are no disputed factual issues in the case. Since the purpose of a trial is to resolve factual disputes, in such a case a trial is unnecessary and a party can request that judgment be entered immediately. In fact, that party is entitled to a judgment as a matter of law. The request for such a judgment is known as a **motion for a summary judgment**. The moving party in such a motion must show the court that no factual dispute exists.

This can be done by submitting affidavits in support of the motion. This can also be done by submitting depositions, answers to interrogatories, or answers to requests for admissions. Depositions, interrogatories, and requests for admissions are methods of discovery and are discussed in subsequent chapters. Along with these documents, the moving party will also submit a memorandum of points and authorities. In most cases, a party opposing a motion for summary judgment will present the court with opposing papers supported by affidavits, depositions, answers to interrogatories, or answers to request for admissions. The opposing party will also file a legal memorandum. All affidavits filed in support or opposition to a motion for summary judgment must show that the persons making the affidavits are competent to testify to the matters stated within the affidavits, that the matters are within their personal knowledge, and that if they were testifying in court the statements would be admissible in evidence. In ruling on a motion for summary judgment the court scrutinizes the various papers to see if a factual dispute does exist. At this point the court does not weigh the evidence or resolve a factual dispute. If a legitimate and genuine factual dispute exists the motion must be denied, even if one side has overwhelming evidence.

A motion for summary judgment need not be directed to all of the issues in the case. A party can request a partial summary judgment or a summary judgment on certain issues in the case. For example, in a personal injury case there may be no factual dispute about liability, but a dispute may exist as to the amount of damages to which the plaintiff is entitled. If such a summary judgment is rendered, a trial is held to decide those issues that remain.

In making a motion for summary judgment you must be careful to check the appropriate statute for time requirements. There are generally limits on how soon after the commencement of the action this type of motion can be made. Notice requirements for such a motion may differ from other motions. For example, under Rule 56 of the Federal Rules of Civil Procedure a motion for summary judgment must be served at least ten days prior to the time fixed for hearing rather than the five days required for other motions.

Trial Motions

At the beginning of a trial, before any evidence is ever introduced, attorneys sometimes need to resolve questions or issues regarding matters of trial procedure. These often involve questions regarding the admissibility of certain kinds of evidence. For example, in a wrongful death case, the defendant

motion to quash the return of the service Made by a defendant who claims he was improperly served with the summons and complaint.

discovery The legal process by which the parties to a lawsuit search for facts relevant to a particular case.

motion to compel A request by one party to the court for an order requiring the other side to comply with a discovery request.

motion for a protective order A motion made during discovery asking the court to limit a discovery request.

motion for a summary judgment A motion requesting that judgment be entered immediately because there are no disputed factual issues in the case.

may anticipate that the plaintiff's attorney is going to introduce photographs of the decedent that are graphic and inflammatory. The defendant might feel that these photos are too prejudicial and should be excluded from evidence. The defense attorney would therefore request that the court order that the evidence is inadmissible. This type of request or motion is not usually made at the time of trial, but before the trial actually commences. If it is a jury trial, it is important that these motions not be made in front of the jury. Motions such as this, made at the commencement of trial, are often referred to as **motions in limine**. Since all parties are present in court, no prior notice need be given, nor do they have to be in writing. (Although attorneys sometimes submit a memorandum of points and authorities in support of their position.)

Likewise, motions made during the course of the trial itself will differ from pretrial motions. Trial motions are often made in immediate response to testimony or other evidence that is offered into evidence. Obviously there is no opportunity to prepare written papers. Since all sides are already present in court, no need for any prior notice of the motion arises. Sometimes, however, the attorneys do know ahead of time that they are going to make a particular motion. One such motion is a **motion for a directed verdict**. A motion for a directed verdict is a motion in a jury trial in which one party is requesting that the court order or direct the jury to decide the case in a particular way. Such a motion is proper where one side has failed to produce any legally sufficient evidence to support his position. Although the attorney can make this motion without a written motion or notice, the attorney may want to present the judge with a memorandum of points and authorities to support the motion. As a litigation paralegal you might be asked to help research the law and prepare such a memorandum.

Post-Trial Motions

Motions made after the trial has occurred often are directed at the judgment that the trial court has rendered. However a post-trial motion may also relate to the assessment of costs against the party who has lost the case.

Motion for Judgment Notwithstanding the Verdict. In a jury trial, all parties normally present evidence to prove their claims and defenses. Where the evidence conflicts, which it usually does, the jury decides the true facts and reaches an appropriate verdict. Sometimes it is clear that only one side has produced any real evidence and that only one judgment is possible. In such a case, the judge could grant a motion for a directed verdict as described above. However, if a directed verdict is overturned on appeal the whole case would have to be retried because the jury was not allowed to decide the case. Therefore many judges are reluctant to grant directed verdicts, hoping that the jury will agree that only one verdict is correct. But sometimes juries are swayed by sympathy or prejudice and do not fairly decide the case. Where there is evidence to support only one verdict, but the jury fails to return that verdict, the judge has the power to order a **judgment notwithstanding the verdict**. Such an order is usually made in response to a motion by a party. Some courts require that as a prerequisite to this motion the moving party must have made a motion for a directed verdict. A motion for a judgment notwithstanding the verdict must normally be made soon after the judgment. Rule 50(b) of the Federal Rules of Civil Procedure provides that such a motion must be made within ten days after judgment. This time limit is very important.

Motion for a New Trial. The party who loses in a civil trial has the right to appeal that decision to a higher court. However, the appellate process is lengthy and costly. Prior to any appeal, that party also has the opportunity to request that the trial court itself set aside the verdict or judgment and grant a new trial by making a **motion for a new trial**. Such a request or motion is normally made before the judge who presided over the trial. This motion is proper in both jury trials and court trials (trials in front of a judge only). Grounds for such a motion might include jury impropriety, mistake in law, or newly discovered evidence.

Normally very strict time limits control when this kind of motion can be made. Rule 59(b) of the Federal Rules of Civil Procedure allows a party ten days after entry of judgment to serve such a motion. If you are assisting an attorney in preparing this motion, pay close attention to statutory time restraints and be careful that all papers are promptly filed and served.

Motion to Tax Costs. The prevailing party in a lawsuit is usually entitled to recover his costs in addition to the judgment. Costs include expenses such as filing fees and service fees incurred as part of litigation. The amount of the costs is usually presented to the court in written form when the trial is over (sometimes referred to as a cost bill). If the other party challenges any or all of these costs, that party does so by filing a motion with the court, known as a **motion to tax costs**. As in all post-trial motions, timing of the motion is critical.

motion in limine
A motion or request made of the court, usually at the start of a trial and outside the presence of the jury.

motion for a directed verdict
A motion made during a jury trial, requesting that the judge tell the jury how they should decide the case.

judgment notwithstanding the verdict
An order made by a judge, usually in response to a motion by a party, in cases where there is evidence to support only one verdict, but the jury fails to return that verdict.

motion for a new trial
A motion made after a trial requesting that the judge set aside the verdict or judgment and grant a new trial to the parties.

motion to tax costs
A motion made after trial challenging the costs of suit that are claimed by the prevailing party.

Motions for Relief from Judgment or Order. In the last chapter we discussed the fact that under Rule 60 of the Federal Rules of Civil Procedure a default judgment could be set aside by the court upon a showing that the judgment was entered due to the mistake, inadvertence, surprise, excusable neglect, or fraud of the party or his legal representative. Under Rule 60, the court has the power to set aside any judgment, order, or proceeding for the same reason. A request of the court by one party to do this is a **motion for relief from a judgment or order.** Depending on the law of the jurisdiction, additional grounds for the granting of relief may exist. For example, Rule 60 of the Federal Rules of Civil Procedure provides as follows:

> On motion and upon such terms as are just, the court may relieve party or a party's legal representative from a final judgment, order, or proceeding for the following reasons: (1) mistake, inadvertence, surprise, or excusable neglect; (2) newly discovered evidence which by due diligence could not have been discovered in time to move for a new trial under Rule 59(b); (3) fraud (whether heretofore denominated intrinsic or extrinsic), (4) the judgment is void; (5) the judgment has been satisfied, released, or discharged, or a prior judgment upon which it is based has been reversed or otherwise vacated, or it is no longer equitable that the judgment should have prospective application; or (6) any other reason justifying relief from the operation of the judgment.

Motions for relief are generally required to be filed within a reasonable time, although the term *reasonable* is not defined. Usually, maximum time limits do exist for the filing of such motions.

In granting or denying a motion for relief, especially on the grounds of mistake or excusable neglect, the court has the right to exercise a great deal of discretion. If you are drafting affidavits for this type of motion you should be as detailed as possible in explaining the reasons for making the motion.

SUMMARY

7-1 The application for a court order is known as a motion. Motions are a common occurrence during the course of any litigation and can take place before, during, or after trial. Except for motions made during the trial, motions are generally in writing, filed in court, and served on the opposing attorneys in the case. Even though motions are not pleadings, they are prepared in the same general format as pleadings.

7-2 The general procedure for making a motion involves filing and serving various documents with the court. These include the motion, which describes the nature of the request and the basis for it, the notice of motion, which states the date, time, and place of any hearing on the motion, affidavits in support of the motion, along with a memorandum of points and authorities. Affidavits are statements made under oath before a notary. These statements are used in lieu of testimony. A memorandum of points and authorities is a discussion and analysis of the law controlling the case. A party wishing to oppose a motion does so by filing and serving affidavits and memoranda of points and authorities in opposition to the motion.

7-3 Many motions involve court hearings. Scheduling the motion with the court is often a job for a paralegal. When setting a motion for hearing care must be taken to allow enough time to give proper notice of the hearing to all parties. After the motion is heard, the judge's ruling is put in writing in a document known as an order. An order is normally prepared by the prevailing party. Some courts require that proposed orders be submitted with the moving papers. In order to prevent unnecessary or frivolous motions courts have the power to punish attorneys who abuse the motion process. This punishment, known as sanctions, usually is in the form of attorney fees but can be a finding of contempt of court.

7-4 Motions can be categorized as pretrial, trial, or post-trial. Pretrial motions include motions that are related to the pleadings, such as a motion to dismiss, motion for a more definite statement, motion to strike, motion for judgment on the pleadings, motion for change of venue, motion to quash return of service, and motion to amend. Pretrial motions also include discovery motions and motions for summary judgment. Trial motions differ from other motions in that they usually do not have to be in writing. Because all parties are already in court, no prior notice is required. Nevertheless attorneys sometimes like to present memoranda of points and authorities in support of trial motions. One common trial motion is the motion for a directed verdict. Motions made after trial include motions for judgment notwithstanding the verdict, motion for new trial, motion to tax costs, and motion to set aside a judgment.

motion for relief from a judgment or order A request of the court by one party to set aside any judgment, order, or proceeding.

KEY TERMS

affidavit

certificate of mailing

declaration

discovery

ex parte

memorandum of points and
  authorities

motion

motion for a more definite
  statement

motion for a directed verdict

motion for change of venue

motion for judgment
  notwithstanding the verdict

motion for judgment on the
  pleadings

motion for a new trial

motion for a protective order

motion for a summary
  judgment

motion in limine

motion to amend

motion to compel

motion to dismiss

motion to quash the return of
  the service

motion to strike

motion to tax costs

moving party

notice of hearing on motion

order

order shortening time

proof of service by mail

QUESTIONS FOR REVIEW AND DISCUSSION

1. What is a motion?
2. What is the procedure for making a motion?
3. What is the procedure for opposing a motion?
4. What is an affidavit?
5. What role does the paralegal have in setting motions for hearing?
6. Describe the method for obtaining orders after hearing on the motion.
7. What are sanctions and how are they used in motion practice?
8. What are some common pretrial motions?
9. How do trial motions differ from other motions?
10. What are some common post-trial motions?

ACTIVITIES

1. Check your state laws regarding general motion practice. What forms are required to be filed to make a motion? What forms are generally filed in opposition to a motion? What are the time limits for giving notice of a motion? Are there any time limits for filing papers in opposition to a motion?

2. Determine whether or not the federal district court in your area has any local rules regarding motion practice. If so, review those rules. Are there any special procedures or time requirements that must be followed?
3. Determine whether or not the state court of general jurisdiction in your area has local rules regarding motion practice. If so, review those rules. Are there any special procedures or time requirements that must be followed?

CHAPTER 7 PROJECT—DRAFTING A MOTION

Review the factual situation described in the commentary. Assume that the president of Overland, Owen Young, relates that the complaint and summons were handed to Barbara Dexter, a sales representative in the New York office of the company. Ms. Dexter has no position with the company other than as a salaried employee. This is the only copy of the summons and complaint that were served upon Overland. Your supervising attorney wants to challenge this service as not being in accordance with Rule 4 of the Federal Rules of Civil Procedure. Prepare the appropriate motion, notice of hearing, and affidavits for the attorney's review.

Discovery

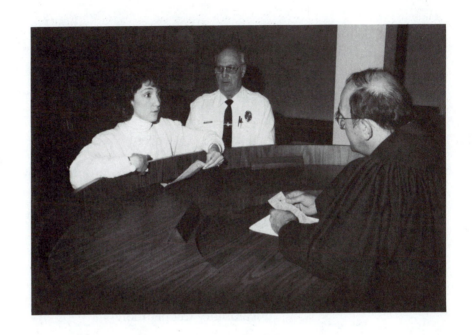

CHAPTER 8
Overview of the Discovery Process

COMMENTARY—THE DALADIER CASE

You have been called into a meeting with your attorney to discuss the details of an important lawsuit. The case involves Charles Daladier, a loan officer with the Dessault Commercial Bank. Daladier has been sued by his former employer, the Clemenceau National Bank. Clemenceau claims that Daladier violated an agreement not to work for a competitor within two years of leaving the bank's employment. The lawsuit has already begun, and your attorney recently filed an answer to the bank's complaint. The case will now proceed to the next major stage of litigation—discovery. This morning you and your attorney will discuss the best discovery devices to use in this case and what steps can be taken to limit the discovery of the other party. You will find that the discovery process takes a great deal of careful planning.

OBJECTIVES

In previous chapters, you had the opportunity to explore the steps involved in the litigation process. In this chapter you will be introduced to another critical part of the litigation process—discovery. After completing this chapter, you will be able to:

1. Define discovery.
2. Identify the five major methods of discovery.
3. Outline the factors involved in choosing discovery methods.
4. Describe the ethical considerations involved in the discovery process.
5. Determine the scope of discovery.
6. Differentiate between the attorney-client privilege, the work product privilege, and the Fifth Amendment privilege against self-incrimination.
7. Explain how expert testimony is subject to discovery.
8. Discuss the purpose of the confidentiality agreement and protective orders.
9. Indicate the objectives of the Federal Freedom of Information Act.
10. Discuss the need for voluntary cooperation in the discovery process.
11. Explain how to obtain a discovery conference.
12. Relate the process used to compel compliance with discovery and the sanctions that result from noncompliance.

8-1 THE NATURE OF DISCOVERY

Discovery is the legal process by which the parties to a lawsuit search for facts relevant to a particular case. Most people who have not been involved in litigation are surprised to learn that both sides in a lawsuit have the opportunity to gather all the facts relevant to that lawsuit. Accustomed as they are to the surprise witness produced at the last minute by Perry Mason and his imita-tors, most people believe that the attorney who wins a case is the one who manages to trap his or her opponent by concealing crucial evidence until the last possible second. The truth is exactly opposite to this fiction. Pretrial discovery is allowed because the law supports the principle that lawsuits should be decided on

discovery
The legal process by which the parties to a lawsuit search for facts relevant to a particular case.

the facts and on the legal merits of the case, rather than on the ability of one attorney to conceal evidence or ambush the other attorney with surprise witnesses. In this part of the chapter, you will explore the objectives of discovery, some preliminary considerations in the discovery process, and some ethical considerations in discovery. The discovery stage is very important not only because it reveals the facts in a suit, but also because it helps shape the direction of the case. The results of an effectively conducted discovery process may encourage your attorney to proceed with the case. However, those results may also indicate that a settlement or a voluntary dismissal is in order.

The Objectives of Discovery

As noted above, one of the primary objectives of discovery is to prevent one of the parties from winning the lawsuit by surprise or trickery. However, this is not the only objective. Another goal is to determine the truth or the falsity of the alleged facts that form the basis of the suit. A third objective of discovery is to examine the facts and weigh the advisability of proceeding with the case or settling early. Frequently a case that looks promising in the opening stages will lose its viability as more and more facts come to light. For example, in the Daladier case, if, during discovery, your attorney uncovers evidence that Daladier unfairly refinanced several loans that he had negotiated while working for Clemenceau, she may elect to move toward a settlement offer, or even a voluntary dismissal of the case. In contrast, early discovery may reveal that your client's case is so strong that there is no need to proceed to trial. In such a situation, your attorney may decide to file a summary judgment motion. For instance, in the Daladier case, your attorney may discover that the restrictive employment covenant was not a part of Daladier's original contract but, rather, was added later without his knowledge. In such a situation, the law would clearly be on his side, and a summary judgment motion would be in order. A final objective of discovery is to preserve testimony that might be lost should a witness disappear or become incapacitated or should records be lost or destroyed.

Preliminary Decisions Regarding Discovery

Discovery may be an expensive and time-consuming process. Because of this, during the preliminary stages in a case an attorney must decide which discovery techniques are best suited to the lawsuit. In making this decision, the attorney must consider the cost and the amount of time involved.

Choice of Discovery Methods.   An attorney has five methods of discovery from which to choose: the deposition, interrogatories, a request for the production of documents and entry upon land for inspection, a request for physical or mental examinations, and a request for admissions. In federal court, the discovery process is regulated by Rules 26 through 37 of the Federal Rules of Civil Procedure. (See Figure 8–1.) Rule 26 sets out the general provisions concerning discovery. Rules 27 through 36 explain the various discovery techniques that can be used by litigants in federal court. The final rule, Rule 37, outlines the sanctions that are available when a party does not cooperate with discovery. A **deposition** is the oral or written testimony of a party or witness given under oath outside a courtroom. Depositions are regulated by Rules 27 through 32 of the Federal Rules of Civil Procedure. **Interrogatories** are written questions requiring written answers under oath and directed to a party in which another party seeks information related to the litigation. Interrogatories are governed by Rule 33 of the federal rules. A **request for the production of documents and entry upon land for inspection**, which is covered by Rule 34, asks for the inspection or duplication of documents or other materials that are relevant to the subject matter of the litigation. As the name implies, this request may also seek permission to enter land for inspection purposes. A **request for a physical or mental examination** asks a party to submit to such an examination to determine the extent of the physical or mental injuries claimed by that party. A **request for admission** asks a party to admit the truth of certain facts or the genuineness of a document so that these issues do not have to be proven at trial. An attorney must take into consideration both the expense and the time available in choosing from among these methods. These two types of requests are regulated by Rule 35 and Rule 36, respectively.

Expense of Discovery.   Discovery can be a very expensive proposition for both sides in a lawsuit. However, some techniques are less expensive than others. For instance, sending a set of interrogatories to a party would be considerably less expensive than having that party sit for an oral deposition. The oral deposition would necessitate paying a court reporter to administer the oath and to transcribe the question-answer period. Oral depositions also involve more of an attorney's time since the attorney would have to be physically present to interrogate the party. In contrast, the interrogatories would simply involve determining the questions to ask, typing those questions, mailing them to the party, and reviewing the answers when returned.

---

deposition
The oral or written testimony of a party or witness given under oath outside a courtroom.

interrogatories
Written questions submitted by one party in a lawsuit to another party in that suit, which must be answered in writing and under oath.

request for the production of documents and entry upon land for inspection
A request for the inspection or duplication of documents or other materials that are relevant to the subject matter of the litigation, including a request for permission to enter land for inspection purposes.

request for a physical or mental examination
A request for a party to submit to a physical or mental examination to determine the extent of the physical or mental injuries claimed by that party.

request for admission
A request filed by one party in a lawsuit asking the second party in the lawsuit to admit to the truthfulness of some fact or opinion.

RULE 26. **GENERAL PROVISIONS GOVERNING DISCOVERY**
Rule 26 covers the history of the Rule, discovery methods, protective orders, the sequence and timing of discovery, the discovery conference, an analysis and the purpose of the deposition and discovery rules, discovery of trial preparation materials, governmental privilege, waiver of privilege, and other general provisions.

RULE 27. **DEPOSITIONS BEFORE ACTION OR PENDING APPEAL**
Rule 27 allows the perpetuation of testimony even though an action cannot be presently brought to court or when an appeal is pending.

RULE 28. **PERSONS BEFORE WHOM DEPOSITIONS MAY BE TAKEN**
Rule 28 specifies that a deposition must be taken before an officer authorized to administer oaths and take testimony. The rule also outlines the persons before whom a deposition can be taken in a foreign country. The rule also eliminates persons who are related to or employees of the parties or the attorneys as well as people who have a financial interest in the action.

RULE 29. **STIPULATIONS REGARDING DISCOVERY PROCEDURES**
Rule 29 allows the parties to an action to modify in writing the discovery procedures outlined in the rules.

RULE 30. **DEPOSITIONS UPON ORAL EXAMINATION**
Rule 30 explains when depositions can be taken, notice requirements, examination and cross examination, objections, motions to terminate or limit examination, failure to attend or failure to serve a subpoena, and exhibits, among other things.

RULE 31. **DEPOSITIONS UPON WRITTEN NOTICE**
Rule 31 discusses the service of depositions upon written questions, as well as the notice requirements, among other things.

RULE 32. **USE OF DEPOSITIONS IN COURT PROCEEDINGS**
Rule 32 outlines the circumstances under which a deposition can be used in court. For example, a deposition can be used to contradict or impeach the testimony of a witness. A deposition can also be used if the witness is dead, is located farther than 100 miles from the place of the trial, or is unable to testify because of age, illness, infirmity, or imprisonment. Also, the deposition will be allowed if the party who wants to introduce the deposition has been unable to make the witness attend by subpoena.

FIGURE 8–1
Federal Rules of
Civil Procedure.

RULE 33.   **INTERROGATORIES**
Rule 33 explains the procedure for using interrogatories, the allowable scope of the interrogatories, and the use of interrogatories at trial. The rule also indicates when business records can be produced in lieu of answering interrogatories.

RULE 34.   **PRODUCTION OF DOCUMENTS AND THINGS AND ENTRY UPON LAND**
Rule 34 explains the scope of this discovery device as well as the process for its use. The rule specifies that this request can be made of non-parties.

RULE 35.   **PHYSICAL AND MENTAL EXAMINATIONS OF PERSONS**
Rule 35 explains when a physical and/or mental examination can be ordered. It also explains the disposition of the report of the examining physician.

RULE 36.   **REQUESTS FOR ADMISSION**
Rule 36 outlines the procedure for requesting admissions. It also explains the effects of an admission.

RULE 37.   **FAILURE TO MAKE DISCOVERY: SANCTIONS**
Rule 37 presents the procedure for filing a motion for an order compelling discovery. It also details the negative consequences of failing to comply with such an order, among other things.

FIGURE 8–1
(continued)

Amount of Time.   If time is a more critical element than expense, the attorney might make an entirely different decision in choosing a method of discovery. Under the pressure of time, having the party sit for a deposition would be much more advantageous than sending interrogatories and waiting for written responses. In addition, the Federal Rules of Civil Procedure allow parties at least thirty days to respond to a set of interrogatories. Defendants receive a forty-five-day period if the discovery tool is served at the same time as the complaint and the summons. Most states allow similar lengths of time. Moreover, while it is possible for courts to shorten this time limit, it is also possible for the court to extend that time, causing further delay.

Ethical Considerations in Discovery

As noted earlier, the primary objective of discovery is to ensure that lawsuits are decided on the facts and on the legal merits of the case, rather than on surprise or trickery. For such an objective to be met, however, all parties must treat the discovery process with the highest ethical regard. It is considered highly unethical for an attorney to stop the other party from obtaining evidence or to destroy that evidence before the other party can see it. For example, in the Daladier case it would be unethical for your attorney to destroy a letter that she finds confirming the fact that Daladier unfairly refinanced the loans of several of Clemenceau's customers. Similarly, it is a violation of ethical principles to falsify evidence or to help someone else falsify evidence. It is also un-ethical for an attorney to make a discovery request that is unwarranted or to request much more information than is really necessary for the case. Naturally, since the paralegal's activities are actually an extension of the attorney's, he or she is also bound by these same ethical principles.

8–2 THE EXTENT OF ALLOWABLE DISCOVERY

The Federal Rules of Civil Procedure limit discovery to the subject matter of the litigation. Most states impose similar limitations. Nevertheless, the extent of the discovery process is quite broad, broader in fact than the extent to which evidence can be introduced in a case once it has reached the trial stage. There are, however, several limits on the discovery process, including the attorney-client privilege, the work product privilege, the Fifth Amendment privilege against self-incrimination, controlled access to expert testimony, confidentiality agreements, and protective orders.

The Scope of Discovery

The amount and type of evidence that can be sought during the discovery process is much vaster than that which be introduced at trial. Of course, the evidence sought during discovery must be relevant to the subject matter of the case. Evidence is considered relevant if it tends to prove or to disprove facts that are necessary to determine the final outcome of the case. However, under Rule 26 of the Federal Rules of Civil Procedure the evidence sought during discovery need not be admissible at the time of the trial, as long as it is reasonably calculated to lead to the discovery of evidence that can be introduced at trial. For example, most hearsay evidence is not admissible at trial. This ban against hearsay evidence means that in most situations a witness at trial cannot testify about the truth of what he or she heard someone else say. For instance, in the Daladier case it would be hearsay evidence to try to prove that Daladier offered to refinance loans held by Clemenceau by allowing a witness to testify that someone else said that Daladier had offered to refinance the loans. However, such a statement would be within the scope of discovery because it could lead to admissible evidence, namely, the testimony of the party who actually overheard Daladier offer to refinance the Clemenceau loans.

Limits on Discovery

While the scope of discovery is quite broad, it is by no means infinite. Discovery is limited by several principles, including the attorney-client privilege, the work product privilege, and the Fifth Amendment privilege against self-incrimination. Limits are also placed on the access to expert testimony. In addition, the parties can draw up confidentiality agreements or can ask the court to issue protective orders.

The Attorney-Client Privilege.   The **attorney-client privilege** prevents the forced disclosure of written or oral communications between an attorney and a client or a prospective client. For a communication to be protected by the privilege, it must be made between the client and the attorney or the attorney's subordinate. This means that the privilege extends to communications made to the paralegal when the paralegal is acting as an agent of the attorney. The communication must also be made within the context of the attorney-client relationship. In other words, information revealed while seeking legal advice would be protected by the privilege, but statements made at a social gathering during polite conversation would not. The privilege belongs to the client, not the attorney. For example, in the Daladier case, should Daladier have no objection to the revelation of the contents of a discussion he had with your attorney, then she could not assert the privilege herself. Certainly, she can advise Daladier to assert the privilege. However, as the client, he has the final decision.

It is also important to know that the attorney-client privilege may be lost or waived by the client if the client does not intend the communication to be confidential, discloses the communication to others, or refuses to assert the privilege. Also, if a third party who is not related to the client is present during an attorney-client discussion, the privilege has been waived by the client. Naturally, such a waiver would not occur if the third party who is present is another attorney in the firm, a paralegal employed by the firm, or a legal secretary who works for the attorney. Thus, if you are asked to be present during a meeting between your attorney and Daladier, he would not have waived his attorney-client privilege.

In a large and complex case, privileged documents may be disclosed inadvertently. Such disclosure could have serious results. To avoid this problem, it is possible to enter into an

attorney-client privilege
A privilege preventing the forced disclosure of written or oral communications between an attorney and a client or prospective client.

agreement with opposing counsel that the inadvertent production or disclosure of privileged information will not result in waiver of the privilege. This agreement may be incorporated in the protective order discussed later in this chapter. (See Figure 8–2.)

Work Product Privilege. The **work product privilege** prevents the opposing party in a lawsuit from using the discovery process to obtain letters, memos, documents, records, and other tangible items that have been produced in anticipation of litigation or that have been prepared for the trial itself. If, for instance, in the Daladier case, your attorney were to take notes during her interview with Daladier, those notes would be considered *work product* and would, therefore, be protected by the privilege.

One problem with the work product privilege is determining what documents actually were prepared in anticipation of litigation. For example, in most hospitals it is common practice for health care professionals to make out "incident reports" when an error has been made. Thus, a nurse who accidentally gives a patient the wrong medication would have to fill out one of these reports. If the patient was hurt by the error and litigation results, the hospital attorney would argue that the incident report was prepared in anticipation of litigation, while the patient's attorney would maintain that it was not. The judge would determine whether or not the incident report is covered by the work product privilege.

Another problem with the work product privilege is that it is not an absolute privilege. Under Rule 26 of the Federal Rules, disclosure may be compelled by showing that the party seeking discovery has a substantial need for the documents or materials in the preparation of his case and that he cannot, without undue hardship, obtain the equivalent of that material by any other means. Most courts continue to provide protection for the portion of work product that consists of "mental impressions, conclusions, opinions, or legal theories of an attorney or other representatives of a party concerning the litigation." Although the attorney is responsible for determining what confidential client material may be revealed, the paralegal should be constantly alert to protecting the attorney-client or work product privilege.

Protection of Expert Testimony. Expert testimony is frequently indispensable in a lawsuit. In the Daladier case, for example, it would be difficult for the jury to determine the practices, procedures, policies, and techniques that are appropriate to a loan officer, without the use of expert testimony. Consequently, although expert testimony is subject to discovery, the means of obtaining that expert testimony is limited. According to Rule 26 of the Federal Rules of Civil Procedure, the only way to uncover information about expert witnesses is through interrogatories. Under this rule, the identities of all experts who will testify at trial must be revealed in response to any interrogatory requesting such information. In addition, interrogatories can seek to uncover the subject matter about which the experts will testify. If an expert is not going to testify at trial, however, then the opposing party can obtain information about that expert's findings only if the court is convinced that "exceptional circumstances" have prevented that party from obtaining the information in any other way.

The Fifth Amendment Privilege Against Self-Incrimination. The Fifth Amendment to the United States Constitution states that "No person . . . shall be compelled in a criminal case to be a witness against himself." This is referred to as the Fifth Amendment **privilege against self-incrimination.** Since the privilege is specifically aimed at self-testimony in a criminal case, it is usually not available as a privilege in a civil lawsuit if the only object of the suit is to seek compensatory damages. Some courts have held, however, that if a civil lawsuit seeks to protect the public, then the privilege may be successfully invoked. For example, if a civil suit is brought by a private party under federal antitrust law, the privilege may be successfully raised. This is because the purpose of antitrust law, like the purpose of criminal law, is to protect the public at large. Antitrust laws protect the public by imposing triple damages and thus discouraging antitrust activity. Furthermore, if a government agency is the plaintiff in the suit, it is also possible to invoke the Fifth Amendment privilege because such agencies are, by definition, designed to protect the public interests. This is also because a suit involving a government agency as the plaintiff is very similar in character to a criminal prosecution, which is also brought by the government. Similarly, if a witness could demonstrate that responding to a particular discovery request could expose him or her to a potential criminal prosecution, then the privilege may also be successfully invoked.

Confidentiality Agreements and Protective Orders. Often, a lawsuit will involve matters that one party wants to keep as secret as possible. For example, in the Daladier case, Clemenceau may allege that Daladier used certain trade secrets while working for Dessault, in violation of the restrictive employment covenant. Determining the authenticity of this claim would probably require a disclosure of the trade secret. In order to protect that trade secret, Clemenceau would want to limit the people who would have access to that secret, or the circumstances under which it is to be revealed. Such limitations can be imposed voluntarily through a

work product privilege
A privilege preventing the opposing party in a lawsuit from using the discovery process to obtain letters, memos, documents, records, and other tangible items that have been produced in anticipation of litigation or that have been prepared for the trial itself.

privilege against self-incrimination
A privilege that prevents a person in a criminal case from being a witness against himself.

confidentiality agreement or by a court decree through a **protective order.** Confidentiality agreements and protective orders cover a wide spectrum. Some agreements and orders completely prevent all discovery of the secret material. Others will designate a particular place and time for the revelation of the protected information. Still others might indicate that only certain named parties can be present when the confidential matter is revealed. It is even possible for the agreement or order to stipulate that the information be enclosed in sealed envelopes to be opened only at the judge's direction. Documents that fall into the category of "confidential" should be stamped with this designation prior to their production or disclosure to the other side. Protective orders are permitted under Rule 26 of the Federal Rules of Civil Procedure. Figure 8–2 represents an example of a protective order.

Federal Freedom of Information Act

Strictly speaking, the Federal Freedom of Information Act is not solely a discovery tool. Rather, it was designed to help ensure that federal government offices will be accountable to the public they are supposed to serve. The act allows individuals to obtain copies of the documents and records produced and held by the offices, departments, and agencies of the federal government. However, since a wide variety of information is available through the provisions of this act, it can also be used during the discovery process. For instance, in the Daladier case, several government agencies may have information on file that might be relevant to the lawsuit. Should the case call for gaining access to government records under the Federal Freedom of Information Act, the job of soliciting that information may fall to the paralegal. In such a situation, the paralegal would draft a letter specifying the nature of the information and records sought. Figure 8–3 is an example of just such a letter. Naturally, the paralegal should realize that the act does not allow access to all information held by the government. The act includes a list of items that cannot be obtained by the public. Included on that list are secret documents related to national security, internal personnel policies and practices, trade secrets and other confidential information, personnel records, and medical records, among others.

confidentiality agreement
An agreement that prevents discovery of confidential information or trade secrets.

protective order
An order protecting disclosure of confidential material or trade secrets from production.

8–3 COOPERATING WITH DISCOVERY

It is to everyone's benefit that the discovery process runs as smoothly as possible. For this reason most parties cooperate freely with discovery requests. However, there are times when a party or parties will refuse to cooperate. The rules of civil procedure provide methods for compelling discovery and sanctions for those who refuse to cooperate.

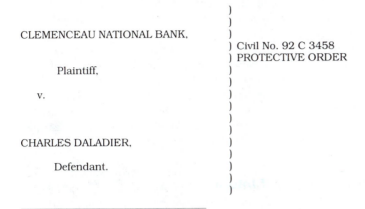

IN THE UNITED STATES DISTRICT COURT

CLEMENCEAU NATIONAL BANK,	)))) Civil No. 92 C 3458) PROTECTIVE ORDER
Plaintiff,	))
v.	)))
CHARLES DALADIER,	))
Defendant.	))))

PURSUANT to Rule 26(c) of the Federal Rules of Civil Procedure, and stipulation of the parties, IT IS HEREBY ORDERED as follows:
1. This Protective Order (the "Order") shall govern all documents and other products of discovery obtained by the Plaintiff or Defendant, all information derived therefrom and all copies, excerpts or summaries thereof, including but not limited to, documents produced pursuant to Rule 33(c) or Rule 34 of the Federal Rules of Civil Procedure, answers to requests for admissions, answers to interrogatories, documents subpoenaed in connection with depositions, and deposition transcripts (referred to collectively herein as Discovery Material). Any motions, briefs, or other filings incorporating Discovery Material are also governed by this Order.
2. All Discovery Material shall be treated as confidential, both during the pendency of and subsequent to, the termination of this action. Discovery Material will be used solely for the purpose of this action and not for any other purpose. No Discovery Material will be disclosed to anyone except in accordance with the terms of this Order.
3. Disclosure of Discovery Material shall be made only to attorneys of record for parties in the litigation; in-house counsel for the parties; persons employed by the law firms of the attorneys retained by the parties whose assistance is required by said attorneys in the preparation for trial of this case; expert witnesses and consultants who are retained by the parties in connection with this proceeding. Counsel for the party making disclosure to any of the aforementioned individuals shall first obtain the written

FIGURE 8–2
Sample Protective Order.

agreement of any such individual to whom disclosure is made to be bound by the terms of this Order. This requirement may be satisfied by obtaining the signed acknowledgment on a copy of this Order that he or she has read the Order and understands its provisions.

4. Counsel for the parties making disclosure of Discovery Material to a party shall first obtain a written agreement of the party producing said Discovery Material. Written agreement shall be obtained from any such party to whom Discovery Material is disclosed to be bound by the terms of the Order. This requirement may be satisfied by obtaining a signed acknowledgement on a copy of this Order that he or she has read the Order and understands its provisions.

5. Discovery Material shall be conspicuously marked by the producing party or witness "Confidential-Subject to Protective Order of the United States District Court."

6. In the event a party inadvertently produces for inspection privileged or potentially privileged documents, such production shall not constitute waiver of the attorney-client privilege, the work product privilege, or any other privilege with respect to the document or portion thereof, or with respect to any other document or testimony relating thereto. In the event that a document that is privileged, in whole or in part, is inadvertently produced, the party claiming privilege shall promptly identify each document being withheld as privileged, and the inspecting party shall forthwith return such document or documents.

7. Within thirty (30) days after the termination of this action, all confidential information, and copies thereof, including but not limited to any notes or other recording made hereof, shall be returned to counsel for the party who initially produced such documents.

8. Nothing in this Order shall prevent any party or non-party from seeking a modification of this Order or from objecting to discovery which it believes to be otherwise improper.

DATED this ___ day of _____, 19___

SIGNED BY: U.S. MAGISTRATE

APPROVED AS TO FORM AND CONTENT BY:
(ALL COUNSEL OF RECORD)

FIGURE 8–2
(continued)

LAW OFFICES OF

PALENCIA, LAURITEG, BOTERUS, AND SELAN
PROFESSIONAL ASSOCIATION

Holis Palencia	83924 Superior Avenue	Robert B. Boterus
Mary Lauriteg	Richmond, Virginia 23219	Hilda J. Selan
	(804) 555-3222	

September 9, 19___

U.S. Comptroller of the Currency
Department of the Treasury
Washington, D.C. 20219

Dear Sir:

Please send me copies of the following documents, records, and reports. I make this request under provisions of the Federal Freedom of Information Act.

To prevent delay, the list which follows should be very precise.

Should you decide that you cannot send the documents that I have requested, please explain the reason for your decision so that I can prepare an appropriate appeal.

Also, please let me know if any fees are involved in obtaining the documents, before you conduct the search. To allow me ample time to review these documents, I would like to receive them by September 19, 19___.

Thank you for your time and effort in this matter.

Cordially,

Stephanie J. Sherman

Stephanie J. Sherman
Paralegal

FIGURE 8–3
Sample Request Letter Under Freedom of Information Act Provisions.

Voluntary Cooperation

Most of the time attorneys involved in litigation will find the other attorney and the other party cooperating with the discovery process. Parties cooperate generally for several reasons, all of which are based on enlightened self-interest. First, under the principle of reciprocity, each side knows that any attempt to disrupt the discovery process may result in a similar attempt by the other side. Second, each side knows that the court disapproves of any attempt to interfere with discovery. Finally, the rules of civil procedure provide severe sanctions for those parties who refuse to obey discovery orders made by the court. For these reasons, if one side resists the discovery process or any part of that process, the other side should make inquiries about the reason for such resistance. Often such problems can be resolved informally. For example, a party may resist sitting for a deposition because it is scheduled at an inconvenient time or place. A minor problem like this can be solved by explaining the importance of the discovery process to the party and rescheduling the deposition for a more acceptable time and place.

Discovery Conferences

Rule 26 of the Federal Rules of Civil Procedure allows the court to direct the parties to come to the court to discuss the discovery process. Such a meeting is called a **discovery conference**. Generally such an order follows a motion filed by one of the parties requesting such a conference. Rule 26 states that such a motion must include:

1. A statement of the issues as they appear;
2. A proposed plan and schedule of discovery; any limitation proposed to be placed on discovery;
3. Any other proposed order with respect to discovery; and
4. A statement showing that the attorney making the motion has made a reasonable effort to reach agreement with opposing attorneys on the matters set forth in the motion.

During the discovery conference, the issues that will be subject to discovery should be agreed to by the parties. Also a discovery schedule should be decided upon as well as a division of the expenses that will be involved in the process.

Involuntary Cooperation

Despite the inclination toward cooperation, there are times when parties may feel they have legitimate reasons for resisting discovery. In such cases, the parties must turn to the court for a resolution of the differences.

Orders to Compel Discovery. If one of the parties in the litigation refuses to comply with a discovery request, the other party must move to force compliance. Under Rule 37 of the Federal Rules of Civil Procedure, the party seeking cooperation must file a motion with the court asking the judge to compel discovery. The judge will then decide whether to grant the motion. It is possible for the non-complying party to have a legally sufficient reason for denying the discovery request. For example, the noncomplying party may claim that certain documents requested by the other party fall outside the scope of discovery; that is, they are not relevant to the subject matter of the litigation, or they could not lead to admissible evidence. If the objection is valid, the judge will deny the motion. If it is not valid, however, the judge will grant the motion and issue the order compelling cooperation with the discovery process.

Sanctions Against Noncomplying Parties. If, after an order compelling cooperation is issued, a party still refuses to comply, then the court can levy certain sanctions against the noncomplying party. Under Rule 37, the sanctions include but are not limited to a dismissal of the action, the granting of a default judgment, the granting of reasonable expenses, including attorney's fees, caused by the failure to cooperate, and a contempt of court ruling against the noncomplying party. Sanctions are permitted against either or both the attorney and the client. This possibility should be considered when drafting a discovery plan. Discovery is an effective and necessary litigation tool. Abuse of discovery results in a protracted and complicated lawsuit.

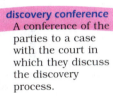

discovery conference
A conference of the parties to a case with the court in which they discuss the discovery process.

THE COMPUTERIZED LAW FIRM—
Word Processing to Prepare Discovery Documents

SCENARIO

Your attorney has called you into her office to discuss the Daladier case. She informs you that in addition to calling several of the officers and other employees of the Clemenceau National Bank in for depositions, she also intends to serve them with interrogatories and requests for the production of documents. To avoid any delays she wants to draw up the interrogatories and the request as soon as possible. Since she must be at an afternoon hearing at the courthouse for another case, she leaves you with the task of drawing up a preliminary set of interrogatories and a draft copy of a request for production of documents. She wants to review these as soon as she returns to the office at 4 p.m. To help you in this task she directs you to the file of another case entitled *Highland Electronics, Inc. v. Javorak.* Since this case also involved the alleged violation of a restrictive employment by a former employee, she feels that looking at the file will help guide you. Before leaving, however, she cautions you not to simply hand her the Javorak interrogatories or the Javorak request. She wants a brand new set of interrogatories and a newly drafted request for production of documents specifically designed for the Daladier case.

PROBLEM

You retrieve the Javorak file and locate the interrogatories. The questions prove to be very similar to the questions that you think should be asked in the Daladier case. However, many of the names in the questions must be changed. You also locate the request for production of documents that was used in the Javorak case. However, since the Javorak case involved an electronics firm, and the Daladier case involves a bank, the types of documents that you must request are different. You also notice that both documents contain lengthy instructions and definition paragraphs that could be reproduced exactly as they are, if you did not have to produce completely new documents. The interrogatories are twelve pages in length, while the request is eight pages. It is already 1:30 p.m. Do you have any way of producing the lengthy documents in just under three hours?

SOLUTION

As explained in the **Computerized Law Firm** feature at the end of chapter 6, word processing ranks number one in computer applications in the law firm. In this case, the Javorak interrogatories and request for production of documents are probably stored on the word processor's hard drive or on a floppy disk. It is also possible that your firm owns a WordPerfect software package. By using the law firm's word processor you will be able to access either the Javorak interrogatories or a generalized interrogatories format on WordPerfect. In either case you will not need to retype the instructions and definitions paragraph for the new documents. As far as the interrogatories themselves are concerned, you will have to add individualized references in the text. Similarly, in the request for production of documents, you will have to identify the specialized documents that you will need to see in the Daladier case.

A variety of word processing packages are used in the legal profession. However, as noted above and in chapter 6, the most widely recognized is Wordperfect 5.0. Appendix B lists software available for IBM, Macintosh, Apple, and other computer hardware. In addition to in-house training on the word processing software, local community colleges, technical colleges, vocational schools, and non-credit programs offer beginning, intermediate, and advanced classes on numerous word processing packages.

SUMMARY

8–1 Discovery is the legal process by which the parties to a lawsuit search for facts relevant to a particular case. The primary objective of discovery is to prevent one of the parties from winning the lawsuit by surprise or trickery. An attorney has five methods of discovery from which to choose: the deposition, interrogatories, a request for the production of documents, a request for physical or mental examinations, and a request for admission. An attorney must take into consideration the expense involved and the time available in choosing from among these five methods. Ethical considerations also play a part in conducting discovery.

8–2 The information sought during discovery must be relevant to the subject matter of the case and, at the very least, reasonably calculated to lead to evidence that can be introduced at trial. There are several limits on the discovery process, including the attorney-client privilege, the work product privilege, limited access to expert testimony, the Fifth Amendment privilege against self-incrimination, confidentiality agreements, and protective orders. The Federal Freedom of Information Act allows individuals to gain access to the documents and records produced and held by the offices, departments, and agencies of the federal government.

8–3 Most of the time, attorneys involved in litigation will cooperate with one another during discovery. Those who do not may be compelled by the court to cooperate.

KEY TERMS

attorney-client privilege
confidentiality agreement
deposition
discovery
discovery conference
interrogatories
privilege against
  self-incrimination

protective order
request for admission
request for a physical or mental
  examination
request for production of
  documents and entry upon
  land for inspection
work product privilege

QUESTIONS FOR REVIEW AND DISCUSSION

1. What is discovery?
2. List the five major methods of discovery.
3. What factors must be considered when choosing among discovery methods?
4. Name five unethical practices involved in the discovery process.
5. Explain what types of evidence can be legally obtained during the discovery process.
6. What is the difference between the attorney-client privilege, the work product privilege, and the Fifth Amendment privilege against self-incrimination?
7. How do the Federal Rules limit access to expert testimony?
8. Explain the purpose of confidentiality agreements and protective orders.
9. What is the purpose of the Federal Freedom of Information Act?
10. Why is voluntary cooperation necessary for the discovery process?
11. How can a discovery conference be arranged?
12. What consequences can result from a refusal to cooperate with an order compelling discovery?

ACTIVITIES

1. Obtain a copy of the pertinent federal rules and a copy of the rules of your state governing discovery. Compare the two sets of rules and note any important differences.
2. Research your state's rules on the attorney-client privilege. Prepare a summary of those rules. Do the same for the rules governing the work product privilege.
3. Find a set of form books in your law library that provides sample forms for use in the courts of your state. Review the forms for a confidentiality agreement and a protective order. List and explain the different options that are available for drafting these documents.

CHAPTER 8 PROJECT—DRAFTING A DISCOVERY LETTER

Review the details of the Daladier case. Draft a letter to Mr. Daladier in which you explain the different types of privileges that may be available to limit Clemenceau's discovery process as it relates to his case. Explain to Mr. Daladier why each privilege would or would not be applicable in his situation.

OUTLINE

COMMENTARY—THE DeMARCO CASE

Your attorney has called you into her office to tell you about a medical malpractice case that she has agreed to handle. Her client, Lisa DeMarco, was a patient at Hampton General Hospital (HGH). During her stay at HGH, she was injected with a contrast medium prior to undergoing several diagnostic x-rays conducted by Dr. Philip Masterson, one of the defendants in the case. A contrast medium is a dye injected into a patient to help a radiologist visualize the patient's internal organs. DeMarco, in this case, had an allergic reaction to the contrast medium and, as a result, almost died. This morning your attorney will be taking the oral deposition of Gary Eckerson, a young radiologic technologist who is employed by HGH and who was present during the incident. Eckerson is not a party to the action, but is a witness who is expected to testify as to certain irregularities in Dr. Masterson's procedure. Your attorney asks you to organize the litigation file, summarize all previous discovery, and draft a deposition outline. This assignment is the beginning of your participation in the taking of an oral deposition.

OBJECTIVES

In chapter 8 you were introduced to the discovery process. The deposition is an important discovery tool. After reading this chapter, you will be able to:

1. Define deposition.
2. Contrast the advantages and disadvantages of the oral deposition.
3. Outline three new trends in oral depositions.
4. Explain the notice of intent to take an oral deposition.
5. Identify the responsibilities of the paralegal in preparing for an oral deposition.
6. Relate the duties a paralegal might perform during an oral deposition.
7. Discuss the paralegal's role in making transcript arrangements.
8. Explain the different types of deposition summaries.
9. Determine the advantages and disadvantages of taking a deposition upon written questions.
10. Recognize the advantages and disadvantages of the telephone deposition.

9-1 THE DEPOSITION

A **deposition** is the written or oral testimony of a witness or party given under oath outside the courtroom. It is one of the most important and widely used pretrial discovery tools. As explained in chapter 8, the use of depositions in federal court is regulated by Rules 27 through 32 of the Federal Rules of Civil Procedure. The purpose of the deposition is to uncover and explore all facts known by a party to the lawsuit or by a non-party witness involved in the lawsuit. A party or non-party witness who is questioned during a deposition is called a **deponent**. As noted in chapter 8, under Rule 26 of the Federal Rules the scope of testimony during discovery is much broader than the scope of testimony during trial. During the taking of a deposition an attorney is allowed to ask questions that could not be asked at trial because these questions seek evidence that is not admissible.

Moreover, according to Rule 26, during a deposition the attorney may ask the deponent not only any questions involving admissible evidence, but also any questions that could reasonably lead to the discovery of admissible evidence. The three types of depositions are the oral deposition, the deposition on written questions, and the telephone deposition.

9–2 THE NATURE OF THE ORAL DEPOSITION

During an **oral deposition**, the deponent is actually present in the attorney's office, at the courthouse, or at some other convenient location to answer an attorney's questions aloud. Rule 30 of the Federal Rules of Civil Procedure regulates the use of oral depositions. Your attorney may be involved in an oral deposition in one of two ways. First, he or she may ask questions of the opposing party or a non-party witness. In this situation, your attorney is said to be *taking the deposition.* If, on the other hand, your attorney's client is being questioned, then your attorney will be present at the deposition to protect the best interests of that client. In this role, your attorney is said to be *defending the deposition.*

Another individual who is always present at a deposition is the **court reporter** or *certified shorthand reporter.* The court reporter will place the deponent under oath, will take a word-for-word account of the proceeding, and, if required, will produce a written copy of the deposition. This written copy of the deposition is known as the **transcript**.

Advantages of the Oral Deposition

One major advantage of the oral deposition is that it gives the attorney taking the deposition the opportunity to see how well a witness or the opposing party will perform on the witness stand. This insight may help the attorney determine how best to handle the party or witness should he or she actually testify at trial. For example, should the deponent appear unsure about certain aspects of his or her testimony, the attorney could be prepared to convince the jury at trial that the witness should be considered unreliable. In contrast, an attorney defending a deposition can see

deposition
The oral or written testimony of a party or witness given under oath outside a courtroom.

deponent
A party or non-party witness who is questioned during a deposition.

oral deposition
A deposition at which the deponent is actually present to answer an attorney's questions aloud.

court reporter
An individual present at deposition to place the deponent under oath and take a word-for-word account of the proceeding and, if required, produce a written copy of the deposition.

transcript
The official daily record of the court proceedings; the verbatim copy of a deposition.

how well the client reacts to questions under pressure. This knowledge will enable the attorney to help the client improve performance when that client must testify in court.

Another advantage of the oral deposition is that it commits a deponent to one version of the facts. Often a deponent will rethink answers to the questions asked during the deposition. The deponent may even decide to change some of the answers should the same questions be asked at trial. For example, in the DeMarco case in the opening commentary, your attorney might elect to take the deposition of Dr. Masterson. In his initial deposition, the doctor may try to explain some of his actions by saying that he did not feel well at the time of the DeMarco examination. If Dr. Masterson changes his testimony at trial your attorney can use these alterations to demonstrate to the jury that Dr. Masterson's testimony is unreliable.

Disadvantages of the Oral Deposition

One primary disadvantage of the oral deposition is that it is inconvenient. Frequently the deposition must be taken at times and places that disrupt the regular office routine. Oral depositions are also expensive and time-consuming. In addition, the oral deposition allows the defending attorney to gain insight into the other attorney's case and strategy. The oral deposition also allows deponents to rehearse their testimony before the trial. Such rehearsals often destroy the element of spontaneity.

Trends in Oral Depositions

The video age has contributed a great deal to the taking of oral depositions. Today attorneys may purchase videotaped depositions that instruct potential deponents on the deposition process. These instructions help deponents prepare for their own depositions by giving them pointers explaining how to act during the deposition. Attorneys defending the deposition can also videotape their own clients during deposition rehearsals. The client can then watch the tape and make adjustments that will help improve performance during the actual deposition. Finally, an attorney taking a deposition can videotape that deposition. This videotaped deposition can be used at trial to dramatically demonstrate the inconsistency of an ill-prepared or unreliable witness.

9–3 THE PARALEGAL'S ROLE BEFORE THE ORAL DEPOSITION

You may be asked to assist the attorney in the preparation of the deposition. Since you'll be handling the procedural details of the deposition process, the attorney will be free to concentrate on developing the substantive legal issues to be explored during the deposition. In the preparation of a deposition, you may be asked to handle both the notice and subpoena requirements. You may also be asked to prepare questions.

Notice Requirement

Professional courtesy dictates that the attorney taking the deposition should contact the defending attorney to schedule mutually acceptable dates and times for taking the depositions of the defending attorney's clients. Sometimes securing a mutually acceptable date is a difficult process. Because of their different strategic concerns in planning their cases, the two attorneys may have conflicting preferences as to who should take depositions first. Such conflicting strategic concerns are usually resolved by the attorneys themselves through friendly compromise. It is also possible that the party or witness will resist the prospect of having to sit for a deposition either because he or she is apprehensive about the process itself or because he or she sees the deposition as providing assistance to the opposition. It is even possible for the potential deponent to feel that the deposition is an inconvenient and unnecessary burden that infringes on his work or leisure time. In such cases, it is the job of the defending attorney to allay the apprehensions of the client. Nevertheless, the attorney taking the deposition should make every effort to be flexible in scheduling a date and a time that is convenient for the party or witness.

The federal rules and the rules of most other jurisdictions require that formal notice of a deposition be given to the deponent and to each party. The length of time between the date that notice is required and the date of the deposition will be determined by the jurisdiction in which the case is being heard. Once an agreement on the deposition date has been reached, you may be asked to arrange for preparation and service of a **notice of intent to take oral deposition**. (See Figure 9–1.) This notice will set the date, time, and place of the deposition, the name of the attorney taking the deposition, and the name and address of the person whose deposition is to be taken. If the name of the deponent is unknown, a general description identifying the person or entity, such as controller, marketing director, or accounts payable supervisor, will suffice.

Documents may also be obtained from a party to the litigation by serving a request for that party to bring those documents to his or her deposition. Rule 30(b)(5) of the Federal Rules of Civil Procedure allows for this process. However, the procedures of Rule 34, Production of Documents, must also be followed whenever this is

notice of intent to take oral deposition
A notice of an intent to take the deposition of a party or witness, which includes the date, time, and place of the deposition, the name of the attorney taking the deposition, and the name and address of the person whose deposition is to be taken.

HAMPTON COUNTY COURT OF COMMON PLEAS

LISA DEMARCO,)
) Civil Action No. 92-7507
     Plaintiff,)
) NOTICE OF INTENT TO TAKE
     v.) ORAL DEPOSITION
)
HAMPTON GENERAL HOSPITAL, et al.,)
)
     Defendants.)
)
)
)

To: Jane K. Gould, Attorney for Defendant,

      PLEASE TAKE NOTICE that pursuant to Rule 30 of the Ohio Rules of Civil Procedure, Perry Matthews will take the oral deposition of Gary Eckerson before a notary public on January 9, 1993, at 4 p.m. and thereafter from day to day until completed, at the law offices of Matthews, Davidson, & Turner, 5477 East Ninth Street, Hampton, Ohio 44124.

                          Respectfully submitted,

                          _____

                          Perry A. Matthews
                          Attorney for Plaintiff

                   Certificate of Service
              I hereby certify that a true and correct copy of the foregoing Notice of Intent to take Oral deposition has been furnished to counsel of record on this the twenty-first day of December, 1992.

                          _____

FIGURE 9–1
Notice of Intent to Take Oral Deposition.

done. Thus, the specific documents or the categories of documents to be produced must be included in the deposition notice of attachment. For example, in the DeMarco case, your attorney may want to see DeMarco's medical chart, her admissions record, and any incident report filed by the hospital personnel. In preparing a notice of deposition for Dr. Masterson, you might ask him to produce all documents related to the case to which he has access. A request for records and documents at the time of a deposition is not, however, always the best way to handle discovery. If an attorney must wait to see the requested documents until the deposition, he or she may have to spend precious time reviewing the documents as the deposition proceeds. Moreover, subsequent examination of the documents often reveals information about which the deponent should have been questioned. This may necessitate the scheduling of another deposition.

Subpoena Requirement

When the attorney taking the deposition is requesting a non-party witness to testify, securing the deponent's presence will be necessary. The legal means for securing the presence of such a witness is a **subpoena**. (See Figure 9–2.) A subpoena is an official document issued by the clerk of court commanding a person to be present at a deposition.

To obtain a subpoena for a deponent in a federal lawsuit, you must provide a copy of the notice to take deposition to the clerk in the district where the deposition is to be taken. In state court, the state rules of civil procedures must be checked to determine who may serve a subpoena. In most states, a subpoena may be served by a sheriff, a bailiff, or any person eighteen years of age or older. Your attorney may request that you serve the subpoena.

In addition to the court costs incurred for a subpoena, it may also be necessary to reimburse the deponent for his or her appearance. For example the witness may be entitled to reimbursement for mileage and meals. These costs would be in addition to the mandatory witness reimbursement fee provided by many states. Prior to obtaining the subpoena, check with the clerk of courts to determine all the fees involved in the process. Make certain that a check in the correct amount is furnished to the clerk issuing the subpoena.

A non-party witness can be subpoenaed to produce documents at his or her deposition according to Rule 45 of the Federal Rules of Civil Procedure. This can be accomplished by serving the non-party witness with a **subpoena duces tecum**. The subpoena duces tecum will contain a specific listing of the documents that the non-party witness must produce at his or her deposition. For example, in the DeMarco case your attorney may want Eckerson to produce all documents related to the case to which he has access. She might also ask him to produce a copy of the hospital's procedure manual.

subpoena
An official document issued by the clerk of court commanding a person to be present for deposition or trial.

subpoena duces tecum
A subpoena listing documents that the non-party witness must produce at his or her deposition.

Preparation for the Deposition

Once the deposition has been scheduled and notice has been given to the potential deponent, preparation for the deposition begins. The nature of the preparation process depends on whether

No. **264**

Doc. **92-7507** Page **991**

COURT OF COMMON PLEAS

HAMPTON County, Ohio

Lisa DeMarco

Plaintiff

vs.

Hampton General Hospital

et al. Defendant

SUBPOENA

Returned and Filed

Ralph Knox

Clerk

By **Harriet Wilshire**

Deputy Clerk

SHERIFF'S RETURN

Rev. Code, Secs. 2317.14; 2335.07, .31

................................Ohio,..........................., 19........

Received this writ..................................., 19.........., at
.............o'clock.........M., and afterwards I served the same in
the manner and at the time shown below, that is I read this
writ to those witnesses whose names are marked R; I delivered a copy of it personally to those whose names are marked
P; and I left a copy of it at the usual place of residence of
those whose names are marked C. They are entitled to the
number of miles set opposite their respective names. The
others are not found.

NAMES OF WITNESSES	Miles	How Served	When Served 19........

FEES

Service and return........persons, each

Mileage,...............miles, at

Total

....Sheriff

....County, Ohio

By...

Deputy

FIGURE 9–2
Subpoena.

your attorney will be taking the deposition or defending it. If your attorney is taking the deposition, she will prepare to question the opposing party or a non-party witness. If she is defending the deposition, she will prepare her own client to answer questions posed by the opposing attorney.

Preparation for Taking the Deposition. If your attorney is preparing to take a deposition, you have to do a variety of tasks designed not only to gather background information but also to plan the actual deposition. In gathering background information, you will be

Form No. CB-1

SUBPOENA—CIVIL CASE
Rev. Code, Secs. 2317.11, .13, .15

CASE NO. **92-7507**

To the Sheriff of **HAMPTON** County, Ohio.

You are commanded to make due service and return of this Subpoena:

The State of Ohio, **HAMPTON** County, ss. COURT OF COMMON PLEAS

To **GARY ECKERSON**
9601 Concord Avenue
Hampton, Ohio

You Are Hereby Required to attend before the Court of Common Pleas at the Court House in **HAMPTON** County, on the **9th** day of **February** 19**93**, at **1:00** o'clock **P.** M., to testify as witness in behalf of the **Plaintiff** in a certain cause pending in said Court, wherein **Lisa De Marco** Plaintiff, and **Hampton General Hospital** Defendant, and not depart the Court without leave.

Herein fail not under penalty of the law.

WITNESS my signature and the seal of said Court, this **30th** day of **January** 19

Ralph Knox
Clerk

By **Harriet Wilshire**
Deputy Clerk

ATTY. **Perry A. Mathews**

FIGURE 9–2
(continued)

required to review documents related to the deponent, to develop a history of events as they involve the deponent, and to summarize prior discovery pertaining to the deponent. In planning the deposition, you may be called upon to prepare a deposition outline and to plan the questions that your attorney will ask the deponent. During this step you may also be asked to prepare any exhibits that may be used during the deposition. For example, in the DeMarco case you may be asked to compile DeMarco's statements, medical bills, and medical history prior to Eckerson's deposition. You may also be asked to arrange for the hiring of a court reporter to place the deponent under oath, to record the question-answer session, and to provide the necessary transcripts.

The site of the deposition will also have to be arranged. In determining how far a potential deponent can be required to travel to sit for a deposition, Rule 45 of the Federal Rules of Civil Procedure distinguishes between potential deponents who are residents and those who are not residents of the district in which the lawsuit was brought. (See chapter 2, "The Courts and Jurisdiction," for a discussion of the place of the district courts in the structure of the federal court system.) Residents of the district can be subpoenaed to appear at a deposition in the county where they reside, work, or transact business. The rule, however, does allow the court to choose another location that would be convenient to the deponent. A resident of another federal court district can be required to attend a deposition in the county where he or she is subpoenaed or within a forty mile radius of that place. Again, the rule allows the court to set some other convenient location. As far as the actual physical setting of the deposition, there are no rules about this. The deposition may be held at the attorney's office, at the courthouse, or at some neutral site, such as a hotel or motel meeting room.

Preparation for Defending the Deposition.   Should your client be asked to appear for a deposition, you may want to consult with your attorney to determine if any preliminary objections should be raised. For example, if your client has been asked to bring documents, records, letters, memos, or any other form of real evidence to the deposition, your attorney may, depending on the circumstances, decide that certain objections are in order. As noted in chapter 8, such objections can be based on the attorney-client privilege, the work product privilege, or the Fifth Amendment privilege against self-incrimination.

A party or a non-party witness who is asked to produce documents at the deposition may also object on the grounds that the request is **overbroad**. Such an objection claims that the request seeks more information than could ever be used. Another additional objection that can be raised is that the request is **duplicative**. This means that the other party has asked for the same information a number of different times in a number of different ways.

As chapter 8 explained in some detail, the scope of discovery is much broader than the scope of evidence that can be introduced at trial. Documents, reports, letters, and other forms of real evidence that would not be admitted at trial must be produced at a deposition, if they are reasonably calculated to lead to admissible evidence. In contrast, items of real evidence that cannot be calculated to lead to admissible evidence are not subject to discovery. Thus your attorney can object on these grounds. Your attorney could also object on grounds that the real evidence asked for is irrelevant to the litigation. If any of these objections are appropriate, written notice of these objections will have to be sent to the other party's attorney. Recall also that your attorney may seek a confidentiality agreement or a protective order to preserve the privacy of certain sensitive documents that your client has been asked to bring to the deposition.

Once the preliminary discussion concerning objections is complete, you will need to prepare the client for the deposition. This will require an initial conference with the client. At the conference, your attorney will explain the deposition process to the client and will review anticipated areas of questioning. Usually such a conference should be scheduled prior to the day of the deposition. Such an early meeting will give the attorney time to react should the client be unable to produce a needed document, or should the client's planned testimony appear to contradict the testimony of another witness. If your attorney prefers extensive deposition planning, he or she may want to prepare an outline predicting the strategy of her opponent. You may be called upon to write a plan that anticipates the opposing attorney's questions. You may also be asked to organize any documents the witness has been asked to produce.

Many attorneys now conduct mock depositions. The purpose of the **mock deposition** is to prepare the client for the actual deposition. Such preparation will help the client know what to expect when his deposition is taken. This rehearsal not only relaxes the client, but also helps him recall the events about which he will be questioned. In the mock deposition, the client will be questioned by your attorney or another attorney in the firm. The format of the mock deposition should closely follow that of an actual deposition.

You may be asked to evaluate the effectiveness of the client during the mock deposition. In such an evaluation, the following questions should be considered: Is the client believable? Does the client answer questions completely? Does the client volunteer information not called for in the question? Many law firms provide a checklist for potential deponents explaining deposition procedure and outlining pitfalls to avoid. See the checklist on page 216.

9–4 THE PARALEGAL'S ROLE DURING THE ORAL DEPOSITION

Notice of the deposition has been given, and preparation for the deposition is complete. Deposition time has arrived. Your job at the deposition will vary, based on your experience, the

overbroad
A discovery request seeking much more information than the other party needs or could ever use.

duplicative
A request for production of information that has already been requested.

mock deposition
A deposition rehearsal to prepare the client for the actual deposition.

**WITNESS CHECKLIST FOR
DEPOSITION TESTIMONY**

1. Dress neatly but conservatively.
2. Listen to the question carefully. Take your time in answering.
3. Answer each question aloud. Avoid head nodding and shaking.
4. Answer the question asked, not the question you wish had been asked.
5. Do not volunteer information.
6. Be courteous, but not overly friendly.
7. Do not be argumentative. Do not lose your temper.
8. Do not interrupt the attorney's question.
9. If you do not understand the question, ask that it be repeated.
10. Listen carefully to any rephrasing of your answer. Correct any inaccurate rephrasing.
11. If you need to review a document to answer a question, request permission to do so.
12. If you do not know the answer to the question, say so. Do not guess or estimate. "I don't recall" is an acceptable answer.
13. Do not look at your attorney for help in answering a question.
14. Do not be distracted by objections made by your attorney.
15. If your attorney advises you not to answer a question, follow that advice.

---

complexity of the case, and the attorney's division of responsibilities. Your duties will also vary depending on whether your attorney is taking or defending the deposition. In either case, you will be asked to take notes and evaluate the witness. However, the focus of the notetaking and the evaluating will depend on whether your attorney is taking or defending the deposition. You may also be called upon to control or produce documents and exhibits depending upon your attorney's role in the deposition.

Notetaking

One of the most critical functions at the deposition is taking notes. Your notetaking will free your attorney to concentrate on the questions and the topics covered. If your attorney is taking the deposition, follow the deposition outline to make certain all questions are asked. Also, make certain the deponent answers each question. Use your notes to call incomplete or inconsistent answers to your attorney's attention. If your attorney is defending the deposition, note what facts the other attorney tends to focus upon as he or she questions your client. Moreover, try to determine whether the attorney's questioning pattern reveals her legal strategy in the case. Also, remember that your attorney is allowed to object to any question that he or she feels violates one of the privileges or principles discussed earlier in this chapter and in chapter 8. Make certain that you accurately record these objections.

Witness Evaluation

You may be asked to assist in evaluating the effectiveness of a witness. If your attorney is taking the deposition, look for weaknesses in the deponent's testimony. The following questions should be addressed:

1. Has the deponent contradicted himself or herself?
2. Does the deponent seem hesitant about certain aspects of his or her testimony?
3. How often does the deponent need to refer to notes or documents in order to answer your attorney's questions?
4. Is the deponent intimidated by your attorney?
5. How often does the deponent say that he does not remember certain facts?

Your evaluation will help your attorney determine how to use the deponent's testimony and how to treat the deponent should he be called on to testify at trial. For example, in the DeMarco case, your observations might reveal that Eckerson's description of the events surrounding DeMarco's examination differs from the account given by Dr. Masterson in his deposition. This information will help your attorney prepare her examination of Eckerson at trial.

If your attorney is defending the deposition, your evaluation will be aimed at helping the witness improve his testimony. In this situation, the following questions should be addressed:

1. Does the deponent seem convincing?
2. Does he take his time in answering questions?
3. Does he volunteer information unnecessarily?
4. Is the deponent argumentative or overly friendly?
5. Does the deponent answer questions aloud or does he rely on head nodding and shaking?
6. Is the deponent consistent in his testimony?

Your evaluation will help your attorney review her client's testimony as she plans her strategy leading to trial. In the DeMarco case, for example, your evaluation of DeMarco's deposition might help your attorney decide that she should have her client review the deposition before trial to prevent any contradictions on the witness stand.

THE COMPUTERIZED LAW FIRM—Full Text Retrieval

SCENARIO

It is the day of the DeMarco trial. Dr. Masterson has just been examined by Bernie Cole, the attorney for Hampton General Hospital. Dr. Masterson has testified that on the day of the DeMarco examination he had eight hours of sleep prior to the session and was in perfect health. Your attorney recalls that at some time during Dr. Masterson's deposition, he said that he had just finished an eight hour shift when he was called back to HGH to cover the second shift because the physician scheduled for that shift had been involved in an accident. Your attorney also recalls that at another point in the deposition Dr. Masterson had tried to explain some of his behavior by saying that he felt "flu-like symptoms accompanied by some dizziness." Unfortunately your attorney cannot recall exactly where in the depositions these remarks were made. Your attorney asks for and is granted a half-hour recess before beginning the cross examination of Dr. Masterson.

PROBLEM

Your attorney wants you to locate the discrepancies in Dr. Masterson's deposition. You have less than thirty minutes to search through a 157 page deposition. Conventional techniques prove useless. Your chronological summary provides no help. Paging through the deposition is too time-consuming. The clock is ticking. Precious seconds are being lost. What can you do to save your client's case?

SOLUTION

The computerized law office offers a management tool for data contained in a deposition. Recent computer technology includes a *full text retrieval* program for deposition and trial transcripts. The program works like this. The court reporter transcribes verbatim testimony onto a machine that generates a computer tape. The tape is then transcribed into computer format and output onto a disk. This disk is then installed on the law firm's computer. You will be able to search the full text of Dr. Masterson's deposition to locate references to his physical condition on the date of the DeMarco examination. Full text retrieval allows you to summarize the deposition and pull together all testimony on a particular topic on the actual deposition page. Accuracy and speed of full text retrieval cannot be duplicated with a manual deposition or a summary system. Appendix C lists full text retrieval packages that are normally available from the court reporter free or at a nominal cost.

9–5 THE PARALEGAL'S ROLE AFTER THE ORAL DEPOSITION

Your responsibilities in the deposition process do not end with the final question. Post-deposition tasks may include assuming responsibility for the transcript and preparation of a deposition summary. This will require you to be familiar with the various types of deposition summaries that are available. If problems arise the paralegal may also be involved in drafting and defending motions.

Transcript Arrangements

Both the attorney taking the deposition and the attorney defending the deposition may need to see a transcript. To obtain copies of the transcript, you must contact the court reporter to find out when the transcript will be ready. Many reporters will provide a copy of the deposition on a disk that facilitates summaries or even allows for the use of deposition summary software. Naturally, whether the reporter provides you with a disk or a hard copy of the deposition, you will be charged for the service. Moreover, if your attorney needs to see a copy immediately, the court reporter will probably charge an additional fee for having to speed up the process. You must also arrange for the appropriate number of copies, handle billing for the court reporter's services, and secure an appropriate date and place for delivery.

When you receive the deposition from the court reporter, you should distribute a copy to your attorney. The deposition should be reviewed for errors or significant omissions prior to summarizing it. This process can be speeded up if you compare the transcript with your deposition notes. You should also check the spelling of all unusual legal and medical terms.

If your attorney defended the deposition, you should arrange for the client to review and correct the transcript. Any errors in the transcript should be corrected by the deponent. The deposition transcript will contain a space at the end of the testimony for necessary changes and the reason for the change. The deponent must also sign the deposition. Should the deponent decide that he or she does not want to sign the deposition, the court reporter must sign it and should record any explanation that the deponent gives for refusing to sign. You must arrange for the signed and corrected deposition to be returned to the court or court reporter as required by court rules.

The Deposition Summary

The **deposition summary** is a written record that reduces many hours of testimony to a few concisely drawn, easily read, and quickly understood pages. A properly written deposition summary can organize selected topics or subject matter into an orderly arrangement. Once the testimony has been arranged in the deposition summary according to a particular plan, inconsistent testimony may become evident. A well-drawn summary could also point out missing pieces of evidence that might lead your attorney to conduct further discovery.

deposition summary
A written record that reduces many hours of testimony to a few concisely drawn, easily read, and quickly understood pages.

page-line deposition summary
A summary covering the deposition testimony in the order in which it occurred in the deposition itself.

topical deposition summary
A deposition summary that organizes the testimony into specific subject areas.

chronological deposition summary
The organization of deposition testimony according to a particular time sequence.

Pre-Summary Considerations. Before writing your deposition summary, determine the date your attorney needs it. Determine the format to be used, the amount of detail required, and the issues or testimony your attorney wants pinpointed. It may be necessary to find out whether your attorney prefers a completely paraphrased summary or one that includes direct quotes from the deponent. Also, make certain you know whether your attorney wants you to write in phrases or complete sentences. Finally, determine which type of deposition summary your attorney wants you to use.

Types of Deposition Summaries. Basically, you will have three types of deposition summaries from which to choose: the **page-line deposition summary**, the **topical deposition summary**, and the **chronological deposition summary**. The page-line deposition summary will cover the testimony as it occurred in the deposition itself. (See Table 9–1.) Such a summary is helpful when the attorney is uncertain about just how to use the deponent's testimony. The page-line summary allows her to review the testimony quickly and focus on areas that she wants to explore further. The topical deposition summary organizes the testimony into specific subject areas. (See Table 9–2.) Such a deposition is useful when the attorney knows what areas she needs to concentrate on in planning her legal strategy. Finally, the chronological

TABLE 9–1

PAGE-LINE DEPOSITION SUMMARY

Page	Line	Topic	Summary
4	9	Test	Patient DeMarco was scheduled for an intravenous polygram
8	17	Antidote	The antidote had to be retrieved from the pharmacy.

---

deposition summary organizes the testimony according to a particular time sequence. (See Table 9–3.) Such a summary is needed when the chronology of events is of critical importance to the case.

The type of summary that you use in a case will depend not only on the facts involved but also on the legal issues that your attorney will want to emphasize. For instance, in the DeMarco case, your attorney may be primarily interested in demonstrating that Dr. Masterson was negligent in the procedure that he followed in administering the contrast medium. Therefore your attorney would be interested in tracing the steps followed by Dr. Masterson. In such a case, the chronological summary would be most helpful.

TABLE 9–2

TOPICAL DEPOSITION SUMMARY

Topic	Page	Summary
Education	1	He received an associate's degree from Hampton County Community College.
Employment Experience	1	Eckerson was employed by Hampton General Hospital 6/5/62 as a radiologic technologist.
Certification	2	He became a certified radiologic technologist in 1991.
Patient's Chart	6	Eckerson identifies contents of DeMarco's chart.
Patient's Condition	8	DeMarco suffered cardiac arrest.

TABLE 9–3

CHRONOLOGICAL DEPOSITION SUMMARY

Date	Event	Page
1990	Graduated from College.	1
1990	Employed at Hampton General	3
1991	Certified as R.T.	2

9–6 SPECIAL TYPES OF DEPOSITIONS

While the most common type of deposition is the oral deposition, there are occasions when your attorney will be required to use the deposition upon written questions or the telephone deposition.

The Deposition Upon Written Questions

A **deposition upon written questions** is a discovery tool that requires the deponent to orally answer written questions in the presence of a court reporter. Although the deponent is physically present at this type of deposition, the attorney who prepared the questions is not. Instead, he or she has submitted the written questions prior to the deposition. Rule 31 of the Federal Rules of Civil Procedure regulates the use of this type of deposition. Depositions upon written questions are easy and inexpensive. They are used primarily to obtain business records and testimony from a minor witness whose oral deposition could be very expensive because of the witness's distant location. While this type of deposition is inexpensive, it does have certain disadvantages. For example, since the questions are written in advance, there is no way to ask follow up questions based on the witness's answers. Similarly, there is no opportunity to observe the witness during the deposition.

Your attorney may request that you prepare the **notice of intent to take deposition upon written questions**. This notice is similar to the notice of intent to take oral deposition. It lists the name and address of the person who must answer the questions and the name of the officer before whom the deposition is to be taken. Also, if the deponent is a non-party, a subpoena must be served.

An additional responsibility you may be asked to assume is the drafting of the written questions. To draft these questions, you should first review the pleadings and previous discovery. Determine the areas of examination to be included in the questions, draft the questions, and furnish them to your attorney for review and revisions. Once your attorney's changes have been made, incorporate those changes into your draft questions and arrange the written questions in final order.

The Telephone Deposition

In the **telephone deposition,** the deponent and the attorney defending the deposition are present in one location and the attorney taking the deposition is in another location asking the questions by telephone. The deponent's answers are recorded by a court reporter who could be at either location. Rule 30 of the Federal Rules of Civil Procedure permits the use of the telephone deposition.

A telephone deposition is the least common of all depositions. Its cost savings is offset by the inability to evaluate the appearance and effectiveness of the deponent. Moreover, there is always the possibility of telephone communication difficulties. This method is useful, however, to obtain an inexpensive deposition of a minor witness. It avoids travel-related deposition costs and reduces the time involved in taking the deposition.

Your attorney may request that you set up the deposition in the court jurisdiction where the deponent is responding to the questions, arrange for the reporter and telephone hook-up, and assist in drafting questions for the deposition.

SUMMARY

9–1 A deposition is the written or oral testimony of a witness or party given under oath outside the courtroom. A person questioned during a deposition is a deponent. The scope of testimony during a deposition is much broader than the scope of testimony during trial.

9–2 During an oral deposition the deponent is actually present to answer the attorney's questions aloud. The attorney who asks the questions during the deposition is said to be taking the deposition. If the attorney's client is being questioned, the attorney is said to be defending the deposition. There are both advantages and disadvantages to oral depositions. One advantage of the oral deposition is that it gives the attorney taking the deposition the opportunity to see how well a witness or opposing party will perform on the witness stand. Another is that the oral deposition commits a deponent to one version of the facts. A third advantage is that the attorney defending the deposition can see how well her client reacts to questions

deposition upon written questions
A discovery tool that requires the deponent to orally answer written questions in the presence of a court reporter.

notice of intent to take deposition upon written questions
Notice of the intent to take a deposition by written questions, listing the name and address of the person who must answer the question and the name of the officer before whom the deposition is to be taken; if the deponent is a non-party, a subpoena must be served.

telephone deposition
A deposition during which the deponent and the attorney defending the deposition are present in one location and the attorney taking the deposition is in another location asking the questions by telephone; the deponent's answers are recorded by a court reporter who could be at either location.

under pressure. One disadvantage of a deposition is that it is inconvenient. Second, oral depositions are expensive and time-consuming. Finally, the oral deposition allows a deponent to rehearse his testimony before trial. The use of video-taped depositions, as models, records, and rehearsals, is rapidly increasing.

9–3 The role of the paralegal in the preparation of the deposition is quite diverse. The paralegal may be asked to arrange for the preparation and service of a notice of intent to take an oral deposition. The paralegal may also be asked to obtain subpoenas for several deponents. Finally, the paralegal may be called upon to help prepare for the deposition. The exact nature of this preparation will depend upon whether the attorney is taking or defending the deposition.

9–4 During the actual deposition, the paralegal may be asked to take notes. The paralegal may also be asked to evaluate the effectiveness of the deponent.

9–5 After the deposition, the paralegal may have to obtain a transcript of the deponent's testimony. The paralegal may also have to write a deposition summary. There are three types of deposition summaries: The page-line deposition summary, the topical deposition summary, and the chronological deposition summary.

9–6 A deposition upon written questions is a discovery tool that requires the deponent to orally answer written questions in the presence of a court reporter. In the telephone deposition, the deponent and his attorney are present in one location, and the attorney taking the deposition is in another location asking the questions by telephone.

KEY TERMS

chronological deposition
  summary
court reporter
deponent
deposition
deposition summary
deposition upon written
  questions
duplicative
mock deposition
notice of intent to take
  deposition upon written
  questions

notice of intent to take
  oral deposition
oral deposition
overbroad
page-line deposition summary
subpoena
subpoena duces tecum
telephone deposition
topical deposition summary
transcript

QUESTIONS FOR REVIEW AND DISCUSSION

1. What is a deposition?
2. Name three advantages and three disadvantages of the oral deposition.
3. Name three modern trends in conducting oral depositions.
4. What is a notice of intent to take an oral deposition?
5. What responsibilities does a paralegal have in preparing for a deposition?
6. What responsibilities does a paralegal have during an oral deposition?
7. Explain the paralegal's role in arranging for a transcript.
8. Identify three types of deposition summaries.
9. What are the advantages and the disadvantages of taking a deposition upon written questions?
10. What are the advantages and the disadvantages of taking a telephone deposition?

ACTIVITIES

1. Review the laws of your state and find all state laws that deal with depositions. Check your local court rules to see if any local rules of court in your area regulate who may be present during the taking of a deposition. Also check local rules to see who may be present to record the questions and answers to a deposition.
2. Contact your local bar association. Try to find out how many local attorneys are using video equipment to instruct clients on how to conduct themselves during a deposition. Also find out if any local attorneys are using video equipment to help clients rehearse for their own depositions.

CHAPTER 9 PROJECT—EVALUATING THE DEPONENT

Review the DeMarco case in the opening commentary. Recall that your attorney will be conducting the deposition of Gary Eckerson, the young radiologic technologist. After doing so, draft a checklist for evaluating Eckerson.

CHAPTER 10
Interrogatories

COMMENTARY—THE MERCHANTS GROCERY CASE

On the morning of March 17 of last year, Marilyn Mason, age seventy-nine, went on her weekly grocery shopping trip to the Merchants Grocery. While in the produce section of the store, she allegedly slipped on a wet spot on the linoleum floor and fell, breaking her right leg and hip. About six months later she elected to sue the grocery store. Your firm has been retained to represent Merchants Grocery in this "slip and fall" case. Your attorney has asked you to draft interrogatories to be answered by Mrs. Mason. The goal here is to obtain additional information about the basis of her allegations, the extent of her injuries, and the expert and lay witnesses that her attorney intends to call. You will also assist in preparing answers to the interrogatories sent to your client by Mrs. Mason's attorney.

OBJECTIVES

The preceding chapters gave you an overview of the discovery process and introduced you to the tools of discovery. Interrogatories are another effective discovery device. After reading this chapter, you will be able to:

1. Define interrogatories.
2. Explain the various purposes of interrogatories.
3. List the advantages of using interrogatories.
4. Outline the disadvantages of using interrogatories.
5. Explain the form and content of the parts of a set of interrogatories.
6. Describe the specific types of interrogatories.
7. Explain the options available when a party refuses to answer an interrogatory.
8. Outline the duty to supplement interrogatory answers.
9. Describe when it would be appropriate to produce business records instead of a written interrogatory response.
10. Explain the form of the interrogatory answer.
11. Outline the objections that can be raised to interrogatories.

10–1 INTERROGATORIES

Interrogatories are written questions submitted by one party in a lawsuit to another party in that suit. The responding party must answer these questions in writing and under oath. Rule 33 of the Federal Rules of Civil Procedure regulates the use of interrogatories in federal courts. As we have seen earlier in the text, many states have adopted the federal rules as their own. Still, you must always check for variations in state and local rules governing the use of interrogatories. According to Rule 33, interrogatories may be served on any party to a lawsuit. Unlike depositions, however, interrogatories cannot be served on non-party witnesses involved in the lawsuit. Rule 33 also allows interrogatories to be served at the same time that the complaint is served. When interrogatories are served with the complaint, the party has forty-five days to provide his or her answers. Otherwise, the party has thirty days to provide those answers.

interrogatories
Written questions submitted by one party in a lawsuit to another party in that suit, which must be answered in writing and under oath.

Scope and Number of Interrogatories

You will recall from our earlier discussions on the scope of discovery that the type and the amount of evidence that can be sought by discovery is much broader than that which could be produced at the trial. A reference in Rule 33 to Rule 26(b) makes it clear that this broad scope of discovery applies to interrogatories. The rule states that: "Interrogatories may relate to any matter which can be inquired into under Rule 26(b), and the answers may be used to the extent permitted by the rules of evidence." Naturally, answers sought by interrogatories must be relevant to the pending lawsuit. However, those answers need not be admissible at the time of the trial, as long as they are reasonably calculated to lead to the discovery of evidence that can be submitted at trial.

All the interrogatories sent to a party at one time constitute a set. Multiple sets of interrogatories, however, can be served on the parties to a lawsuit. Within each set, each interrogatory is numbered for convenient reference. The federal rules require sequential numbering throughout all sets. For example, if, in the Merchants Grocery case in the opening Commentary, the first set of interrogatories contained twenty interrogatories, the second set would begin with number twenty-one. In federal court there is no limit on the number of interrogatories per set or the number of sets which may be served on a party. However, in the interests of efficiency and economy, some state courts do set such limits.

Purposes of Interrogatories

The primary purpose of interrogatories is to obtain information on the basic facts in a case including any other people who may be involved in the lawsuit. Interrogatories may also be used to determine the party's contentions and to locate relevant documents. A set of interrogatories may also disclose the identities of both lay and expert witnesses that the other party intends to call to the stand at trial. This last point is especially critical in the identification of expert witnesses because Rule 33 allows interrogatories to explore not only the opinions of the expert but also how he or she reached those opinions.

Properly drafted interrogatories can also help to narrow the issues and facts in preparation for trial. Also, like the deposition, interrogatories can be used to impeach a witness at the time of the trial. Finally, interrogatories may facilitate a settlement of the case.

Advantages of Interrogatories

Interrogatories offer substantial advantages over other discovery methods. First of all, they are simple, inexpensive, and efficient. For instance, since a party answers interrogatories at his own pace, there is no need to schedule a special session convenient to all those involved. Interrogatories, therefore, avoid the logistical problems associated with depositions. Second, a set of interrogatories can be more thorough than a deposition. This is because interrogatories must be answered and verified by the party. The answering party has a duty to obtain the answer to an interrogatory if that information is either in the possession or the control of that party. The responding party also has the duty to provide the identity of the person who does have custody of a document if the party does not have it. A final advantage is the fact that interrogatories complement the other discovery techniques. For example, interrogatories may determine the identities of future deponents. They may also reveal documents that should be included in a subsequent request for production of documents.

Disadvantages of Interrogatories

Like the other discovery devices, interrogatories are not without their disadvantages. The first disadvantage is that they are limited to the parties to a lawsuit. Consequently, the use of interrogatories may not eliminate the need to take depositions at a later date. In fact the use of interrogatories does not even eliminate the need to take the deposition of a party. Second, interrogatories lack spontaneity. Therefore, a party responding to a set of interrogatories has the time to draft self-serving answers. In addition, the answers are often edited by the attorney or the paralegal before they are sent out. Moreover, since the answers are written, they do not allow for immediate follow-up questions. Certainly, follow-up questions can be drafted and submitted, but this does not eliminate the possibility of further self-serving answers. Another disadvantage is that interrogatories may help the opposing attorney by motivating him to begin the preparation of his case earlier than he might ordinarily be inclined to proceed. In line with this, interrogatories can also alert the opposition to the direction of your case. In spite of these disadvantages, interrogatories are an effective discovery device.

10–2 DRAFTING INTERROGATORIES

Paralegals are often asked to participate in drafting interrogatories. Your involvement in drafting the interrogatories will free your attorney's time so that he or she can concentrate on other matters. The drafting of interrogatories is one of the most important jobs that you may have during the litigation process, because properly drafted interrogatories not only provide information themselves, but also indicate the need to use other discovery devices. Your role in drafting interrogatories may later be expanded to include drafting a motion to compel the other party to respond to some of the interrogatories that have not been properly answered. You may also be responsible for reviewing the other party's response.

Preliminary Steps in Drafting Interrogatories

Before you can draft an effective set of interrogatories, you must take the time to familiarize yourself with the facts of the case. To do this properly, review the pleadings, the correspondence file, the attorney's notes, and the research notebook. Your review should be an active one. Take notes as you review the material and consider the types of questions you will want to ask the other party. In the Merchants Grocery case, for example, as a paralegal for the firm representing the grocery store, you would want to ask Mrs. Mason about the extent of her injuries and about the treatment that she may have received from her physician. Other questions may involve the circumstances surrounding the accident itself. Upon the termination of the preliminary review you will be ready to draft the interrogatories.

Form and Content of Interrogatories

The format that you will have to use in drafting the interrogatories will be mandated by federal or state rules. Make certain to consult the appropriate court rules to determine the form that is required in your jurisdiction. Most jurisdictions will require a title, an introductory paragraph, definitions, instructions, specific interrogatories, signature, and certificate of service.

Title of the Interrogatories and Introductory Paragraph. Discovery will always involve the production of a wide variety of pleadings, motions, and requests. For this reason all documents should carry an appropriate title. This procedure allows participants in the action to identify a document that they have in their hands just by glancing at the title. The Federal Rules of Civil Procedure, as well as most state rules, also require the use of such titles. The title of the interrogatories should identify the party serving the interrogatories, the party receiving the interrogatories, and the number of the set of interrogatories:

**DEFENDANT MERCHANTS GROCERY'S
FIRST SET OF INTERROGATORIES**

TO PLAINTIFF MARILYN MASON

The rules do not require an introductory paragraph. Nevertheless, tradition dictates including an introductory paragraph immediately after the caption of the case and the title of the interrogatories. Usually this paragraph identifies the recipient of the interrogatories. It will also indicate that an answer is required within a specified period of time. The introductory paragraph should also state the appropriate federal or state rule under which the interrogatories are presented. Finally, the introduction may set forth the number of interrogatories permitted and the statutory requirements for supplemental answers. Figure 10–1 is an example of the introductory paragraph.

Definitions.   The definition section should be distinct so that the responding party can easily locate it. The heading "definitions" should be placed in the center of the page in bold-faced lettering. Definitions can be used to clear up discrepancies among words that have several meanings. They can also be used to establish the meaning of a word that is used frequently throughout the interrogatories. For example, in the Merchants Grocery case, the word "accident" may be repeated several dozen times. To avoid confusion, the definition section of the interrogatories might establish the definition in the following way: " 'accident' refers to the incident during which the plaintiff, Marilyn Mason, was allegedly injured on the premises of Merchants Grocery at 455 West Fifth Street, Dallas, Texas." The definition section also conserves space and shortens the questions by eliminating the need to repeat the meaning of a word that appears throughout the interrogatories. Finally, properly drafted definitions can enlarge the number of questions asked by defining a word to include several subtopics. For example, as indicated in Figure 10–2, the words "identify" and "identity," when effectively defined, can result in an abundance of information about the people and the documents involved in a case.

Instructions.   Instructions prevent confusion and help the party preparing the interrogatories to obtain the needed information. When drafting the instructions, be sure to include instructions for

---

Pursuant to Rule _____, _____ Rules of Civil Procedure, you are to answer the interrogatories hereinafter set forth, separately, fully, in writing, and under oath. You should deliver a true copy of your answer to the undersigned attorney within thirty days after the date of service of these interrogatories.

FIGURE 10–1
Introductory Paragraph for Interrogatories.

1. To "identify" a document or state the "identity of" a document shall mean to state with respect thereto:
   (a) The identity of the person who prepared it;
   (b) The identity of the person who signed it or over whose signature it was or is issued:
   (c) The identity of each person to whom it was addressed or distributed;
   (d) The nature and substance of the document with sufficient particularity to enable it to be identified:
   (e) The date, if any, which the document bears; and
   (f) The present location of the document, including the identity of its custodian or custodians; or in lieu thereof, attach a copy of said document to your response to these interrogatories.
2. To "identify" or to state the "identity of" a person shall mean with respect thereto:
   (a) The person's full name;
   (b) The person's title and business or professional affiliation, if any, as of the time to which the answer relates; and
   (c) The person's present title and business or professional and residence addresses.

FIGURE 10–2
Definitions.

any desired action by the other party. Also make certain to offer the opposing party the opportunity to attach documents instead of answering an interrogatory. This will save time and avoid the need to file a request for production of documents.

It is also important in drafting the instructions to consider the time period that the interrogatories will cover. Your request should seek not only information about the incident that gave rise to the lawsuit, but also information about past conduct, conditions, and activities. For example, in the Merchants Grocery case, the accident took place on March 17, 1991. Your instructions may indicate that the applicable time period for all answers will extend from March 17, 1990, to the date the plaintiff actually answers the interrogatories. This may allow you to detect some preexisting condition that contributed to the accident in question. Drafting these instructions must be done with care, however. The inquiry must be comprehensive enough to discover relevant information, yet narrow enough to avoid an objection that the request is overbroad and burdensome.

Another topic often included in the instructions is the duty to supplement answers when additional information is received or there is a change in the content of any previous answer. However, it is important to note that not all states recognize this duty to supplement. The instructions should also explain how to deal with any objections that the responding party has to the interrogatories. For example, should the responding party object to part of a question, he or she should be instructed to answer any other part of that question that is not objectionable. A special instruction may also be used to inquire about any information that is withheld under a claim of the attorney-client privilege or the work product privilege.

Since the instruction section of the interrogatories is a crucial part of this document, that heading should be centered and placed in bold-faced type. Some law firms will combine definitions and instructions, so check on the accepted procedure in your office. Figure 10–3 contains examples of the instructions that you might incorporate in the interrogatories directed at the plaintiff in the Merchants Grocery case.

Specific Interrogatories.   Several types of interrogatories may be asked. Each of these is designed to elicit different forms of information related to the lawsuit. These special interrogatories include interrogatories that identify people, interrogatories that establish facts or lead to the discovery of facts, interrogatories that identify documents, and interrogatories that identify contentions.

1. Interrogatories that Identify People. The identities of the people who are involved in the lawsuit are very important. For example, in the Merchants Grocery case, you will need to determine the identities of any witnesses to the accident. You will also need to identify the physicians who have treated the plaintiff. It would also be helpful if you could uncover the identities of individuals who have direct knowledge of Mrs. Mason's condition before and after the accident.

Another area of questions about people concerns the identities of all people who have given statements to the other party's attorney. For example, has the opposing attorney taken statements from witnesses, physicians, neighbors, safety experts, etc.? Once you receive this information, you will be able to schedule any depositions that your attorney decides are necessary. You will also be able to draft any document production requests that appear appropriate.

Finally, interrogatories can be used to identify the expert witnesses that the opposition intends to call at trial as witnesses. In fact, in federal court under Rule 26(b)(4), the only method for obtaining information about the identity of these experts is through interrogatories. Under this rule, you can discover not only the identity of the expert, but also the subject matter about which he or she will testify, and the grounds for that expert's opinion. Figure 10–4 gives an example of this type of interrogatory.

It is important to note that such an interrogatory can be asked only about an expert that will be called to testify at trial. If

A. You are required by Rule _____ of the _____ Rules of Civil Procedure to:
   1. Answer fully and factually each of the interrogatories hereinafter set out.
   2. Furnish all information called for by said interrogatory.
   3. Sign your response.
   4. Swear to your response.
   5. Serve same upon the undersigned attorney within thirty (30) days after the date of service of these interrogatories. You are further instructed:
B. Every interrogatory herein shall be deemed a continuing interrogatory, and you are to supplement your answers promptly if and when you obtain relevant information in addition to, or in any way inconsistent with, your initial answer to any interrogatory.
C. If you object to, or otherwise decline to answer, any portion of an interrogatory, provide all information called for in that portion of the interrogatory to which you do not object or to which you do not decline to answer. If you object to an interrogatory on the grounds that to provide an answer would constitute an undue burden, provide such requested information as can be supplied without undertaking an undue burden. For those portions of any interrogatory to which you object or otherwise decline to answer, state the reason for such objection or declination.
D. The applicable period of time, unless otherwise provided, shall be from _____ to the date of answering these interrogatories.
E. If any answer is refused in whole or in part, on the basis of a claim of privilege or exemption, state the following:
   (1) the nature of the privilege or exemption claimed;
   (2) the general nature of the matter withheld (e.g., substance of conversation of the withheld information, name of originator);
   (3) name(s) of person(s) to whom the information has been imparted; and
   (4) the extent, if any, to which the information will be provided subject to the privilege or exemption.

FIGURE 10–3
Instructions.

an expert will not be called to testify, this information is not discoverable. It is protected by the work product privilege.

2. Interrogatories to Establish Facts. Some of the questions in any set of interrogatories will seek to uncover facts surrounding the allegations in the pleadings. These questions should always be aimed at the most recent pleading filed by the opposition. Thus, if the plaintiff has filed an amended complaint, that amended complaint becomes the target of the fact-finding interrogatories, rather than the original complaint. Fact-finding interrogatories should cover the who, what, when, where, why,

State the name, business address, title, and qualifications of each and every person whom you intend to or may call as an expert witness during the trial of this case. With respect to each such expert, state the following information:

(a) Describe in detail the subject matter about which he is expected to testify;

(b) Each and every mental impression and opinion held by the expert with respect to this lawsuit and all facts known by the expert (regardless of when the actual knowledge was acquired) that relate to or form the basis of such mental impressions and opinions;

(c) The style, case number, and court of each and every case in which such expert has previously provided expert testimony, whether by deposition or at trial;

(d) List and describe completely all facts provided to the expert witness for his use in connection with his analysis of all or any portion of the issues in this case. For any such facts that are in document form, you may instead attach a copy of such document to your response to these interrogatories; and

(e) If the expert has submitted a report, please recite verbatim all contents thereof or, if you prefer, a copy of same may be attached to your response to these interrogatories.

FIGURE 10–4
Expert Witness
Interrogatory.

and how of the allegations. This is known as seeking the "five W's and an H." Figure 10–5 lists possible subject categories of questions directed to the plaintiff in the Merchants Grocery case.

3. Interrogatories that Identify Documents. Interrogatories that are directed at uncovering documents may seek information about medical reports, medical bills, earning statements, and income tax returns. Such questions may also seek to discover any statements received or given in connection with the accident. Pleadings and prior discovery are additional documents that interrogatories may ask about.

4. Interrogatories that Identify Contentions. Rule 33 of the Federal Rules of Civil Procedure permits interrogatories to ask for "an opinion or contention that relates to fact or the application of law to fact." This is a crucial part of the interrogatories because it requires the disclosure of not only the contention, but also the basis for that contention. For example, in the Merchants Grocery case, your interrogatories might seek the following contention.

Do you contend that Defendant, Merchants Grocery, was negligent by failing to maintain safe premises for its customers?

If so, please state:

Identification of Parties
Identification of Witnesses
Identification of Expert Witnesses
Identification of Statements Given
Insurance Coverage
    Company
    Type of Coverage
    Amount
Physical and Emotional Condition of Party
    Events Leading up to Accident
    Physical Handicaps
    Visual Impairments
    Medical or Alcohol Consumption
    Type of Clothing and Shoes
    Articles in Hands
Accident Site
    Floor Condition
    Foreign Objects on Floor
    Construction or Maintenance
Physical Evidence
    Photographs
    Inspection of Site
    Witness and Fact Statements
Possible Causes of Accident
Medical Treatment Received
    Doctors
    Hospital
    Ambulance
    X-ray
    Lab
    Nurses
Medical Reports and Records
Injuries
    Nature
    Prognosis-Extent of Disability
Damages
    Medical Expenses
    Lost Wages
Previous Accidents
    Describe
    Identify Parties Who Rendered Medical Treatment
    Injuries
    Extent of Disability
Duty of Care
Breach of Duty

FIGURE 10–5
Subject Categories—Slip and Fall Interrogatories.

a. On what do you base your contention?
b. What is the identity of every person who has knowledge or information relating to those facts?
c. Whether any statements have been given by persons you identified in (b) above relating to those facts.

d.   What is the identity of any documents or evidence that you believe support your contention?

The answers to these questions may not be obvious early in the lawsuit. Therefore, this type of question is of greater value in a set of interrogatories filed toward the end of the discovery process.

Summary Paragraph.   No matter how careful you are in drafting interrogatories, you will not cover all the information you will need to help your client in the lawsuit. A summary paragraph can be used to request any information that may be relevant to the suit. Such a summary question might read, "Do you have any additional information relevant to the subject of the lawsuit which has not been previously covered in your foregoing answers to these interrogatories? If so, please state that information." There are problems, however, with using this type of summary question. While there is no harm in asking such a question, the responding party may object on the grounds that it is either overbroad or vague.

Signature and Certificate of Service.   At the end of the specific questions, a signature line for the attorney and the firm's address should be included. Following the signature block, a certificate of service sets out the date, type of service, and to whom service of the interrogatories was made. Interrogatories are not filed in the federal court. You should consult your state and local rules to determine if filing is necessary in your jurisdiction. Figure 10–6 is a checklist for the paralegal's use in drafting interrogatories.

Motion to Compel

Usually the party responding to the interrogatories will cooperate fully. If there are objections to certain questions, such objections can frequently be resolved on a friendly basis. However, there are times when the other party does not cooperate. The motion to compel can help remedy this situation.

Once the opposing party 's answers are received, you should promptly read each answer, review the objections, and note any answer that is incomplete, unclear, evasive, or non-responsive. Your attorney will decide whether an informal effort will be made to obtain the missing information or to clarify the problem areas. A follow-up set of interrogatories may be all that is required. However, if agreement cannot be reached between the parties, you may be asked to draft a motion to compel.

Rule 37 of the Federal Rules of Civil Procedure allows for the filing of a motion to compel the uncooperative party to respond to the interrogatories. Sanctions are available under Rule 37 if the

1. Read the documents—correspondence, pleadings, statements, documents produced, etc.
2. Understand what the attorney wishes to accomplish with this particular set of interrogatories.
3. Read the pertinent court rules to determine such items as format and number of interrogatories permitted.
4. Consult form interrogatories.
5. Draft preliminary portions of request: title of document, introductory paragraph, definitions and instructions, including time covered, continuing nature of interrogatories, procedure to be followed for objections, and permission for the party to provide a document instead of describing same.
6. Draft interrogatories that are directed to your facts and issues. Remember to identify facts and expert witnesses and documents that form the basis for the party's allegations or defenses. Include interrogatories that ask for legal and factual contentions.
7. Keep the interrogatories simple.
8. Organize interrogatories into categories.
9. Make certain the interrogatories ask the who, what, when, why, where, and how questions.
10. Request all facts relied upon in the last pleading filed.
11. Interrogatories should not be excessive in length or number.
12. Read the interrogatories for possible objections. Revise to avoid objections, if possible.
13. Proofread carefully prior to submitting to attorney for review, signature, and execution of certificate of service.
14. Arrange for service and filing, if necessary.
15. Calendar the answer date and follow up for same.
16. Consult with the attorney regarding the possibility of filing a motion to compel.

FIGURE 10–6
Tips for Drafting
Interrogatories.

responding party fails to properly and completely answer the interrogatories. Normally the courts are reluctant to grant sanctions unless efforts have been made by the parties to resolve the problem.

10–3 DRAFTING ANSWERS TO INTERROGATORIES

Like all other forms of discovery, responding to interrogatories requires patient and careful planning. Since your client is responsible for answering the questions, it is essential that he or she be contacted immediately upon the receipt of a set of interrogatories. Working with the client, you can then determine how much time is needed to respond, how each question should be answered, which questions must be supplemented, which questions are best answered with business records, and which questions require objections.

Determining Time Limits

As soon as your office receives a set of interrogatories you should contact the client and forward a copy of those interrogatories to him or her. Remember that the deadline for responding is normally thirty days after the interrogatories have been received. In the case of the defendant the period may be forty-five days, if the interrogatories were served with the summons and the complaint. Whatever the case, time will be short. Most interrogatories cannot be answered quickly. Therefore you will have to consult with the client to determine if the time allowed is realistic. If you and the client conclude that more time is required, your attorney will have to negotiate an extension of that time period. It is important to take care of this immediately, because in some jurisdictions the failure to respond on time may waive the right to object to any interrogatory for which a proper objection might have been made in a timely fashion. Figure 10–7 is a checklist for use in drafting interrogatory answers.

Answering the Interrogatories

Interrogatories directed to an individual must be answered by that individual in writing under oath. Interrogatories addressed to a corporation may be answered by any officer, agent, or employee who has the requested information.

1. Calendar deadline for answering interrogatories. Place several interim reminders into the system.
2. Send a copy of the interrogatories to the client and schedule a meeting to begin working on the answers.
3. Make another copy of interrogatories. Put one interrogatory on a page for drafting purposes. Place a copy of each interrogatory into a file. Any information or documents received that relate to that interrogatory should be placed in the file also.
4. Note on the individual interrogatories the names of individuals who might have the information to answer the interrogatory and the location of that information.
5. Review pleadings file for any previous answers to avoid contradictions.
6. Review possible objections to interrogatories.
7. Draft interrogatory answers after information is received from the client.
8. Review with client and attorney. Arrange for signing, filing, if necessary, and service of interrogatories.
9. Remember to update interrogatory answers.

FIGURE 10–7
Checklist for Drafting Interrogatory Answers.

Form of the Answers. The client is responsible for answering the interrogatories. The client normally supplies the information to the attorney or the paralegal, who drafts the answers. Each interrogatory must be answered separately, in writing. The answers should be **engrossed** by restating the interrogatory to be answered. The form of the answer must duplicate the interrogatory. For example, if the interrogatory contains six sub-parts, the answer contains six sub-parts. Some states, notably California, do not require that answers be engrossed. There is no rule that requires the answers to be complete sentences. Your attorney decides matters of writing style.

Content of the Answers. A party answering the interrogatories has a duty to make a reasonable investigation to obtain all information requested. Interrogatory answers must be straightforward and complete. On some occasions, however, you may need to qualify a response or indicate that the answer is unknown at this time. If the answer is unknown at the response time, you may state that fact and supplement the answers later if so required. If you do not answer a question because of lack of sufficient information, you must include the reason for failing to answer. If the answer to an interrogatory has been given in a previous response, you may refer to that prior response. All hearsay information should be designated accordingly. This can be done by beginning the answer with a qualifying statement such as, "I have no personal knowledge, but have been informed by . . ." A qualified response such as, "Upon information and belief . . ." should be adopted if you are not sure of your information or source.

You should disclose as little harmful information as possible. However, you must never deliberately conceal information that is requested in an interrogatory. Your attorney's role is to place the client in the best possible light in each answer without either distorting or misrepresenting the facts. One word of caution is appropriate here. Interrogatory answers are admissible only against the interest of the responding party. This means that you cannot use your client's answers to prove the facts in your case. However, because your client was under oath, the opposition may use them to impeach the testimony of your client. Naturally, not all interrogatories can be used in this fashion. Some interrogatories ask for relevant but inadmissible information.

Fulfilling the Duty to Supplement

Federal and state rules may vary on the duty of a party to supplement interrogatory answers. In federal court, the following situations require that interrogatory answers be supplemented:

1. Answers to questions addressing the identity and location of persons with knowledge of the case and the identity and opinions of experts; or
2. When a party obtains information that shows a previous response was incorrect when made or the response, though correct when made, is no longer true and failure to amend would amount to "knowing concealment"; or
3. By order of the court or by agreement of the parties.

Because the duty to supplement interrogatory answers is a statutory requirement, your attorney will determine when updated answers are needed. However, you can assist in supplementing answers by maintaining a file on interrogatories which may need to be updated.

Using Business Records Instead of a Written Response

Rule 33 of the Federal Rules of Civil Procedure provides for an alternative to answering an interrogatory in writing. A responding party may identify specific documents where information might be found that would answer the question. The responding party must also pull the information together, identify the particular documents that answer the question, and give the other party the opportunity to review those documents.

Objecting to Interrogatories

Objections to interrogatories may be served with the answers or in a separate pleading. As might be expected, the same objections that are available in response to the other discovery devices are available in response to interrogatories. Rule 33 of the Federal Rules of Civil Procedure does require that objections be signed by the attorney. As noted in previous chapters, the grounds for such objections include arguing that the answer to a particular question would provide information that is protected by the attorney-client privilege or the work product privilege. You may also argue that an interrogatory is irrelevant, overbroad, vague, or unintelligible. Another objection is that the interrogatories are unduly burdensome.

The Attorney-Client Privilege and the Work Product Privilege.
Recall that the attorney-client privilege seeks to protect any and all types of communication between the attorney and the client. In the same way, the work product privilege protects letters, notes, memos, documents, records, and other items that are prepared by

engrossed
Restating the interrogatory to be answered.

an attorney in anticipation of a lawsuit. Should an interrogatory ask for information that would violate either of these privileges an objection can be raised.

Inadmissible and Irrelevant Evidence.   As we saw earlier in this chapter, the scope of discovery is much broader than the scope of evidence that can be presented at trial. Still, even the search for evidence during discovery has its limits. Any interrogatory must be reasonably calculated to lead to admissible evidence. If the answer to an interrogatory cannot be reasonably calculated to lead to admissible evidence, you may object to it. Also, should an interrogatory ask for information that is irrelevant to the subject matter of the lawsuit, you may object on that basis.

Overbroad, Vague, and Unintelligible Interrogatories.   An overbroad interrogatory is one that is not narrowly defined and that is, therefore, difficult, if not impossible, to answer. A vague interrogatory is one that does not clarify exactly what information is sought. An unintelligible interrogatory is one that cannot be understood. All provide appropriate grounds for an objection.

Unduly Burdensome Objections.   The exact definition of an **unduly burdensome** set of interrogatories is elusive. Generally the courts will ask the following questions to determine whether a set of interrogatories is unduly burdensome:

1. Will an excessive amount of time be required to answer the questions?
2. Will the expenses involved in finding the answers be excessive?
3. Does the question seek information for which there is no compelling need?
4. Will the burden placed on the responding party outweigh the benefit gained by the requesting party?
5. Has the information already been disclosed in other discovery requests?

The more of these questions to which the court can say "yes," the more likely it is that the interrogatories will be found to be unduly burdensome.

Confidentiality Agreements and Protective Orders.   As noted in previous chapters, often a lawsuit will involve matters that one party will want to keep as secret as possible. For example, one party may have a trade secret that needs protection or a customer list that it

---

unduly burdensome
An objection to answering a set of interrogatories because of such factors as an excessive amount of time required to answer, excessive expenses involved in finding the answer to the interrogatories, a request for information for which there is no compelling need, placing a burden on the responding party that outweighs the benefit gained by the requesting party, and disclosure of information that has already been disclosed in other discovery requests.

en camera
A private viewing by the judge to determine the validity of the objection based on privileged information or work product.

wants to keep as confidential as possible. Such limitations can be imposed voluntarily through a confidentiality agreement or by a court decree through a protective order. Interrogatories that seek information covered by a protective order or a confidentiality agreement should be answered in accordance with the terms of the order or agreement.

Burden of Proof. The party objecting to an interrogatory has the burden to prove the validity of the objection. Thus, the specific and particular grounds for the objection must be explained. The amount of detail required to sustain an objection in a hearing varies, depending on the nature of the objection. An objection based on privileged information or work product may be resolved by the judge's inspection of the documents **en camera**, a private viewing by the judge to determine the validity of the objection.

THE COMPUTERIZED LAW FIRM—Using a Macro

SCENARIO

Your attorney has asked you to draft the interrogatories in the Merchants Grocery case. You are about to begin working on the project when she calls you into her office and tells you that one of the other paralegals in the firm has just called in sick. Your fellow paralegal was also working on several sets of interrogatories that your attorney needs by 1:00 p.m. She asks that you draft not only the interrogatories for Mrs. Mason but also the ones on which the absent paralegal was working. You take a look at the preliminary work that has been done on the interrogatories and you see that many of the parts of each are repeated in each set. For example, you note that the caption of the case, several form interrogatories, the certificate of service, and the law firm's signature block are all repeated with only minor variations.

PROBLEM

It will be very time-consuming and quite repetitive to have to retype all of these nearly identical parts. The problem is compounded by the fact that you must have all three sets completed by 1:00 p.m. Is there any shortcut that you can take that will allow you to complete all three sets of interrogatories in the allotted time frame?

SOLUTION

WordPerfect offers a time-saving device for the creation of repetitive forms of discovery, including interrogatories. This time-saving device is known as a macro. A macro will store frequently used keystrokes that make up phrases or paragraphs. If your law firm has WordPerfect word processing software, you may find that a macro file has been established. Usually, the firm will have on file a list of all macros along with a printout of the particular macro that will facilitate the drafting of the repetitive parts of interrogatories. The printouts of the individual macros should be filed alphabetically, with a master index to facilitate easy and rapid retrieval. If you need assistance in locating the name of a particular macro, WordPerfect's List Files menu permits a user to view the names of all macros that have been created. Advanced legal application manuals and a technical 800 hotline will assist you in creating useful macros for interrogatories and other repetitive forms of discovery.

SUMMARY

10-1   Interrogatories are written questions submitted by one party to another party. The responding party must answer these questions in writing and under oath. Rule 33 of the Federal Rules of Civil Procedure regulates the use of interrogatories in federal courts. Answers sought by interrogatories must be relevant to the pending lawsuit. However, those answers need not be admissible at the time of the trial, as long as they are reasonably calculated to lead to the discovery of evidence that can be submitted at trial. The primary purpose of interrogatories is to obtain information on the basic facts in a case including any other people who may be involved in the lawsuit. Interrogatories may also be used to determine the party's contentions and to locate relevant documents. A set of interrogatories may also disclose the identities of both lay and expert witnesses that the other party intends to call to the stand at trial. Interrogatories offer substantial advantages over other discovery methods. However, they also have distinct disadvantages.

10-2   Most jurisdictions will require a title, an introductory paragraph, definitions, instructions, specific interrogatories, signature, and certificate of service. Several types of interrogatories may be asked. Each of these is designed to elicit different forms of information related to the lawsuit. These special interrogatories include interrogatories that identify people, interrogatories that establish facts or lead to the discovery of facts, interrogatories that identify documents, and interrogatories that identify contentions.

10–3 Since the client is responsible for answering the questions, it is essential that he or she be contacted immediately upon the receipt of a set of interrogatories. Working with the client, the paralegal can then determine how much time is needed to respond, how each question should be answered, which questions must be supplemented, and which questions are best answered with business records.

KEY TERMS

en camera

engrossed

interrogatories

unduly burdensome

QUESTIONS FOR REVIEW AND DISCUSSION

1. What are interrogatories?
2. What are the purposes of filing interrogatories on the opposing party?
3. What are the advantages of using interrogatories?
4. What are the disadvantages of using interrogatories?
5. What is the proper form for a set of interrogatories?
6. What are the specific types of interrogatories that can be asked?
7. What options are available to the requesting party should the responding party refuse to answer an interrogatory?
8. When is it necessary for the responding party to supplement an answer to an interrogatory?
9. When would the responding party substitute a business record instead of filing a written answer to an interrogatory?
10. What objections to interrogatories can be raised by the responding party?

ACTIVITIES

1. Review any state rules that relate to interrogatories. Check local court rules to see if there are any restrictions on the number of interrogatories and or the number of sets of interrogatories that can be filed in a lawsuit.
2. Prepare a chart of the objections to interrogatories that are permitted in the federal and state courts in your area.

CHAPTER 10 PROJECT— DRAFTING INTERROGATORIES

In your state's form book, locate a sample set of interrogatories for a case involving the type of accident that occurs in the Merchants Grocery case. Draft a set of interrogatories to the plaintiff Marilyn Mason, in which you request all information relating to the accident. Also request information relating to the identity of all experts who will be called to testify at trial. Include questions on the subject matter about which each expert will testify, all opinions that each expert has on the matter, the case number and court of each case in which each expert has testified, and all facts provided to each expert witness for use in the analysis of the case. Also request a copy of any reports the expert witness has prepared in connection with the case.

CHAPTER 11
Physical and Mental Examinations

OUTLINE

COMMENTARY—THE SHIRER CASE

Your attorney has decided to take a personal injury case. She has called you into her office to explain the details of the case. It seems that her client, Patrick Shirer, was struck and injured by an automobile driven by the defendant, Dana Sedgewick. The complaint has already been filed, and the defendant has responded. Discovery has also begun. Ms. Sedgewick's attorney has asked your client to submit to a medical examination. Your attorney suspects that the opposing attorney in the case is going to try to prove that some of your client's alleged injuries are not as serious as he contends. Your attorney has also asked Ms. Sedgewick to undergo a medical examination. This decision was made because your attorney has evidence that the accident may have occurred because Ms. Sedgewick had failed to take her medication and, as a result, had an epileptic seizure that made her lose control of the vehicle. Ms. Sedgewick, however, has repeatedly denied having any form of epilepsy. Your attorney has asked you to cooperate with the opposing counsel in scheduling Mr. Shirer's examination. She also asks for you to arrange for Ms. Sedgewick's medical exam.

OBJECTIVES

Chapters 8, 9, and 10 introduced two specialized types of discovery, depositions and interrogatories. The request for physical or mental examination is another effective tool in the discovery process. After reading this chapter, you will be able to:

1. Define physical and mental examination.
2. Outline four types of cases in which the physical and mental examination may be used.
3. Explain the purposes for requesting a physical or mental examination.
4. Outline the procedure for obtaining a physical or mental examination if the parties cannot agree to the examination.
5. Define the concepts of "good cause" and "in controversy."
6. Relate the responsibilities a paralegal might perform in the physical and mental examination process.
7. Determine the possible consequences of a party's refusal to submit to a physical or mental examination.

11-1   THE PHYSICAL AND MENTAL EXAMINATION

A **physical or mental examination** is the examination of a party in a lawsuit to determine factual information about the physical or mental condition of that party. Such an examination is used when that physical or mental condition is an important factor in a lawsuit. One party to a lawsuit can request that the other party undergo a physical or mental examination. The request can be made even if the party who is to undergo the examination is a minor, in the custody of a parent, or a legally incapacitated person under the legal control of a guardian. Physical and mental examinations will, by their very nature, invade the privacy of the person undergoing the examination. For this reason, among others, this discovery tool is used only in certain types of cases.

Types of Cases Using Physical or Mental Examinations

Physical and mental examinations are often used in personal injury cases. In such cases, the physical or mental condition of a party can be very important in establishing the personal liability of the defendant or in determining the extent of the injuries suffered by the plaintiff. For example, in the Shirer case your attorney has requested a physical examination to determine whether or not Ms. Sedgewick has epilepsy. Since your attorney has alleged that Ms. Sedgewick's failure to take her medication contributed to the accident and since Ms. Sedgewick denies being epileptic, a physical examination would be in order here. On the other hand, Ms. Sedgewick's attorney has asked Mr. Shirer to undergo a physical examination to determine whether his alleged injuries are really as serious as he contends.

Physical or mental examinations are not limited to personal injury cases, however. A physical exam might be requested to confirm the extent of the injuries in an industrial accident case. Such an examination may also be requested to determine the identity of the father of a child in a paternity suit or to establish whether a plaintiff is eligible for payments under the terms of a disability insurance policy. Whether or not an examination will be requested often depends upon the purpose that the attorneys have in mind when they are planning the legal strategy in a lawsuit.

Reasons for Allowing Physical and Mental Examinations

One reason the law allows physical and mental examinations is to establish the truth about the plaintiff's allegation of physical or mental injuries. For example, in the Shirer case, if Mr. Shirer claims to have a pinched nerve as the result of the car accident, a physical examination could help determine whether or not he is telling the truth. Another reason for permitting physical and mental examinations is to discourage plaintiffs who have filed false or exaggerated claims. When plaintiffs are told that they must undergo a physical or a mental exam, they may decide to drop the suit rather than risk exposure as a fraud. In fact, the very existence of a rule allowing such examinations may deter the initial filing of fraudulent or exaggerated lawsuits. If a potential plaintiff finds out that the court may order a physical examination, that potential plaintiff may decide not to file that fictitious or exaggerated claim. One final reason for allowing such examinations is to uncover inconsistencies between a plaintiff's subjective complaints and the objective nature of the injury. In the Shirer case, for instance, Mr. Shirer may complain of severe back pain. An examination could uncover whether there is an objective medical condition causing that pain.

physical or mental examination
  The examination of a party in a lawsuit to determine factual information about the physical or mental condition of that party.

11–2 FILING A MOTION FOR COMPULSORY EXAMINATION

Most physical and mental examinations are scheduled by mutual agreement of the attorneys for the parties. In such cases this mutual agreement should be set out in a letter or formal stipulation filed with the court. If agreement cannot be reached, however, a formal **motion for compulsory examination** will be necessary. Such a motion must establish good cause for the requested physical or mental examination. Figure 11–1 is an example of a motion for compulsory examination.

RAYFIELD COUNTY COURT

PATRICK SHIRER,	)
	) Civil Action No. 93-61491
Plaintiff,	)
	) MOTION FOR PHYSICAL
v.	) EXAMINATION
	)
DANA SEDGEWICK	)
	)
Defendant.	)
	)
	)
	)
_____	)

TO THE HONORABLE JUDGE OF SAID COURT:
COMES NOW Dana Sedgewick, the Defendant in the above cause, and files this Motion under Rule 35 of the State Rules of Civil Procedure, to require Patrick Shirer, the Plaintiff in the above cause, to submit to a physical examination by Andrew Altick, M.D., at 9785 Lorain Avenue, in the city of Spartanville, and respectfully show the Court as follows:

I.
This is a case in which the Plaintiff alleges that he suffered permanent and disabling injuries as a result of an automobile accident on May 27, 1992, in the city of Athens in this state. The Plaintiff alleges that said accident was directly and proximately caused by the negligence of the Defendant.

II.
Defendant denies the allegations made by the Plaintiff concerning his injuries and disabilities. Accordingly, the physical condition of the Plaintiff is in controversy.

III.
Defendant has heretofore requested the Plaintiff to submit to a voluntary examination, and that request has been denied.

FIGURE 11–1
Motion for a Physical Examination.

IV.
Defendant requests that the Plaintiff be ordered by the Court to submit to an independent medical examination at the offices of Andrew Altick, M.D., 9785 Lorain Avenue, in the city of Spartanville in this state, on March 25, 1993, at 2 p.m.

WHEREFORE, the Defendant herein, prays that the court grant this Motion in all respects and award all other and further relief to which Defendant is justly entitled.

Respectfully submitted,

_____

Ruth Montgomery
Attorney for Defendant

Certificate of Service

I hereby certify that a true and correct copy of the foregoing Motion for Physical Examination has been furnished to counsel of record on this the twenty-first day of February, 1993.

_____

FIGURE 11–1
(continued)

Rule 35(a) of the Federal Rules of Civil Procedure details the prerequisites for the content of a motion requesting an order for a physical or a mental examination. The party requesting the examination is responsible for giving notice to the person to be examined as well as to all the other parties or their attorneys. **Notice** is a formal written notification to the person to be examined and to the other parties. The moving papers, which are filed with the court and which give notice to the other party and the examiner, must specify the time, place, manner, conditions, scope of the examination, and the name of the person conducting the examination.

The motion must be specific. In the Shirer case, for example, a broad request for Ms. Sedgewick to undergo "neurological testing" would be too vague and may not be ordered by the court. The particular test or tests required should be stated. For example, instead of simply asking for "neurological testing," the motion would ask the court to compel Ms. Sedgewick to submit to a CAT scan at a particular time and place.

motion for compulsory examination
A motion asking the court to order a requested physical or mental examination.

notice
A formal, written notification to the person to be examined and to the other parties.

11-3 REQUIREMENTS FOR GRANTING THE MOTION FOR A COMPULSORY EXAMINATION

Rule 35 of the Federal Rules of Civil Procedure sets down the conditions under which a motion for a physical or mental examination will be granted by the trial judge. The rule gives the trial judge total discretion in determining whether the request for a physical or mental examination meets two essential requirements. These requirements are that there is "good cause" for the examination and that the nature of the condition is "in controversy."

Evidence of Good Cause

As noted earlier, both a physical and a mental examination will, by necessity, invade the privacy of the person submitting to the examination. For this reason, the courts tend to define good cause very strictly. In general, the court will decide that **good cause** exists to order such an examination only if the same information cannot be found in any other way. Still, good cause is a flexible concept that varies from one case to another and from one type of examination to another. For example, in the Shirer case, because the physical condition of Mr. Shirer is an important aspect of the case, the need for an examination is obvious. This may not be true in other lawsuits, such as one involving the question of whether a person was mentally competent to enter a contract.

THE COMPUTERIZED LAW FIRM—The Administrative Database

SCENARIO

You have been given a last-minute assignment in the Shirer case by your attorney. She has just met with Dr. David Weinstein of the Euclid Clinic. Dr. Weinstein has turned over to your attorney a complete set of medical records for Mr. Shirer. Your attorney has handed over the record to you and has asked you to organize the material so that she can dig into the file and quickly retrieve information by date, by the name of the attending physician, by injury, or by the name of various medications.

PROBLEM

The file your attorney hands you is at least an inch thick. You are at a loss as to where to begin organizing the records. As you glance through the file you realize that Mr. Shirer has been treated by six different physicians, has been a patient in four different hospitals for a total of ten weeks, and has been given eight different medications. Sorting all this out in the time allotted seems to be an impossible task. How will you solve the problem?

SOLUTION

If your law firm has a general database for its administrative functions you can use this database to prepare for Mr. Shirer's physical examination. Your firm may even have a simple software program for litigation applications. Information that should be captured for future litigation purposes includes the dates of all visits to the doctor, the name of each doctor, the names and quantities of all medications taken, the medical problem for which each medication was prescribed, the doctor prescribing the medications, the dates and places of all hospitalizations, the attending physicians and nurses, the medication and the treatment received in the hospital, the patient's discharge date, and the nurses' and doctors' notes relating to the patient. Inputting all this data into the computer will assist your attorney in preparing for the medical examination. It may also indicate any problem areas such as potential drug addictions or the failure to follow a doctor's orders for future therapy and exercise. Once the data is in the computer your attorney will be able to quickly retrieve information by date, by the name of the attending physician, by injury, or by the name of various medications. Appendix B lists software packages that will assist you in the area of requests for physical and mental examinations.

Condition in Controversy

Rule 35 also requires that the physical or mental condition to be examined by the medical professional must be in controversy. To be **in controversy**, the condition to be examined must be at the heart of the dispute. For example, a request for an order compelling a plaintiff to submit to a blood test would have nothing to do with a claim that his or her injuries prevent the performance of certain types of work. Such a request would not be ordered. In contrast, a request for an order to compel a defendant in a paternity suit to undergo a blood test to determine whether he could be the father of a child would be at the heart of the dispute. Such a request would be granted. Similarly, a request for a mental examination would not be granted if neither mental nor emotional injuries have been alleged. However, if a plaintiff claims to be the victim of intentionally caused emotional distress, a mental

good cause
Sufficient cause for a court to order a physical and mental examination in a case.

in controversy
A requirement that the condition to be examined in a physical or mental examination must be at the heart of the dispute in the case.

examination would be appropriate. In the Shirer case, since your attorney intends to prove that Ms. Sedgewick's alleged epilepsy contributed to the accident and since Ms. Sedgewick has denied having epilepsy, the matter is in controversy. Similarly, the extent of Mr. Shirer's injuries is also in controversy.

11–4 GRANTING A MOTION FOR A COMPULSORY EXAMINATION

As noted above, Rule 35 gives the trial judge total discretion to decide if the party seeking a physical or mental examination has good cause for the request and whether the examination involves a condition in controversy. This discretion, however, does not mean that the moving party must prove his case on the merits as he would have to do at a trial. Nor does this discretion automatically mean that a hearing will be held prior to entry of an order for the examination. In some cases a hearing may be required. In others, the judge may decide these requirements have been met on the basis of an affidavit filed by the attorney or a physician who believes that the examination is vital to establishing the claims or defenses of the case.

If the court decides to grant the motion for the compulsory examination, then it will issue an order compelling the party to submit to the examination. Usually when the party seeking the order files the original motion, a proposed order will be included at the same time. Figure 11–2 is a sample form of a proposed order for entry by the trial judge. The judge may or may not enter the proposed order as submitted. In fact, the judge could even change the number or the type of examinations asked for in the motion. For instance, in the Shirer case, the judge might order several examinations of Mr. Shirer to determine the nature and the extent of his injuries. The court also has the authority to order subsequent examinations if it feels the facts require further validation. In the Shirer case, for example, part of Ms. Sedgewick's defense may be that Mr. Shirer's problems stem from a previous industrial accident and not from his collision with her automobile. In such a case the judge might order several examinations to help validate or invalidate that defense.

11–5 THE PARALEGAL'S ROLE IN PHYSICAL AND MENTAL EXAMINATIONS

Your role as the paralegal in the request for a physical or a mental examination will depend upon whether your attorney or the opposing attorney has requested such an examination.

Arranging for the Examination of an Opposing Party

If your attorney has requested an examination of an opposing party, you may be asked to schedule the actual examination. In such a situation, you should contact the opposing counsel to see if there are any objections to the examination. If the other party is not agreeable, you may be asked to draft the motion for compulsory physical exam and a proposed order, as shown in Figure 11–2.

RAYFIELD COUNTY COURT

PATRICK SHIRER,	)
	) Civil Action No. 93-61491
Plaintiff,	)
	) ORDER
v.	)
	)
DANA SEDGEWICK,	)
	)
Defendant.	)
	)
	)
_____	)

This matter being heard on Defendant's Motion to compel the physical examination of Plaintiff, all parties having been given notice, and the court having heard arguments, it is hereby ordered that:

1. Plaintiff Patrick Shirer be examined by Andrew Altick, M.D., at 9785 Lorain Avenue, in the city of Spartanville in this state, on March 25, 1993, at 2 p.m. unless the Plaintiff and Dr. Altick mutually agree to an earlier date and time.

2. Plaintiff shall submit to such neurological examinations and tests as are necessary to diagnose and evaluate Plaintiff's back and legs, so that Dr. Altick can reach opinions and conclusions about the extent of any injuries, their origin, and prognosis.

3. Dr. Altick shall prepare a written report detailing his findings, test results, diagnosis, prognosis, and opinions along with any similar reports on the same conditions, and deliver it to Defendant's attorneys on or before March 25, 1993.

Signed this 28th day of February, 1993.

_____
JUDGE

FIGURE 11–2
Order.

Fortunately, however, most physical and mental examinations are conducted by voluntary arrangement. If your attorney has requested the examination, it will normally be conducted by a physician of his or her choice, unless the party to be examined has a valid objection to that selection. This selection is not an absolute right, however. If the parties cannot agree on a physician, the court will make the selection. Check your local court rules to determine if they include an approved list of impartial experts from whom the examining physician must be selected.

Convenience should be a major criterion in the selection. If the party to be examined lives in Albany, New York, and the party requesting the examination selects a physician in New York City, the court could refuse to approve the physician selected. Parties may, however, be required to come to the city where the suit is filed for the physical or mental examination, even though they reside in another city.

Assuming that everyone involved is agreeable up to this point, your next job would be to contact the physician or laboratory to discuss the purpose of the examination and the nature of the case. Arrangements for payment of the physician or laboratory should also be discussed at the time of the initial contact.

Following the examination, you should contact the physician or laboratory and request a copy of the report. Once you have received the report, review it with the attorney and, when the report has been approved, pay the physician or the laboratory. Remember also to add that amount to the client's ledger for billing. Your attorney will direct when and where a copy of the medical report should be sent. Your attorney may also ask you to review the medical report and prepare a summary by chronology of events or category of injury. The fact that you have received a written report from the physician who examined the opposing party does not affect your attorney's ability to depose the examining physician. The independent examination under Rule 35 is not a substitute for discovery through a deposition or other available discovery tool.

Preparing the Client for an Examination

If your client has been requested to undergo a physical or mental examination, you should notify the client immediately. Your attorney will have explained to the client in the initial interview that such an examination is possible. However, the client may have some apprehension about the actual examination. Explaining the purpose and procedure to be utilized may give the client some comfort. This explanation can take the form of a letter to the client setting out the details concerning the examination. Figure 11–3 is an example of such a letter to the client.

LAUREY, POPOVICH, MONTGOMERY, AND HUDSON
2785 Middleton Avenue
Spartanville, New Jersey 07503

March 4, 1993

Mr. Patrick Shirer
P.O. Box 200
Athens, New Jersey 07506

Dear Mr. Shirer:

You may recall that attorney Hudson mentioned in your initial visit to our office that the other side may request an examination by a physician of their choosing to confirm the existence and the extent of your injuries. Ms. Ruth Dunbar, attorney for defendant Dana Sedgewick, has requested such an examination.

The examination is tentatively scheduled for March 25, 1993, at 2:00 p.m. The examining physician is Dr. Andrew Altick. His office is located at 9785 Lorain Avenue, Spartanville, New Jersey. Please be at his office several minutes prior to that time so that the examination can begin on schedule.

This examination will consist of an examination of your neck and back injuries as well as several diagnostic x-rays. The examination should last no longer than one hour.

Before the examination, you should review the medical recap sheet that you have prepared so that you may respond quickly and correctly to the physician's questions about prior illnesses, injuries, medication, etc.

Please cooperate with the physician, but do not volunteer any information not specifically requested. Do not exaggerate or minimize any medical problem about which you are asked.

Attorney Hudson believes this examination will be beneficial in establishing the damages you have suffered to this date. If you have any questions about the examination, please let me know.

Thanks for your time.

Sincerely,

Paula K. Pepperton

Paula K. Pepperton
Paralegal

FIGURE 11–3
Sample Letter to Client Concerning Physical Examination.

You may be asked to meet with the client prior to the examination and review the types of information he or she can expect to be asked by the physician. Caution your client to refrain from telling the examiner anything he or she has discussed with your attorney. It is also a sound practice to warn your client not to discuss the facts of the case with the examining physician. However, the client should be reminded to review all facets of his or her medical history, including the names of all doctors and hospitals who have treated the patient, the nature of the illness or injury, the names of medications, and the dates of all illnesses, injuries, or hospitalizations. In the Shirer case, for example, Mr. Shirer should not discuss with the physician anything that he has talked over with you or your attorney about the suit he has filed against Ms. Sedgewick. Nor should he discuss the accident itself. He should, however, be prepared to intelligently discuss his own medical history.

If you furnish the client with a medical summary sheet such as in Figure 11–4, it will help the client recall information that will probably be covered in the physical examination. However, the client probably should not take this summary into the examination room. Using such a written record to answer questions in the presence of the examiner may cast some doubt on your client's ability to independently recall his or her own medical history. Such a revelation may hurt your client's credibility, should it somehow come to the jury's attention at trial.

Your client may request that his or her own physician be present during the examination. That request must be made through the opposing attorney. Permission for the examining physician to attend is solely in the discretion of the trial judge, under the provisions of Rule 35. Some states, California, for example, also allow the paralegal to accompany the client.

Sanctions.   Hopefully your client will demonstrate no resistance to submitting to the requested examination. However, if your client does indicate that he or she intends to refuse to submit to the examination, then you should point out that such a refusal carries with it very severe sanctions or penalties.

Permitted sanctions include an order striking all or parts of pleadings, staying the proceedings until the order for the examination is obeyed, entry of a judgment by default against a defendant who refuses to submit to the examination, or the dismissal of a plaintiff's case, if the plaintiff refuses to submit to the examination. Your client may also be ordered to pay the physician's fee if the client fails to appear for an appointment, and it must be rescheduled.

Distributing the Medical Records.   You must be very cautious when asking for a copy of the physician's report or the laboratory test results after the examination of your client has been conducted. This caution is necessary because the discovery provisions of Rule 35 are reciprocal. This means if you request a copy of the report on your client's examination, then the other side can request copies of all reports in your possession that deal with the same condition, regardless of when those reports were made. Because of this, you should consult with your attorney before you

Medical Recap

PHYSICIANS:

Name	Date of Visit	Diagnosis/Treatment
Sergei Gagarin Athens General Hospital 24771 Eastway Drive Athens, New Jersey (609) 433-5656	May 27, 1992	Broken Leg Sprained Neck Concussion
Donald O'Brien Athens General Hospital	May 28, 1992 to June 14, 1992	Treatment for above noted injuries
Donald O'Brien 7786 Broadway Avenue Spartanville, New Jersey (609) 263-9988	June 27, 1992	Cast removed
Karla Bonfiglio 1524 East 310 Street Spartanville, New Jersey (609) 263-7689	June 30, 1992 to September 9, 1992	Physical Therapy

PRESCRIPTIONS:

Name	Date	Drug Prescribed/Reason
Sergei Gagarin Athens General Hospital 24771 Eastway Drive Athens, New Jersey (609) 433-5656	May 27, 1992	Tylenol w/Codeine Pain
Donald O'Brien 7786 Broadway Avenue Spartanville, New Jersey (609) 263-9988	June 27, 1992	Vasotec/Hypertension

HOSPITALS/CLINICS:

Name	Date	Reason for Visit
Athens General Hospital 24771 Eastway Drive Athens, New Jersey (609) 433-5656	May 28, 1992 to June 14, 1992	Treatment for injuries noted above
Medtech Clinic 4444 Flowers Road Athens, New Jersey (609) 263-6714	June 30, 1992 to September 9, 1992	Physical Therapy

LABORATORIES/DIAGNOSTIC SERVICES:

Name/Referring Physician	Date	Service/Reason
Sergei Gagarin Athens General Hospital 24771 Eastway Drive Athens, New Jersey (609) 433-5656	May 28, 1992	Diagnostic X-rays

FIGURE 11–4
Medical Recap.

request a copy of the medical report on your client. Although the reports in your possession do not have to be automatically produced, your request allows the opposing counsel to gain access to them as requested. Your attorney may not want to open that window of opportunity to the opposition. Because of this, you should consult with your attorney before you request a copy of the medical report on your client's examination.

On the other hand, the rules of your state may allow the opposing counsel access to your client's medical records regardless of any request on your part. This is especially true if your client is the plaintiff in a personal injury case. In such a situation you would want to request a copy of the report. Again you should consult with your attorney and check the rules of your particular state before making such a request.

SUMMARY

11–1 A physical and mental examination is the examination of a party to a lawsuit to determine factual information about the physical or mental condition of that party. The request can be made even if the party is a minor, in the custody of a parent, or a legally incapacitated person under the control of a guardian. The examination is a tool used to establish the validity of allegations of mental or physical injuries.

11–2 Most physical and mental examinations are scheduled by mutual agreement. If an agreement cannot be reached, however, a formal motion for a compulsory examination must be filed with the court.

11–3 Rule 35 of the Federal Rules of Civil Procedure sets down the conditions under which a motion for a physical or mental examination will be granted by the trial court. These requirements are that there is "good cause" for the examination and that the nature of the condition is "in controversy."

11–4 The trial judge has total discretion as to whether the party seeking a physical or mental examination has good cause for the request and whether the examination involves a condition in controversy. If the court decides to grant the motion for the examination, it will issue an order compelling the party to submit to the examination.

11–5 The paralegal's role in the request for a physical or mental examination depends on whether the paralegal's attorney or the opposing attorney has requested the examination. The paralegal's role will also depend on whether the examination is proceeding by agreement or by a motion filed with the court.

KEY TERMS

good cause
in controversy
motion for a compulsory
   examination

notice
physical and mental
   examination

QUESTIONS FOR REVIEW AND DISCUSSION

1. Define physical and mental examination.
2. Name four types of cases in which a physical or mental examination might be requested.
3. Identify four reasons why the law allows one party to compel another party to submit to a physical or mental examination.
4. Give an example of a party "in the custody of" or "under the legal control" of another person.
5. Explain the concepts of "good cause" and "in controversy" as they relate to the physical and mental examination.
6. What is the procedure for obtaining a physical or mental examination if the parties cannot agree?
7. Explain the paralegal's role in arranging for the physical or mental examination of an opposing party.
8. Explain the paralegal's role in preparing the client to undergo a physical or mental examination.
9. What are the considerations to be evaluated prior to requesting a copy of the examinee's medical report?
10. What are the possible consequences of a party's refusal to submit to a physical or mental examination ordered by the court?

ACTIVITIES

1. Review the laws of your state and find all state laws that deal with requests for physical and mental examinations. Check your local court rules to see if any local rules of court in your area regulate any aspect of the request for a physical or mental examination.
2. Find the form books in your law library that provide sample forms for use in the drafting of legal documents in your state. Find a sample motion for a physical examination and a sample proposed order compelling such an examination. How do they compare to the samples found in this chapter?

CHAPTER 11 PROJECT—PREPARING THE CLIENT AND ADVISING THE ATTORNEY

Review the Shirer case in the commentary at the beginning of this chapter. Draft a checklist of duties that you expect to assume in preparing Mr. Shirer for his physical examination. Also draft a memo to your attorney exploring the issue of whether you should request a copy of Mr. Shirer's examination results in light of the laws of your particular state.

OUTLINE

COMMENTARY—THE DIETER CASE

The Dieter Financial Bank lent several million dollars to Haubrich Industries so that Haubrich could purchase a French petrochemical plant. In making the loan to Haubrich, Dieter relied on financial statements that were drawn up by the accounting firm of Wellington, Judgson, and Davies. Haubrich defaulted on the loan, and Dieter has retained your firm to bring suit. Your attorney requests that you assist with all discovery matters, including drafting a request to be served on both Haubrich and Wellington, Judgson, and Davies for the production of documents.

OBJECTIVES

In chapters 8, 9, 10, and 11 you were introduced to depositions, interrogatories, and requests for physical and mental examinations. The next discovery technique is the request for documents. After reading this chapter, you will be able to:

1. Define a request for production of documents.
2. Differentiate among the alternative methods of obtaining documents.
3. Determine when a request for production of documents should be served.
4. Identify the different approaches to document requests.
5. Explain the attorney-client privilege and the work product privilege.
6. Determine when confidentiality agreements or protective orders should be sought.
7. Explain what objections are available to prevent the production of documents.
8. Identify the duties of the paralegal in requesting the production of documents.
9. Relate a paralegal's duties in responding to a request for production of documents.
10. Explain the duties of the paralegal in organizing the documents from both sides.
11. Explain when a party can request an inspection of property.

12-1 THE REQUEST FOR DOCUMENTS

A **request for documents** is a request by one party in a lawsuit to another party in that suit to allow the first party access to documents that are relevant to the subject matter of the suit. Besides the formal request for documents there are other discovery procedures for obtaining documents needed for litigation. Before examining the request for documents, we will explore these alternatives.

Alternative Methods of Requesting Documents

In federal court, as well as in many state courts, in addition to using a request for documents, the parties to a lawsuit can request documents at the deposition of a party, or they can use a subpoena duces tecum to compel a non-party to produce documents at the time of a deposition. The use of interrogatories may also result in the production of documents.

Request for Documents at the Deposition of a Party. Documents may be obtained from a party by serving a request for that party to bring those documents to his or her deposition. Rule 30(b)(5) of the Federal Rules of Civil Procedure allows for this alternative. The specific documents or the categories of documents to be produced must be included in the deposition notice of attachment. Figure 12–1 is an example of this.

A request for documents at the deposition of a party is not always the most efficient way to handle document discovery. If an attorney must wait to see the requested documents until the deposition, he or she may have to spend precious time reviewing the documents as the deposition is in progress. Moreover, subsequent examination of the documents often reveals information about which the deponent should have been questioned. This may necessitate scheduling another deposition, which may or may not be allowed by the court.

Subpoenas Duces Tecum for a Non-Party to Produce Documents at a Deposition. A non-party can be subpoenaed to produce documents at his or her deposition according to Rule 45 of the Federal Rules of Civil Procedure. The deposition notice served on the non-party will contain a specific listing of the documents to be produced. That list is repeated in the deposition subpoena served on the non-party. This method of document production is handicapped by the same shortcomings that plague the request for documents at the deposition of a party. If the attorney is viewing the documents for the first time, he or she will waste valuable time at the deposition. Moreover, a later review of the documents may suggest the need to schedule another deposition. Again, the court may or may not allow a second deposition.

Interrogatories and the Production of Documents. Sometimes the use of a set of interrogatories results in the production of

request for documents
A request by one party in a lawsuit to the other party in that suit to allow the first party access to documents that are relevant to the subject matter of the suit.

COURT OF COMMON PLEAS
CUYAHOGA COUNTY
STATE OF OHIO

DIETER FINANCIAL BANK, Plaintiff,	))
	) Civil Action No. 93-77976
	) NOTICE OF TAKING
vs.	) DEPOSITION UPON
	) ORAL EXAMINATION
	)
HAUBRICH INDUSTRIES, et al.,	)
Defendants.	)
	)
	)
	)
	)

TO: Jeremy Wickard, Attorney of Record for Defendant, Haubrich Industries, in the above styled and numbered cause.

Please take notice that the deposition of Helen Haubrich, President and Chief Executive Officer of Haubrich Industries, whose address is 2168 Gibson Industrial Park, Mayfield Heights, Ohio, will be taken upon oral examination on October 31, 1993, beginning at 9 a.m., and continuing from day to day until completed.

The witness is requested to bring with her to the deposition those items in her custody or subject to her custody, care, or control, identified in Exhibit "A" attached hereto.

You are hereby invited to attend and cross-examine.

Respectfully submitted,

_____

Giacomo Striuli
Striuli, Grazak, and Usalis
2233 Hamilton Avenue
Cleveland, Ohio 44119
Attorneys for Plaintiff
Dieter Financial Bank

CERTIFICATE OF SERVICE

I hereby certify that a true and correct copy of the foregoing has been mailed by first class mail, postage prepaid to Jeremy Wickard, 54392 St. Clair Avenue, Cleveland, Ohio, 44118, on this 29th day of September, 1993.

_____

FIGURE 12–1
Request for Production of Documents at Deposition of a Party.

documents. This is because Rule 33(c) of the Federal Rules of Civil Procedure allows a party answering a set of interrogatories to produce business records if the examination of those records will provide the answer to an interrogatory.

Request for Documents to Parties. Despite these other techniques, the request for documents still remains the most efficient and effective way to obtain documents. A request for documents served on a party may be made at the time that the party is originally served with process. If this is the case, then the party has forty-five days to respond to the request. Otherwise, the party has thirty days to respond. The court, however, may shorten or lengthen these time periods. The opposing attorney's response to the request must indicate that his or her client will comply with the request or should indicate the grounds for any objection to the request. Figure 12–2 is an example of the opening paragraph in a request for documents.

In order for the responding party to comply with the request as efficiently as possible, the request must specify with "reasonable particularity" the general categories of documents or the particular documents that the other party wishes to inspect. The request should also specify a reasonable time, place, and manner of production. Naturally the attorneys may alter these arrangements to make the production more convenient to all those involved in the process. The manner of production is also determined by negotiation and agreement between the attorneys. Sometimes the original documents will be required while at other times copies will be sufficient. The Federal Rules of Civil Procedure do not limit the number of requests for production. Several requests may be needed in a complicated lawsuit involving many parties located across the country.

As might be expected, the term "documents" has a wide variety of meanings. Rule 34(a) of the Federal Rules of Civil Procedure defines **documents** to include such diverse items as photographs, graphs, computer printouts, calendars, and accounting records, among others. The scope of the rule extends not only to documents in the actual custody of the party, but also to those documents under the "control" of that party. This means that the requesting party has the right to obtain some documents that are actually in the possession of a third individual, such as the other party's tax consultant. The rule also allows the requesting party to inspect and copy those documents.

documents
Such diverse items as photographs, graphs, computer printouts, calendars, and accounting records.

The paralegal's role in a request for production of documents will depend on whether your attorney has made the request or must help his or her client respond to the request. Often the paralegal will have to fill both roles in the same lawsuit. Thus, you

COURT OF COMMON PLEAS
CUYAHOGA COUNTY
STATE OF OHIO

DIETER FINANCIAL BANK, Plaintiff,	))) Civil Action No. 93-77976) REQUEST FOR) DOCUMENTS)
vs.	))
HAUBRICH INDUSTRIES, et al., Defendants.	))))))

TO: Jeremy Wickard, Attorney of Record for Defendant, Haubrich Industries, in the above styled and numbered cause.

Pursuant to Rule 34 of the Ohio Rules of Civil Procedure, Dieter Financial Bank, plaintiff in the above cause, requests that Haubrich Industries, defendant in the above cause, produce for inspection and copying by Dieter, within thirty days of service hereof or at such other time as may be agreed upon by counsel for the parties, originals or legible copies of the documents requested herein. You are also requested to serve upon plaintiff within thirty (30) days after service of this request a written response in accordance with Rule 34 of the Ohio Rules of Civil Procedure.

FIGURE 12–2 Introductory Paragraph for a Request for Documents.

must know how to review, organize, and analyze the documents that you have received from the other party. However, you must also know how to help your client to produce the documents that the other party has requested.

Preliminary Decisions Regarding Requests for Documents

In the opening commentary, your client, Dieter Financial Bank, has elected to sue a borrower, Haubrich Industries, and the accounting firm of Wellington, Judgson, and Davies, which issued an unqualified opinion about the accuracy of Haubrich's financial records. In this case your attorney will have to make some preliminary decisions regarding any request for documents to be served on the defendant. Two crucial considerations involve the timing of the request and the potential cost of the production of the documents.

Timing of the Request. Rule 34 of the Federal Rules of Civil Procedure allows a request for documents to be served at the same time that the complaint is served. Sometimes your attorney will want to serve the request at this early stage, because he or she will want to use those documents in preparing the questions to be asked at any planned depositions. On the other hand, since your attorney may not know what documents are available, he or she may wish to conduct the deposition first. This approach allows the attorney to ask the deponent what documents are involved in the case. Armed with this information your attorney will be able to draw up a more detailed, specific, and, therefore, productive request.

Cost of the Production. Your attorney should also consider the cost involved in having the documents inspected and reproduced. Since it is possible that your client will have to pay any expenses involved in photocopying, reproducing video or audio tapes, or having duplicate photographs made, your attorney must consider this factor carefully. In fact, it would be advisable to consult with the client and inform him or her of the extra costs that may be involved in the document production request.

Approaches to Document Production

An attorney's approach to document production is based on two factors. When responding to a document request, the attorney must decide on the organizational approach that will best serve his or her purposes. Similarly, the attorney must frequently decide on the number of documents to be produced.

Organization of the Documents. The Federal Rules of Civil Procedure provide that a party producing documents has a choice of two organizational approaches. The documents may be produced either as they are kept in the usual course of business or according to the categories specified in the document request.

Producing the documents as they are kept in the usual course of business requires less time and effort by the responding party. If an enormous amount of information is requested by the other party, this approach would be appropriate. However, do not make the mistake of thinking that the term "in the usual course of business" allows the responding party to shuffle the documents in order to hide pertinent information.

Producing the documents according to the categories in the request requires additional time and effort for the responding party. Still, such an organizational effort can be managed if relatively few documents are requested. Naturally, the party initiating the request usually prefers this approach because it reduces the time and effort required to sift through the documents in an effort to organize and analyze them. Moreover, the party producing the documents may also prefer this technique because it forces him or her to review all the requested documents, lessening the chance of inadvertently revealing privileged documents.

The Number of Documents. The party responding to the request has three options available in producing the documents. These three options are the warehouse approach, the broad production approach, and the limited approach. Each has its own particular advantages and disadvantages.

In the **warehouse approach,** all documents, both relevant and irrelevant, are produced without any type of organization. The advantage for the producing party here is a saving in the time and effort that would be involved in organizing the documents. However, this approach does not relieve the attorneys and paralegals of the need to review the documents before releasing them. Also, by releasing all the documents available to the party, some documents that appear irrelevant early in the litigation may later be discovered to be highly relevant. These apparently innocent documents could disclose information to which the requesting party is not entitled. Such a disclosure might assist the opposing party in preparing his or her case for trial.

In a **broad production** all documents even remotely relevant are produced, even those not directly requested. This approach is advantageous because it can save time and effort later. The underlying premise is that all these documents will be requested later anyway. By releasing them now we eliminate the need to repeat the process of combing through the files a second and possibly even a third time. The disadvantage is that the responding party may release documents that the other party would never have requested.

A **limited production** is one in which only those documents requested are produced. The advantage here is the protection of relevant documents that the other party has yet to request. An attorney might elect this approach if the request is very limited in scope or if it is drafted poorly. However, the disadvantage is that later document searches may be necessary as subsequent requests are received.

12–2 PROTECTION OF DOCUMENTS

As noted earlier a party served with a request for documents has either thirty or forty-five days to respond to that request. The response must indicate either that the party will comply or that the party objects to the request or to part of the request. Grounds for such objections include arguing that complying with the request will violate either the attorney-client privilege or the attorney-work product privilege. Other objections include that the request is overbroad, duplicative, or irrelevant. If none of these objections are suitable, the documents may still be kept private by using a confidentiality agreement or a protective order.

The Attorney-Client Privilege

As explained in chapter 8, the attorney-client privilege prevents the forced disclosure of communication between an attorney and a client. Like the other forms of discovery, a request for documents is limited by the attorney-client privilege. This extends to communications to or from both inside and outside counsel. In the Dieter case, for example, if the in-house counsel of Haubrich wrote an internal memo to the company's CEO concerning the potential of facing a lawsuit over the company's default, that memo would be protected.

At an early stage in the discovery process, the paralegal should draw up a list of all attorneys who represented the client in matters relevant to the lawsuit. The list will be used to identify documents that should be withheld from the other party on the basis of the attorney-client privilege. Recall that the attorney-client privilege is waived if a document is disclosed to a third party. Care should therefore be taken to limit access to these protected documents.

The Work Product Privilege

As pointed out in the discovery overview chapter, the work product privilege prevents the opposing party from obtaining through discovery letters, memos, documents, records, and other tangible items that have been produced in anticipation of litigation or that have been prepared for the trial itself. Since the work product privilege protects tangible evidence, it is especially applicable to a request for documents. Investigator's reports and

warehouse approach The type of document production in which both relevant and irrelevant documents are produced without any type of organization.

broad production A document production in which all documents even remotely relevant are produced, even those not directly requested.

limited production A document production in which only those documents requested are produced.

materials prepared by expert consultants who will not testify at trial are examples of protected work product. Handwritten notes penned by the attorney during office visits or phone conversations with the client would also be considered work product. Similarly, lists made by the client in response to a request by the attorney would be protected.

Unlike the attorney-client privilege, the work product privilege is not an absolute privilege. Disclosure of some documents may be compelled if the party requesting production of the documents has a substantial need for the documents and cannot, without undue hardship, obtain the equivalent of the material by any other means. Calculating the time period when a document could be considered work product can be difficult. Is a document prepared by in-house counsel six months prior to the beginning of the lawsuit protected by the work product privilege? Probably, if the attorney gives any legal advice or discusses potential litigation. If, however, in-house counsel sends a memo on the general legal risks involved in assuming too much debt, that memo would probably not be protected by the privilege even if sent six weeks before the lawsuit is brought against the company.

Overbroad and Duplicative Requests

A party who is responding to a request for documents may also object on the grounds that the request is **overbroad**. Such an objection would claim that the request seeks much more information than the other party needs or could ever use. In the Dieter case, for example, if Dieter requested all the corporate minute books of Haubrich Industries, Haubrich's attorney would be justified in objecting on the grounds that the request is overbroad.

Usually such an objection is accompanied by an alternative suggestion. Thus, Haubrich's response to Dieter's request would refuse to produce all the minute books but would promise to produce any minutes that expressly refer to the loan from Dieter, the purchase of the petrochemical plant, and the audit by Wellington, Judgson, and Davies, all of which would be relevant to the lawsuit. Another objection to a request for production is that the request is **duplicative**. This objection argues that the other party has already asked for that information in another part of the request.

Inadmissible and Irrelevant Evidence

As we learned in chapter 8, the scope of discovery is much broader than the scope of evidence that can be introduced at trial. Documents that would be inadmissible at trial can still be requested if those documents are reasonably calculated to lead to admissible evidence. However, documents that cannot be reasonably calculated to lead to admissible evidence are not subject to discovery. Thus the producing party may object to a request on those grounds. The producing party may also object on the grounds that the documents sought are irrelevant to the lawsuit. Thus, in the Dieter case, Haubrich Industries might object to a request for its certificate of incorporation on the grounds the certificate is irrelevant to the lawsuit.

Confidentiality Agreements and Protective Orders

The secrecy of documents may be difficult to preserve during discovery. In the Dieter case, for example, at least three law firms, one for Dieter, one for Haubrich, and one for Wellington, Judgson, and Davies would be working on the case. Each law firm will probably have several attorneys and paralegals involved in the suit. In addition, legal secretaries, word processing personnel, copy center personnel, and receptionists, among many others, will have access to the documents. How can the privacy and secrecy of documents be preserved in this type of atmosphere? One way to maintain privacy and secrecy is to have everyone who works on the case sign a confidentiality agreement. Another way is to seek a protective order from the court that would limit the people who could see the document or the circumstances under which the contents of the document would be revealed.

Inadvertent Production

Despite the most stringent safeguards, privileged documents will be sent to the other party inadvertently. In complex litigation, parties often provide for this eventuality by an agreement to notify the other party of the accidental production of documents and request a return of all copies of the documents. Unfortunately, the parties to a lawsuit are not always cooperative. If a party in possession of inadvertently released documents refuses to return those documents, your attorney will have to file a motion asking the court to compel the return of those documents. If, however, the documents were released as a result of your negligence, the court may not be sympathetic and might very well refuse to grant your attorney's motion.

12-3 REQUESTING THE PRODUCTION OF DOCUMENTS

As a paralegal you will often be involved in the drafting of requests for documents. Naturally, before you begin drafting a

overbroad
A discovery request seeking much more information than the other party needs or could ever use.

duplicative
A request for production of information that has already been requested.

request, you should develop a working knowledge of the case. You can gain this understanding of the case by reviewing the pleadings binder, the correspondence file, the attorney's notes, and the research notebook. As you review these files, you should take notes of the possible types of documents or particular documents that are relevant to the case. In the Dieter case, for example, as a paralegal for the firm representing the Dieter Financial Bank, you might want to see the debtor's cash ledger books, checkbooks, corporate minute books, bank statements, stock transfer books, monthly statements, state and federal income tax returns, annual reports, correspondence relating to the loan, and internal memos involving the loan.

Once you have done this initial research, you will be ready to draft the request. However, your responsibilities will not end with the drafting of the request. As we shall see later in this section of the chapter, you may also need to draft a motion to compel the other party to produce the documents, and you may be responsible for reviewing the documents once they are received.

Form and Content of the Request

Before sitting down to draft the request, you might locate sample requests for documents in form books or in the firm's word processing form file. Of course, since no two cases are exactly the same, you will have to modify any form or sample request to the particular facts and issues in the case. Still, forms and samples can often be utilized for the basic areas of the request, such as the introductory paragraph and the definitions of terms. You will also need to be familiar with the pertinent court rules involving discovery. Each court may have individual rules relating to the number of requests allowed, the time allowed for responding to requests, the manner of objecting to requests, and the availability of a motion to compel the production of the requested documents.

Title of the Document and Introductory Paragraph. Document production often involves many parties and several requests. Your draft request for the production of documents should identify the party making the request, the party receiving the request, and the number of the request:

**PLAINTIFF DIETER FINANCIAL BANK'S FIRST
REQUEST FOR
PRODUCTION OF DOCUMENTS TO DEFENDANT
HAUBRICH INDUSTRIES**

Using this type of detailed title avoids confusion and eliminates the need to read the entire request to determine the parties involved. The introductory paragraph of your request should list the applicable federal or state authority and the time and place of the production.

Definitions. The definition section is a pivotal area of the request. The heading "definitions" should be placed in the center of the page in bold-faced lettering. This emphasis will direct the party answering the request to that section for clarification of any ambiguous terms. Having a separate section devoted solely to definitions avoids the need to include this information in the body of the request. Some of the terms that may be defined include "agreement," "document," and "report," among others.

Instructions. Since the instruction section of the request is also crucial, its heading should be placed in the center of the page in bold-faced lettering. Some law firms will combine the definition and instruction sections of the request, so make certain that you check on your firm's procedure. The instruction section will specify the time period in which the documents should be produced. For example, in the Dieter case if your client's loan to Haubrich Industries was made on September 9, 1992, the request should cover at least the period from January 1, 1992, to the date of the upcoming production of documents. This entire period should be included because negotiations and correspondence that preceded the signing of the loan agreement are critical in litigating your client's case.

The instructions may also indicate whether the requesting party wants to see originals or copies of the documents. It is also customary to ask for the identity of anyone who has any of the documents requested not in the custody, possession, or control of the party served with the request. The instructions should also remind the responding party of the duty to supplement the production of documents with any documents found or created after the first production takes place. This can usually be done by labeling the request as a "continuing request." It is also customary to remind the responding party to correct any errors uncovered after the original production of documents.

Documents Requested. Rule 34 of the Federal Rules of Civil Procedure states that a request for documents must specify with "reasonable particularity" the general categories of documents or the individual documents that the requesting party wishes to inspect. This is accomplished in the section headed "documents requested." Generally, this section consists of a list of numbered paragraphs, each one specifying a document or a category of documents. Since the preceding paragraphs have explained the definitions and instructions, the job of listing the documents in this section has been considerably simplified. Figure 12–3 is an example of a request for production of documents that might be filed in the Dieter case.

Final Responsibility in Drafting the Request

Responsibility for the final review and signature of the request for documents rests with the attorney. Once the request has been signed, you will have to arrange for service on the other party or parties. Under the Federal Rules of Civil Procedure a request for production of documents need not be filed with the court. However, since some states do have this filing requirement, you should check your state and local rules on this matter. After the other party has been served with the request, place a reminder of the response due date in the firm's tickler or calendar system. If a timely response is not received, you might check with your attorney to determine if an extension of time has been granted. If an extension has not been granted then it may be necessary to file a motion to compel.

Motion to Compel

Usually, all the parties in a lawsuit will be cooperative during the discovery process. Dates and times for the production of documents are negotiated and adhered to with great regularity. Even when a party objects to the production of a document on the grounds that it is irrelevant, the document is often produced anyway. Similarly, objections on the grounds that the request is overbroad will often be followed by a narrowed response. However, sometimes the other party refuses to cooperate or makes invalid objections to the request. For this situation the law provides the motion to compel. Rule 37 of the Federal Rules of Civil Procedure allows a party to file a motion asking the court to compel the uncooperative party to produce the document requested. As the paralegal, you may be asked to draft this motion. Again, in preparation for the drafting of this motion, review your firm's form books or document file. Generally, however, your attorney will avoid the motion to compel as much as possible. Such motions are not favored by the court and should only be used when your

COURT OF COMMON PLEAS
CUYAHOGA COUNTY
STATE OF OHIO

DIETER FINANCIAL BANK,　　　　　)
　　　Plaintiff,　　　　　　　　　　　)
　　　　　　　　　　　　　　　　　　) Civil Action No. 93-77976
　　　　　　　　　　　　　　　　　　)
　　vs.　　　　　　　　　　　　　　　)
　　　　　　　　　　　　　　　　　　)
　　　　　　　　　　　　　　　　　　)
HAUBRICH INDUSTRIES, et al.,　　　　)
　　　Defendants.　　　　　　　　　　)
　　　　　　　　　　　　　　　　　　)
　　　　　　　　　　　　　　　　　　)
　　　　　　　　　　　　　　　　　　)
　　　　　　　　　　　　　　　　　　)

PLAINTIFF DIETER FINANCIAL BANK'S FIRST REQUEST FOR
PRODUCTION OF DOCUMENTS TO DEFENDANT
HAUBRICH INDUSTRIES

TO:　Jeremy Wickard, Attorney of Record for Defendant, Haubrich
　　　Industries, in the above styled and numbered cause.

Pursuant to Rule 34 of the Ohio Rules of Civil Procedure, Dieter
Financial Bank, plaintiff in the above cause, requests that Haubrich
Industries, defendant in the above cause, produce for inspection
and copying by Dieter, within thirty days of service hereof or at such
other time as may be agreed upon by counsel for the parties,
originals or legible copies of the documents requested herein. You
are also requested to serve upon plaintiff within thirty (30) days
after service of this request a written response in accordance with
Rule 34 of the Ohio Rules of Civil Procedure.

DEFINITIONS AND INSTRUCTIONS

　　1.　Unless specified otherwise, documents requested herein
include all those which were dated, written, rewritten, modified, sent
or received from January 1, 1992 to September 9, 1992.
　　2.　The following definitions apply to this request:
　　　　a.　The term "agreement" means any document or oral
statements that constitute or purport to be in whole or in part a
contract, lease, or license, and includes all changes, amendments,
covenants, alterations, modifications, interpretations, and drafts
thereof, whether or not carried out.
　　　　b.　The term "document" means any written, recorded,
taped, typed, or word processed, whether produced, reproduced,

FIGURE 12–3
Request for
Documents.

filed, or stored on paper, cards, disks, tapes, belts, charts, films, cassettes, or any other medium, and shall include books, booklets, pamphlets, brochures, statements, speeches, memos, notebooks, agreements, appointment calendars, working papers, contracts, notations, records, telegrams, journals, diaries, or summaries, cash ledger books, checkbooks, corporate minute books, bank statements, stock transfer books, monthly statements, city tax returns, state tax returns, federal tax returns, and annual reports, and shall also include all drafts, originals, and copies.

c. The term "report" means any written, recorded, taped, typed or word processed, whether produced, reproduced, filed, or stored on paper, cards, disks, tapes, belts, charts, films, cassettes, or any other medium, and shall include books, booklets, pamphlets, brochures, statements, speeches, memos, notebooks, agreements, appointment calendars, working papers, contracts, notations, records, telegrams, journals, diaries, or summaries, cash ledger books, checkbooks, corporate minute books, bank statements, stock transfer books, monthly statements, city tax returns, state tax returns, federal tax returns, and annual reports, and shall also include all drafts, originals, and copies.

d. The term "defendants" means Haubrich Industries; Wellington, Judgson, and Davies, including their directors, officers, employees, and agents.

e. The phrases "relate to" and "relating to" shall be construed to include "refer to," "summarize," "contain," "include," "mention," "explain," "discuss," "define," "describe," "point out," "comment on," or "remark."

f. The words "and" and "or" shall be interpreted in such a way as to bring within the scope of the specification all responses that otherwise might be interpreted as being outside its scope.

g. The term "each" shall be interpreted to include the word "every," and the word "every" shall be interpreted to include the word "each."

h. The word "any" shall be interpreted to include the word "all," and the word "all" shall be interpreted to include the word "any."

i. A plural noun will be interpreted to be a singular noun, and a singular noun will be interpreted as a plural noun, whenever needed to bring within the scope of the specification all responses that otherwise might be interpreted as being outside its scope.

3. Produce each and every document in its original file folder, cover, envelope, or jacket, and write on that folder, cover, envelope, or jacket, the person or the corporate office, department, subdivision, or subsidiary, for which, by which, and/or in which the file is maintained.

FIGURE 12–3
(continued)

4. Should you be unable to produce any of the documents called for in this request, explain the reason that you cannot comply.

5. Should you be unable to produce any of the documents called for in this request, because such documents are no longer in your custody, control, or possession, please identify the document and the reason that you no longer have custody, control, or possession of said document or documents.

6. Should you be unable to produce any of the documents called for in this request, because such documents are no longer in your custody, control, or possession, please identify the document, and the person, department, subdivision, or subsidiary that does have custody, control, or possession of said document.

7. Should you wish to assert the attorney-client privilege, the work product privilege, or any other privilege as to any of the documents called for in this request, then as to each document subject to such privilege, please provide the plaintiff with an identification of such documents, including the name of the document, the date of the document, the type of document, the author of the document, the receiver of the document, the names of all people receiving copies of the document, the names of all people who saw the original document, and a summary of the subject of the document in sufficient detail to allow the Court to determine the validity of the assertion of the privilege, should a motion to compel be filed.

8. Each paragraph in this request should be interpreted independently and not in relation to any other paragraph for the purpose of limiting the request.

9. This request is to be considered a continuing request requiring the defendant to supplement the production of document with any documents found or created after the first production takes place.

10. The defendant has the additional duty to correct any errors that are uncovered after the original production of documents takes place.

11. Any questions that may arise as to this request for documents may be directed by the counsel for the defendant to the undersigned representative of the plaintiff before the dates set for the production of the documents that are the subject matter of this request.

<u>DOCUMENTS REQUESTED</u>

1. All documents, reports, and agreements that relate to and involve the corporate organization of Haubrich Industries.

FIGURE 12–3
(continued)

2. All documents, reports, and agreements that relate to the corporate organization of Wellington, Judgson, and Davies, C.P.A.s, Inc.

3. All documents, reports, and agreements directed to or received by Haubrich Industries from Wellington, Judgson, and Davies.

4. All documents, reports, and agreements that Haubrich Industries directed to or were received by Wellington, Judgson, and Davies.

5. All documents, reports, and agreements that relate to contracts, proposed contracts, draft contracts, negotiated contracts, contemplated contracts, or offers of contracts that passed between Haubrich Industries and Wellington, Judgson, and Davies.

6. All documents, reports, and agreements that constitute or relate to any and all communication between Haubrich Industries and Wellington, Judgson, and Davies.

7. All documents, reports, and agreements that relate to the audit conducted by Wellington, Judgson, and Davies on the financial condition of Haubrich Industries.

8. All documents, reports, and agreements that constitute internal communication within Haubrich Industries that relate to Wellington, Judgson, and Davies.

9. All documents, reports, and agreements that constitute internal communication within Wellington, Judgson, and Davies, that relate to Haubrich Industries.

10. All documents, reports, and agreements that constitute or relate to any and all communication between Haubrich Industries and Wellington, Judgson, and Davies concerning the Dieter Financial Bank.

11. All documents, reports, and agreements that relate to the audit conducted by Wellington, Judgson, and Davies on the financial condition of Haubrich Industries and that specifically refer to The Dieter Financial Bank.

12. All documents, reports, and agreements, that constitute internal communication within Haubrich Industries that relate to The Dieter Financial Bank.

13. All documents, reports, and agreements that constitute internal communication within Wellington, Judgson, and Davies that relate to The Dieter Financial Bank.

14. All documents, reports, and agreements that relate to the unqualified opinion issued by Wellington, Judgson, and Davies on the financial health of Haubrich Industries.

15. All documents, reports, or agreements that relate to the audit conducted by Wellington, Judgson, and Davies on Haubrich

FIGURE 12–3
(continued)

Industries and that refer to The Dieter Financial Bank that are not covered by the prior requests herein.

16. All documents, reports, or agreements that relate to the audit conducted by Wellington, Judgson, and Davies on Haubrich Industries and that refer to any and all other potential investors in and creditors of Haubrich Industries that are not covered by the prior requests herein.

17. All documents, reports, and agreements that relate to the financial structure of Haubrich Industries that are not covered by the prior requests herein.

Giacomo Striuli
Striuli, Grazak, and Usalis
2233 Hamilton Avenue
Cleveland, Ohio 44119
Attorneys for Plaintiff
Dieter Financial Bank

CERTIFICATE OF SERVICE

I hereby certify that a true and correct copy of the foregoing has been mailed by first class mail, postage prepaid to Jeremy Wickard, 54392 St. Clair Avenue, Cleveland, Ohio, 44118, on this 29th day of September, 1993.

FIGURE 12–3
(continued)

attorney feels there is no other way to obtain information that is vital to the successful outcome of the lawsuit.

Reviewing the Documents of the Opposing Party

Once the documents requested have been received in your office, you may be asked to review those documents, either alone or with an attorney. Naturally, a knowledge of the facts, issues, and parties in the case is essential to a successful document review. However, it is also important for you to have an understanding of what your attorney is looking for as you inspect and review the documents. Therefore, you should ask your attorney for guidance in reviewing the documents. For example, it would be helpful for you to know which of the files must be read in depth and which can be merely scanned. You might also want to know if your attorney is interested in a particular category of documents or in the documents produced by a particular individual.

Since reviewing a large volume of documents is a time-consuming and tedious task, you will want to try various techniques for expediting the job. One technique is to dictate file labels and a brief summary of the contents of each file. This will help you review more documents over a shorter period of time. Another technique is to keep a record of the files that you have reviewed. This will help you recall the precise location of documents that you have seen and considered crucial to the case.

If you are dealing with original documents, your attorney may want to have copies made of the more important documents. Your attorney will set the parameters for the documents that he or she will want you to copy. However, if there is any doubt about the value of a document to your case, designate the document for copying.

12–4 RESPONDING TO A REQUEST FOR DOCUMENTS

A document production is only as successful as the planning that precedes it. The first action that you should take once you have been served with a document request is to determine if the production date is realistic. Other important ingredients in the successful production process are categorizing the documents, involving the client, and organizing the documents.

Determining a Target Date

Whether or not the requested target date is feasible depends to a great extent on the number of the documents in your client's possession and the number of people in the law firm who will assist in the production. However, estimating the volume of documents in a document production can be difficult. Often the first estimate will be revised several times as you locate and review pertinent documents. Nevertheless, you must make some initial assessment of the feasibility of meeting the deadline indicated in the request. Consulting with other paralegals who have been through several document productions may help you evaluate the deadline date.

Categorizing the Documents

You can make the task of documentation production easier if you divide the request into several general categories. For example, you might divide the request into the following categories:

Request 1 Accounting Information
Request 2 Marketing Plans and Correspondence

THE COMPUTERIZED LAW FIRM—Document Summary

SCENARIO

You and your attorney are in the middle of a deposition. The deponent is Frank K. Wellington, a CPA who is a partner in the accounting firm of Wellington, Judgson, and Davies. Wellington has just indicated that he had no idea that the financial report that his firm issued on Haubrich Industries would be seen and relied upon by the Dieter Financial Bank. Your attorney, however, recalls seeing a letter that was written by Wellington and addressed to Helen Haubrich, the president of Haubrich Industries. In the letter Wellington referred to a list of third parties who would probably receive copies of the report. Included on that list was Frederick J. Dieter, the founder and president of the Dieter Financial Bank. Before continuing with the deposition, your attorney would like to see that letter. She instructs you to return to your office and to bring her a copy of the correspondence. Unfortunately, your attorney cannot recall the exact date or the primary subject of the letter. Nevertheless, she expects you to return with the letter within the next fifteen minutes.

PROBLEM

Document production in massive and complex litigation is time-consuming and cumbersome. Organizing thousands of documents for fast and accurate retrieval presents a challenge for you and your attorney. When you return to your office you realize the immensity of the task you face. Literally thousands of documents are stacked in boxes in your office and piled on shelves in your attorney's office. How are you going to locate a single letter?

SOLUTION

Fortunately for you, your law firm recently introduced automated litigation support, a computer application for litigation tasks. Consequently, you have already analyzed and extracted the pertinent data from the documents produced by the parties in this case. You have also placed this summary into the firm's computer. Your computer has stored in its memory valuable information about each document, including the Bates number, the date, the author, the recipient, carbon copy recipients, subject matter, type of document, marginalia, and attachments. The high-speed search capacity of the computer permits you to locate the letter from Wellington to Haubrich, dated March 17, 1992, in which Dieter is named on a list of probable recipients of the financial report. Searching a database of 10,000 documents, the computer identifies this critically important document in a matter of minutes. Selecting the proper software for document summary may depend on a number of factors such as the type of hardware, the number of litigation matters handled by the law firm, and the personnel available to support computerized litigation. Your law firm's general database may be sufficient to handle the demands of a litigation support system. If that is not a viable choice, the law firm's computer programmer might adapt the specialized requirements of a document summary database. Excellent software programs available for document summary include Summation II, Paradox, and BRS. Vendors for document summary software are found in Appendix B.

Request 3   Corporate Minutes, Bylaws, and Articles of Incorporation
Request 4   Research and Development
Request 5   Sales Projections

Once the general categories are developed, subcategories can be easily defined. These categories and subcategories will give your document search a controlling structure that will guide your work.

Involving the Client in Document Production

Although you have established categories of the documents that you believe are responsive to the request, you must remember that only the client knows what types and how many documents actually exist. Also remember that only the client can make the documents available to the law firm for production. Therefore the client must be involved in the production process as early as possible. You might begin by sending the client a copy of the request as soon as you have received it. Make certain that you point out the date when the production is to be made so that the client is aware that the process should not be delayed. Next, schedule a meeting with the client as soon as possible to plan the document production.

Making Document Production a Joint Effort with the Client.   Sometimes clients suggest that they conduct the document search without the aid of someone from the law firm. There are several disadvantages to this approach. First, clients are often unaware of the attorney-client privilege and the work product privilege and may, therefore, not recognize protected documents. Second, clients may also fail to recognize the documents they actually must produce. Third, clients often do not comprehend the amount of time and effort involved in a document production. Finally, the client probably doesn't realize that sanctions can result if he or she does not produce all the documents requested. Pointing out these disadvantages to the client should help convince him or her to make the document production a joint effort with the law firm. Your client may also suggest hiring an independent contractor to conduct the document search. While there are reputable firms that can conduct such a search, it is generally not a good idea for your firm to relinquish control over the process.

Selecting a Client's Representative for Document Production. The client should designate a representative to coordinate the document production with the legal team. Often it is advantageous if that representative is a member of the client's in-house legal department. Whatever the case, the person chosen should know about the client's business during the entire period of time covered by the document request. Since the client's representative must devote a significant amount of time to the document production project, there is a tendency for clients to appoint junior executives who are new to the corporation. Such a move can be a mistake, not only because the junior executive will not be familiar with the entire case, but also because the other employees may refuse to cooperate with the "outsider." If you find yourself in this uncomfortable situation, you may seek the help of the client's in-house legal department to find a replacement. The replacement should be someone who is more familiar with the case and who will command the respect needed in such a sensitive operation.

Organizing the Document Production

Organization is a key factor in conducting a successful document production. One effective way to organize is to gather all the required documents in one central location. Figure 12–4 is a checklist you might follow to locate and gather in one location all the documents from your client's executive offices and branches.

Controlling the Documents. Control is also an important factor in effective document production. You must be able to determine the location of any document among the thousands of documents that you will have compiled. For example, when your attorney asks for a one-page opinion that is part of a closing binder, you will be expected to locate the pertinent document quickly. Or if the client's loan officer needs to review a loan committee minutes file before a loan committee meeting, you must know exactly where that file is and make certain that the loan officer has it in time for

1. Review request for production and determine time and personnel required.
2. Forward request for production to client and request a client's representative be named to assist with the production.
3. Determine if the originals or copies of the documents will be produced.
4. Determine if the documents will be produced as kept in the ordinary course of business or by document request number.
5. Determine if only relevant documents will be produced or if the production will be a "warehouse" production.
6. Meet with the client's representative to begin planning the collection and organization of client's files for production. Request an organization chart to determine departments and employees where responsive documents may be located. Ask for a dedicated work room for the production, including telephones, office furniture, and supplies.
7. Search all of the pertinent files in the client's offices. Draw a map of each office or department to indicate the location and titles of files and file cabinets.
8. List all files removed on the Document Production Log, and indicate the employee from whom the files were received, in addition to the date the files were received.
9. Request a copy of the client's document retention policy to determine the length of time various types of documents are retained and the storage and destruction policies of the client.
10. Request an index to the archived files to determine files that might pertain to the litigation. Order those files brought from archives to the production site.
11. Number each box as it is brought into the work area. Place that number on the log and index all files within the box, including source.
12. Review the contents of each box of documents. Create new file folders labeled "Produce," "Non-produce," "Privilege/Work Product." Place a colored sticker or flag on each document about which there is a question. Ask the supervising attorney to review those documents immediately to determine the appropriate folder. In the case of documents that require redaction, make a copy of the original before doing the redaction, note the redaction at the top of the document, make a copy of the document with the redaction and place it in the "Produce" file; place the original and the original redacted copy in the "Non-produce" or "Privilege/Work Product" folders, as applicable.
13. Remove the privileged document folders from the work room. Once the attorney has reviewed the documents and determined that the privilege designation is correct, these documents may be numbered with a different numbering prefix from the documents to be produced. A notation should be made on the production log to indicate privileged documents, the original files from which they came, and their document numbers once they are assigned.

FIGURE 12–4
Checklist for Production of the Client's Documents.

14. After the document review has been completed, all documents to be produced should be copied and numbered. The document number can indicate the source of the documents. For example, documents from defendant A begin with "1," from defendant B with "2," and third-party defendant "X" begin with "3."
15. Prepare a privilege list to attach to the response to the request for production.
16. Prepare the response to the request for production.
17. Index produced documents.
18. Produce documents to the opposing party. The paralegal should remain in the production room at all times. No copies should be removed by the opposing party or its counsel.
19. Copy documents the opposing party designates for copying. Review the documents and notify your attorney of the documents requested by the opposing party. Forward the copies and a statement for the copying costs to the counsel for the opposing party. Make a notation on the production log of all copies received by the opposing party.
20. Return original documents to the client's office. Place a notation in the file that no documents are to be added to or taken from this file because the matter is in litigation. Begin a new file with the same file label for all new correspondence and documents. In the event of a supplemental request for production, you may be able to avoid reviewing files previously reviewed.
21. Make additional copies of documents produced and organize in chronological, subject matter, or witness order for later deposition exhibit, trial exhibit, or general trial preparation use.
22. Produce documents.

FIGURE 12–4
(continued)

the meeting. Figure 12–4 includes steps that will help in the organization of the document production process.

Copying the Documents.   The decision of when to copy the documents must be made early in the document production process. Usually, it is not advisable to release original documents because the release of such documents can handicap the daily operation of the client's business. Also, when original documents are released there is always the possibility that they may be lost. Finally, government regulations may prohibit the removal of some documents from the principal place of business.

Unfortunately, copying thousand of documents can be expensive and time-consuming. Therefore, the legal team should

Bates numbering
A system for placing a number on a document by machine.

document production log
A log used to track the production of documents, including the source of the document, the file in which the document is located, and whether the document is to be produced or excluded on the basis of privilege or work product.

privilege log
A log listing all documents identified as being protected from discovery under either the attorney-client privilege or the work-product privilege.

responsive documents
Documents that are responsive to a request for

always be aware of ways to reduce this expense. For example, time and money can be saved by waiting until the opposing counsel designates the documents that he or she wants copied. A disadvantage to this approach is that you may miss some documents that could be helpful to your client's case. Opposing counsel will have little interest in copying documents that will support your client's position.

Numbering the Documents. Numbering and control are synonymous. Without an identifying number, it is virtually impossible to organize and control a document production. A number assigned to a document during the production process should remain with the document throughout the lawsuit. One technique for numbering the documents is the Bates numbering system. The **Bates numbering** system involves placing a number on a document by machine. The Bates system served as the primary means of numbering documents for many years. Recently, however, computer-generated numbers on peel-off labels have replaced the Bates numbering system. The system is different, but the result is the same. Documents can be identified quickly and easily.

Alpha prefixes can be used to identify the source of a document. For instance, the plaintiff's documents might begin with "A," while the defendant's begin with "B." However, you should not act too quickly in the numbering of the documents. All privileged documents must be removed from the production before the numbering to avoid suspicious gaps in the numbering system. Figure 12–5

STYLE OF CASE: _____ REVIEWER: _____ REVIEW DATE: _____

BOX NO. _____ SOURCE _____

FILE NAME	SOURCE	PRODUCE	NON-PRODUCE	PRIVILEGE	BATES NOS.	PRODUCED	OPPOSING PARTY

FIGURE 12–5 Document Production Log.

represents a sample **document production log** to assist you in organizing the documents for production.

It is also wise to make out a **privilege log,** indicating all documents that you have identified as being protected from discovery under either the attorney-client privilege or the work product privilege. Figure 12–6 will help you compile such a log.

Reviewing, Labeling, and Filing Documents Before Removal. A paralegal and an attorney should review all documents before they are removed from the client's office. Sometimes one or more of the client's original files will contain documents that you must produce, other documents that you don't have to produce, and still others that are protected by privilege. The documents that you will have to produce are called **responsive documents**, while the documents that you don't have to produce are called **non-responsive documents**. The protected documents are called **privileged documents**.

To separate these documents, set up three duplicate files. Place copies of the documents to be produced in one of the folders and give it the same title as the client's original file. Place the non-responsive documents in the second file and label it "non-responsive" or "non-produce." The term **non-produce** is simply a synonym for non-responsive. Place the privileged documents in the third file and label it "privileged." All privileged files should be removed from the area where the responsive documents are kept. This simple precaution will prevent them from being inadvertently sent to the other party.

---

production of documents and must be produced to the party initiating the request for production.

non-responsive documents
Documents that are not responsive to a request for production of documents and thus do not have to be produced to the party initiating the request for production.

privileged documents
Documents that are protected from production because of attorney-client privilege.

non-produce
Documents that are not produced to a party initiating a request for production of documents because they are not responsive to the request.

BATES NO.	DATE	DOC. TYPE	AUTHOR	RECIPIENT COPIES	SUMMARY	TYPE PRIVILEGE

FIGURE 12–6 Privilege Log.

Sometimes a single document will contain information that you must produce and information that you need not produce. The same document may also include information that is protected by privilege. In such a case, cover the irrelevant or the protected information before making a photocopy. Place the notation "deletion" on the covered portion. This deletion process is referred to as **redact**. Make two copies of the **redacted page**. Place one of the redacted copies in the file that is marked as the client's original file is marked. Place the other redacted copy in the non-responsive file or the privileged file, whichever is appropriate.

12–5 ORGANIZING AND INDEXING THE DOCUMENTS AFTER PRODUCTION

As the paralegal, you will have several duties following the production of your client's documents and the review of the opposition's documents. Since there will often be thousands of documents involved in the litigation, control problems will be very serious. You can aid in establishing a tight control over these documents by organizing and indexing them.

Organizing the Documents After Production

redact
> The process of deleting irrelevant or privileged information on a document before copying the document for production to the party initiating the request for production of documents.

redacted page
> A page on which information on a document is deleted before copying the document for production to the party initiating the request for production of documents.

Before the mass of information in these documents can be used properly, they must be organized. Organizational plans will vary from case to case. Some cases turn on chronological events. Documents in such cases are ordered by dates. Other cases may be broken down into several subject categories. The documents would therefore be organized by those subjects. In other cases you will be asked to organize the documents in anticipation of the upcoming depositions. In such a case, you will need to pull together all documents related to the testimony of each deponent to be called. The method of organization is less important than the fact that the documents are organized in a way that will help you instantly locate a document when asked to do so.

If the case is going to be managed manually, without the aid of a computer, several copies of each document should be made. One set can be placed in chronological order, a second set in subject order, and a third set in deponent order. Keep the copies separate from the original numbered set and limit access to that original set. A missing original that is incorrectly numbered may disappear forever. The absence of that crucial document could have a severe impact on the case. Remember, control and organization are the keys to effective document management in any successful litigation.

Indexing the Documents After Production

An index of the documents produced by all parties is critical to controlling the files throughout the lawsuit. This index can be limited to the document number, date, author, recipient, document type, and a brief summary of its content. If you place the document in word processing or on the firm's computer, a particular document can be located quickly by any of the identifying labels. The index is your final control measure. However, this does not mean that you should minimize its importance. It may be a difficult job at the outset of the lawsuit, but it is much less difficult than trying to search for a document by trial and error later in the case.

12-6 INSPECTION OF PROPERTY

The request for documents is directed only to documents. However, often a case involves tangible property, such as a piece of equipment or a parcel of real estate. Rule 34 of the Federal Rules of Civil Procedure provides for a procedure through which the parties or their representatives can inspect property for the purposes of measuring, photographing, or testing.

Obtaining an Inspection

Normally, the demand for inspection is made informally by letter. The letter will also designate a date and place of inspection. If the date and time specified in the letter are inconvenient for the other party, another time and place can be set. In some instances, the party who has custody or possession of the property in question is reluctant to allow the other parties access to the property. Rule 34 of the Federal Rules of Civil Procedure provides the procedure by which a party may demand that the party with the custody of the property relevant to the case shall produce the property for inspection. The court will usually grant the inspection if it determines the inspection is calculated to lead to the discovery of evidence that will be admissible at trial.

The procedure for gaining access to property in the possession of another party is simple. A **demand for inspection** must be prepared and served upon all parties in the litigation even if it is directed only to the party that has the custody of the property at issue. The property must be identified with reasonable particularity, and the demand must not be overly broad or vague. A demand for inspection may be made only upon the parties to the litigation. As in the case of depositions, a subpoena duces tecum must be prepared to require non-parties to produce tangible items for

demand for inspection
A demand for access to inspect a property that is relevant to the case, served upon all parties in the litigation even if it is directed only to the party who has custody of the property at issue.

inspection at the time of deposition or trial. The subpoena duces tecum cannot be used to obtain access to real property.

Responding to a Demand for Inspection

Under Rule 34, the respondent has thirty days to respond to the demand for inspection or forty-five days if the demand is served upon the defendant with the summons and the complaint. The respondent may agree to the inspection, limit or place conditions on the inspection, or serve formal objections to the requests. Normally, inspections of land, buildings, or equipment must be timed so as not to interfere with the other party's normal use. If a test to be used on the property might destroy that property, the test may be conducted by an expert agreeable to both parties. A video recording may be made of the test.

SUMMARY

12–1 Four ways that documents can be obtained during discovery include a request for documents, a request for documents at the deposition of a party, a subpoena duces tecum for a non-party to produce documents at the time of a deposition, and the option of producing business records as an answer to an interrogatory. A request for documents is a request by one party in a lawsuit to allow the first party access to documents that are relevant to the subject matter of the lawsuit. Two crucial preliminary considerations in a production request are the timing of the request and the potential cost of the production. Documents can be produced either as they are kept in the usual course of business or according to the categories specified in the document request. The three ways to respond to a document request are the warehouse approach, the broad approach, and the limited approach.

12–2 Not all documents requested must be produced. Some are protected by the attorney-client privilege or the work product privilege. Other objections are that the request is overbroad, duplicative, or irrelevant. If none of these objections are available, the documents can still be protected by using a confidentiality agreement or a protective order.

12–3 The paralegal will often be called upon to draft the request for production of documents. The parts of the request include the title, the definitions, the instructions, and a list of documents requested. The paralegal may also need to draft a motion to compel the other party to produce the documents requested. The paralegal may be required to review and organize the documents once they arrive.

12–4 The paralegal will also be involved in responding to a request for documents. The steps in this process include determining a realistic production date, categorizing the documents, involving the client, and organizing the documents.

12–5 After document production by all parties, the paralegal may be required to organize the documents by various categories.

12–6 The request for documents is directed only to documents. Often a case involves tangible property such as a piece of equipment or a parcel of real estate. The Federal Rules of Civil Procedure stipulate a procedure through which the parties or their representatives can inspect property for purposes of measuring, photographing, or testing.

KEY TERMS

Bates numbering
broad production
demand for inspection
document production log
documents
duplicative
limited production
non-produce
non-responsive documents

overbroad
privileged documents
privilege log
redact
redacted page
request for documents
responsive documents
warehouse approach

QUESTIONS FOR REVIEW AND DISCUSSION

1. Name three alternative methods for obtaining documents besides serving a request for documents.
2. What is a request for documents?
3. Explain the factors to be considered in deciding whether to serve the other party with a request for the production of documents.
4. What are the three basic approaches to document production?
5. Distinguish between the attorney-client privilege and the work product privilege.
6. When should a confidentiality agreement or a protective order be sought?
7. What objections can be raised to a request for production of documents?

8. What are the duties of the paralegal in requesting the production of documents?
9. What responsibilities does the paralegal have in responding to a request for the production of documents?
10. What are the paralegal's duties in organizing the documents produced by both sides?
11. What procedure can be used to obtain an inspection of property?

ACTIVITIES

1. Review the laws of your state and find all state laws that deal with requests for the production of documents. Check your local court rules to see if any local rules supplement or alter the state laws.
2. Obtain the form books in your law library that provide sample forms for use in drafting the legal documents in your state. Find a sample request for production of documents, and compare it with the sample found in this chapter.
3. Review the laws of your state and find out whether your state allows the same objections to the request for documents that are outlined in this chapter.

CHAPTER 12 PROJECT—ORGANIZING AND INDEXING DOCUMENTS AFTER PRODUCTION

Review the Commentary at the beginning of this chapter. Recall that your firm has been retained by the Dieter Financial Bank to bring suit against Haubrich Industries for defaulting on a loan. Review the sample request for production of documents in this chapter or the one that you located in your state's form book. Assume that the defendant, Haubrich Industries, has responded to the request for documents and has delivered the documents that you asked for. Now you and your staff face the unenviable task of organizing and indexing these documents. You cannot handle the task by yourself, but the only other paralegal available has never had the opportunity to be involved in document indexing. Draft a memorandum in which you explain in detail to the new paralegal the process that the two of you must follow in organizing and indexing the documents that your firm has received from Haubrich Industries. Assume that you are going to have to organize the documents manually, without the aid of a computer. Be sure to ask the paralegal for his or her input into the organizational principle that will best fit this case.

CHAPTER 13

Request for Admissions

OUTLINE

COMMENTARY—THE ALVAREZ CASE

Your firm has been retained to represent Maria Alvarez, a chemical engineer, who believes that she has been unjustly dismissed by her employer, Wyandott-Von Maitlin Pharmaceuticals, Inc., where she was head chemist for twelve years. At this point in the case, the discovery process has been substantially completed. As you and your attorney are reviewing the evidence, she sees the need to establish that certain documents are genuine. She also wants to make sure that several facts are accurate. As a result your attorney asks you to draft a request for admissions to be served on Ernst Weissler, the chief executive officer (CEO) of Wyandott-Von Maitlin. The next day your firm receives a request for admissions from Dirksen, Vannice, and Raeder, the law firm representing the company. Your attorney asks you to contact Dr. Alvarez and prepare a response to this request. In order for you to complete these assignments, you will be required to review the applicable court rules, including your local rules, and to review the pleadings, critical documents, and prior discovery. You will also need to consult either a form book or your law firm's word processing file.

OBJECTIVES

Now that the discovery process has been nearly completed, you may need to establish the truthfulness, accuracy, and genuineness of the evidence that you and your attorney have compiled. For that purpose, you may need to file a request for admissions. After reading this chapter, you will be able to:

1. Define request for admission.
2. Relate the purposes for filing a request for admissions.
3. Explain the uses of the request for admissions.
4. List the advantages of the request for admissions.
5. Identify the procedures involved in drafting a request for admissions.
6. Explain the content of each section of a request for admission.
7. Differentiate among the responses and the objections to a request for admissions.

13-1 THE REQUEST FOR ADMISSIONS

The **request for admissions** is a request filed by one party in a lawsuit on another party in that lawsuit asking the second party to admit to the truthfulness of some fact or opinion. The request may also ask the party to authenticate the genuineness of a document. According to Rule 36 of the Federal Rules of Civil Procedure, a request for admissions may be served on any party in a lawsuit. However, the request may not be served on a non-party. Rule 36 allows a request for admissions to be served at the same time that the complaint is served. In such a case, the party has forty-five days to respond to the request. If the request for admissions is served after the complaint is served, the party has thirty days to respond. The federal rules place no limit on the number of requests that can be filed. However, some states, California, for example, do have a limit on the number of requests that can be filed.

The request for admissions differs from all of the other discovery tools that we have examined thus far. In fact, some legal scholars would argue that the request for admissions is not, strictly speaking, a discovery tool at all. This argument is based on the fact that the request for admissions seeks a commitment regarding information that has already been discovered. Thus, it does not, in itself, "discover" anything. Nevertheless, it is a very powerful tool that can be used to great advantage.

Purposes of the Request for Admissions

The primary purpose of the request for admissions is to simplify a lawsuit by reducing the number and nature of the points in controversy. The simplification of the points in controversy has a "ripple effect," simplifying many of the other matters involved in the suit. For example, if there are fewer points in controversy, fewer witnesses will be necessary should the case reach the trial stage. The fewer witnesses that are needed, the more money that can be saved. These savings can be especially lucrative if the need for a variety of expert witnesses is eliminated. Simplifying the points in controversy could also lead to an early settlement of the case. This is because claims and defenses that have no legal merit evaporate quickly under the scrutiny of a well-drafted request for admissions. Finally, a carefully drafted request for admissions can emphasize important factual information that is buried in volumes of documents and testimony.

Uses of the Request for Admissions

A request for admissions can be used in three different ways. First, it might be used to authenticate the genuineness of certain important documents. Second, the request can authenticate the truthfulness of certain facts or opinions. Finally, it can be used to authenticate the application of the law to the facts. A single request for admissions can be used to fulfill all of these uses.

Authenticating the Genuineness of Documents. One of the most widely recognized purposes of the request for admissions is to authenticate the genuineness of a document. For example, in the case in the opening commentary, it would be very helpful if Mr. Weissler, the CEO of Wyandott-Von Maitlin, were to authenticate the genuineness of the letter of dismissal sent to Dr. Alvarez, the company's progressive disciplinary procedure, and the evaluation records kept on Dr. Alvarez. Naturally, such documents could be authenticated at trial, but only after overcoming a number of evidentiary hurdles. These hurdles can be reduced in a request for admissions. It is important to note, however, that an individual may admit to the genuineness of a document and still object to its admissibility. Thus, in the Alvarez case, Mr. Weissler may

request for admission
A request filed by one party in a lawsuit asking the second party in the lawsuit to admit to the truthfulness of some fact or opinion.

authenticate the document outlining the company's disciplinary procedure but object to its relevance and admissibility in this case. It is also important to note that a party who admits to the genuineness of a document does not at the same time admit to the truthfulness of the contents of the document. For example, in the Alvarez case, Dr. Alvarez might be asked to admit to the genuineness of a letter dismissing her for failing to follow company policies and procedures. In admitting to the genuiness of the letter, she is not admitting to any of the alleged rule violations outlined in the letter.

Authenticating the Truthfulness of Facts and Opinions. A second use for a request for admissions would be to authenticate the truthfulness of certain facts or opinions. In the Alvarez case, for instance, your attorney may ask the CEO to authenticate that he signed every employment evaluation of Dr. Alvarez and that each of those employment evaluations stated that she had done outstanding work for the company. These admissions, however, only authenticate the content of the evaluations and the fact that they were signed by Mr. Weissler. They do not admit anything about the actual quality of Dr. Alvarez's job performance. Thus your attorney might also ask Mr. Weissler to admit that Dr. Alvarez did outstanding work. Note the differences among these admissions. The admissions about the content and the signature authenticate facts, while the admission about the actual quality of Dr. Alvarez's job performance authenticates Mr. Weissler's opinion. Factual admissions are usually easier to obtain than those that state an opinion.

Admissions about the truthfulness of facts and opinions in response to a request for admissions carry much more weight than an admission made using some other form of discovery. Anything that is admitted in a deposition, for example, can be altered or denied when the party takes the witness stand. While this may make the witness look a bit less credible in the eyes of the judge and the jurors, they must still weigh the alterations and denials against the rest of witness's testimony. Such is not the case with an admission made in response to a request. Such an admission is taken as proven. Court permission is required in order for a party to withdraw the admission. Thus such admissions can be very effective for the party obtaining them and very damaging to the party giving them.

Authenticating the Application of the Law to Facts. A request for admissions can also combine the authentification of the facts in a case with the law that applies to those facts. For instance, in the case in the opening commentary, your attorney may request

Mr. Weissler to admit that Dr. Alvarez was employed by Wyandott-Von Maitlin on a contractual basis, and was therefore subject to the provisions of the employee policy manual, including the provision regarding progressive discipline. Such an admission would cut down on the time and effort needed to prove the legal status of Dr. Alvarez's employment. However, such an admission would not prove that she was unjustly discharged, since other issues, such as whether the disciplinary policy was followed properly or whether, under the circumstances, she was entitled to its protection, must still be proven.

Advantages of the Request for Admissions

The request for admissions offers several advantages over other discovery devices. One principal advantage is that a request for admissions cannot be ignored or overlooked. This is because of the **deemed admitted** rule. Under this rule any request that is not denied is deemed to be admitted. Also, if the response to the request does not conform to the requirements of Rule 36, the court may order that the fact has been admitted. For example, in the case in the opening commentary, if Mr. Weissler's denial of the request to authenticate Dr. Alvarez's status as a contractual employee is not specific enough, the court may rule that he has admitted that she is a contractual employee. Similarly, if Mr. Weissler were to claim that he is unable to admit or deny whether Dr. Alvarez performed her job well, and that claim is not detailed enough, the court may order that the matter has been admitted. In both of these examples, the court could instead order Weissler to file an amended response to the request. Some states have altered the deemed admitted rule. In California, for example, nothing is deemed admitted unless the propounding party makes a motion to that effect.

An advantage that the request for admissions shares with interrogatories is that parties cannot refuse to respond simply because they lack the information needed to make the response. Rather, they must make a reasonable attempt to obtain the missing information. Moreover, a party cannot refuse to cooperate merely because the other party could obtain the information another way. Furthermore, although a request for admissions is usually made toward the end of the discovery process, such requests can be made at any time, even with the service of the summons and complaint. Thus, since a total knowledge of the facts is not a prerequisite for the request, it can be used as a learning tool. Finally, as noted earlier, in federal court there is no limit to the number of requests that can be filed. Some states, however, do place limits on the number of requests for admissions.

deemed admitted
The rule stating that any request for admissions that is not denied is deemed to be admitted.

13-2　DRAFTING THE REQUEST FOR ADMISSIONS

As a paralegal you may be called upon to draft a request for admissions. This responsibility is extremely important because, as we have seen previously, properly drafted requests can save time and money and can often lead to an early settlement of the lawsuit. Consequently, great care must be taken in preparing for and actually drafting the request.

Preliminary Steps in Drafting the Request for Admissions

Before you sit down to draft the request, you should do some preliminary work. First, discuss the matter with your attorney so that you have an understanding of the goals and objectives of the request. Then make certain that you review all previous pleadings and important documents as you assemble the facts. Also take some time to look over the applicable federal or state and local court rules so that you can accurately determine response deadlines and procedural details.

As a final step before drafting the request, list and organize the admissions that you would like the other party to make. For example, as we have seen in the Alvarez case, it would be very helpful if Mr. Weissler would admit that Alvarez was a contractual employee, that she was protected by the provisions of the company's progressive disciplinary policy, that her job performance evaluations had always been favorable, that he had signed those favorable evaluations, and that he personally believed her job performance to be satisfactory. With these suggested admissions in hand double check with your attorney to make certain that you have not overlooked anything.

Form and Content of the Request for Admissions

With your preliminary list of desired admissions in hand, locate a sample request in a form book or in your firm's word processing file. Naturally, no two situations are exactly the same, so you will have to modify the form to fit the facts of your particular case. Nevertheless, we can make some general statements about the title, the introductory paragraph, the definitions and instructions, and the specific request.

Title of the Request and the Introductory Paragraph.　The title of your request should reflect the party making the request, the party receiving the request, and the number of the request:

PLAINTIFF ALVAREZ'S FIRST REQUEST FOR ADMISSIONS
TO DEFENDANTS ERNST WEISSLER AND
WYANDOTT-VON MAITLIN PHARMACEUTICALS, INC.

Make certain that you cite the appropriate court rules in the introductory paragraph. If you follow the actual language of the rule, you will avoid any possible misunderstanding. The introductory paragraph should also include a demand for written answers to the request within the applicable time limits. Figure 13–1 includes a typical introductory paragraph for the request.

UNITED STATES DISTRICT COURT

MARIA ALVAREZ,	)
	) Civil Action No. 92-31753
Plaintiff,	)
	)
v.	)
	)
ERNST WEISSLER AND	)
WYANDOTT-VON MAITLIN	)
PHARMACEUTICALS, INC.	)
	)
Defendants.	)
	)

      PLAINTIFF, Maria Alvarez ("Alvarez"), requests that the DEFENDANTS, Ernst Weissler ("Weissler") and Wyandott-Von Maitlin Pharmaceuticals, Inc. ("Wyandott"), within thirty days after the service of this request separately admit in writing, pursuant to Rule 36 of the Federal Rules of Civil Procedure and for the purposes of this action only, the truth of the following statements;

      A. That each of the following documents listed below, the best copies of which are attached as Appendix A

      (1) is genuine and is a complete and accurate representation of the actual writing which the document purports to represent;

      (2) was prepared or sent by an officer or employee of Wyandott during the existence of his or her employment with Wyandott;

      (3) was directed to or concerned matters within the scope of the employment of said officer or employee of Wyandott;

      (4) was written and sent on or about the date listed on the document;

      (5) was written on the basis of the officer's or employee's firsthand knowledge of the matter contained therein;

      (6) was written in the ordinary course of business of Wyandott;

FIGURE 13–1
Request for Admissions.

(7) was kept as part of the routine employee evaluation process at Wyandott:

    (a) Alvarez employee evaluation of September 9, 1990.
    (b) Alvarez employee evaluation of October 31, 1990.
    (c) Alvarez employee evaluation of January 19, 1991.
    (d) Alvarez employee evaluation of February 7, 1991.
    (e) Alvarez employee evaluation of March 17, 1991.
    (f) Alvarez employee evaluation of April 23, 1991.
    (g) Memo of February 21, 1991.
    (h) Memo of February 28, 1991.
    (i) Memo of March 27, 1991.
    (j) Memo of April 1, 1991.
    (k) Memo of August 19, 1991.

B. That the best copies of each of the documents listed below are attached as Appendix B

(1) is genuine and is a complete and accurate representation of the actual writing which the document purports to represent;

(2) was prepared or sent by an officer or employee of Wyandott during the existence of his or her employment with Wyandott;

(3) was directed to or concerned matters within the scope of the employment of said officer or employee of Wyandott;

(4) was written and sent on or about the date listed on the document;

(5) was written on the basis of the officer's or employee's firsthand knowledge of the matter contained therein;

(6) was written in the ordinary course of business of Wyandott;

(7) was sent as part of the dismissal process involving Alvarez:

    (a) Letter of September 9, 1991.
    (b) Letter of September 15, 1991.
    (c) Letter of December 23, 1991.
    (d) Letter of January 29, 1992.
    (e) Letter of February 14, 1992.
    (f) Letter of March 17, 1992.
    (g) Letter of June 16, 1992.
    (h) Letter of August 31, 1992.

C. That the document entitled WYANDOTT-VON MAITLIN PHARMACEUTICALS, INC. EMPLOYEE HANDBOOK, the best copy of which is attached as Appendix C

(a) is genuine and is a complete and accurate representation of the actual writing that the document purports to represent;

(b) was distributed to all employees at Wyandott between August 19, 1989 and September 19, 1989;

(c) was received by Alvarez on August 19, 1989.

D. That each of the following documents listed below, the best copies of which are attached as Appendix D

(1) is genuine and is a complete and accurate representation of the actual writing that the document purports to represent;

(2) was prepared or sent by an officer or employee of Wyandott during the existence of his or her employment with Wyandott;

FIGURE 13–1
(continued)

(3) was directed to or concerned matters within the scope of the employment of said officer or employee of Wyandott;

(4) was written and sent on or about the date listed on the document;

(5) was written on the basis of the officer's or employee's firsthand knowledge of the matter contained therein;

(6) was written in the ordinary course of business of Wyandott;

(7) was kept as part of the routine employee evaluation process at Wyandott:

    (a) Research report on Biomiocin dated September 23, 1991.
    (b) Research report on Biomiocin dated October 19, 1991.
    (c) Research report on Biomiocin dated November 30, 1991.
    (d) Research report on Biomiocin dated March 28, 1992.
    (e) Research report on Biomiocin dated August 19, 1992.
    (f) Research report on Biomiocin dated December 2, 1992.
    (g) Research report on Biomiocin dated December 15, 1992.
    (h) Research report on Biomiocin dated December 31, 1992.

E. That each of the following documents listed below, the best copies of which are attached as Appendix E

(1) is genuine and is a complete and accurate representation of the actual writing which the document purports to represent;

(2) was received by an officer or employee of Wyandott during the existence of his or her employment with Wyandott;

(3) was received within the scope of the employment of said officer or employee of Wyandott;

(4) was received on or about the date listed on the document;

(5) was kept in the ordinary course of business of Wyandott;

(6) was kept as part of the routine employee evaluation process at Wyandott:

    (a) Letter of September 12, 1991.
    (b) Letter of September 20, 1991.
    (c) Letter of December 27, 1991.
    (d) Letter of January 1, 1992.
    (e) Letter of February 18, 1992.
    (f) Letter of March 27, 1992.
    (g) Letter of June 19, 1992.
    (h) Letter of September 2, 1992.

F. That each of the following statements is true:

(1) Wyandott is incorporated under the laws of the state of Delaware and has its principal place of business in Seattle, Washington.

(2) Wyandott is and was during the calendar years of 1989-1992, engaged in the manufacture and sale of Biomiocin.

(3) The Food and Drug Administration banned the manufacture and sale of Biomiocin on or about September 9, 1991.

(4) Biomiocin has not yet been reclassified as a safe drug by the FDA.

FIGURE 13–1
(continued)

(5) Alvarez was discharged on or about September 9, 1991.

(6) Alvarez received favorable employee evaluations from September of 1989 to September of 1991.

(7) Alvarez received all scheduled pay increases between September of 1989 and September of 1991.

(8) Alvarez received all scheduled promotions between September of 1989 and September of 1991.

DATED: Portland, Oregon
March 27, 1993.

> Kent, Freidman, Hedges, and Cole
>
> BY _____
> A member of the firm
>
> Attorneys for the Plaintiff
> Dr. Maria Alvarez
> 750 Maple Street
> Portland, Oregon

TO: Dirksen, Vannice, and Raeder
Attorneys for Defendant
Wyandott-Von Maitlin Pharmaceutical, Inc. and
Ernst Weissler, CEO of Wyandott-Von Maitlin
17810 Brinkerhoff Blvd.
Seattle, Washington

FIGURE 13–1
(continued)

Definitions. As in the request for production of documents covered in chapter 12, the definition section of the request for admissions may have a separate heading placed in the center of the page in bold-faced lettering. Terms that may be defined include such words as "document," "letter," "memorandum," and "report," among others.

Instructions. The heading "instructions" may also be placed in the center of the page in bold-faced letters. The instructions will specify any procedures that should be followed in responding to the request. Often the request for admissions is so complex that it is not possible to include a separate instructional paragraph at the beginning of the request. In such a case the instructions must be included with each category of documents examined and with the list of facts that are to be admitted. For instance, in the Alvarez case, the introductory section leading to a request to authenticate the genuineness of certain documents may have to specify that Mr. Weissler is to admit that the documents in question were written by Wyandott employees, that the documents were sent to the named recipients, that they were sent on the dates noted on the documents, etc. In contrast, the instructions leading to the list of facts and opinions to be admitted may simply read that Mr. Weissler is to admit "that each of the following statements is true." (See Figure 13–1.)

Specific Requests.   The request itself should be as simple as possible. That part of the request that lists the documents should be very specific as to the identity of each of those documents. It is best to list each document separately. Combining documents can cause confusion and can also open the request to objections. If possible include any identifying dates or numbers found on the documents. Copies of the documents in the list must be gathered together and attached to the request with an appropriate identifying heading. For example, in the Alvarez case, should you request the authentification of certain internal memos that passed between Mr. Weissler and the Human Resources Director at Wyandott-Von Maitlin, and the authentification of certain letters that passed between Mr. Weissler and Dr. Alvarez, you would include two separate lists, each with its own instructional paragraph. In turn, copies of the memos and letters would be attached to the request and labeled as such. The memos might be labeled "Appendix A," while the letters would be labeled "Appendix B."

That part of the request that lists the facts and opinions to be admitted should also be very carefully worded. Each fact and opinion should be listed separately. All facts that are undisputed should be included in this list. By identifying and including those facts in the request, you may avoid having to argue those facts at the time of the trial. Also include facts that you know are true, but that you might have a difficult time proving at trial. If you can get an admission now, you will save a lot of work later. However, you should be very careful to avoid topics that will elicit an appropriate objection from the other party.

13–3 RESPONDING TO THE REQUEST FOR ADMISSIONS

Make certain that when you receive a request for admissions you determine that the target date is reasonable. Once you have established that the target date is reasonable, place a reminder of the due date on the firm's calendar. If you have the responsibility of drafting the response, you should meet with the client to cover the alternatives available in responding to each request. You should also consider any objections that you might raise to the request.

Alternative Responses to the Request for Admissions

Your response to the request must be filed on time. This may mean that you must work quickly. However, because of the finality of an admission, you should never sacrifice care and accuracy for speed. Before beginning the drafting process, you should review the applicable court rules relating to the format and procedure. The alternatives available in a response are:

1. to admit;
2. to deny;
3. to refuse to either admit or deny; or
4. to object.

When you draft the response, first copy each statement to which you are responding, exactly as it appears on the original request. If a statement is true, you must respond by admitting that it is true. However, if reasonable doubt exists as to the truthfulness of a particular statement, you may deny it. A statement that has been admitted is called a judicial admission. A **judicial admission** is one that is placed into evidence and that can be presented to the court at the time of the trial.

Any statement that is not truthful should be denied. However, you should resist the temptation to deny a statement on a technicality, such as a misspelled word or an obvious typographical error. On the other hand, should the error actually alter the substance of the statement, you may consider denying it. For instance, in the Alvarez case, if your client is mistakenly identified as Mary Alvarez rather than Maria Alvarez, you probably would not be justified in denying the statement. However, if a statement listed her as Ms. Alvarez rather than Dr. Alvarez, you might be justified in denying the statement, provided that a legal question as to her professional expertise was at the heart of the case. Such questions, however, are best discussed with your attorney. Be careful in your denials because the other party may ask the court to compel your client to pay the cost of proving a matter that should not have been denied in the first place. Interestingly, even the losing party can make this request to the court.

Sometimes when the deadline for a response is approaching you may deny all requests and later amend your response, admitting those requests that should have been admitted in the first place. This practice has its dangers, however. The chief danger is the deemed admitted rule. As we have seen, under this rule unless a party delivers a written denial or a detailed reason why that party cannot admit or deny a statement, that statement is deemed admitted.

The third alternative is to refuse to either admit or deny a request. However, the Federal Rules of Civil Procedure do not allow you to do this unless you have made a reasonable inquiry into the subject. Moreover, a lack of personal knowledge is not a proper basis for refusing to respond, unless the party has reason to doubt the credibility of the source of the information. Your response to the request for admission does not require verification in federal court. However, since some state and local rules demand such verification, you should check on the proper procedure in your area.

Objections to the Request for Admissions

Basically, the same objections that are available in response to the other discovery techniques are available in response to a request for admissions. As we have seen in previous chapters, the grounds for such objections include stating that complying with the request would violate the attorney-client privilege or the work product privilege. Other objections are that the request is overbroad, irrelevant, or duplicative. You may also object on the grounds that the statement is a compound request.

The Attorney-Client Privilege and the Work Product Privilege. As we have seen previously, the attorney-client privilege prevents the forced disclosure of communication between an attorney and a client. Similarly, the work product privilege protects letters, memos, documents, records, and other tangible items that have been prepared in anticipation of litigation. If a request for admissions would violate either of these privileges, you could lodge an appropriate objection on those grounds.

Inadmissible and Irrelevant Evidence. You will recall that the scope of discovery is much broader than the scope of the evidence that can be introduced at trial. Despite this broad scope, however, any discovery request must be reasonably calculated to lead to admissible evidence. Should a request for admissions ask your client to respond to the truthfulness of a matter that could not be reasonably calculated to lead to admissible evidence, you may object on those grounds. Similarly, a request for admissions must address a fact, opinion, or document that is relevant to the lawsuit. The request for admissions must further the discovery process. If it does not, you may object.

Overbroad and Duplicative Requests. An overbroad request is one that is not narrowly defined. For example, in the Alvarez case, the lawsuit involves her employment with Wyandott-Von Maitlin Pharmaceuticals. If the opposing party sought admissions regarding every employment evaluation ever filed on Dr. Alvarez,

judicial admission
An admission that is placed into evidence and that can be presented to the court at the time of the trial.

even those involving part-time jobs when she was in high school, college, and graduate school, an objection that the request is over-broad would be in order. Another objection is that the request is duplicative or repetitious. This objection argues that the request includes one item for admission that is repeated over and over. Your duty extends to only one request. Often the request will be varied slightly to elicit a different answer. You should object to every variation of the request.

Compound Requests.   The **compound request** is a request that asks a party to admit to two or more facts in one statement. The compound request makes a response tricky, if not impossible. Your objection should address the compound nature of the request and explain the difficulty that it presents in framing an accurate response. This objection may not, however, prevent the ultimate need to respond to the subject matter of the statement, since the opposing party can file an amended request.

> **compound request**
> A request for admission that asks a party to admit to two or more facts in one statement.

THE COMPUTERIZED LAW FIRM—Word Processing

SCENARIO

Your attorney has called you into her office to discuss the Alvarez case. She lets you know that she intends to serve Ernst Weissler, the CEO of Wyandott-Von Maitlin Pharmaceuticals, Inc., with a request for admissions. She is going to ask that he admit to the genuineness of Dr. Alvarez's employee evaluation record and to the genuineness of the Wyandott-Von Maitlin employee handbook. In addition, she will want to request the authentication of several dismissal letters sent to Dr. Alvarez. To expedite matters she asks that you draw up the request as soon as possible. Since she must be at a continuing education seminar all afternoon, she leaves you with the job of drawing up a draft of a request for admissions. She asks you to have the request on her desk by 8 a.m. the next day. To give you some direction in this job, she tells you to look up the case of *Justinian v. The Biotechnology Engineering Research Center*, another unjust dismissal lawsuit that she handled last year. Your attorney is certain that looking at the file will help guide you. However, a newly drafted request for admissions specifically designed for the Alvarez case should be developed.

PROBLEM

You look up the Justinian file and locate the request for admissions. However, since the Justinian case did not involve the employee's performance evaluation records, the request for admissions will have to be worded differently. You also notice that the Justinian case involved a series of memos and employee bulletin board announcements rather than statements in an employee manual. Again, this means that the Alvarez request must be reworded. The request is seventeen pages in length. It is already 2:30 p.m. Do you have any way of producing the request by 8 a.m. tomorrow?

SOLUTION

As outlined in the **Computerized Law Firm** features at the end of chapters 6, 7, and 8, word processing is a very important computer application in the law firm. In this case, the Justinian request for admissions is likely stored on the word processor's hard drive or on a floppy disk. Your firm may also own a WordPerfect software package. By using the law firm's word processor you can call up either the Justinian request for admissions or a generic request format on WordPerfect. In either case you will not need to re-keyboard the entire document. You will simply have to identify the specialized documents that must be authenticated in the Alvarez case.

Several word processing packages are available for the computerized law firm. However, as noted above and in chapters 6 and 8, the most frequently used is WordPerfect 5.0. Software available for IBM, Macintosh, Apple, and other computer hardware is listed in Appendix B. As noted in chapter 8, local community colleges, technical colleges, vocational schools, and non-credit programs offer beginning, intermediate, and advanced classes on numerous word processing packages.

SUMMARY

13–1 A request for admissions is a request filed by one party in a lawsuit on another party in that suit asking the second party to admit to the truthfulness of certain facts or opinions or to authenticate the genuineness of certain documents. The primary purpose of the request is to simplify the points in controversy. An admission made in response to a request for admissions cannot be withdrawn without the court's permission. Any request that is not denied is deemed admitted.

13–2 In preparing to draft a request for admissions, the paralegal should discuss the matter with the attorney, review all pleadings, and look over the applicable court rules. The actual request for admissions will include the title, the introductory paragraph, the definitions and instructions, and the specific request. Copies of any documents involved in the request must be attached to the request.

13–3 The alternatives available in responding to a request for admissions are to admit, to deny, to refuse to either admit or deny, or to object. Grounds for objecting include arguing that complying with the request would violate the attorney-client privilege or the work product privilege. Other objections are that the request is overbroad, irrelevant, or duplicative. A final objection is that the statement is a compound request.

KEY TERMS

compound request

deemed admitted rule

judicial admission

request for admissions

QUESTIONS FOR REVIEW AND DISCUSSION

1. What is a request for admissions?
2. On whom may a request for admissions be served?
3. What is the principal purpose for filing a request for admissions?
4. What advantages does the request for admissions have over other discovery tools?
5. What preliminary steps should be taken before drafting a request for admissions?
6. List the parts of a request for admissions.
7. Explain the content of each part of a request for admissions.
8. List the possible responses to a request for admissions.
9. Point out the danger of not responding to a request for admissions.
10. List the possible objections to a request for admissions.

ACTIVITIES

1. Review your state's rules relating to the request for admissions. Prepare a summary of the differences between the federal and the state rules. Also check your local court rules and do the same.
2. Prepare a chart of the objections to the request for admissions that are permitted in the federal and state courts in your area.

CHAPTER 13 PROJECT—DRAFTING A REQUEST FOR ADMISSIONS

Review the Commentary at the beginning of this chapter. Recall, that in this case, your firm is representing Dr. Maria Alvarez in a wrongful discharge suit against her former employer, Wyandott Von-Maitlin Pharmaceuticals, and its CEO, Mr. Ernst Weissler. Locate a sample request for admissions in your state's form book. Draft a request for admissions in which you request that Mr. Weissler admit that he signed all of Dr. Alvarez's employee evaluation forms, that all of those forms indicated that she did outstanding work for the company, that Dr. Alvarez is a contractual employee, and that he personally believed that her job performance was satisfactory. Also request that he authenticate the attached document purporting to be the company's progressive disciplinary procedure. Also request that he authenticate the letter that he sent to Dr. Alvarez announcing her termination and the internal memo that he sent to the company's Human Resources Director informing him of her termination.

Pre-Trial, Trial, and Post-Trial

CHAPTER 14

Settlements and Dismissals

COMMENTARY—THE KOWALSKI CASE

Clark Kowalski is a nuclear physicist who is employed by Americans for Environmental Safety (AES), an independent organization of individuals devoted to protecting the environment. The Cuyahoga Valley Nuclear Power Plant, located on the outskirts of Cleveland, Ohio, and owned and operated by the Everett-Stimson Power and Light Company, had wanted Dr. Kowalski to inspect the power plant. The objective of the inspection was to reassure AES and the public that the plant was safe. Unfortunately, during the inspection tour, Dr. Kowalski was severely injured in an explosion. Shortly after the accident, a reporter asked Dr. Kowalski for an interview, during which he revealed some very damaging information about the plant's safety procedures. Shortly after the news story appeared, Dr. Kowalski decided to bring a lawsuit against Everett-Stimson. Because Everett-Stimson has filed a counterclaim against Dr. Kowalski for libel, your attorney thinks it would be a good idea to explore the possibility of settling some of these claims out of court. Accordingly, she asks you to organize the litigation file in preparation for a possible settlement. Depending on the outcome of the preliminary investigation, you may also be called upon to prepare a settlement summary, a settlement letter, or a settlement brochure. If a settlement is actually reached you may also be required to draft a settlement agreement. This chapter will cover the details surrounding the settlement process.

OBJECTIVES

In Section 3, you were introduced to the discovery process. Like the discovery process, the settlement process is an integral part of any lawsuit. After reading this chapter, you will be able to:

1. Define settlement.
2. Identify the preliminary decisions regarding settlement.
3. Discuss the work that must be done in a preliminary investigation in the settlement process.
4. Differentiate between a settlement summary and a settlement letter.
5. Relate the duties a paralegal might perform in compiling a settlement brochure.
6. Outline the nature of a settlement agreement.
7. Explain the differences among general releases, partial releases, and mutual releases.
8. Discuss the nature of a stipulated dismissal.
9. Define the voluntary dismissal on notice.
10. Explain a court ordered involuntary dismissal.
11. Discuss the nature of a consent decree.
12. Explain the need for a settlement proceeds statement.

14–1 THE SETTLEMENT

A **settlement** is an agreement or a contract between parties that terminates their civil dispute. Many civil cases end in a settlement. Often settlement negotiations are conducted simultaneously with the active preparation of the lawsuit. In fact, the preparation of the lawsuit may actually lead to the settlement. This is because as the attorney gathers information about the suit, he or she may decide that a settlement is in the client's best interests.

settlement
An agreement or contract between disputing parties in which differences are resolved.

In such a case, the lawsuit is settled quickly. If, however, the attorney decides not to settle, no time has been lost in the litigation process. In order to be an effective paralegal, you must understand the factors to consider in making a settlement decision. It also will be very helpful for you to know how to conduct a preliminary investigation.

Decisions Regarding Settlement

An attorney must consider a number of factors before deciding to settle a case. Perhaps the two most obvious factors are time and money. Since the legal system is overburdened with a heavy case load, it is not uncommon for a court's calendar to be backed up for months. Some courts in large metropolitan areas have dockets that are backed up for years. This type of overcrowding may mean that a trial date cannot be set for months or even years after the original complaint has been filed. If your client cannot afford to wait that much time for a judgment, then your attorney may elect to settle the case without going to trial.

Also recall that a lengthy and involved discovery procedure may be needed to gather the facts required to prove your client's case at trial. The more involved the discovery process, the more expensive the lawsuit becomes. For example, in the Kowalski case, discovery may be necessary to uncover not only the facts surrounding the explosion itself, but also the circumstances leading to the explosion. In addition, discovery will also be needed to uncover whether the defendants had any knowledge of similar incidents involving the type of pump that exploded and harmed Dr. Kowalski. This will mean not only taking multiple depositions, but also serving interrogatories and requests for production of documents. Your client may have to undergo a physical examination, and your attorney will probably want to inspect the site of the explosion. All of this costs money, which will erode the value of any final judgment rendered by the court.

Another settlement factor may be the particular court's decisions in similar cases. In the Kowalski case, for example, you may find that the court recently rendered a judgment favorable to a utility company in a case that involves facts very similar to the facts in your case. In such a situation it may be in your client's best interest to engage in settlement negotiations.

Finally, the subsequent tactics of the other party's attorney may motivate a client to seriously consider a settlement. Recall, for example, that the defendant, in responding to a lawsuit, may elect to file a counterclaim against the plaintiff. The legitimacy of the counterclaim and the degree to which the defendant may succeed in presenting that counterclaim would be critical factors to consider in making any settlement decision. In the Kowalski case, for instance, Everett-Stimson has filed a counterclaim for libel against Dr. Kowalski. Such an event may motivate your attorney to consider the possibility of settling the case without proceeding to trial.

Preliminary Investigative Work

Generally, an offer to settle originates with the plaintiff. This is because the plaintiff's attorney is in the best position to assess the injuries to the client and can, thus, set a reasonable figure as the basis for the settlement. Naturally this means that some preliminary assessment work is in order. Usually this preliminary investigative work will be the responsibility of the paralegal. During this stage you will have to obtain a personal history of the client, a preliminary assessment of the client's present health, and a medical history of the client. You may also be required to calculate the damages in the case. You may have to probe some collateral areas to get an accurate picture of the probability of your client prevailing should the case go to trial.

The Client's Personal History.   One of the preliminary steps in the settlement investigation is to obtain an accurate personal and financial history of the client. This would include the client's family information, education, employment record, and religious, professional, and civic organization memberships. It might also be helpful to determine if your client has any hobbies or if he participates in sports. For example, in the Kowalski case, it might be helpful to know that Dr. Kowalski was an avid tennis player prior to sustaining the injuries caused by the explosion in the power plant. Such information may be helpful later in calculating the damages that your attorney will seek in this situation.

The Client's Present Health and Medical History.   The client's medical history before and after the accident are key ingredients in the case. You will have to determine the nature and the extent of the injuries the client has suffered. You will also need to find out what treatment he or she has undergone and will be compelled to undergo in the future. It will also be helpful to know what diagnostic tests were performed on the client and what therapy, if any, was performed. Furthermore, your attorney will want to know if the client was disfigured and if he or she has suffered any temporary or permanent disability as a result of the accident. Don't overlook any psychiatric or psychological damage that may have resulted from the accident. It is often advisable to have the client keep a medical diary on a daily or a weekly basis. Instruct the client to record any symptoms related to the accident and any medical visits to physicians, chiropractors, psychologists, and physical therapists.

Calculating Damages. If, as the paralegal, you are asked to calculate the damages in the case, make sure to organize and review all checks, receipts, income tax returns, and paycheck stubs furnished by the client. This will ensure that you have presented a concise and accurate picture of the damages. Extreme care should be exercised in this calculation because damages are often a substantial part of any settlement agreement.

Investigating Collateral Matters. Before your attorney can make an informed decision he or she must take into consideration certain collateral matters. Collateral matters are considerations that go beyond the facts and the merits of the case but that, nevertheless, have a very real impact on the decision to settle or to proceed with the suit. For example, the attitude of the trial judge assigned to the case may play an important factor in the decision. If, in the Kowalski case, you learn that the trial judge tends to rule in favor of utility companies in tort suits of this nature, your attorney may decide that a settlement would be in your client's best interests.

Another collateral area to look at is the experience or inexperience of the opposing attorney. If in the Kowalski case you're dealing with an attorney who has a strong record representing utility companies in this type of suit, your attorney will approach him or her with a different strategy than the strategy that would be used if the attorney were inexperienced.

Recent statutes and court rulings involving this area of the law must also be researched to help your attorney determine if any recent trends in the law would make it advisable to settle the suit. For example, in the Kowalski case it would be essential for your attorney to know whether there have been any changes in the law of Ohio that would affect the outcome of your case. This information will be helpful to your attorney when she negotiates for a settlement with Everett-Stimson.

14-2 SETTLEMENT OFFERS

As a paralegal, your talents may be used in a number of ways as your attorney prepares a settlement offer. Often the paralegal will be asked to draft a settlement summary, a settlement letter, or a settlement brochure. The complexity of the lawsuit and the amount of money involved will be primary factors in determining which of the three will be used in a given case.

Settlement Summaries and Letters

Once the preliminary investigative work has been completed, the information must be pulled together into a useful report. This report must convince the defendant that a settlement would be in his or her best interests. Depending on the situation you may be charged with writing a settlement summary or a settlement letter. The objective of each is to persuade your opponent to agree to your settlement terms. The choice of which format to use is based on the complexity of the case and the amount of money involved. Drafting settlement summaries and settlement letters is an important part of the paralegal's role in the overall settlement process. The law firm's form files and personal injury form books should be used to prepare the initial draft of the settlement summary or the settlement letter.

Settlement Summaries. Simple cases involving relatively inexpensive claims may be settled early primarily because the cost of such litigation outweighs the benefit of a long and expensive suit. In such a case a short settlement summary may be drafted by the paralegal. The **settlement summary** would pull together all essential information outlining the benefit of settling the case at an early stage in the litigation. Settlement summaries are usually not much longer than one page. Figure 14–1 is an example of a settlement summary for the Kowalski case.

Settlement Letters. Cases that involve complex issues and an extensive list of damages may require the writing of a settlement letter. The **settlement letter** is a much more detailed account of the essential information needed to determine the benefit of settling a case. Often it is several pages in length. This is because it must cover a variety of material with much more detail than that required by the settlement summary. The settlement letter will begin with a statement of the facts involved in the case. Naturally, this statement of the facts must be written from the perspective of the defendant's potential liability. The letter will also include a detailed assessment of your client's injuries. This should include your client's medical history, present medical condition, and future medical prognosis. To be convincing, the letter should also reveal the plaintiff's legal theory or theories of recovery. The amount of money spent by your client because of his injuries should be included as well as the amount of any wages he has lost because of those injuries. Finally, the settlement letter should present to the defendant a statement of the amount that your client is prepared to ask as a reasonable settlement. Figure 14–2 is an example of a settlement letter sent by Dr. Kowalski's attorney to the Everett-Stimson Power and Light Company.

settlement summary
A summary of all essential information outlining the benefits of settling the case at an early stage in the litigation.

settlement letter
A detailed account of the information needed to determine the benefit of settling a case.

Kowalski v Everett-Stimson Power and Light Company
Common Pleas Court
Cuyahoga County, Ohio
Case No. 93-GD-980

Settlement Summary

On the morning of November 27, 1992, at approximately
11:45, the plaintiff, Dr. Clark Kowalski, acting as a representative
of Americans for Environmental Safety, and plant technician
Samuel Kirk were making an inspection of the cooling system at
the Cuyahoga Valley Nuclear Power Plant. An incident report filed
by Samuel Kirk indicates that Dr. Kowalski had followed all proper
safety procedures as he conducted his inspection. The incident
report filed by Mr. Kirk also indicates that at approximately 11:47
that morning, while he and Dr. Kowalski were preparing to
complete their inspection, a nearby hydraulic pump
malfunctioned, causing an explosion that threw both Dr. Kowalski
and him to the floor. Dr. Kowalski had been facing Mr. Kirk, with
his back to the pump, and thus took the full force of the explosion
in the upper back. Dr. Kowalski's has testified that at
approximately 11:47 on the morning of November 27, 1992, he
was struck in the back by an explosive force. Dr. Kowalski
has stated that at no time was he in any way in contact with
said pump.

Dr. Kowalski may recover in tort law under two theories:
(a.) The defendants knew about the dangerous condition of the
pump and negligently failed to remedy the situation or to warn Dr.
Kowalski; and (b.) the defendants should have known about the
dangerous condition of the pump but did not because of a
negligently conducted inspection.

Dr. Kowalski suffered third-degree burns across the upper
one-half of his back. The plaintiff also received a broken arm and a
broken wrist. Dr. Kowalski also suffered a minor concussion, a
sprained neck, and received minor cuts and abrasions to his face
and hands. He also lost three teeth and will require a series of
corrective dental operations as well as restorative plastic surgery.
The medical expenses incurred by Dr. Kowalski total $52,440. The
plaintiff also intends to seek $235,000 in damages for pain and
suffering, plus $500,000 in punitive damages under the theory
that the defendant's conduct was intentional. The plaintiff has also
incurred lost wages amounting to $8,000.

The plaintiff is asking for a total of $795,440 in damages.
Because of the climate of anti-utility, anti-nuclear sentiment
prevalent in Ohio at the present time, it is anticipated that the jury
will award the full amount. However, in the interest of a speedy
and just end to the suit, the plaintiff is willing to settle for an
award of $400,000. This represents just slightly more than one-
half the anticipated recovery should the matter go to trial. The
plaintiff is also willing to negotiate a payment plan, provided that
he can receive an immediate cash payment of the first $100,000.

FIGURE 14–1
Settlement
Summary.

LAW OFFICE OF

EDWARDS, BLAKE, FITZSIMMONS, AND MYLORIE
31753 EAST CLOVER AVENUE
CLEVELAND, OHIO 44121

March 17, 1993

Ms. Charlene Bannister
Andrews, Bannister, Vilnius, and Friedman
The Billings Building Suite 81989
2748 West Lexington Blvd.
Cleveland, Ohio 44117

RE: Kowalski v. Everett-Stimson Power and Light Co.
Common Pleas Court
Cuyahoga County, Ohio
Case No. 93-GD-980

Dear Ms. Bannister:

In the interests of bringing the case of Kowalski v. Everett-Stimson to a speedy and just conclusion, I have been authorized by my client, Dr. Clark Kowalski, to make the following settlement offer to your client. Please consult with your client, give this settlement offer all due consideration, and contact my office with your response within fourteen days from the receipt of this letter.

Plaintiff's Background—Clark Kowalski was born on February 9, 1948, the first of seven children born to Mr. and Mrs. Vytautus Kowalski. The plaintiff attended St. Mary Magdalene Grade School in Willowick, Ohio; St. Joseph High School in Cleveland; John Carroll University in Cleveland; and Case Western Reserve University, also in Cleveland. He received his doctorate in nuclear physics from Case Western Reserve University in June of 1974. Dr. Kowalski has taught at a number of universities and colleges over the course of the last twenty years. He is an acknowledged expert in the field of nuclear physics, having no fewer than thirty scholarly articles to his credit. Prior to his accepting employment as a nuclear physicist with Americans for Environmental Safety (AES), he directed the research department at the prestigious North Central Institute of Technology (NCIT).

Medical History—Dr. Kowalski's medical history is notable for its lack of incident. He suffered a knee injury while playing tennis at St. Joseph High School in 1966. Aside from that, he has a mild case of hypertension that is kept under control by the daily administration of the minimum dose of Vasotec. He has no previous history of head, back, or arm injuries. Before the accident he was, in fact, in good enough health to win the Cleveland-Akron-Toledo Tri-City Amateur Tennis Championship for three years in a row.

The Facts Surrounding the Accident—On the morning of November 27, 1992, at approximately 11:45, Dr. Kowalski was making an inspection of the cooling system at the Cuyahoga Valley Nuclear Power Plant. The inspection of the plant by an AES representative had been arranged by Everett-Stimson to reassure AES and the public that the plant was safe. The attached incident report filed by Samuel Kirk indicates that Dr. Kowalski had followed all proper safety procedures as he conducted his inspection. The incident report filed by Mr. Kirk also indicates that at approximately 11:47 that morning, while he and Dr. Kowalski were preparing to

FIGURE 14–2
Settlement Letter.

complete their inspection, a nearby hydraulic pump malfunctioned, causing an explosion that threw both Dr. Kowalski and him to the floor. Dr. Kowalski had been facing Mr. Kirk with his back to the pump and thus took the full force of the explosion in the upper back. Dr. Kowalski's position shielded Mr. Kirk from the force of the explosion.

Dr. Kowalski's deposition, a copy of which is attached, also indicates that at approximately 11:47 on the morning of November 27, 1992, he was struck in the back by an explosive force. Dr. Kowalski has stated that at no time was he in any contact with said pump. He has indicated that he was talking to Mr. Kirk as they were preparing to complete their inspection when he was suddenly thrown from his feet by a sudden hot blast. He was looking at Mr. Kirk at the time and had no warning that the pump was about to explode.

Theories of Recovery—Dr. Kowalski may recover in tort law under two theories:

    a. The defendants knew about the dangerous condition of the pump negligently failed to remedy the situation or to warn Dr. Kowalski.

    b. The defendants should have known about the dangerous condition of the pump but did not because of a negligently conducted inspection.

The first theory will be proven by an examination of the accident records of the Everett-Stimson Power and Light Company, which will clearly indicate that identical explosions involving identical pumps taken from the same lot number occurred at two other nuclear power plants owned and operated by Everett-Stimson. Testimony from Dr. Kowalski, Mr. Kirk, and from Julius Angelitis, the director of the Cuyahoga Valley Nuclear Power Plant, will indicate that neither Dr. Kowalski nor Mr. Kirk was informed of the previous accidents, despite Mr. Angelitis's knowledge of the accidents and his knowledge that Dr. Kowalski and Mr. Kirk would be working in the vicinity of the suspect pump. Such a failure to warn of impending danger would amount to negligent conduct, making the company liable for Dr. Kowalski's resulting injuries.

The defendants may wish to argue that Mr. Angelitis did not inform Dr. Kowalski about the dangerous pump because a recent inspection had revealed that the pump was not flawed. The defendants may argue that because of this favorable inspection they did not know that harm to the plaintiff would occur. If this is the argument presented by the defendants, then the plaintiff will call upon his second theory. That theory suggests that the inspection performed by the defendants must necessarily have been conducted in a negligent manner. The plaintiff will submit evidence that will convince a jury that even a cursory examination of the pump would have revealed the same flaw in this pump which caused the other two pumps to explode. The plaintiff will submit further convincing evidence that will prove that this pump exploded in the same manner and as a result of the same flaw that caused the other two pumps to explode.

Injuries to the Plaintiff—The initial medical examination conducted by Dr. Wesley Forbes, the staff physician at Cuyahoga Valley, indicated that Dr. Kowalski suffered third-degree burns across the upper one-half of his back. Dr. Forbes's initial assessment also indicated that the plaintiff received a broken arm and a broken wrist. The plaintiff was air-lifted to the Burn Unit at Cleveland Metropolitan General Hospital, where the diagnosis of his burns and broken bones

FIGURE 14–2
(continued)

was confirmed. Dr. Michelle Gonzales also found that Dr. Kowalski had suffered a minor concussion, a sprained neck, and had received minor cuts and abrasions on his face and hands. He also lost three teeth and will require a series of corrective dental operations as well as restorative plastic surgery. The reports issued by Dr. Forbes, Dr. Gonzales, and the dentist, Dr. Herman Kleinhenz, are attached.

Medical Expenses—The medical expenses incurred by Dr. Kowalski have been itemized on the attached forms. However, a general summary of those expenses includes the following items:

a.	Medivac Transportation to Cleveland Metro	$ 1,000
b.	Emergency Room Treatment	$ 2,300
c.	One-Week Hospital Stay at Metro	$ 9,800
d.	Orthopedic Treatment	$ 7,900
e.	Burn Unit Treatment	$ 8,000
f.	Radiology Department	$ 1,000
g.	Dr. Kleinhenz's Examination	$ 1,500
h.	Anticipated Oral Surgery	$ 2,400
i.	Anticipated Cosmetic Surgery	$ 9,900
j.	Anticipated Treatment	$ 8,640
	TOTAL	$52,440

Further Damages—The plaintiff, Dr. Kowalski, also intends to seek $235,000 in damages for pain and suffering plus $500,000 in punitive damages. The plaintiff has also incurred lost wages amounting to $8,000.

Proposed Settlement—The plaintiff is asking for a total of $795,440 in damages. Because of the climate of anti-utility, anti-nuclear sentiment prevalent in Ohio at the present time, it is anticipated that the jury will award the full amount. However, in the interest of a speedy and just end to the suit, the plaintiff is willing to settle for an immediate cash award of $400,000. This represents just slightly more than one-half the anticipated recovery should the matter go to trial.

As counsel for the plaintiff, I urge you to take this settlement offer to your client in the spirit in which it is offered. I will look forward to your affirmative response.

Very truly yours,

Terry A. Mylorie

Terry A. Mylorie

TAM/skg
Enclosures
CC: Dr. Clark Kowalski with enclosures

FIGURE 14–2
(continued)

Settlement Brochures

The **settlement brochure** is a multiple page portfolio that seeks to compile all the information relevant to settlement negotiations. Naturally, the objective and the basic content of a settlement summary or a settlement letter and a settlement brochure are the same. They differ, however, in the amount of the material presented and in the format used. The settlement brochure tends to be more elaborate in that it includes photographs, charts, graphs, newspaper articles, witness statements, medical reports, and the like. It is frequently made more striking by its use of multi-colored graphs and charts. A settlement brochure can be a very persuasive settlement tool. However, it is also expensive and is thus used most effectively in lawsuits seeking fairly large settlements. The individual parts of a settlement brochure should include a statement of the facts, the client's personal history, the client's medical history and medical condition, the damages suffered by the client, and an evaluation of the case and statement of the settlement. Figure 14–3 is an example of a table of contents that might be used for a settlement brochure in the Kowalski case.

Statement of the Facts. Like the settlement letter, the settlement brochure will begin with a **statement of the facts** involved in the case. Again, this statement of the facts must be written from the perspective of the defendant's potential liability. However, the settlement brochure can also include witness statements, medical reports, newspaper articles, and photographs. The use of newspaper articles and photographs can be an especially effective way of creating a vivid effect. Consider, for example, the dramatic impact in the Kowalski case of including in your settlement brochure a front page news story of an accident at the Cuyahoga Valley Plant

---

FIGURE 14–3
Table of Contents—Settlement Brochure.

I.	Description of the Accident
	Witness Statements
	Photos of the Accident Scene
	Photos of the Plaintiff before the Accident
	Photos of Plaintiff after the Accident
II.	Statement of the Facts
III.	Plaintiff's Personal History
IV.	Medical History of the Plaintiff
V.	Medical Condition of the Plaintiff
VI.	Medical Expenses
VII.	Evaluation of the Claim

and color photographs of the accident site and the injuries to Dr. Kowalski. Such a package can be very sobering to the defendant, who realizes that these same photographs may be presented to jury members who may live near the Cuyahoga Valley Plant.

Client's Personal History.   The **client's personal history** should also be included in the settlement brochure. To complete this section of the settlement brochure, you should review the preliminary investigative work that you did in the case. The personal history would include the client's family information, education, employment record, and religious, professional, and civic organization memberships. It might also be helpful to include information about your client's hobbies or participation in sports. As in the case of the facts, photographs can also be used here. Photographs may be helpful later in calculating the damages that your attorney will seek in this situation.

Client's Medical History and Medical Condition.   Like the settlement letter, the settlement brochure will also include a detailed assessment of your **client's medical history and medical condition**. Again, this should include the injuries suffered by the client as well as any future medical prognosis. To be convincing, this section of the settlement brochure can include the hospital records, the reports filed by any physicians and therapists involved in the case, as well as the client's medical diary. Again, photographs of the plaintiff's injuries can be a very effective supplement in this section of the brochure.

Damages, Evaluation, and Settlement.   In a separate section devoted to **damages**, the amount of money spent by your client because of his injuries should be included as well as the amount of any wages he has lost because of those injuries. All checks, receipts, income tax returns, and pay stubs furnished by the client must be organized and totaled to present a precise and accurate picture of the damages. Finally, the settlement brochure should include an **evaluation of the claim** and present to the defendant a **statement of the settlement** that your client believes is reasonable.

14–3   SETTLEMENT AGREEMENTS AND RELEASES

If the parties reach an agreement based on the settlement offer, then it will be necessary to place the details of that settlement into some permanent written form. The complexity of the case and the settlement arrangement will determine whether the parties will want to draft a settlement agreement or a release.

---

settlement brochure
A multiple page portfolio that seeks to compile all information relevant to settlement negotiations.

statement of the facts
A narrative of all facts involved in the case.

client's personal history
A listing of the client's family information, education, employment record, and church, professional, and civic organization memberships in a settlement brochure.

client's medical history and medical condition
A section of the settlement brochure that sets out the injuries suffered by the client and any future medical prognosis.

damages
The amount of money spent by a client because of injuries and all wages lost because of the injuries.

evaluation of the claim
A recap of the perceived value of a claim.

statement of the settlement
A recap of the settlement client believes is reasonable.

Settlement Agreements

A **settlement agreement** is actually a contract between the parties. As such, it must meet all the legal requirements of a contract. This means that it must involve the voluntary mutual assent of the parties. It must involve the give-and-take element of consideration. Also, the agreement must be legal and must be made by parties with the capacity to contract.

Voluntary Mutual Assent. Since a settlement agreement is a contract, it must be made with the voluntary mutual assent of both parties. If the client is against the settlement, the attorney cannot agree to it no matter how lucrative and beneficial it may appear to be. In fact, the rules of ethical conduct that guide attorneys also specify this limitation on the attorney's power to represent a client. Similarly, to be voluntary, the settlement agreement must not result from duress or undue influence. Threats of bodily harm or threats to property would constitute duress.

Consideration. Because the settlement agreement is a contract, it will not be valid unless each side gains something and each side gives up something. This exchange of values is called **consideration**. Money is the most common form of consideration. In the Kowalski case, for example, your attorney may decide to ask Everett-Stimson for a $400,000 settlement to compensate your client for the injuries he suffered as a result of the explosion of the hydraulic pump used in the Cuyahoga Valley Nuclear Power Plant. Money, however, is not the only form of consideration. A promise to act or not to act may also be consideration. In the Kowalski case, for example, the consideration offered by Dr. Kowalski is his agreement to drop the lawsuit. Once the settlement has been agreed to, it is binding even if Dr. Kowalski later finds out that he had no legal basis for bringing the suit against Everett-Stimson.

Capacity and Legality. In order for the settlement to be enforceable in court, it must be made by parties who have the legal capacity to enter into a contract. If one of the parties is a minor, the parent or the guardian enters into the settlement agreement and obtains the court's approval on behalf of the minor. Naturally, the terms of the settlement must not require either party to do something that is illegal.

Form of the Settlement Agreement. The settlement should be structured to include the identities of the parties, the action that gave rise to the claim, the type and the extent of the injuries

settlement agreement
A contract between two or more parties to settle a case; it involves the voluntary, mutual assent of the parties and the give-and-take element of consideration; the agreement must be legal and must be made by parties with the capacity to contract.

consideration
The exchange of values in a contract.

caused, the consideration given for the settlement, the time and the circumstances under which any and all payments will be made, and any special conditions that have been agreed to by the parties. If a dispute arises over any part of the agreement, a court will interpret its provisions. If the court finds that a term of the agreement is vague or ambiguous, it may seek additional testimony or evidence to determine the intent of the parties at the time that they entered the agreement. Figure 14–4 presents an example of a settlement agreement in the Kowalski case.

COURT OF COMMON PLEAS
CUYAHOGA COUNTY
STATE OF OHIO

CLARK KOWALSKI   )
        Plaintiff,   )
) Civil Action No. 93-GD-980
    vs.   ) SETTLEMENT AGREEMENT
)
)
EVERETT-STIMSON, et al.   )
        Defendants.   )
)
)
)

     THIS ACTION, Kowalski v. Everett-Stimson Power and Light Co., Case No. 93-GD-980, was brought in the Common Pleas Court of Cuyahoga County, Ohio by Clark Kowalski, hereinafter called "plaintiff," against Everett-Stimson Power and Light Company, hereinafter called "defendant." The plaintiff brought this action to recover damages for injuries received in an explosion at the Cuyahoga Valley Nuclear Power plant, a facility owned and operated by the defendant. Subsequent to the filing of this action, the defendant in its answer filed a counterclaim against the plaintiff for libel relating to certain remarks made to a reporter for the Cleveland Daily News, and which appeared in that paper in a story dated December 19, 1992.
     THIS AGREEMENT has been made and entered into at Cleveland, Ohio this 15th day of May, 1993.

WITNESSETH

     WHEREAS, the parties desire to settle and adjust all matters relating to this action, all property rights, all payments in the nature of damages, or other allowances that each might be entitled to, and
     WHEREAS, each of the parties is fully advised as to the extent of the injuries, the value of the property, and the prospects of the other,

FIGURE 14–4
Settlement Agreement.

NOW, THEREFORE, in consideration of the mutual covenants and agreements herein contained, the parties hereby acknowledge and agree as follows:

a. The plaintiff agrees to accept the sum of Four Hundred Thousand Dollars ($400,000) in full satisfaction of all claims in the complaint filed against the defendant in Case No. 93-GD-980 in the Common Pleas Court of Cuyahoga County, Ohio.

b. The defendant agrees to pay the plaintiff the sum of Four Hundred Thousand Dollars ($400,000) payable as follows: the sum of $100,000 payable in cash when the settlement agreement is final and signed, the sum of $300,000 payable over a seven year period with a 10 percent interest per annum, with the first payment of $4,000 beginning on the first day of the month following the signing and finalizing of this agreement and continuing at a rate of $4,000 per month on the first day of every month thereafter until paid in full.

c. The plaintiff agrees that there will be no prepayment penalty should the defendant decide to pay the balance early.

d. Contemporaneous with the signing of this agreement, the defendant shall execute a note payable to the order of the plaintiff, providing for the payment of the $400,000 as indicated above.

e. The parties agree that with the signing and execution of this agreement and of the aforementioned note, the parties shall cause the complaint in the action to be dismissed with prejudice.

f. The parties agree that with the signing and execution of this agreement and the aforementioned note, the parties shall cause the defendant's counterclaim in this action for libel to be dismissed with prejudice.

g. The plaintiff agrees that the payment of the sum of $400,000 is also in full satisfaction for all wrongful discharge claims that the plaintiff may have against the defendant.

h. The plaintiff shall sign and execute all releases prepared by the attorney for the defendant, provided that those releases are consistent with the provisions of this agreement.

i. The defendant is to pay court costs of the action.

It is further agreed that the forthgoing provisions are in full settlement of all claims that either party might assert against the other.

IN WITNESS WHEREOF, the parties hereto have executed this agreement on the day and the year first above written.

SIGNED AND ACKNOWLEDGED
IN THE PRESENCE OF

_____   _____
                                 Clark Kowalski, Plaintiff

_____   _____
                                 President and CEO
                                 Everett-Stimson Power and Light

FIGURE 14–4
(continued)

Releases

If the facts and the legal issues involved in the lawsuit are not overly complex, the parties may be satisfied to settle the case by using a release, rather than a settlement agreement. Although a release is also a contract and, as such, accomplishes essentially the same thing as a settlement agreement, the release is much simpler and much shorter than the settlement agreement and, therefore, much more efficient. The two most common releases are the general release and the partial release. If both parties have agreed to release each other from any and all claims, then a mutual release would be appropriate.

General Release.   A **general release** is used for full and final settlements. In a general release, all possible claims against all possible persons who might be liable for the plaintiff's injuries have been settled. This type of release is advantageous for the defendant because he or she can rest assured that no further action will be taken by the plaintiff in relation to the subject matter of the lawsuit. In the Kowalski case, for example, a general release would cancel all claims that Dr. Kowalski has or may have relating to the explosion at the Cuyahoga Valley Nuclear Power Plant. Figure 14–5 is an example of a general release form that might be used in the Kowalski case.

COURT OF COMMON PLEAS
CUYAHOGA COUNTY
STATE OF OHIO

CLARK KOWALSKI)
    Plaintiff,)
) Civil Action No. 93-GD-980
  vs.) GENERAL RELEASE
)
EVERETT-STIMSON, et al.)
    Defendants.)
)
)
)

_____

    Clark Kowalski, Plaintiff, in the above case, hereby releases the Defendants and all other persons, known or unknown, who may have contributed to the incident which forms the basis of this lawsuit, from all claims and demands for any act or matter whatsoever which may have arisen or may arise in the future.
    Signed and sealed this 26th day of April, 1993, at Cleveland, Ohio.

_____

---

general release
  A release granting full and final settlement, including all possible claims against all possible persons who might be liable for the plaintiff's injuries.

FIGURE 14–5
General Release.

Partial Release. In a complex lawsuit involving multiple claims, a party may elect to relinquish some claims while retaining others. In such a situation a **partial release** would be appropriate. This type of release is advantageous to the plaintiff because it preserves some of the grounds that he or she has for bringing a subsequent lawsuit against the defendant. However, the defendant also benefits because at least a portion of his or her potential liability has been eliminated. For example, in the Kowalski case, in addition to the negligence suit for the injuries suffered as a result of the explosion at the power plant, your client may have also filed an invasion of privacy suit against Everett-Stimson for making illegal tapes of his private phone conversations. Should Dr. Kowalski decide to settle the negligence suit against Everett-Stimson while maintaining the invasion of privacy suit, he would use a partial release.

Mutual Release. If the defendant in a lawsuit has filed a counterclaim against the plaintiff, then both parties in the case may find themselves in the position of relinquishing part or all of their claims in the suit. If this is the case, then a mutual release would be used. In a **mutual release,** each party relinquishes its claims against the other party. This type of release benefits both parties, because each of them can be assured that all potential liability in regard to this particular lawsuit has been eliminated. For example, in the Kowalski case Everett-Stimson filed a counterclaim against Dr. Kowalski for libel, claiming that he made false statements to a newspaper reporter about certain inadequate safety procedures followed at the plant. If both Dr. Kowalski and Everett-Stimson agree to release each other they would use a mutual release.

Form of the Release. Regardless of the type of release needed in a given case, it should include the identities of the parties, the action that gave rise to the claim, the consideration given for the release, and a specifically worded explanation of the claim that has been relinquished. Naturally, the release should also be signed by the parties. As in the case of the settlement agreement, if the court finds that a term of the release is vague or ambiguous, it may seek additional testimony or evidence to determine the intent of the parties at the time that they negotiated the release.

14–4 DISMISSALS, CONSENT DECREES, AND DISTRIBUTION OF FUNDS

Once a lawsuit has been settled, an order for dismissal will be drawn up. As an alternative to a dismissal, the parties may prefer to file a consent decree with the court. Finally, a statement outlining how the settlement funds will be distributed should be drawn up and delivered to the client.

Dismissals

There are three major types of dismissals: a stipulated dismissal, a voluntary dismissal on notice, and a court-ordered involuntary dismissal.

Stipulated Dismissals. The parties to a lawsuit may stipulate to a dismissal at any time and on any terms. A stipulated dismissal may be either with prejudice or without prejudice. A stipulated dismissal **with prejudice** means that the claim cannot be brought to court again at any time in the future. In contrast, a stipulated dismissal **without prejudice** means that the lawsuit can be brought at another time in any court that has the jurisdiction to hear the case. If the parties fail to stipulate the form of the dismissal, the court presumes the dismissal is without prejudice. In a stipulated dismissal, it is not necessary to state the terms and the conditions of the settlement. This type of dismissal avoids the disclosing in public records of the amount of the settlement. It also preserves the confidentiality of the terms surrounding the settlement. Figure 14–6 is a stipulated dismissal.

Voluntary Dismissal on Notice. Rule 41 of the Federal Rules of Civil Procedure permits a plaintiff to voluntarily dismiss a claim without order of the court by filing a motion of dismissal "at any time before service by the adverse party of an answer or of a motion for summary judgment, whichever comes first." Although not required under the terms of Rule 41, the plaintiff should serve a copy of the dismissal upon the defendant. As in the case of the stipulated dismissal, this dismissal can be with prejudice or without prejudice. The presumption is that the dismissal is without prejudice unless the court order of dismissal specifically states that it is with prejudice. Figure 14–7 reflects a dismissal without prejudice.

Court-Ordered Involuntary Dismissal. The court has the authority to dismiss an action if a party has failed to proceed with an action or if the party has failed to comply with a court order. For example, in the Kowalski case, if your client fails to comply with a court order compelling him to respond to repeated discovery requests from Everett-Stimson, the case may be dismissed by the court. In addition, the court may dismiss if the plaintiff's evidence is insufficient to establish liability against the plaintiff. A dismissal marks

partial release
The relinquishment of some claims and the retention of others by a party.

mutual release
The process of each party relinquishing its claims against the other party.

with prejudice
A stipulated dismissal by which the claim cannot be brought to court again at any time in the future.

without prejudice
A stipulated dismissal by which the lawsuit can be brought at another time in any court that has the jurisdiction to hear the case.

COURT OF COMMON PLEAS
CUYAHOGA COUNTY
STATE OF OHIO

CLARK KOWALSKI
    Plaintiff,

      vs.

EVERETT-STIMSON, et al.
Defendants.

)
)
) Civil Action No. 93-GD-980
) STIPULATED ORDER OF
) DISMISSAL
)
)
)
)

On this 26th day of April, 1993, it is stipulated between counsel for the Plaintiff, and counsel for the Defendant that this action be dismissed without prejudice regarding all claims and counterclaims of the parties.

_____
Attorney for Plaintiff

_____
Attorney for Defendant

FIGURE 14–6
Stipulated Order
of Dismissal.

COURT OF COMMON PLEAS
CUYAHOGA COUNTY
STATE OF OHIO

CLARK KOWALSKI
    Plaintiff,

      vs.

EVERETT-STIMSON, et al.
Defendants.

)
)
) Civil Action No. 93-GD-980
) VOLUNTARY DISMISSAL
) WITHOUT PREJUDICE
)
)
)
)
)

Having reviewed the Plaintiff's Motion for Voluntary Dismissal Without Prejudice in this action, it is hereby

ORDERED this 26TH day of APRIL, 1993, that this action be dismissed without prejudice regarding all claims and counterclaims of the parties.

_____

FIGURE 14–7
Voluntary
Dismissal Without
Prejudice.

the end of the case. Normally, it does not result in the court's entry of a judgment. Figure 14–8 gives an example of a court-ordered involuntary dismissal.

Consent Decrees

As an alternative to a dismissal, the parties may elect to use a consent decree. A **consent decree** outlines the details of the settlement agreed upon by the parties. The parties file the decree with the court, requesting that the judge examine the agreement and either approve or disapprove the terms that they have set forth. Most of the time the judge will have no hesitation in rendering his or her approval. Once it has been approved by the court, the consent decree is just as effective as a judgment would have been, had the case gone to trial. Unlike the terms of a stipulated dismissal, the settlement terms of a consent decree become a public record. Because of the official nature of the consent decree, should one of the parties violate the terms of a decree, that party may be held in contempt of court.

Distribution of Settlement Funds

Distribution of funds is often made at the time that the stipulated dismissal is signed or when the court has approved of the

---

COURT OF COMMON PLEAS
CUYAHOGA COUNTY
STATE OF OHIO

CLARK KOWALSKI)
    Plaintiff,)
) Civil Action No. 93-GD-980
  vs.   ) COURT ORDERED
) INVOLUNTARY DISMISSAL
)
EVERETT-STIMSON, et al.)
    Defendants.)
)
)
)

_____

Upon consideration of the failure of the Plaintiff to timely prosecute this action, it is hereby
    ORDERED this 26th day of April, 1993, that the complaint filed in this action against the Defendants is hereby dismissed.

_____

consent decree
An outline of the details of the settlement agreed upon by the parties.

FIGURE 14–8
Court-Ordered Involuntary Dismissal.

consent decree. A settlement proceeds statement should be prepared, similar to a closing statement in a real estate transaction, to account for the receipt of all proceeds. Such an accounting avoids later problems or questions by a party as to the payment of any expense involved in the settlement.

THE COMPUTERIZED LAW FIRM—Document Generator

SCENARIO

At 1:00 p.m. on Friday, your attorney calls you into her office. She has just received a call from Charlene Bannister, the attorney for Everett-Stimson Power and Light. Apparently, Everett-Stimson has decided to settle the case for $400,000. Your attorney has already talked to Dr. Kowalski, who has given his permission to accept. Your attorney is anxious to conclude the settlement before Ms. Bannister leaves for the Middle East on Monday morning.

PROBLEM

Your attorney is scheduled to return to the county courthouse on another matter at 1:30 p.m. She asks that you draft all settlement documents and deliver them to the courthouse during an anticipated recess at 3:00 p.m. so that she can review them. You will need to fax the documents to Ms. Bannister for approval and put them in the final form for execution of the settlement documents on Saturday morning. Drafting the lengthy, complicated settlement documents is time-consuming. The time to complete the project is limited. How can you accomplish this mammoth undertaking in less than two hours?

SOLUTION

The computerized law firm includes a word processing tool for drafting long documents. Recent advances in computer technology have developed a software package called the *document generator*. The document generator is a questionnaire-predicated software package that asks targeted questions in order to assemble a document to incorporate those answers. A document generator is similar to a building block. One answer determines the next question. The word processing part of the program will then take all the applicable paragraphs to build the settlement agreement. The speed, accuracy, and completeness that can be obtained by using the document generator cannot be obtained with standard word processing programs. Appendix B lists document generator software packages that can be purchased at a nominal fee.

SUMMARY

14–1   A settlement is an agreement or a contract between parties that terminates their civil dispute. Most civil cases end in a settlement. The preliminary investigative work in the settlement process is often the responsibility of the paralegal. The paralegal will have to obtain a personal history of the client, a preliminary assessment of the client's present health, and a medical history of the client. In addition, the paralegal may be required to calculate the damages in the case. There are also some collateral areas that the paralegal may have to probe to get an accurate picture of the probability of the client prevailing should the case go all the way to trial.

14–2   Once the preliminary investigative work has been completed, the information must be pulled together into a settlement report. This report must convince the defendant that a settlement would be in his or her best interests. Depending on the situation you may be charged with writing a settlement summary, a settlement letter, or a summary brochure.

14–3   A settlement agreement is actually a contract between two or more parties. As such, it must meet all the legal requirements of a contract, including the voluntary mutual assent of the parties, the element of consideration, legality, and capacity. If the facts and the legal issues involved in the lawsuit are not overly complex, the parties to the suit may be satisfied to settle the case by using a release rather than a settlement agreement. The two most common releases are the general release and the partial release. If both parties have agreed to release each other from any and all claims, a mutual release would be appropriate.

14–4   There are three major types of dismissals: a stipulated dismissal, a voluntary dismissal on notice, and a court-ordered involuntary dismissal. The parties to a lawsuit may stipulate to a dismissal at any time and on any terms. A stipulated dismissal may be either with prejudice or without prejudice. Rule 41 of the Federal Rules of Civil Procedure permits a plaintiff to voluntarily dismiss a claim without order of the court by filing a motion of dismissal. The court has the authority to dismiss an action if a party has failed to proceed with an action, if the party has failed to comply with a court order, or if the plaintiff's evidence is insufficient to establish liability against the defendant. As an alternative to a dismissal, the parties may elect to use a consent decree. A consent decree outlines the details of the settlement agreed upon by the parties. The parties file the decree with the court, requesting that the judge examine the agreement and either approve or disapprove the terms that they have set forth. At the time that the stipulated dismissal is signed or when the court has approved of the consent decree, a settlement proceeds statement should be prepared to account for the receipt of all proceeds.

KEY TERMS

client's medical history
  and medical condition
client's personal history
consideration
consent decree
damages
dismissal with prejudice
dismissal without prejudice
document generator
evaluation of the claim
general release
mutual release

partial release
release
settlement
settlement agreement
settlement brochure
settlement letter
settlement summary
statement of the facts
statement of the settlement
with prejudice
without prejudice

QUESTIONS FOR REVIEW AND DISCUSSION

1. What is a settlement?
2. What are some of the preliminary decisions surrounding settlement?
3. What areas must be investigated before a settlement offer is made?
4. What is the difference between a settlement summary and a settlement letter?
5. How does a settlement brochure differ from a settlement summary and a settlement letter?
6. What is a settlement agreement?
7. What is a release? What types of releases are available?
8. What are the advantages of a stipulated dismissal?

9. When is a voluntary dismissal on notice allowed?
10. Under what circumstances can a court order an involuntary dismissal?
11. How does a consent decree differ from a stipulated dismissal?
12. What is a settlement proceeds statement?

ACTIVITIES

1. Review the laws of your state and find all state laws that deal with settlements. Check your local court rules to see if there are any specific rules of court in your area regulating settlements.
2. Prepare an interoffice memorandum in which you explain the preliminary investigative work that you would have to do in the Kowalski case.

CHAPTER 14 PROJECT—PRELIMINARY DECISIONS REGARDING A SETTLEMENT

Review the Kowalski case in the opening commentary. Recall that Dr. Kowalski has elected to sue the Cuyahoga Valley Nuclear Power Plant and its owner and operator, the Everett-Stimson Power and Light Company, for the injuries that he sustained in the explosion of a hydraulic pump. Also recall that he is considering an additional lawsuit for invasion of privacy against Everett-Stimson. Note also that Everett-Stimson has brought a counterclaim against him for libel. Draft a memo in which you explore the factors to be taken into consideration in a decision regarding the possibility of offering to settle.

CHAPTER 15
Trial Techniques

COMMENTARY—THE LERMENTOV CASE

You have been called into a meeting with your attorney to discuss the details of an an upcoming trial. The trial involves your client, a certified public accountant named Mikhail Lermentov, who was injured in a fire last year while he was conducting an audit at the laboratories and main offices of Billicheck-Kendall Pharmaceuticals, Inc. The company has attempted to deny liability for Lermentov's injuries by claiming that all maintenance and security work done in their building is performed by two independent companies, Sergi Selinkov Security, Inc. and the Kolata Maintenance Corporation. Although the trial date is three months away, your attorney is concerned about the heavy work load that she has in several other cases. Therefore, she requests that you immediately begin to assist in preparing the Lermentov case for trial. Your responsibilities will include handling the file organization, preparing a trial notebook, coordinating witness preparation, selecting and organizing trial exhibits, and assisting in obtaining jury information.

OBJECTIVES

In the first two sections you explored the litigation process, the beginning of a lawsuit, the pleadings, and motion practice. In section 3 you were introduced to the details of the discovery process. As you can well imagine, this preliminary work and the discovery process can produce volumes of documents as well as significant information about the facts in the case. Before trial, this diverse information and these volumes of documents must be organized. Other pretrial matters must also be taken care of. In this chapter you will be introduced to the preparations that must be made before the trial. After reading this chapter, you will be able to:

1. Explain the paralegal's role in organizing the file and amending pleadings.
2. Describe the purpose and content of the trial notebook.
3. Outline the paralegal's role in preparing witnesses for trial.
4. List the standards by which a trial exhibit should be tested.
5. Explain the paralegal's participation in preparing trial briefs.
6. Determine the paralegal's logistical duties in preparing for trial.
7. Describe the paralegal's role in the jury process.
8. Discuss the paralegal's function at trial.

15–1 PRELIMINARY PREPARATION FOR TRIAL

The preparation for trial actually begins at the initial client interview. It is at this point that the attorney begins to assess the merits of the case to determine what course of action to take. Each of the processes and tasks that we have examined thus far in the text advances the prosecution or the defense of the case. Although most cases are settled or dismissed before reaching the trial stage, you must proceed on the assumption that eventually the case will reach trial. Some preparation tasks may be performed several months in advance of trial, while others must be handled at the last minute.

Whatever the case, your client will prevail only if you and your attorney are thoroughly prepared for all eventualities. One task that you can perform to aid in this preparation is to prepare a trial checklist. The checklist should include all the tasks that must be performed before the trial and the time frame for completion of those tasks. If you monitor this checklist faithfully and regularly, you will ensure that the case is truly ready for the trial. Figure 15–1 is an example of a trial checklist.

File Organization

One of the tasks in trial preparation that can be completed during the preliminary stages is the organization of the litigation

---

1. Calendar trial date and dates trial preparation tasks must be completed.
2. Notify the client and witnesses of trial date and need for meeting to prepare for trial testimony.
3. Review litigation file and organize. Complete any action necessary on this file.
4. Prepare and serve trial subpoenas.
5. Review chronology and cast of characters, and update if necessary.
6. Complete trial notebook.
7. Designate and organize trial exhibits. Prepare trial exhibit log.
8. Assist with trial brief.
9. Visit the courtroom and diagram location of trial exhibits, documents, briefcases, etc.
10. Locate a "war room" at a nearby hotel. Arrange for food to be delivered during the trial.
11. Arrange travel and hotel for client and witnesses.
12. Pull the documents to be introduced by a witness, according to the examination outline in the trial notebook. Assist with preparing the witness for testimony at trial.
13. Assist with collecting jury demographics data. Determine the juror profile for your case.

FIGURE 15–1
Trial Preparation
Checklist.

files. Naturally, it is best if the files are kept current as the case develops. For example, each time a pleading is filed by either side it should be immediately placed in the pleadings binder. However, the hectic pace of most law firms will challenge even the most efficient paralegal. Consequently, not all litigation files are kept up to date. The setting of the trial date, however, signals the need to organize the litigation file. This will mean reviewing all the pleadings and motions that were filed in the case. It will also necessitate locating all documents, records, deposition transcripts, and interrogatories produced during discovery. You may also have to transcribe all witness interview notes that you have not yet examined. Reviewing the litigation files at an early stage will probably add a number of items to the "to do" list on the trial preparation checklist (see Figure 15–1 above). This should not overly concern you, however. The only thing that you should be concerned about is the thorough preparation of your case.

Amending the Pleadings

One problem that might surface during the organization of the file is the need to amend the pleadings in the case before the time to do so expires. According to Rule 15 of the Federal Rules of Civil Procedure, once a case has been placed on the trial calendar, the pleadings in that case can be amended only with permission of the court or with the written consent of the opposing party. Fortunately, most state courts do not have this strict requirement. However, it's best to check local court rules to determine the procedure that must be followed should you find that a pleading in your case must be amended after the trial date has been set.

The Trial Notebook

The trial notebook, a vital part of any trial preparation, is usually the paralegal's responsibility. The **trial notebook** is a binder that contains, in complete or summary form, everything necessary to prosecute or defend a case. Preparation of the trial notebook, like the preparation of the trial itself, begins with the initial client interview. The contents and the organization of the trial notebook are determined by the individual preferences of the attorney or the paralegal. The form of the notebook is dictated by the type of case, the number of pleadings, the complexity of the legal issues, the number of exhibits and witnesses, and the anticipated length of the trial. However, most trial notebooks will include the following basic sections: (1) the parties and the attorneys; (2) the pleadings and motions; (3) the witnesses; (4) the expert witnesses; (5) document indexes; (6) deposition

trial notebook
A binder that contains, in complete or summary form, everything necessary to prosecute or defend a case.

summaries; (7) chronology; (8) the cast of characters; (9) legal research; (10) jury profiles and instructions; (11) the trial outline; (12) the attorney's notes; and (13) the "things to do" list.

The Parties and the Attorneys. The first entry in the trial notebook is a list of all the parties and attorneys involved in the lawsuit. This list can also function as a service list. In addition to the names and addresses of the attorneys, the list should include the telephone and fax numbers of their law firms. Updating this list is extremely important. Each time a pleading is received, you should check to determine that the attorney's name, firm, address, and client represented are correct on your list of parties and attorneys. If you don't take this simple precaution, you may mail a pleading to the wrong address. Such an error is not only embarrassing and costly, but also grounds for a potential malpractice action.

Pleadings and Motions. In a simple case, a copy of all the pleadings and motions would be filed in the trial notebook. However, in a complex case only pertinent pleadings, such as the complaint and the answer, would be placed in the notebook because of space limitations.

Witnesses. This section should include a list of all witnesses, their telephone numbers and addresses, and a copy of their trial subpoena, if one was issued. If possible, also include a summary of the factual areas that each witness is expected to cover in his or her testimony. Your attorney will also benefit from an outline of the questions that the witnesses will be asked at trial. Figure 15–2 is an example of a witness list that contains the type of information that will help you locate a witness rapidly, either before or during the trial.

Expert Witnesses. At the beginning of this section, place a list of all expert witnesses that each side intends to call at trial. As in the case of the factual witnesses, include their addresses and telephone numbers. Copies of each expert's curriculum vitae should also be included. A **curriculum vitae** will list the expert's professional credentials. The list will include each witness's educational and professional credentials as well as a summary of his or her publications and research projects. If the witness has written any reports regarding the present case, they should also be included in this section. You may also want to include a list of any other cases in which the expert has testified. A major component of this section is the list of questions that each expert will be asked at trial.

curriculum vitae
A list of an expert's professional credentials, including each educational and professional credential, and a summary of publications and research projects.

Name and Address	Tel #	Role	Subpoena Served/ Returned
Yuri Vilnius	542-4999	CEO of Sergi Selinkov, Inc. Finances and Organization of Sergi Selinkov	9/9/92 9/15/92
Maria Mendez	756-9989	Secretary at Billicheck-Kendall Witness to fire	9/15/92 9/17/92
Carl Loggia	756-9989	CPA at Billicheck-Kendall Finances of B-K	9/15/92 9/17/92
Lon Robertson	756-9989	Janitor at Sergi and Kolata Witness to fire	9/15/92 9/16/92
Julius Vilnius	756-9989	CEO of Billicheck-Kendall Organization Chart For B-K	9/15/92 9/25/92
Kay Vilnius	756-9989	Treasurer of Billicheck-Kendall Organization Chart For B-K Finances of B-K	9/15/92 9/25/92
Albert Vilnius	481-9997	CEO of Kolata Maintenance Organization Chart For Kolata Finances of Kolata Vice President of Billicheck-Kendall Organization Chart For B-K Finances of B-K	9/15/92 9/25/92
Vytautas Vilnius	481-9997	Treasurer Kolata Maintenance Organization Chart For Kolata Finances of Kolata Vice President of Billicheck-Kendall Organization Chart For B-K Finances of B-K	9/15/92 9/25/92
Rachel Friedman, M.D.	825-1409	Physician at Red Forest County Hospital	9/15/92 9/17/92
Jay Kellerman, M.D.	825-1409	Physician at Red Forest County Hospital	9/15/92 9/17/92
Abe Greenstein	825-3800	Professor Auburn University	9/16/92 9/18/92

FIGURE 15–2
Witness List.

Document Indexes. In a simple case the trial notebook may contain all documents that are produced in the case. However, in the more complex cases, an index of all documents produced by each party should be sufficient. A comprehensive but clear **document index** will enable you to quickly yet unobtrusively locate a document during trial, when time and discretion are of the essence.

Deposition Summaries. A complex case may require a separate binder for the deposition summaries. You will recall from our discussion in chapter 9 on depositions that a deposition summary is a written record that reduces many hours of testimony to a few concisely drawn, easily read, and quickly understood pages. The three types of deposition summaries are the page-line deposition summary, the topical deposition summary, and the chronological summary. The **page-line deposition summary** covers testimony as it occurred in the deposition itself. The **topical deposition summary** organizes the material into specific subject areas. Finally, the **chronological deposition summary** organizes the testimony according to a particular time sequence. A complex case involving numerous depositions would require an index of these summaries. The index should be arranged in alphabetical order by the last name of each deponent. In simple cases involving only a few depositions, an index is not needed.

Chronology. Another important tool in the trial notebook is the **chronology**. The chronology is the listing of what happened, when it happened, where it happened, and who was involved. A properly constructed chronology will also include source documents that indicate how each of these facts was learned. A chronology moves from the first dated piece of information on the litigation to the most current event in the case. As the trial approaches, you must review the chronology for completeness by checking key documents, pleadings, witness interviews, depositions, and exhibits to make sure that all dates have been taken from these sources and placed in the chronology. An effective chronology contains only the most pertinent dates. A chronology that is filled with unnecessary information can be a hindrance rather than a help at trial. Figure 15–3 represents a well-written chronology.

The Cast of Characters. The **cast of characters** is a roster of all key players in the case. This list can be drawn from witness interviews, documents, depositions, exhibits, and pleadings. In a case with a crowded list of key players, the cast of characters can provide valuable identification. As is true of the chronology, you must be careful to update the cast of characters as new information is

document index
An index of documents produced in a case.

page-line deposition summary
A summary covering the deposition testimony in the order in which it occurred in the deposition itself.

topical deposition summary
A deposition summary that organizes the testimony into specific subject areas.

chronological deposition summary
The organization of deposition testimony according to a particular time sequence.

chronology
A list of what happened, when it happened, where it happened, and who was involved in a case.

cast of characters
A roster of all key players in a case, which may be drawn from witness interviews, documents, depositions, exhibits, and pleadings.

case on point
A case that has been decided in your jurisdiction and that involves both facts and legal principles that are so similar to the facts and principles in the present case that the attorney feels the court will be bound to follow the court's ruling in that earlier case.

DATE	EVENT	SOURCE	NOTES
4/25/90	Incorporation of Sergi Selinkov, Inc.	Secretary of State's Records/Delaware	*formed to provide security for B-K*
4/26/90	Incorporation of Kolata Maintenance	Secretary of State's Records/Delaware	*formed to provide maintenance for B-K*
4/29/90	Shareholders meetings for both Kolata and Sergi Selinkov canceled	Carl Loggia	*initial indication that the two new corporations will not become separate entities*
5/5/90	Bank accounts opened for Kolata and Sergi Selinkov	Carl Loggia	*Both accounts Undercapitalized*
2/7/91	Semi-annual safety inspection of B-K performed jointly by employees of Kolata and Sergi Selinkov	Kolata and Sergi Selinkov records Lon Robertson	*Inspection not carried out properly indicates negligence*
2/7/91	Repairs performed on heating unit in storeroom	Lon Robertson	*Indicates that repairs were done negligently*
2/28/91	Lermentov arrives at B-K for audit	Lermentov, et al.	*Indicates lawful presence*
3/4/91	Date of fire	Lermentov, et al.	*Several people will testify as to the events surrounding the fire*
3/4/91 to 5/11/91	Lermentov's hospital stay	Hospital records Several physicians	*Extent of injuries must be explained*

FIGURE 15–3
Chronology of
the Case.

received. The failure to include one name in the cast may be a critical omission that could cause serious problems at trial.

Legal Research. This section of the trial notebook should contain copies of all cases that are on point with the legal issues involved in the present case. A **case on point** is one that has been decided in your jurisdiction and that involves both facts and legal principles that are so similar to the facts and principles in the present case that your attorney feels the court will be bound to follow the court's ruling in that earlier case. If the cases on point are numerous and lengthy, the paralegal should include a summary of each and a citation to the case and maintain the actual case in a separate, clearly marked binder.

Jury Profiles and Instructions.   This section of the trial notebook consists of two parts. The first part is a jury profile. The **jury profile** will give a narrative description of the characteristics of the ideal jury that you would like to assemble in the case. For example, you might want the jury to include people with a certain background, or with a certain level of education. Figure 15–4 is a sample that you might use to develop a profile of your ideal juror.

The second part of this section is the jury instructions. **Jury instructions** will explain the legal principles that the jury must apply to the facts in the case in reaching the verdict. Jury instructions also outline the procedures that the jury must follow as they attempt to reach a verdict. Although these will change during the course of the trial, drafting a proposed set of jury instructions and placing them in the trial notebook will save a substantial amount of time during the trial. The ultimate responsibility for giving the jury instructions lies with the judge. However, attorneys are permitted to suggest the substance of those instructions to the judge and may object when they feel the judge has not properly instructed the jury. Attorneys who fail to object to jury instructions cannot on appeal raise the inaccuracy of the instructions as an issue.

Trial Outline.   A trial outline is a chronological listing of the tasks that must be performed just prior to and during the trial. Such a chronological outline is a vital part of the trial notebook. This is because it simplifies and organizes the tasks facing the paralegal and the attorney as the trial date approaches. For example, the paralegal may be asked to assist in drafting the questions to be used during voir dire. (**Voir dire** is the process by which the jurors are questioned to determine any bias that they might have that would affect their ability to be fair and impartial in the case.) The paralegal may also be asked to draft the opening statement, the questions to be used during the examination of friendly witnesses, the questions to be asked during the cross-examination of the opposing witnesses, and the closing argument. All of these tasks would be listed on the trial outline. Allow space on the trial outline for annotations and changes. (Note: At this point you may want to refer to Appendix C, The Trial Process. This appendix covers the actual steps of a trial in some detail.

jury profile
A narrative description of the characteristics of the ideal jury that you would like to assemble in the case.

jury instructions
An explanation of the legal principles that the jury must apply to the facts of a case in reaching the verdict, and the procedures that the jury must follow as they attempt to reach a verdict.

voir dire
The process by which jurors are questioned to determine any bias that they might have that would affect their ability to be fair and impartial in the case.

Case Name: _____

Case Number: _____

Juror Name: _____ Juror No. _____

Age : _____ Sex: _____ Marital Status: _____

Cultural Background: _____ Religion: _____

Nationality: _____

Education: _____ Economic Status: _____

Physical Appearance: _____ Dress: _____

Body Language/Facial Expressions: _____

Behavioral Information (drinking, law enforcement background, etc.):

_____

_____

_____

Personality Characteristics: _____

Prior Jury Experience: _____

Litigation (Plaintiff or Defendant): _____

_____

Other Information: _____

_____

_____

_____

_____

_____

_____

_____

_____

_____

FIGURE 15–4
Juror Profile.

Attorney's Notes. Blank pages should be inserted in this section of the trial notebook for the attorney's notes about witnesses, legal issues, or other general information to be used during the trial.

Things To Do List. In addition to the trial preparation checklist, you will discover tasks that must be performed in the case. You should make notes of these items as they arise, then transfer them to the trial calendar specifically developed for the case.

15–2 PREPARATION OF WITNESSES

As a paralegal, you will be instrumental in preparing the witnesses for trial. One task that you may have to perform is arranging for the sending of subpoenas to certain select witnesses. You may also be charged with communicating the details of the trial to the witnesses. Finally, you may be required to arrange and attend all witness preparation meetings.

Subpoena of Witnesses

You must consult with your attorney to determine if any witnesses will require a subpoena. In some instances, attorneys prefer to subpoena only witnesses who are not considered "friendly." However, a friendly witness may request a subpoena to present to an employer as evidence that he or she has been ordered to appear and testify.

Trial subpoenas require the same procedure as deposition subpoenas. You should review your state and local rules to determine if there are any unusual requirements for subpoenas. Generally, any person eighteen years of age or older may serve subpoenas. In state courts the sheriff, a sheriff's deputy, or a local constable may also perform this task.

In federal courts, the subpoena process is governed by Rule 45 of the Federal Rules of Civil Procedure. According to Rule 45, the clerk of court is responsible for issuing subpoenas. In addition to compelling a witness to appear for oral testimony, Rule 45 can also compel the production of books, papers, documents, or other tangible items. Figure 15–5 is an example of this type of subpoena.

In federal court under Rule 45, a federal marshal can serve a witness with a subpoena. However, the rule also states that any person who is eighteen years of age or older can also serve a subpoena. A witness who has been subpoenaed and who has been requested to produce documents may object to the document request within ten days of service. The objection must be in writing and must be served on the attorney who made the original document request.

A trial subpoena must be personally served on the witness. In addition, all mileage and witness fees required must be tendered to the witness. Finally, the return of service information on the subpoena must be completed and filed with the court before the subpoena is valid.

Communicating with Witnesses

The preparation of a witness for trial is much more involved and generally much more critical than the preparation of the

AO 89 (Rev. 10/82)   ⊕   SUBPOENA

United States District Court	DISTRICT

	DOCKET NO.

V.

TYPE OF CASE
☐ CIVIL   ☐ CRIMINAL

SUBPOENA FOR
☐ PERSON   ☐ DOCUMENT(S) or OBJECT(S)

TO:

   YOU ARE HEREBY COMMANDED to appear in the United States District Court at the place, date, and time specified below to testify in the above-entitled case.

PLACE	COURTROOM
	DATE AND TIME

   YOU ARE ALSO COMMANDED to bring with you the following document(s) or object(s):[1]

☐ *See additional information on reverse*

   This subpoena shall remain in effect until you are granted leave to depart by the court or by an officer acting on behalf of the court.

U.S. MAGISTRATE(2) OR CLERK OF COURT	DATE
(BY) DEPUTY CLERK	

This subpoena is issued upon application of the:

   ☐ Plaintiff   ☐ Defendant   ☐ U.S. Attorney

ATTORNEY'S NAME AND ADDRESS

(1) If not applicable, enter "none."
(2) A subpoena shall be issued by a magistrate in a proceeding before him, but need not be under the seal of the court. (Rule 17(a), Federal Rules of Criminal Procedure.)

FIGURE 15–5 Subpoena.

RETURN OF SERVICE(3)

RECEIVED BY SERVER	DATE	PLACE
SERVED	DATE	PLACE

SERVED ON (NAME)	FEES AND MILEAGE TENDERED TO WITNESS(4)
	☐ YES ☐ NO AMOUNT $_____

SERVED BY	TITLE

STATEMENT OF SERVICE FEES

TRAVEL	SERVICES	TOTAL

DECLARATION OF SERVER(4)

I declare under penalty of perjury under the laws of the United States of America that the foregoing information contained in the Return of Service and Statement of Service Fees is true and correct.

Executed on _____
Date

_____
Signature of Server

_____
Address of Server

ADDITIONAL INFORMATION

(3) As to who may serve a subpoena and the manner of its service see Rule 17(d), Federal Rules of Criminal Procedure, or Rule 45(c), Federal Rules of Civil Procedure.
(4) "Fees and mileage need not be tendered to the deponent upon service of a subpoena issued on behalf of the United States or an officer or agency thereof (Rule 45(c), Federal Rules of Civil Procedure; Rule 17(d), Federal Rules of Criminal Procedure) or on behalf of certain indigent parties and criminal defendants who are unable to pay such costs (28 USC 1825, Rule 17(b) Federal Rules of Criminal Procedure)".

FIGURE 15–5 (continued)

witness for the deposition. For this reason it is usually advantageous for the paralegal to work with the witnesses in the case from the time of the initial interview. This early involvement will build a relationship that will facilitate communication and will help put the witness at ease while working with the paralegal.

As the paralegal, you may be asked to communicate with the witnesses early in the trial preparation period about the basic details of the trial, including the date, the location, and the anticipated length of the testimony. The witnesses should also be informed that they may have to meet with the attorney and the paralegal closer to the time of the trial. Remind the witnesses to review their depositions at least once before the meeting.

Figure 15–6 is an example of a letter that transmits to a witness basic information about the trial and his or her role in the case. By signing the letter and agreeing to remain in touch with you for availability at trial, the witness may feel committed to whatever length of time is required for his or her testimony.

It is essential that the paralegal be able to reach witnesses to advise them of changes in the trial schedule. The trial notebook should contain the address and the telephone number of each witness. Also, the client and all the witnesses should be given a designated contact person at the law firm. Each morning and afternoon during the trial the client and the witnesses should check with this person to make certain that there have been no changes in the schedule.

Witness Preparation Meeting

Shortly before trial, you should arrange a meeting between each witness and your attorney. Before the meeting, you may be asked to collect all documents that refer to the witness. You should review the witness's deposition and note any areas that gave the witness difficulty or that may require further clarification. Prepare an outline or actual questions that your attorney anticipates asking each witness during the trial. Make sure that you also correlate the necessary trial exhibits with that outline. During the witness preparation meeting, your attorney will explain the trial process to each witness. She will also explain what is expected from each witness. Many attorneys will also conduct mock questioning sessions so that the witnesses will know exactly what questions will be asked during direct examination. Your attorney may request that you videotape this mock questioning session for evaluation of the witness's appearance and testimony prior to trial.

POPSON, PIERCE, RUEBER, AND BURKE

5293 St. Clair Avenue
Red Forest, Alabama 36107

Mr. Carl Loggia
Certified Public Accountant
4226 Superior Avenue
Red Forest, Alabama 36107

RE: Lermentov v. Billicheck-Kendall Pharmaceuticals, Inc.

Dear Mr. Loggia:

The trial in the above captioned case has been scheduled for
January 19, 1993, at the Red Forest County Court House, in
Courtroom Number 1, 96 Public Square, Red Forest, Alabama.

We would appreciate your keeping us informed of your location at
all times because there may be a change in the trial starting date.
If for any reason you will be unable to attend to testify during the
period of January 19 to February 7, please let us know
immediately.

By signing a copy of this letter at the space indicated below, you
agree to comply with the terms of this letter.

Sincerely,

Laura Burke

Laura Burke
Attorney-at-Law

ACCEPTED AND AGREED TO
THIS _____ DAY OF _____ , 19____ :

_____

FIGURE 15–6
Letter to Witness
Regarding the
Trial.

15–3 PREPARATION OF EXHIBITS AND BRIEFS

Often the paralegal is called upon to gather and organize the
exhibits in a case. This responsibility may require obtaining enlarged exhibits or unusual graphics. The paralegal may also have
to set up a chronology or organize a set of statistics. Whatever the
case, it helps to know what to look for in the evaluation of those
exhibits. It is also possible that the paralegal may be called upon
to help conduct research for the trial brief.

Preparing Trial Exhibits

Many of the trial exhibits will be used at trial. In some jurisdictions, court rules require that the parties exchange lists of all the trial exhibits before the trial. Once you have established the documents or the materials that your attorney will introduce at trial, you may begin to prepare a trial exhibit's log that will trace the trial exhibit's progress throughout the trial. Such is the case whether you are working with enlarged exhibits, unusual graphics, or a chronology of the case. It is also important for the paralegal to know how to determine the effectiveness of a document that may be used as a trial exhibit.

Enlarged Exhibits and Unusual Graphics. It may be necessary for you to obtain enlarged exhibits or unusual graphics. For example, in the Lermentov case, your attorney may request that you have Mr. Lermentov's x-rays enlarged for the jurors to view during his testimony. In addition, many litigation support services offer models of various parts of the human anatomy, created to show the effects of certain types of injuries to various parts of the body. You should also obtain printed copies of any charts or diagrams that will be used as exhibits. For instance, if you use a large chart to portray the extent of Mr. Lermentov's medical expenses in this case, you should prepare a printed copy for the jury to take into the jury room when deliberations begin. Photographs should also be reproduced by a photocopy machine. All of these exhibits must be secured several weeks in advance of the trial. Once your attorney has selected the exhibits that she plans to use, you should immediately locate companies that can produce effective trial exhibits.

Preparing a Chronology of the Case. A chronology of the case, especially in a tort suit like the Lermentov case, is an effective trial exhibit. You should review the litigation files and documents and construct the critical events in the case. The chronology should include the date of the accident, the days that Mr. Lermentov spent out of work, the dates of all doctor visits and periods of hospitalization, the dates of all physical therapy treatments, and the date that he finally returned to work.

Evaluating Documents as Trial Exhibits. In most lawsuits the discovery process will produce a mountain of documents. Not all of these documents, however, make effective trial exhibits. Consequently it is crucial that the paralegal ask the following questions to evaluate how effective a document will be as a trial exhibit.

1. Is the document relevant?
2. Is the document admissible?
3. Is the document necessary?
4. Does the document support the cause of action?
5. Is the document confusing?
6. Does the document contain repetitive information?
7. Will the document detract from the testimony of the witness?
8. Does the document increase the effectiveness of the witness's testimony?
9. Is the document easy to read from the jury box and counsel table?
10. Is the document accurate?
11. Does the document have an attractive appearance?
12. Is the document clear?
13. Can a clear and readable copy of the document be made?
14. Can the procedural foundation be laid for the document's introduction at trial?

If the document meets these tests, it is marked as a trial exhibit and entered on the trial exhibit log. You should also make copies of the exhibit and place those copies in manila folders. Label the files by trial exhibit number and by the name of the witness through whom the exhibit will be produced. Make copies of each exhibit for all of the attorneys, a copy for the judge, a copy for the trial notebook, and at least two extra copies. Figure 5–7 is an example of a trial brief.

Researching for the Trial Brief

If your jurisdiction requires the filing of a trial brief, you may be asked to assist with its preparation. A **trial brief** explains the legal issues that are involved in the case and the law that demonstrates the validity of the position your attorney has taken in relation to those issues. The purpose of the trial brief is to inform the trial judge of the legal arguments your attorney intends to make at trial.

Your role in the preparation of the trial brief may consist of legal and factual research. For example, your attorney may request that you locate specific testimony from a particular witness's deposition. You may also be asked to determine the validity of the cases cited in the brief. This task is known as a **cite check**.

The paralegal is often responsible for coordinating the preparation and filing of the brief with the court. You should be familiar with your local court rules pertaining to the form of the brief, the number of copies needed, and the time for filing.

trial brief
A legal brief explaining the legal issues involved in the case and the law that demonstrates the validity of the position the attorney has taken in relation to those issues.

cite check
The process of determining the validity of cases cited in the brief.

COUNTY COURT
RED FOREST COUNTY
STATE OF ALABAMA

MIKHAIL LERMENTOV Plaintiff,	) Civil Action) No. 93-71891)) PLAINTIFF'S
vs.	) TRIAL BRIEF)
BILLICHECK-KENDALL PHARMACEUTICALS, INC. Defendant,	))))
et al.	)

BACKGROUND

This is a personal injury action arising out of a fire that occurred on March 4, 1991, at the headquarters of Defendant
Billicheck-Kendall Pharmaceuticals, Inc., in Red Forest, Alabama.
The fire started in a storeroom when a portable heating unit that
had been recently repaired by Lon Robertson, an employee of Defendant Kolata Maintenance Corporation, ignited. The fire rapidly
spread to combustible chemicals that were left in the storeroom,
causing a dangerous flame to envelope the fourth-floor offices. A
safety inspection, conducted jointly on 2/7/91 by employees of Defendant Kolata Maintenance Corporation and Defendant Sergi
Selinkov Security, Incorporated, failed to note the accumulation of
dangerous, highly combustible chemicals in the storeroom.

Plaintiff Mikhail Lermentov, a certified public accountant,
hired as an independent contractor by Defendant Billicheck-Kendall
Pharmaceuticals, Inc., was conducting an annual financial audit in
an office adjacent to the storeroom at the time of the occurrence and
was severely injured. Plaintiff sustained third-degree burns over his
chest, hands, forearms, and legs, necessitating two full months of
hospitalization and treatments.

LIABILITY OF DEFENDANTS

Plaintiff contends that both Defendant Kolata Maintenance
Corporation and Defendant Sergi Selinkov Security, Incorporated
are subsidiaries that were formed, financed, and operated solely for
the benefit of the parent corporation, Defendant Billicheck-Kendall
Pharamceuticals, Inc. Defendant Kolata Maintenance Corporation
was incorporated and provides maintenance and janitorial services
strictly for the parent corporation. Likewise, Defendant Sergi
Selinkov Security, Incorporated, was created solely to provide security and protection services for the parent corporation and does no
work for any other entity. Both subsidiaries were formed in a feeble
attempt to shield the parent corporation from legal liability as a
result of claims arising from the performance of faulty or negligent
repair work and security services, as in the instant case.

The Defendant Billicheck-Kendall Pharmaceuticals, Inc.
maintains that the inspection and repair work were carried out by
employees of the security firm of Sergi Selinkov Security, Incorporated and the maintenance firm of Kolata Maintenance Corporation,

*Normally an employee can-
not sue his or her employer.*

*An independent contractor
has a different relationship
with its employer and may
bring a legal claim.*

*Plaintiff demonstrates
reasons to the court for
holding parent corporation
liable.*

*The subsidiary corporations
are virtually assetless,
making any judgment
against them worthless.*

*Defendant tries to escape
blame by looking to other
Defendants.*

FIGURE 15–7
Trial Brief.

Piercing the corporate veil is a term used when the court is willing to look beyond the name of a corporation to assess damages and liability against the individual directors and officers, or to treat one corporation as one and the same as another corporation, such as when a parent/subsidiary relationship exists and one corporation serves as a mere agent for the other corporation.

Plaintiff could also have brought a claim against the individual officers and directors of Defendant Billicheck-Kendall Pharmaceuticals, Inc. under the theory of piercing the corporate veil.

In the event the court applies the law to the facts of the case and draws a different conclusion, Plaintiff is offering alternate theories of law for recovery.

who were hired as independent contractors, thereby exonerating Defendant Billicheck-Kendall Pharmaceuticals, Inc. from any and all liability. Plaintiff denies this claim and will prove at the time of trial that both subsidiaries acted as mere empty shells and that they are corporations in name only, entitling Plaintiff to "pierce the corporate veil" and hold Defendant Billicheck-Kendall Pharmaceuticals, Inc. completely responsible for Plaintiff's injuries.

The injuries sustained by Plaintiff on the morning of March 4, 1991, were the direct result of the fire that broke out at the corporate headquarters of Defendant Billicheck-Kendall Pharmaceuticals, Inc. Said fire was caused by the negligence and carelessness of the Defendants Billicheck-Kendall Pharmaceuticals, Inc., Sergi Selinkov Security, Incorporated, and Kolata Maintenance Corporation, and their agents, servants, and/or employees. Defendant Billicheck-Kendall Pharmaceuticals, Inc. knew or should have known of the dangerous and defective conditions existing on its premises and warned the Plaintiff. Defendant Billicheck-Kendall Pharmaceuticals, Inc. was further negligent in that Defendant, its agents, servants and/or employees failed to perform or negligently and carelessly performed safety inspections of the premises, and failed to detect or correct safety hazards that might endanger persons lawfully on the premises. In addition, Defendant, its agents, servants, and/or employees failed to repair or negligently and carelessly repaired the defective heating unit, creating a dangerous and hazardous condition that seriously and permanently injured and damaged the Plaintiff.

As the evidence clearly shows, neither Sergi Selinkov Security, Incorporated nor Kolata Maintenance Corporation was an independent corporation. At all times from the date of their incorporation to the date of the fire that severely injured Plaintiff, both corporations were acting as a part of the overall operation of Billicheck-Kendall Pharmaceuticals, Inc. In fact, the sole purpose for incorporating the two entities was to protect the parent corporation from liability in two areas, maintenance and security. In the interests of justice, the court must pierce the corporate veil and reach Billicheck-Kendall Pharmaceuticals, Inc. as the parent corporation of both Sergi Selinkov Security, Incorporated and Kolata Maintenance Corporation.

In the alternative, counsel for the plaintiff will demonstrate that, even if the corporate veil is not pierced and the court concludes that both subsidiaries are independent contractors, Billicheck-Kendall Pharmaceuticals, Inc. should still be held liable for the injures suffered by Plaintiff. The duty of a landowner to maintain his or her property in a reasonably safe condition, the duty of proprietors to protect third parties from injury caused by inherently dangerous activities or conditions, and the duty of employers and suppliers to comply with all safety provisions of the Labor Code are all nondelegable duties.

When Billicheck-Kendall Pharmaceuticals, Inc. gave the maintenance and security responsibilities to its subsidiaries, it was attempting to sidestep these duties. The law in this state is quite clear on this matter. Such duties cannot be delegated. Therefore, despite the independent contractor status of Sergi Selinkov Security, Incorporated and Kolata Maintenance Corporation, Billicheck-Kendall Pharmaceuticals, Inc. is still liable.

The facts will reveal at the time of trial that both Defendant Sergi Selinkov Security, Incorporated and Defendant Kolata Maintenance Corporation are "alter egos" of Defendant Billicheck-Kendall Pharmaceuticals, Inc. In support, Plaintiff will offer the following:

FIGURE 15–7
(continued)

a.) The parent corporation incorporated both subsidiaries, neither of which has assets of its own.

b.) The parent corporation shares common directors and officers with its subsidiaries.

c.) The parent corporation, Defendant Billicheck-Kendall Pharmaceuticals, Inc., owns all stock and finances of both of its subsidiaries, which are grossly undercapitalized.

d.) Neither subsidiary does business with any entity other than the parent corporation.

e.) The directors and officers of both subsidiaries take all orders from the parent corporation and do not act in their corporations' own self-interests, nor do they follow any of the legal requirements for a corporation.

PLAINTIFF'S WITNESSES

WITNESSES (not in order of appearance):

TESTIMONY

a.) Carl Loggia (CPA), former employee of Billicheck-Kendall Pharmaceuticals, Inc.

Neither Sergi Selinkov Security, Incorporated nor Kolata Maintenance Corporation were ever intended to be anything other than a front for Billicheck-Kendall Pharmaceuticals, Inc. in the event of a lawsuit against Billicheck-Kendall Pharmaceuticals, Inc. for any injuries occurring at Billicheck-Kendall Pharmaceuticals, Inc.

b.) Maria Mendez, secretary, employee of Billicheck-Kendall Pharmaceuticals, Inc.

Neither Sergi Selinkov Security, Incorporated nor Kolata Maintenance Corporation were ever intended to be anything other than a front for Billicheck-Kendall Pharmaceuticals, Inc.

c.) Lon Robertson, employee of Sergi Selinkov Security, Incorporated and Kolata Maintenance Corporation

Safety and security inspection procedures used by Sergi Selinkov Security, Incorporated and Kolata Maintenance Corporation; will also testify about the repairs.

d.) Rachel Friedman, M.D., Physician at County Hospital

Extent of Mr. Lermentov's injuries.

FIGURE 15–7
(continued)

e.) Jay Kellerman, M.D., Physician at County Hospital

Extent of Mr. Lermentov's injuries.

f.) Yuri Vilnius, CEO of Sergi Selinkov Security, Incorporated

Sergi Selinkov Security, Incorporated has always been treated as an extension of Billicheck-Kendall Pharmaceuticals, Inc.

g.) Julius Vilnius, CEO of Billicheck-Kendall Pharmaceuticals, Inc.

Organization and operation of Billicheck-Kendall Pharmaceuticals, Inc.

h.) Kay Vilnius, Treasurer of Billicheck-Kendall Pharmaceuticals, Inc.

Financial structure of Billicheck-Kendall Pharmaceuticals, Inc., Sergi Selinkov Security, Incorporated, and Kolata Maintenance Corporation.

i.) Albert Vilnius, CEO of Kolata Maintenance Corporation Vice-President of Billicheck-Kendall Pharmaceuticals, Inc.

Relationship between Billicheck-Kendall Pharmaceuticals, Inc. and Kolata Maintenance Corporation.

j.) Vytautas Vilnius, Treasurer of Kolata Maintenance Corporation Vice-President of Billicheck-Kendall Pharmaceuticals, Inc.

Relationship between Billicheck-Kendall Pharmaceuticals, Inc. and Kolata Maintenance Corporation.

k.) Abe Greenstein Professor at Auburn University

Lost wages and reduction in future earnings potential.

PLAINTIFF'S DAMAGES

The devastating effects of the fire upon Plaintiff is readily apparent. Mikhail Lermentov, who was 35 years old at the time of the occurrence, suffered third-degree burns over 30% of his body. Tragically, his arms were most damaged and will probably always be disabled. Plaintiff had numerous painful operations and procedures during his initial two-month hospitalization and will require many such operations and procedures in the future. Plaintiff's arms are covered with motion-restricting scars. Plaintiff will always suffer from limitation of motion, altered sensation, itching, and skin sensitivity. It is hoped that with continued physical therapy, Plaintiff will be able to resume working in some capacity.

FIGURE 15–7
(continued)

The injured Plaintiff sustained the following:

<u>Hospitalizations</u>

County Hospital	3/4/91 - 5/11/91
County Hospital	5/30/91 - 6/2/91
County Hospital	6/15/91
County Hospital	10/4/91 - 10/6/91

<u>Medical Expenses</u>

County Hospital	$281,112
County Hospital	$3,402
County Hospital	$800
County Hospital	$1,654
Prescriptions	$3,488
Dr. Friedman	$35,000
Dr. Kellerman	$20,008
County Radiologists	$4,213
Physical Therapy Associates	$6,000

APPLICABLE LAW:

The line of cases supporting Plaintiff's claim for piercing the corporate veil are as follows:

Kwick Set Components, Inc. v. Davidson Industries, Inc., 411 S2d 134 (Ala 1982). In this case the Supreme Court of Alabama court pierced the corporate veil of Capital Components, Inc., a wholly owned subsidiary of Kwick Set Components, Inc. Davidson Industries, Inc. had sold goods to Capital Components, Inc., which then delivered them to Kwick Set Components, Inc. Kwick Set Components, Inc. used the goods. Kwick Set Components, Inc. never paid Capital Components, Inc., and Capital Components, Inc. never paid Davidson Industries, Inc. Subsequently, Capital Components, Inc. went out of business. When Davidson Industries, Inc. found out that Capital Components, Inc. had been a subsidiary of Kwick Set Components, Inc. and that all the goods sold to Capital Components, Inc. had gone directly to Kwick Set Components, Inc. without payment, Davidson Industries, Inc. asked the court to pierce the corporate veil and hold Kwick Set Components, Inc. liable. The court agreed for three reasons. First, Kwick Set Components, Inc. and Capital Components, Inc. had the same president and the same directors. Second, all goods used by Kwick Set Components, Inc. were purchased through Capital Components, Inc. Third, the entire purpose of Capital Components, Inc. had been to postpone or totally avoid payment for goods purchased through Capital Components, Inc. This demonstrates that Capital Components, Inc. had no corporate identity separate from Kwick Set Components, Inc. In conclusion, the court quoted an earlier case, *Forest Hill Corp. v. Latter & Blum, Inc.*, 29 S2d 298 (Ala 1947), in which the Supreme Court of Alabama said "the courts will not allow the corporate entity to successfully masquerade through its officers, stockholders, representatives, or associates so as to defeat the payment of its just obligations." Id at 302.

Matrix-Churchill v. Springsteen, 461 S2d 782 (Ala 1984). In this case the court restated and approved the standard it had established in the *Kwick* case.

FIGURE 15–7
(continued)

Messick v. Moring, 514 S2d 892 (Ala 1987). In this case the Supreme Court of Alabama outlined three elements that must be present in order to pierce the corporate veil. These elements are:

1. The dominant party must have complete control and domination of the subservient corporation's finances, policy, and business practices so that at the time of the attacked transaction, the subservient corporation had no separate mind, will, or existence of its own.
2. The control must have been misused by the dominant party. Although fraud or the violation of a statutory or other positive legal duty is misuse of control, when it is necessary to prevent injustice or inequitable circumstances, misuse of control will be presumed.
3. The misuse of control must proximately cause the harm complained of. Id at 895.

Simmins v. Clark Equipment Corp., 554 S2d 398 (Ala 1989). In this case the Supreme Court of Alabama approved of the factors and elements presented in the *Messick* case.

Cohen v. Williams, 318 S2d 279 (Ala 1975). In this case the court held that the plaintiff need not prove that the defendant corporation engaged in fraud to convince the court to pierce the corporate veil. Rather, the court concluded that the court can pierce the corporate veil if it is convinced that upholding the separateness of the entities will cause an injustice. The court stated, "actual fraud is not necessarily a predicate for discarding the theory of separate corporate existence. It may also be discarded to prevent injustice or inequitable consequences." Id at 281.

Woods v. Commercial Contractors, Inc., 384 S2d 1076 (Ala 1980). In this case the court reaffirmed its position in *Cohen v. Williams,* stating that "the theory of corporate existence can properly be discarded, even in the absence of fraud, to prevent injustice or inequitable consequences." *Woods,* 384 S2d at 1079.

Barrett v. Odum, May & DeBuys, 453 S2d 729 (Ala 1984). In this case the Supreme Court of Alabama reaffirmed the principle that corporate existence can be disregarded to prevent injustice even in the absence of fraud.

Deupree v. Ruffino, 505 S2d 1218 (Ala 1987). In this case the Supreme Court of Alabama again reasserted that fraud is not a necessary element in a case involving an attempt to pierce the corporate veil.

United Steelworkers of America v. Connors Steel, 847 F2d 707 (11th Cir 1988). In this case the United States Court of Appeals for the Eleventh Circuit, in interpreting Alabama law, upheld the position that the corporate veil can be pierced to prevent inequity even without a showing of fraud.

In support of the doctrine of non-delegable duties are the following:

Dixie Stage Lines v. Anderson, 134 S 23 (Ala 1931). In this case the Supreme Court of Alabama set down the non-delegable duty exception to the rule that the proprietor is not liable for the negligent acts of an independent contractor. The court said, "a person is responsible for the manner of the performance of his non-delegable duties, though done by an independent contractor, and therefore, that one who by his contract or by law is due certain obligations to another cannot divest himself of liability for a negligent

FIGURE 15–7
(continued)

performance by reason of the employment of such a contractor."
Id at 24.

Arlington Realty v. Lawson, 153 S 425 (Ala 1934). In this case
the court states that landlords have a non-delegable duty to see to it
that proper care is used in making repairs to their property.

Alabama Power Co. v. Pierre, 183 S 665 (Ala 1938). This case
reiterates and approves the non-delegable duty exception laid down
by the Supreme Court of Alabama in the *Dixie Stage Lines* case.

*Knight v. Burns, Kirkley & Williams Construction Company,
Inc.,* 331 S2d 651 (Ala 1976). In this case the Supreme Court of
Alabama cites with approval the nondelegable duty exception estab-
lished in the *Dixie Stage Lines* case.

General Finance Corp. v. Smith, 505 S2d 1045 (Ala 1987). In
this case the court again upholds the nondelegable duty exception.

Boroughs v. Joiner, 337 S2d 340 (Ala 1976). In this case the
Supreme Court of Alabama specifically identifies the performance of
inherently dangerous activities, such as the storing of combustible
materials, as a non-delegable duty. In doing so the court quotes
with favor the Restatement (Second) of Torts Section 427 (1965),
which states, "One who employs an independent contractor to do
work involving a special danger to other which the employers knows
or has reason to know to be inherent in or normal to the work, or
which he contemplates or has reason to contemplate when making
the contract, is subject to liability or physical harm cause to such
others by the contractor's failure to take reasonable precautions
against such danger." Id at 342.

Laura Burke

Laura Burke, Trial Attorney
Attorney for the Plaintiff
Popson, Pierce, Rueber, and Burke
Attorneys at Law
5293 St. Clair Avenue
Red Forest, Alabama 36107
(205)725-8788

FIGURE 15–7
(continued)

15–4 COORDINATING TRIAL LOGISTICS

The paralegal is often responsible for coordinating the logistics of a trial. If the trial is held at the local court where your attorney usually works, coordinating the logistics will be a matter of
routine. However, when the trial is held in another district or
another county or when your client and many of the witnesses are
from out of town, you will have to arrange for accommodations.
Also, for out-of-town trials you will have to examine the courthouse and contact local court personnel.

Arranging for Accommodations

When the trial is to be held in another district or county or when your client and several of the witnesses are from out of town, the paralegal may be responsible for travel, hotel, and food arrangements. Often a suite of offices in a hotel near the courthouse is set up as a *war room.* The war room is an area containing additional trial documents and supplies. It will also double as a conference room where the legal team, the client, and the witnesses may gather during trial recesses or at the end of the trial day to regroup and prepare for the next day of the trial.

You should locate hotels near the courthouse and determine if your firm has a corporate account with any of them. Once the hotel has been selected and the necessary rooms reserved, make any travel arrangements that may be required for the client and out of town witnesses. Make certain to confirm the travel arrangements in writing. Write to the client and the witnesses informing them of the location of the hotel and the details of the travel plans. Remember to enclose the airline tickets along with a map of the area around the courthouse and the hotel.

Once the trial is under way, the paralegal may be called upon to arrange for catered meals in the war room to avoid crowded, noisy restaurants around the courthouse. This arrangement also prevents the awkwardness of being seated in a restaurant next to the opposing counsel or several of the jurors. However, often these arrangements should be delegated to another member of the legal team. This delegation may be especially important at the relatively short lunch breaks that occur during the trial because often the paralegal will be needed elsewhere. For example, the paralegal may have to use this valuable break time to locate a witness, secure another copy of an exhibit, or locate a case for inclusion in the trial brief.

Visiting the Courthouse

If the trial is to be held in another district or another county, or if you have never been to the courthouse where an upcoming trial is scheduled, you should visit that courthouse several weeks before the trial is to be held. Determine the location of telephones, photocopy machines, fax machines, restrooms, and vending machines. You may also need to locate a work area for meeting with the client or witnesses during the trial.

In many courthouses all of the courtrooms are identical. Often, however, a courthouse will have several courtrooms, each of which will be configured differently. Therefore, if possible, you should try to locate and examine the exact courtroom where the trial will be held. Determine the amount of space available for exhibits, briefcases, and supplies. Also check for the location of easels, charts, chalkboards, overhead projectors, slide projectors, video equipment, and audio equipment. This check is critical because you will have to bring any equipment that your attorney will need that is not provided by the court. Look around and note whether the courtroom is equipped with enough electrical outlets for the operation of a VCR or a laptop computer. If you think that the number or location of these outlets is inadequate for your needs, you will have to arrange for adapters or extension cords.

A **trial box**, consisting of all supplies needed during the trial, should be put together after the visit to the courthouse. Any special items noted during the courthouse tour should be included in the trial box. Figure 15–8 indicates the items that you may want to consider placing in your trial box.

Contacting Court Personnel

The paralegal should also schedule a meeting with the court clerk and the court reporter before the trial. Determine if the courtroom will be available the evening before or early the morning of the trial for the delivery of exhibits and documents. You may also need to arrange for security clearance and access to the courthouse elevators and the loading dock after hours.

During the trial, the court clerk will receive many calls and inquiries concerning the case. If the paralegal furnishes the clerk with a list of the law firm personnel who will be present in the courtroom, the possibility of missing an important telephone call is diminished. The court reporter will make a transcript of the trial proceeding. You should meet with the court reporter prior to the trial and give him or her your business card just in case there are any problems in the transcription of trial testimony.

15–5 THE JURY PROCESS

The jury system is a time-honored institution in this country. The Seventh Amendment to the U.S. Constitution guarantees the right to a jury trial in civil lawsuits at common law (as long as the amount in controversy exceeds twenty dollars). In the past, planning for, conducting, and winning a case before a jury were largely matters of chance. Today, however, attorneys have a wide variety of tools at their disposal to help them maximize the effectiveness of a jury trial. These techniques include the jury profile, the mock jury trial, and the shadow jury.

trial box
A box consisting of all supplies needed during the trial.

Court Rules (federal or state and local rules)

Manila Folders

Pencils

Pens

Stapler

Staple Puller

Staples

Rubber Bands

Paper Clips

Binder Clips

Post-It Notes

File Labels

Hole Punch

Yellow Pads

Exhibit Stickers

Roll of Quarters (for copier, vending machines, etc.)

Copy Card (for law library or clerk's office copy machine)

Bus Pass

Aspirin

Cough Drops

Antacid

Kleenex

Extension Cord

Tape Recorder

Blank Tapes

Batteries for Tape Recorder

FIGURE 15–8
Contents of a
Trial Box.

Preparing a Jury Profile

The purpose of the jury profile is to determine a composite profile of the ideal jurors for a particular case. Social psychologists and litigation specialists are equipped to provide law firms with valuable statistics and jury sampling information. These statistics and information are designed to create not only the image of the preferred jurors but also a profile of the jurors that your attorney will want to avoid. For example, in the Lermentov case the litigation specialist may conclude that well-educated, white-collar workers will be more sympathetic to your client. One reason for this may be that your client is a well-educated, white-collar professional. Another reason may be that well-educated jurors tend to be skeptical of the motives of large corporations like the defendants in this case. The social psychologists and litigation specialists may also indicate that lower-income, less-educated jurors may be swayed by the presence of the corporate defendants. Your attorney would therefore try to steer away from including such people on the jury as often as possible. It is also important to remember that the cost of this service may be prohibitive for smaller cases. On the other hand, if the expense results in a favorable decision or reduces the judgment against a client, the cost will certainly be justified.

Holding a Mock Jury Trial

Complex cases often require a jury trial of several months. To help facilitate a favorable jury decision, many firms stage a mock trial prior to the date of the actual trial. A **mock trial** is a practice trial. Again, social psychologists and litigation specialists can be retained to arrange the mock trial. Legal directories are excellent sources for locating companies that specialize in conducting mock trials.

The paralegal is often responsible for arranging the mock trial. The first step in the mock trial is to select the mock jury. A **mock jury** is a group of independent individuals chosen to reflect the probable makeup of the actual jury. Again, social psychologists and litigation specialists can interview and hire the people who will make up the mock jury. Once the mock jury panel is selected, your firm will present the mock trial. Key witnesses and principal exhibits will be presented to the jury in the same way that they will be presented at the actual trial. Part of your legal team will also present the case that you envision being presented by the opposition. For best results the jurors should not know which side your law firm represents. This will ensure an impartial evaluation. The mock jury evaluates the testimony and exhibits and renders the verdict.

Following their decision, the jurors may be questioned about their perceptions of the strengths and weaknesses of the case. For example, in the Lermentov case you may discover that the medical model that you intended to present at trial is far too complicated for the jury to understand. Or you may discover that your attorney's cross-examination of the opposing witnesses offended certain jury members. In contrast, you may find that some of the evidence presented by the corporate defendants was very convincing. You would then want to concentrate your forces on countering this evidence. The period between the mock trial and the actual

mock trial
A practice trial prior to the date of the actual trial.

mock jury
A group of independent individuals chosen to reflect the probable makeup of the actual jury.

trial should be devoted to correcting these and other weaknesses pointed out by the mock jury.

Participating in Jury Selection

As the paralegal assigned to the case, you may be asked to prepare a jury seating chart similar to the one depicted in Figure 15–9. The purpose of this chart is to track voir dire examination. While your attorney is conducting the jury examination, you should note the verbal and nonverbal communication of potential jurors.

Follow the voir dire examination outline from the trial notebook. Note the response of each potential juror. The paralegal and the attorney may confer to compare their observations about the jury panel before the final jury selection.

Using Shadow Juries

The increasing complexity of litigation has resulted in the introduction of a technique known as the shadow jury. A **shadow jury** is a secret jury selected by the law firm or the outside

misdemeanor
6 jurors

Lermentov v. Billicheck-Kendall Pharmaceuticals

Civil Action No. 93-71891

Jury Seating Chart

1.	2.	3.	4.	5.	6.
Pete Anderson	Nancy Rodriquez	Carole Peczniak	Joy Speigel	Gaspar Ortega	Christine Calderone

— Back Row —

7.	8.	9.	10.	11.	12.
Hubert Conaughton	Hedeki Seki	Andrew Glanzburgh	Monroe Szarkowski	Gustave Schoenborn	Clifton Wheeler

— Front Row —

FIGURE 15–9 Jury Seating Chart.

consulting firm. In choosing individuals to serve on the shadow jury, the law firm or the consulting firm attempts to match as closely as possible the individuals serving on the actual jury. The shadow jury then attends the trial. To assure fairness these individuals are not told which side of the lawsuit has retained them. During each break and at the end of each day's court session, the shadow jury reports to another paralegal or legal team member on their impressions of the trial witnesses, the exhibits, and the attorneys. The shadow jury's reports are given considerable weight. Adjustments in the order of witnesses, changes in the trial exhibits, or alterations in the attorney's technique may result from the observations and the suggestions made by shadow jury members. A substantial amount of expense and time is involved in this exercise. If the shadow jury strengthens a case, however, both the expenses and the time are well-spent.

shadow jury
A secret jury selected by the law firm or the outside consulting firm to attend the trial and report on its impression of the trial witnesses, exhibits, and attorneys.

THE COMPUTERIZED LAW FIRM—Legal Research

SCENARIO

Your attorney has asked you to come into the office on a Saturday morning to clear up a few details she has just remembered concerning the Lermentov case. It seems that last night it occurred to her that while Billicheck-Kendall Pharmaceuticals, Inc., has its main office in your home state of Alabama, it is incorporated in Delaware. Perhaps even more significant is the fact that Sergi Selinkov, Inc., and the Kolata Maintenance Corporation are both incorporated in Delaware. Your attorney's case against Sergi Selinkov and Kolata Maintenance involves being able to prove that they are really "dummy corporations" set up to divert liability from Billicheck-Kendall. To prove this your attorney must use the legal doctrine known as "piercing the corporate veil." She is relatively certain that the court will apply the laws of Alabama in interpreting this doctrine. Nevertheless, she is always quite thorough in her legal research, and wants to make absolutely certain that she is well-versed in the laws of Delaware before she goes to trial on Monday morning.

PROBLEM

Your attorney has asked you to double-check on the law regarding "piercing the corporate veil" in Delaware. Your law library does not include much substantive law from Delaware. Since it's Saturday morning, the county law library is closed and will not open until 9 a.m. Monday. Unfortunately, this is also the time that you are scheduled to go to trial. The nearest college of law library is open and could probably help you, but it is 317 miles away. How can you possibly research the extensive case law and statutory law of Delaware on such short notice?

SOLUTION

Fortunately, you are well-versed in the technique of computerized legal research. Your law firm has access to both Westlaw and Lexis, the two main legal research databases. Included in both databases will be the case law and the statutory law on corporations from Delaware. You will be able to access this information with your computer. Using the keyboard attached to your computer, you can use key words to describe the issue that you are researching. Through the phone lines and the modem, your computer is attached to the distant computer storing the database. Once that computer has received the relevant information, it will search the database and locate the relevant source information. That material will be transferred to your computer and can be read on your computer screen. All you'll have to do is print out a copy of the material using the printer attached to your computer. In one short morning session you will have accomplished a task that would have taken your non-computerized predecessors hours and maybe even days.

15-6   THE PARALEGAL'S ROLE AT TRIAL

The paralegal's role at the trial involves the same general areas that the paralegal was involved in during the preparation stages. These areas of participation include witnesses, exhibits, notetaking, and general trial coordination tasks.

Ensuring the Presence of Witnesses

The paralegal may be responsible for locating and having the witnesses present in the courtroom for their testimony. Your witness control log, discussed earlier, will assist you in coordinating the production of witnesses at the appropriate times. You may also be asked to provide for transportation of witnesses. This task may even include picking up out-of-town witnesses arriving at the airport. If possible, you should delegate this responsibility to another member of the legal team so that you are not away from the courtroom for any extended period of time. The paralegal may also be called upon to calm or reassure a nervous witness. It may even be your responsibility to work with hostile witnesses who your attorney is forced to call to the stand. Your demeanor must be firm but relaxed when dealing with hostile witnesses. If a contact person for witnesses has been designated at the law firm, you should check with that person frequently to ensure that all witnesses will be present in court as scheduled.

Keeping Track of Exhibits

During the trial, you must keep track of exhibits introduced by both sides. The exhibit log must be maintained to keep track of which exhibits have been offered and admitted, which exhibits have incurred objections, and whether the exhibit was ultimately admitted into evidence. At each break in the trial you should compare the court reporter's original exhibits against the exhibit log to be sure that all exhibits are accounted for. During the trial you should confer with your attorney at the end of each day to determine which exhibits will be introduced the next day. Review your exhibit files to make certain that adequate copies of these exhibits are ready for the next trial session.

Taking Notes During the Trial

Your attorney's full energy and concentration must be directed toward the witness on the stand, on the objections raised by opposing counsel, and on the court's rulings on particular motions. You should, therefore, assume the responsibility for taking full and accurate notes of the trial proceedings. A lined notebook with a wide left margin will assist you in noting down inconsistencies in testimony, incomplete answers to questions, and exhibits that have not yet been admitted into evidence. You may want to use red ink to record "things to do" that arise during the trial. Note the beginning time of each session and all breaks. These notations will enable you to quickly locate a particular piece of information.

SUMMARY

15–1 One of the tasks in trial preparation that can be completed during the preliminary stages is the organization of litigation files. It is best if files are kept current as the case develops. Each time a pleading is filed by either side it should be immediately placed in the pleadings binder. One problem that might surface during the organization of the file is the need to amend the pleadings in the case before the time to do so expires. The paralegal must check federal or local rules to determine the procedure that must be followed if a pleading must be amended after the trial date has been set. The paralegal must also prepare a trial notebook. The form of the trial notebook is dictated by the type of case, the number of pleadings, the complexity of the legal issues, the number of exhibits and witnesses, and the anticipated length of the trial. However, most trial notebooks will include the following basic sections: (1) the parties and the attorneys; (2) the pleadings and motions; (3) the witnesses; (4) the expert witnesses; (5) document indexes; (6) deposition summaries; (7) chronology; (8) the cast of characters; (9) legal research; (10) jury profiles and instructions; (11) the trial outline; (12) the attorney's notes; and (13) the "things to do" list.

15–2   The paralegal must consult with the attorney to determine if any witnesses will require a subpoena. In some instances attorneys prefer to subpoena only witnesses who are not considered "friendly." However, a friendly witness may request a subpoena to present to an employer as evidence that he or she has been ordered to appear and testify. The paralegal may be asked to communicate with the witnesses early in the trial preparation period about the basic details of the trial, including the date, the location, and the anticipated length of the testimony. The witnesses should also be informed that they may have to meet with the attorney and the paralegal closer to the time of the trial. Shortly before trial the paralegal should arrange a meeting between each witness and the attorney. During the witness preparation meeting, the attorney will explain the trial process to each witness.

15–3   Often the paralegal is called upon to gather and organize exhibits in a case. This responsibility may require obtaining enlarged exhibits or unusual graphics. The paralegal may also have to set up a chronology or organize a set of statistics. Whatever the case, it helps to know what to look for in the evaluation of those exhibits. It is also possible that the paralegal may be called upon to help conduct research for the trial brief.

15–4   The paralegal is often responsible for coordinating the logistics of a trial. Often logistics will be a matter of routine. However, when the trial is held in another district or another county or when the client and many of the witnesses are from out of town, the paralegal will have to arrange for accommodations. Also, on out-of-town trips the paralegal will have to examine the courthouse and contact local court personnel.

15–5 The purpose of the jury profile is to determine a composite profile of the ideal jurors for a particular case. Social psychologists and litigation specialists are equipped to provide law firms with valuable statistics and jury sampling information. These statistics and information are designed to create not only the image of preferred jurors but also a profile of the jurors that your attorney will want to avoid. The paralegal is often responsible for arranging the mock trial. The first step in the mock trial is to select the mock jury. Key witnesses and principal exhibits will be presented to the jury in the same way that they will be presented at the actual trial. The mock jury evaluates the testimony and the exhibits and renders the verdict. Following their decision, the jurors may be questioned about their perceptions of the strengths and weaknesses of the case. The period between the mock trial and the actual trial should be devoted to correcting these and other weaknesses pointed out by the mock jury. The paralegal may also be asked to prepare a jury seating chart to track voir dire examination. While the attorney is conducting the jury examination, the paralegal notes the verbal and the nonverbal communication of potential jurors. The increasing complexity of litigation has resulted in the introduction of a technique known as the shadow jury. A shadow jury is a secret jury selected by the law firm or an outside consulting firm. The shadow jury attends the trial and at breaks and the end of each session is questioned about the effectiveness of the trial procedures.

15–6 The paralegal may be responsible for locating and having witnesses present in the courtroom. During the trial the paralegal must keep track of exhibits. The exhibit log must be maintained to keep track of which exhibits have been offered and admitted, which exhibits have incurred objections from the opposing counsel, and whether the exhibit was ultimately admitted into evidence. The paralegal must assume the responsibility of taking full and accurate notes of trial proceedings. A lined notebook with a wide left margin will assist the paralegal in noting inconsistencies in testimony, incomplete answers, and exhibits that have not yet been admitted into evidence. The paralegal will often use red ink to record "things to do" that arise during the trial.

KEY TERMS

case on point	document index	shadow jury
cast of characters	jury instructions	trial box
chronology	jury profile	trial brief
cite check	mock jury	trial notebook
curriculum vitae	mock trial	voir dire

QUESTIONS FOR REVIEW AND DISCUSSION

1. What are the paralegal's duties in trial preparation?
2. What is the purpose of the trial notebook?
3. What are the contents of the trial notebook?
4. What responsibilities does the paralegal have in preparing witnesses for trial?
5. What are the standards by which a trial exhibit is evaluated?
6. What duties does the paralegal have in preparing the logistics of the trial?
7. What are the paralegal's duties in preparing for the jury process?
8. What duties does the paralegal perform during the trial?

ACTIVITIES

1. Review your local court rules that relate to jury selection. Check to see if these rules differ in any substantial way from the rules enumerated in the Federal Rules of Civil Procedure.
2. Prepare a memorandum describing what a paralegal should look for during a visit to an out-of-town courthouse.

CHAPTER 15 PROJECT—DRAFTING A TRIAL NOTEBOOK MEMORANDUM

In chapter 15, locate the detailed explanation of the contents of a trial notebook. Next, review the facts presented in the Lermentov case, which appears in the opening commentary to this chapter. Draft a memorandum to a new paralegal in your law firm instructing him or her on the contents of a trial notebook for the Lermentov case. Make certain to include instructions for each area of the notebook.

CHAPTER 16
Post-Trial Practice

OUTLINE

COMMENTARY—THE IMPERIAL CASE

A federal court jury recently awarded $10 million to Paragon Centre, a ten-story office building in downtown Houston. The decision stated that the Imperial Gasoline Company, a major national gasoline distributor incorporated in Delaware and headquartered in Pennsylvania, was negligent in permitting a leak from its abandoned gas station a block from Paragon Centre to spread through the elevator shaft of the office complex. The building was evacuated for less than two hours. Three employees in the building suffered nausea and dizziness from the fumes. They were treated and released from a local hospital. There was no structural damage to the building. However, the jury found that the future value of the building was diminished because of the stigma associated with the gasoline incident. The firm that represented Imperial at trial is unable to prosecute an appeal and has withdrawn from its representation of the client. Imperial has hired your local firm to appeal what it feels is an excessive jury award in light of the minimal injury to the building. Imperial also suspects that the large jury award was due in part to local prejudice in Houston against a large, out-of-town corporate entity that the jurors felt damaged a small, local, real estate developer. Your attorney has requested that you immediately obtain a copy of the testimony from the six-week-long trial. This testimony encompasses over twenty volumes and more than 100 exhibits. Accordingly, your attorney asks that you summarize the transcript and draft the necessary post-trial documents. You may also be asked to participate in the preparation of an appellate brief. This chapter will cover the details of the post-trial process.

OBJECTIVES

The post-trial process is the final stage in the litigation process. After reading this chapter, you will be able to:

1. Identify trial and post-trial motions.
2. Define appeal.
3. Identify the two major parties to an appeal.
4. Explain the nature of a notice of appeal.
5. Explain the purpose of a supersedeas bond.
6. Determine the paralegal's duties in drafting an appellate brief.
7. Describe the paralegal's role in the oral argument.
8. Discuss the final procedures in an appeal.

16–1 TRIAL AND POST-TRIAL MOTIONS

While a trial is still in progress, the litigants have the opportunity to end the dispute in a number of different ways. Naturally, as explained in chapter 14, the litigants may settle their dispute at any time, even after the trial has commenced. However, also during the trial, a litigant may attempt to arrive at a speedy conclusion by asking the court to grant a motion for a directed verdict. (At this point, you might want to refer to Appendix C, The Trial Process, for an explanation of how this motion fits into the flow of the trial.) After the trial has ended, a dissatisfied party may file a motion for a judgment notwithstanding the verdict or a motion for a new trial.

Motion for a Directed Verdict

One of the options open to litigants during the trial is to file a motion for a directed verdict. In federal court such a motion is permitted under Rule 50 of the Federal Rules of Civil Procedure. A **motion for a directed verdict** asks the judge to instruct the jury to render a verdict for the party filing the motion. The rule allows this motion to be raised after the opposing party has closed its presentation of evidence. If the motion is denied it can be raised again at the conclusion of the party's own evidence, or after the closing arguments. Naturally, the motion must explain the grounds upon which it has been made.

Motion for a Judgment Notwithstanding the Verdict

Rule 50 of the Federal Rules of Civil Procedure also allows a party to raise a motion for a judgment notwithstanding the verdict. A **motion for a judgment notwithstanding the verdict** asks the court to to have the verdict and its judgment set aside. To grant such a motion the court must be convinced that a group of reasonable individuals would not have reached such a verdict and that the jury's decision is wrong as a matter of law. The judgment notwithstanding the verdict is also known as a motion for a judgment n.o.v. or a motion for a J.N.O.V. These abbreviations come from the Latin phrase *non obstante veredicto*, which means "notwithstanding the verdict."

Motion for a New Trial

Rule 59 of the Federal Rules of Civil Procedure allows a dissatisfied party to file a motion asking for a new trial. A motion for a new trial must state the legal grounds on which a new trial should be granted. The court may grant such a new trial on the following grounds: (1) the verdict was contrary to law; (2) the verdict was totally defective; (3) irregularity in the court proceeding; (4) excessive or insufficient damage awards; (5) jury misconduct; or (6) newly discovered evidence. For example, in the Imperial

motion for a directed verdict
A motion made during a jury trial, requesting that the judge tell the jury how they should decide the case.

motion for a judgment notwithstanding the verdict
A motion asking the court to have the verdict and its judgment set aside because the court is convinced that a group of reasonable individuals would not have reached such a verdict and that the jury's decision is wrong as a matter of law.

non obstante veredicto
Notwithstanding the verdict.

case, your attorney may feel that some irregularity in the court proceedings may have resulted in the excessive damage award. She may, for instance, feel that the closing remarks of Paragon's attorney inflamed the jury, igniting a prejudicial passion against your client. Such a situation would call for the filing of a motion for a new trial.

Under Rule 59 of the Federal Rules of Civil Procedure, a motion for a new trial must be served on the opposing attorney within ten days of the entry of judgment. Some state courts allow a longer period of time. Ohio courts, for instance, allow fourteen days for the filing of a motion for a new trial. Whatever the case, it is important for the paralegal to realize that the actual entry of a judgment could be several weeks or even months after the decision itself has been rendered. You should therefore monitor the court's docket to determine the actual date of the entry of judgment. This date begins the official post-trial time clock.

16–2 THE PRELIMINARY STEPS IN THE APPEAL

As a paralegal, you will be instrumental in preparing the appeal. An appeal is filed by a party who has lost a case or who is dissatisfied with a judgment or a court order. The **appeal** asks that a higher court review the lower court's decision. A person bringing an appeal is referred to as the **appellant**. The person who opposes an appeal is the **appellee**. The appellee may also file a cross-appeal. A **cross-appeal** is an appeal filed by the appellee based on a different legal rationale than the appeal filed by the appellant. Only questions of law are subject to review. The appellate court has no authority to consider questions relating to the facts of a case. For example, in the Imperial case, no facts may be introduced concerning the safety record of Imperial over the ten years it has operated in the Houston area. However, your attorney may argue that the judge erred in his instructions to the jury. This argument relates only to the law that should have been applied in the case. Appeals are expensive, time-consuming, and often unsuccessful. However, the appeal is an essential element in the legal system. Without appeals there would be no check on the legal decision making of the trial courts.

In recent years the appellate process has been simplified in the federal courts. The clerk in the district court supervises the preparation of the court record, all pleadings and transcripts in the case, for an appeal. The clerk also provides the attorneys with the appropriate forms and copies of the local rules. In contrast, involvement in the state appellate process generally requires more attention to the state court procedural rules.

appeal
A request for a higher court to review a lower court's decision.

appellant
A person bringing an appeal.

appellee
The person who opposes an appeal.

cross-appeal
An appeal filed by the appellee based on a different legal rationale than the appeal filed by the appellant.

You should be familiar with federal, state, and local rules for the appellate process. The preliminary steps in an appellate procedure generally include (1) notice of appeal; (2) bond for costs or a supersedeas bond; (3) transcript order and preparation of pertinent record sections; and (4) filing of briefs by both parties. Following these preliminary steps, oral arguments will be presented to the court, and the court will render its decision. Figure 16–1 charts the stages of an appeal in the federal court up to and including the time for the filing of the briefs. The chart also notes

ACTION	TIME DUE	FED. APP. RULE
Notice of Appeal	30 days after entry of judgment or order.	4(a)(1)
	60 days in cases involving U.S., its officers, agencies, or parties.	4(a)(1)
	If timely motion for new trial, JNOV, motion to amend or alter judgment, or motion to amend or make additional findings of fact, time for appeal for all parties runs from entry of order denying.	4(a)(1)
Supersedeas Bond	Supersedeas bond given at or after time of filing notice of appeal or order allowing appeal.	4(a)
Record and Transcript Appellant	Within 10 days after filing notice of appeal, appellant places written order for transcript. At or before time for perfecting appeal, appellant makes written request designating portion.	10(b)
Record and Transcsript Appellee	Within 10 days after service of appellant's order, appellee designates additional parts of transcripts.	10(b)
Transcript-Reporter	If transcript cannot be completed within 30 days of receipt of order, reporter shall request extension of time from clerk of court of appeals.	11(b)
Briefs	Appellant must file a brief within 40 days after record is filed. Appellee must file brief within 30 days after service of appellant's brief. Reply brief must be filed within 14 days after appellee's brief, and at least 3 days before argument.	31(a)

FIGURE 16–1
Appellate Timetable and Procedures—Federal Courts.

the time limits for completing each stage, and the underlying federal appellate court rules.

Notice of Appeal

Only one document is required for the filing of an appeal. That document is the notice of appeal. The **notice of appeal** lists the party or parties taking the appeal, the judgment, the order or the portion of the judgment appealed (including the caption of the case in the trial court), and the court to which the appeal is taken. Figure 16–2 is an example of a notice of appeal.

According to Rule 4(a) of the Federal Rules of Appellate Procedure, the original of the notice of appeal must be filed with the clerk of the district court from which the appeal is taken within thirty days after the entry of the judgment or the order. Rule 4(a) also states, however, that if the United States or one of its agencies or officers is a party in the case, the notice of appeal must be filed within sixty days after entry of the judgment or the order. Another party may file a notice of appeal within fourteen days after the date the first notice was filed, or within the time period prescribed by Rule 4(a) of the Federal Rules of Appellate Procedure.

The appellant must pay a docketing fee to the clerk of the district court upon the filing of the notice of appeal. The district court clerk then forwards this fee to the clerk of the appellate court. The clerk of the district court is required to serve notice of the filing of a notice of appeal by mailing a copy of the notice to counsel of record for each party other than the appellant, or to the last known address of a party not represented by counsel. A note is made in the court docket of the names of the parties to whom the clerk mailed copies of the notice of appeal and the date of the mailing. Docketing an appeal occurs when the notice of appeal and certified copies of docket entries are received by the clerk of the court of appeals.

Appeal Bond

An appeal does not automatically stay, or halt, the judgment or the execution of the judgment in the lower court. A party must apply to the district court for a stay. Therefore, an appellant in a civil case may be required to post a bond to cover the cost of the appeal and a supersedeas bond to stay the enforcement of the judgment. A **supersedeas bond** is a promise, supported by a form of surety, to secure suspension of a judgment and delay execution upon the judgment, pending the outcome of the appeal. The appellant and its surety, usually an insurance company, agree to pay to the appellee the amount of any damages sustained due to the

notice of appeal
The only document required for the filing of an appeal, which lists the party or parties taking the appeal, the judgment, the order or the portion of the judgment appealed (including the caption of the case in the trial court), and the court to which an appeal is taken.

supersedeas bond
A promise, supported by a form of surety, to secure suspension of a judgment and delay execution upon the judgment, pending the outcome of the appeal.

IN THE UNITED STATES DISTRICT COURT
FOR THE SOUTHERN DISTRICT OF TEXAS HOUSTON DIVISION

Paragon Centre,	)
	)
	)
	)
	) CIVIL ACTION NO. 93-81891
Plaintiff,	)
	)
vs.	)
	)
Imperial Gasoline Co.,	)
	)
Defendant.	)
	)
	)
	)

NOTICE OF APPEAL

Notice is hereby given that the Imperial Gasoline Company, Defendant herein, hereby appeals to the United States Court of Appeals for the Fifth Circuit from the final judgment entered in this action on July 18, 1993.

Respectfully submitted.

By: *Mary Beth Musil*
Attorney for the Defendant
Kirchendorfer, Lehane, Zuer, and Musil
216264 Crestview Drive
Houston, Texas 75247

FIGURE 16–2
Notice of Appeal.

delay caused by the appeal if the appellant loses the appeal. The court has the authority to set the amount of the supersedeas bond, based on a monetary value set to the risk taken in the appeal. For example, in the Imperial case, the court may establish a supersedeas bond of $2 million because of the amount of the verdict and because of the additional devaluation of the real estate as the appellate process continues.

Under Rule 7 of the Federal Rules of Appellate Procedure, the district court may require an appellant to file a bond or provide other security in such form and amount as it finds necessary to ensure payment of costs on appeal. Security costs for the appeal include the cost of filing fees for docketing the appeal, the cost of the clerk's preparing and transmitting the record, and the cost attributed to the losing party for transcribing and printing the necessary copies of the briefs, appendices, and records. Costs are eventually paid by the party losing the appeal.

Ordering the Transcript

Under Rule 10(b) of the Federal Rules of Appellate Procedure, within ten days of the filing of the notice of appeal the appellant is responsible for making a written request, on a form supplied by the district court clerk, to the court reporter for the complete transcript, the official daily record of the court proceeding, or desired portions of the transcript. A copy of the request is filed with the clerk of the district court. The appellate must also notify the clerk of the appellant court that the transcript has been ordered.

Responsibilities of the Appellant and the Appellee. According to Rule 10(b) of the Federal Rules of Appellate Procedure, if the entire transcript is not included in the appeal the appellant, within ten days of filing the notice of appeal, must file a statement of the issues that will be presented on appeal. This statement must then be served on the appellee. Under the provisions of Rule 10(b), the appellee then has ten days to file and serve on the appellant a designation of any additional parts of the transcript that the appellee wants included. If the appellant does not order the additional parts, the appellee may order those parts or apply to the district court for an order requiring the appellant to do so.

Responsibilities of the Court Reporter. Under provisions of Rule 11(b) of the Federal Rules of Appellate Procedure, the court reporter must acknowledge receipt of the order for the transcript. According to Rule 11(b) the reporter must also note at the bottom of the order the date on which the reporter expects to complete the transcript. The reporter then transmits the order to the clerk of the court of appeals.

Rule 11(b) also provides that if the transcript cannot be completed within thirty days of the receipt of the order, the court reporter must request an extension of time from the clerk of the court of appeals. The clerk then notes the extension of time granted on the docket and notifies the parties. The court reporter files the completed transcript with the clerk of the district court within thirty days after receipt of the transcript order form and notifies the clerk of the court of appeals of the filing. Under Rule 11(b), if the court reporter does not file the transcript within the allotted time, the clerk of the court of appeals notifies the district judge and takes such steps as may be directed by the court of appeals, including sanctions.

Responsibilities of the Paralegal. As the paralegal, you will have a variety of responsibilities in relation to the transcript. You should, first of all, maintain close contact with the court reporter to make sure of the timely filing of the transcript. Telephone the reporter periodically to determine the projected release time for the transcript. If the reporter is unable to complete the transcript within the designated time frame, designate the order in which you would like to receive parts of the transcript. For example, in the Imperial case, if your attorney plans to base the appeal on the judge's erroneous instructions to the jury and on the opposing attorney's inflammatory closing arguments, you would want to request those portions of the transcript first. Once the transcript has been received, review it for accuracy, comparing the transcript with any notes taken by the attorney or the paralegal from the law firm that originally tried the case.

Transmitting the Record

The district court clerk is responsible for arranging in chronological order the original papers filed with the district court. The clerk must also number and index those documents. Once this has been accomplished, the clerk must transmit the record and a certified copy of the docket entries to the court of appeals. This must be done within fifteen days of the filing of the notice of appeal, or fifteen days after the filing of the transcript, whichever is later. If the deadline cannot be met, the district court clerk must notify the court of appeals of the reasons for the delay and request an extension.

Enlargement of Time

If your attorney determines that the time permitted for the appeal is insufficient, you may be asked to draft a **motion for enlargement of time**. Such a motion is authorized by Rule 26 of the Federal Rules of Appellate Procedure. This motion should set forth the reasons that the additional time is needed and the number of additional days required. The court of appeals will generally grant additional time for a new firm taking over an appeal. This is especially true if the case is lengthy and complex. The motion for enlargement of time must be served on all counsel of record. Figure 16–3 is an example of a motion for enlargement of time.

motion for enlargement of time
A motion requesting additional time for an appeal, including the reasons that the additional time is needed and the number of additional days required.

THE COMPUTERIZED LAW FIRM—Calendar System

SCENARIO

Your attorney calls you into her office and expresses her concerns about the numerous filing deadlines in the Imperial case. The time for perfecting the appeal is short. The volume of work to be done is large. Your attorney asks that you review the court rules to determine all applicable deadlines and place reminders and actual deadlines on a computer calendar system.

PROBLEM

Your numerous responsibilities in the appeal are time-consuming. You need the calendar for future projects, but the time required to secure the deadlines and enter them in the computer will take away from the time for summarizing the transcript and working on the appellate brief. How can you accomplish the task of locating deadlines and installing the reminders and deadlines on the computer?

SOLUTION

The computerized law firm includes a calendar function on the versatile WordPerfect 5.0 office package. With this calendar, you will be able to place multiple reminders in advance of a filing date. The calendar function allows you to print daily, weekly, and monthly reminders. With the computer calendar, you will be able to prioritize the appellate tasks and assure that all deadlines are met. Appendix B lists additional calendar software packages that can be purchased for a nominal fee.

16–3 THE APPELLATE BRIEF

Often the paralegal is called upon to participate in the drafting of the appellate brief. Your research, writing, organizational, and analytical skills must be employed in this vital part of the appellate process. The court of appeals will not hear witnesses nor see evidence. The brief must therefore be well-researched and well-written to have the necessary persuasive power.

IN THE UNITED STATES COURT OF APPEALS FOR
THE FIFTH CIRCUIT

Paragon Centre,
 	
  Plaintiff-Appellee,
 	
vs.
 	
Imperial Gasoline Co.,
 	
  Defendant-Appellant.
	)
	)
	)
	)
	) APPEAL NO. 93-31753
	)
	)
	)
	)
	)
	)
	)
	)
	)
	)
	)

Appeal From the United States District Court
For the Southern District of Texas
Houston Division, Civil Action No. 93-81891

MOTION FOR AN ENLARGEMENT OF TIME

Now comes Appellant, Imperial Gasoline Company, and files this motion to request that the time for filing its brief be enlarged by thirty days, to October 19, 1993, and, in support of this motion, Appellant shows the following:

I.

The judgment from which this appeal is taken was rendered in cause No. 93-81891 in the Federal District Court for the Southern District of Texas, Houston Division, on June 20, 1993. The appeal was perfected on July 18, 1993. The transcript was filed on August 1, 1993, and the statement of facts was filed on August 10, 1993. Appellant's brief is to be filed on or before September 19, 1993.

II.

The undersigned attorney is solely responsible for the preparation of the Appellant's brief.

III.

The undersigned is lead counsel for a medical malpractice action involving complex issues, Cause No. 93-31791, Montgomery v. The Stepford-Carmichael Medical Institute, which is set for trial in the Federal District Court Southern District of Texas, Houston Division, beginning next week. The court has scheduled three weeks on its docket to hear the case.

WHEREFORE, PREMISES CONSIDERED, Appellant requests the court to enlarge the time for filing Appellant's brief to October 19, 1993.

FIGURE 16–3
Motion for an Enlargement of Time.

Respectfully submitted,

By: *Mary Beth Musil*

Attorney for the Defendant-Appellant
Kirchendorfer, Lehane, Zuer, and Musil
216264 Crestview Drive
Houston, Texas 75247

CERTIFICATE OF SERVICE

I hereby certify that a true and correct copy of the foregoing has been mailed by first class mail, postage prepaid, to Simon Zuercher, 35713 Marion Road, Baytown, Texas, on this 9th day of September 1993.

By: *Mary Beth Musil*

Attorney for the Defendant-Appellant

FIGURE 16–3
(continued)

Drafting the Appellate Brief

The appellate brief is an integral part of the appeal. This formal document consists of the legal issues, the important facts, the legal arguments, and the legal authorities. You may be called on to help draft several types of briefs. These are the appellant's brief, the appellee's brief, and the reply brief. It is also possible for your attorney to, at some time, write and file an amicus curiae or intervenor brief. An **amicus curiae** (literally "friend of the court") or **intervenor brief** is one that is voluntarily filed by an attorney who is not a part of the case but who has been granted permission to present some legal argument before the court. Before beginning work on a brief, you should locate and review the format of the appellate briefs filed either in that particular case or in that appellate court. You may be asked to assume the responsibility for compiling and organizing the various sections of the brief.

Format of the Brief. Except by permission of the court or local court rules, the principal brief may not exceed fifty pages, and reply briefs may not exceed twenty-five pages. These page limitations do not include the table of contents, the table of citations, or any required addendum. The brief must be printed or duplicated in at least eleven-point type, with a clear, black image on opaque, unglazed, white paper. Typographic briefs and appendices bound in volumes must be on $6\frac{1}{8} \times 9\frac{1}{4}$ -inch paper, and typewritten matter must be $4\frac{1}{6} \times 7\frac{1}{6}$ inches. All others must be bound and contain

8½ × 11-inch paper, with the typewritten matter 6½ × 9½ inches, double spaced, except for footnotes. Each page must contain no more than twenty-seven typed lines.

Appellate Brief Colors.   The color requirements for appellate brief covers include: (1) appellant—blue; (2) appellee—red; (3) amicus curiae or intervenor—green; and (4) reply—gray. The appendix, if separate from the brief itself, must contain a white cover. Front covers of the brief and appendix must include: (1) the name of the court; (2) the number of the case; (3) the title of the case; (4) the nature of the proceedings; (5) the name of the lower court; (6) the title of the document; and (7) names and addresses of counsel representing the party on whose behalf the brief is filed.

Researching the Law.   An experienced paralegal is often asked to assist in researching the law in preparing the appellate brief. Responsibilities in this regard may include researching potential legal theories, locating supporting authority, researching pertinent parts of the record, and verifying the correctness of both the citations and the brief format.

Drafting the Statement of Facts.   Good writing skills and an analytical mind are requirements for drafting the statement of facts. Knowing where to find the pertinent facts to incorporate in the appellate brief is critical. It is also important to be able to figure out which facts should be included in the relatively short statement of facts. To accomplish these tasks you may be required to summarize the transcript and index testimony for inclusion in the appellate brief. Familiarity with the transcript will enable you to effectively assist your attorney with the drafting of the brief. Indexed summaries of the transcript and exhibits should be incorporated into a three-ring binder and provided to each member of the legal team working on the brief. The binder might also include pertinent pleadings, trial exhibits, statutes, and cases that will be relied on in the brief.

Appellant, Appellee, and Reply Briefs

As noted previously, the three most important briefs that you may be required to work on are the appellant's brief, the appellee's brief, and the reply brief.

Appellant's Brief.   The requirements for the **appellant's brief** vary slightly among the federal circuit courts of appeal, but generally they include the following:

amicus curiae brief
A brief that is voluntarily filed by an attorney who is not a part of the case but who has been granted permission to present some legal argument before the court.

intervenor brief
A brief that is voluntarily filed by an attorney who is not a part of the case but who has been granted permission to present some legal argument before the court.

appellant's brief
Brief of the person bringing an appeal.

1. Certificate of interested persons.
2. Statement regarding oral argument.
3. Table of contents.
4. Table of cases in alphabetical order.
5. List of statutes, treatises, and law review articles, including the author's name where appropriate.
6. Statement of jurisdiction.
7. Statement of issues.
8. Statement of the case, the nature of the case, the course of the proceedings, and disposition in the court below. This section includes the statement of facts that are relevant to the legal issues, including appropriate references to the record.
9. Summary of the argument.
10. The argument, including the reasons for the contentions regarding issues, as well as citations to authorities, statutes, and parts of the record relied upon, and so on.
11. A short conclusion listing the exact relief sought.
12. Certificate of service.

The appellant is also required to file an appendix to its brief, which includes the following parts:

1. Relevant docket entries in the lower court proceeding.
2. Relevant portions of the pleadings, charge, findings, or opinion.
3. Judgment, order, or decision in question.
4. Any other parts of the record to which the parties wish to direct the attention of the court.

Ten copies of the appendix must be filed with the clerk. One copy is served on each counsel of record. Rule 30(d) of the Federal Rules of Appellate Procedure specifies the arrangement of the appendix as follows:

1. List of parts of record contained in the appendix, in order, with page references.
2. Relevant docket entries.
3. Other parts of the record in chronological order.

Exhibits designated for inclusion in the appendix may be placed in a separate volume. Four copies of this separate exhibits volume must be filed with the appendix, and a copy served on counsel for each party.

Appellee's Brief. The appellee's brief should follow the requirements of the appellant's brief, with the exception of the statement of the issues in the case. This section is not necessary unless the appellee disagrees with the appellant's statement. No conclusion is required in the appellee's brief.

Reply Brief. Rule 28(c) of the Federal Rules of Appellate Procedure permits the appellant to file a brief in reply to the appellee's brief. The appellee may also file a cross-appeal. As noted earlier in the chapter, cross-appeal is an appeal filed by the appellee based on a different legal rationale than the appeal filed by the appellant. If the appellee files a cross-appeal, the appellant will file a brief in response to the issues presented in the cross-appeal. The appellee can then file a reply to the appellant's response. No further briefs are permitted, except by leave of the court.

Filing and Service of Appellate Briefs

According to Rule 31 of the Federal Rules of Appellate Procedure, the appellant must file and serve its brief within forty days after the date on which the record is filed. The appellee has thirty days after service of the appellant's brief to file and serve its brief, unless service upon the appellee was by mail. In this case the appellee is allowed three additional days for filing the brief. Under Rule 31(a), the appellant's reply brief is due fourteen days after service of the appellee's brief. It must, however, be filed at least three days before the argument of the case, except for good cause. A brief is deemed timely filed if it is mailed within the time permitted by the pertinent court rule. It does not have to actually reach the clerk's office by that day.

As the paralegal, you should file twenty-five copies of the brief with the clerk of the court of appeals and serve two copies on the counsel for each party, unless the appellate court's local rules stipulate a different number of copies. For example, the Fifth Circuit Court of Appeals requires only seven copies of the brief. If the appellant fails to file its brief within the time allowed, the appellee may move for a dismissal of the appeal. If the appellee fails to file a brief, it will not be heard at the oral argument, except by permission of the court.

16–4 COORDINATING THE ORAL ARGUMENT

The **oral argument** is the presentation of the basis for the appeal before the court of appeals. Oral arguments are permitted in all appellate cases unless, pursuant to local rules, a three-judge panel, after examination of the briefs, unanimously decides that the oral argument is not needed. If such a local rule exists, the party desiring the oral argument may file a statement with the

appellee's brief
Brief of the person who opposes an appeal.

oral argument
The presentation of the basis for the appeal before the court of appeals.

court listing the reasons that it should be granted the oral argument. The court notifies the parties of the date, time, and place of the oral argument. The court also notifies the parties of the amount of time allotted for each side's presentation. The appellant opens and closes the oral argument. Even though the parties do not request oral argument, the court may direct that the case be argued.

Preparing for the Oral Argument

The paralegal's duties related to the oral argument may vary, depending on the complexity of the case, the economic constraints, or the paralegal's experience. As an experienced paralegal, you may be asked to prepare for and attend the oral argument.

Outline of the Argument. You may be requested to assist your attorney in preparing the written outline for the oral argument. This outline is incorporated into the oral argument notebook, which may include copies of pertinent cases and pleadings. Capsule summaries of the trial transcripts may also be included in the oral argument notebook.

Research Notebook for Justices. For the convenience of the court, you may be asked to prepare a notebook of research for each justice, consisting of cases that your attorney anticipates the court will need to consider in its decision. The cases may be indexed by the court rendering the decision or alphabetically by the parties. Additionally, the notebook may include summaries of the records that have been organized and indexed.

Delivery of the Exhibits to Court. You may also be given the responsibility to deliver the exhibits to the court of appeals for the oral argument. You will also have to make arrangements for the prompt removal of these exhibits. This is especially important because Rule 34(g) of the Federal Rules of Appellate Procedure provides that any physical evidence not removed within a reasonable time after notice to the counsel by the clerk is to be destroyed or disposed of "as the clerk shall think best."

Assisting at Oral Argument

As in the deposition or the trial, you may be asked to attend the oral arguments and make complete notes for your attorney's use during her portion of the oral argument. Thus, your attorney will be free to concentrate on her argument, without the distraction of making notes during the opposition's argument.

16–5 FINAL PROCEDURES

We are nearing the end of the litigation process. After the court of appeals has rendered a decision, a dissatisfied party may seek to continue the appellate process. However, should the defendant eventually lose the case, the plaintiff may use certain post-trial judgment procedures to secure payment of the award.

Further Appeal Procedures

Under provisions of Rule 40 of the Federal Rules of Appellate Procedure, if the losing party desires to appeal the decision of the court of appeals, a petition for rehearing should be filed. A **petition for rehearing** asks that a higher court's decision be reviewed. This petition must be filed within fourteen days after the judgment is entered, unless the time is either shortened or enlarged by order of the court. A petition for a rehearing is not a prerequisite to the filing of a petition for certiorari. A **petition for certiorari** is a request for a rehearing before the United States Supreme Court.

Post-Trial Judgment Procedures

Statutory remedies allow for the execution of a judgment within thirty days after the entry of judgment. The party seeking to execute on the judgment is known as the **judgment creditor**. The party who must pay the judgment is known as the **judgment debtor**. Often it is helpful for the judgment creditor to uncover details about the financial condition of the judgment debtor. To facilitate this process, the law permits post-judgment discovery. Post-judgment discovery procedures offer the the judgment creditor a relatively simple and inexpensive method of determining the amount and the location of a party's assets. **Post-judgment interrogatories**, for example, are written questions that the judgment debtor must answer in writing about his or her assets. A **post-judgment deposition** can also be taken after sending the opposing counsel a **notice of intent to take oral deposition by non-stenographic means**. This type of deposition is taken with only a dictating machine or a tape recorder, with no court reporter present. The judgment creditor could also use a post-judgment request for production of documents to obtain necessary financial information from the judgment debtor.

petition for rehearing
A request that a higher court's decision be reviewed.

petition for certiorari
A request for a rehearing before the United States Supreme Court.

judgment creditor
The party seeking to execute on the judgment.

judgment debtor
The party who must pay the judgment.

post-judgment interrogatories
Written questions that the judgment debtor must answer in writing about his or her assets.

post-judgment deposition
A deposition that can be taken after judgment, with only a dictating machine or a tape recorder, with no court reporter present.

notice of intent to take oral deposition by non-stenographic means
A notice sent to an opposing counsel of an intent to take a deposition post-judgment by use of only a dictating machine or a tape recorder, with no court reporter present.

IN THE UNITED STATES DISTRICT COURT
FOR THE SOUTHERN DISTRICT OF TEXAS HOUSTON DIVISION

Paragon Centre,	))))) CIVIL ACTION NO. 93-81891
Plaintiff,	)
vs.	))
Imperial Gasoline Co.,	))
Defendant.	)))))

WRIT OF GARNISHMENT

TO: THE TEXAS LONGHORN BANK AND TRUST COMPANY, 444 Houston Plaza, Houston, Texas, 75429, Garnishee;

1. Paragon Centre is the plaintiff in the case of Paragon Centre v. Imperial Gasoline Company, in Civil Action No. 93-81891, in the Federal District Court for the Southern District of Texas, Houston Division. In this case the plaintiff has a valid, uncollected judgment against the defendant for the sum of $750,000 with interest charged at a rate of 10% per year and costs of the suit.
2. Plaintiff has applied for a writ of garnishment against The Texas Longhorn Bank and Trust Company.
3. You are hereby commanded to appear before this court at 9 a.m. on November 22, 1993. You will at that time be required to answer under oath what property belonging to the defendant you have in your possession or had in your possession when this writ was served upon you, and what money owing to or belonging to the defendant you have in your possession or had in your possession when this writ was served upon you. At that time you will also be required to answer under oath what other persons you know of who have property belonging to the defendant in their possession or had in their possession at the time this writ was served upon you, and what other persons you know of who owe the defendant money or have possession of money belonging to the defendant or had in their possession when this writ was served upon you money belonging to the defendant.
4. The official who served this writ upon you is also charged with serving the defendant, Imperial Gasoline Company, with a true copy of this writ.

Dated and Issued on October 22, 1993.

ATTESTED TO BY:

Hanna Cartwright

Clerk of the Federal District Court,
Southern District of Texas,
Houston Division

Crawford Webster

Presiding Judge

FIGURE 16–4
Writ of
Garnishment.

Without the filing of a supersedeas bond, a writ of execution may be issued ten days after entry of a final judgment order. A **writ of execution** is a court order compelling the seizure of the judgment debtor's property to satisfy the judgment. Proper notice must be given to the public and to anyone who has an interest in that property before it can be sold at a public auction. In addition, the judgment debtor must be given the opportunity to pay the judgment creditor before the auction is held. The law also prescribes the order in which certain types of property can be seized and sold at auction. Usually, personal property is seized and sold before real property is subject to seizure. After the auction has been held and the debt satisfied, any remaining amount goes to the judgment debtor.

Another means by which the judgment creditor could collect is by using a post-trial garnishment. A **post-trial garnishment** is a separate but ancillary lawsuit, filed in the court that rendered the judgment. The garnishment is brought against a third-party garnishee. A **third-party garnishee** is a person or company that is holding assets belonging to the judgment debtor. The judgment creditor must obtain a writ of garnishment. (See Figure 16–4.) The garnishee is then served with the writ and a summons. The garnishee will be compelled to reveal how much of the judgment debtor's money or property is in his or her possession. Once this is known the judgment creditor can seize the money or property or prevent the judgment creditor from receiving any of that money or property. Bank accounts and wages can be the targets of a post-trial garnishment. However, state and federal laws protect a certain percentage of the debtor's income so that he or she can still make a living, despite the garnishment.

SUMMARY

16–1 One of the options open to the litigants during the trial is to file a motion for a directed verdict. A motion for a directed verdict asks the judge to instruct the jury to render a verdict for the party filing the motion. The rules allow this motion to be raised after the opposing party has closed its presentation of evidence. If the motion is denied it can be raised again at the conclusion of the party's own evidence, or after the closing arguments. A motion for a judgment notwithstanding the verdict asks the court to to have the verdict and its judgment set aside. To grant such a motion the court must be convinced that a group of reasonable individuals would not have reached such a verdict and that the jury's

writ of execution
A document issued by a court that allows a party to seize and sell property and use the proceeds to satisfy the judgment.

post-trial garnishment
A separate, but ancillary, lawsuit, filed in the court that rendered the judgment, to permit the judgment creditor to collect on a judgment.

third-party garnishee
A person or a company that is holding assets belonging to a judgment debtor.

decision is wrong as a matter of law. A motion for a new trial will state the legal grounds for the new trial.

16–2 An appeal is filed by a party who has lost a case or who is dissatisfied with a judgment or a court order. The appeal asks that a higher court review the lower court's decision. A person bringing an appeal is referred to as the appellant. The person who opposes an appeal is the appellee. Only questions of law are subject to review. The appellate court has no authority to consider questions relating to the facts of a case. The preliminary steps in an appellate procedure generally include (1) notice of appeal; (2) bond for costs or a supersedeas bond; (3) transcript order and preparation of pertinent record sections; (4) filing of briefs by both parties. Following these preliminary steps, oral arguments will be presented to the court, and the court will render its decision.

16–3 The appellate brief is an integral part of the appeal. This formal document consists of the legal issues, the important facts, the legal arguments, and the legal authorities. There are actually several types of briefs that you may be called on to help draft. These are the appellant's brief, the appellee's brief, and the reply brief. It is also possible for your attorney to write and file an amicus curiae or intervenor brief. An amicus curiae or intervenor brief is one that is voluntarily filed by an attorney who has been granted permission to present some legal argument before the court. The appellee may also file a cross-appeal. A cross-appeal is an appeal filed by the appellee based on a different legal rationale than the appeal filed by the appellant. If the appellee files a cross-appeal, the appellant will file a brief in response to the issues presented in the cross-appeal. The appellee can then file a reply to the appellant's response.

16–4 The oral argument is the presentation of the basis for the appeal before the court of appeals. Oral arguments are permitted in all appellate cases unless, pursuant to local rules, a three-judge panel, after examination of the briefs, unanimously decides that the oral argument is not needed. The paralegal may be requested to assist the attorney in preparing the written outline for the oral argument. This outline is incorporated into the oral argument notebook. For the convenience of the court, the paralegal may be asked to prepare a notebook of research for each justice, consisting of cases that your attorney anticipates the court will need to consider in its decision. The paralegal may also be given the responsibility to deliver the exhibits to the court of appeals for the oral argument. As in the deposition or the trial, the paralegal may be asked to attend the oral argument and make complete notes for the attorney's use during her portion of the oral argument.

16–5 If the losing party desires to appeal the decision of the court of appeals to a higher court, a petition for rehearing should be filed. A petition for rehearing asks that a higher court's decision be reviewed. A petition for certiorari is a request for a rehearing before the United States Supreme Court. Statutory remedies allow for the execution of a judgment within thirty days after the entry of judgment, or sooner. The party seeking to execute the judgment is known as the judgment creditor. The party who must pay the judgment is known as the judgment debtor. Often it is helpful for the judgment creditor to uncover details about the financial condition of the judgment debtor. To facilitate this process, the law permits post-judgment discovery. Without the filing of a supersedeas bond, a writ of execution may be issued ten days after entry of a final judgment order. A writ of execution is a court order compelling the sale of the judgment debtor's property to satisfy the judgment. Another means to collect a judgment is by using a post-judgment garnishment.

KEY TERMS

amicus curiae brief
appeal
appellant
appellant's brief
appellee
appellee's brief
cross-appeal
intervenor brief
judgment creditor
judgment debtor
motion for a directed verdict
motion for a judgment
  notwithstanding the verdict
motion for a new trial
motion for enlargement of time

non obstante veredicto
notice of appeal
notice of intent to take oral
  deposition by
  non-stenographic means
oral argument
petition for certiorari
petition for rehearing
post-judgment deposition
post-judgment interrogatories
post-trial garnishment
supersedeas bond
third-party garnishee
writ of execution

QUESTIONS FOR REVIEW AND DISCUSSION

1. What is a motion for a directed verdict?
2. What is a motion for a judgment notwithstanding the verdict?
3. What is a motion for a new trial?

4. What is an appeal?
5. Who are the parties to an appeal?
6. What is a supersedeas bond? What is its purpose?
7. List and define four types of appellate briefs.
8. What duties does the paralegal have in relation to oral arguments?
9. What post-judgment discovery devices are available to a judgment creditor?
10. What post-trial judgment procedures are available to collect a judgment?

ACTIVITIES

1. Review the laws of your state and find all state appellate court rules. Compare the state and federal court rules to determine the differences between the two.
2. Prepare a memorandum describing the duties of the paralegal during the appellate process in relation to the transcript.

CHAPTER 16 PROJECT—DRAFTING THE APPELLATE BRIEF

Review the Imperial case in the opening commentary. Recall that the case originated in Houston, Texas, and the appeal must therefore be brought in the Fifth Circuit Court of Appeals. Remember also that each circuit has local rules that must be followed in addition to the Federal Rules of Appellate Procedure. Draft a memo in which you tell a new paralegal in your firm about the requirements for the appellant's brief in the Imperial case.

Deposition Style of the Case

LISA DEMARCO,	)
	) Civil Action No. 92-7507
Plaintiff,	) DEPOSITION
	) TRANSCRIPT
v.	)
	)
HAMPTON GENERAL	)
HOSPITAL, et al.	)
	)
Defendants.	)
	)

APPEARANCES:

Matthews, Davidson & Turner
By: Perry A. Matthews
For the Plaintiff

Stephens, Wilcox, Brantley & Matlock
By: Jane K. Gould
For the Defendant

STIPULATIONS:

It is hereby stipulated and agreed by and between counsel that all objections, except to the form of the questions, be reserved until the time of the trial.

Gary Eckerson, R.T., sworn

BY MR. MATTHEWS:

Q. Would you please state your full name for the record?

A. Gary Andrew Eckerson.

Q. Where are you employed, Mr. Eckerson?

A. Hampton General Hospital.

Q. At what address is Hampton General Hospital located?

A. 17810 Glessner Ave., in Hampton.

Q. Mr. Eckerson, would you briefly list your educational background.

A. I attended Hampton County Community College, where I earned an associate of applied science degree in radiologic technology.

Q. Do you have any board certification.

A. Yes. I became a registered radiologic technologist in 1990 and a certified radiologic technologist in 1991.

Q. Would you explain the process required to become a certified radiologic technologist?

A. At least an associate's degree is required, plus satisfactory performance on a state-administered, nationally recognized examination.

Q. How many hours of clinical work were you required to perform as part of your education?

A. I was required to perform 320 hours of supervised radiologic work at an approved center.

Q. At what approved center did you perform your clinical work?

A. At HGH.

Q. And HGH is...

A. I'm sorry. HGH is Hampton General Hospital.

Q. So, prior to being hired by HGH, you had 320 hours of clinical experience in their X-Ray Department.

A. Radiology Department.

Q. I beg your pardon.

A. It's called the Radiology Department.

Q. So, prior to being hired by HGH, you had 320 hours of clinical experience in their Radiology Department?

A. Actually, I had a lot more experience than that.

Q. Why is that?

A. Under state rules, once you're in your second year of an accredited radiologic program, you can work in a department as long as you're under the supervision of a CRT.

Q. What exactly is a CRT?

A. A Certified Radiologic Technologist.

Q. So, you were hired by HGH during your second year in the program at Hampton County Community College?

A. That's correct.

Q. How many hours per week did you work?

A. Well, it varied, but usually around twenty.

Q. So, before being hired on a full-time basis, you had worked how long for HGH?

A. About six months.

Q. When were you hired on a full-time basis?

A. Right after graduation.

Q. Totaling all this time, how long have you worked for the X-Ray, that is, the Radiology Department at HGH?

A. Two years.

Q. Are you familiar with the procedure manual at HGH?

A. Yes. Everyone is required to read it and sign a form that indicates that they have done so.

Q. And did you read it and sign the appropriate form?

A. Yes I did.

(Deposition Exhibit 1 marked for identification)

Q. Mr. Eckerson, I'd like you to take a look at the document that I have marked Exhibit 1 and tell me if that is the form that you signed.

A. Yes. That's it.

Q. And is that your signature?

A. Yes, it is.

(Deposition Exhibit 2 marked for identification)

Q. Mr. Eckerson, I'd like you to take a look at the document that I've marked Exhibit 2 and tell me if that is a copy of the policy and procedure manual used at HGH.

A. Yes, it is.

Q. Mr. Eckerson, in a typical day at the hospital, how many patients do you see in the Radiology Department?

A. Typical day—there's no such thing as a typical day. I probably see on an average of thirty to forty patients a day.

Q. Since you see so many patients, it is unlikely that you'd remember any single patient.

A. That's true.

Q. Mr. Eckerson, do you remember a patient named Lisa DeMarco.

A. I sure do.

Q. But you've just testified that you don't remember most of your patients.

A. She's the first one I ever saw come close to dying so I'll always remember her.

Q. Do you remember why Ms. DeMarco was taken to the Radiologic Department?

A. Yes. She was scheduled for an IVP.

Q. And what is an IVP?

A. An intravenous pyleogram.

Q. Is this procedure dangerous?

A. Not usually.

Q. But it can be.

A. Oh sure, if the patient is allergic to the contrast material.

Q. Mr. Eckerson, let's back up for a moment. Explain the procedure you performed on Ms. DeMarco.

A. Well, we inject the patient with a contrast material. The contrast material acts sort of like a dye. That allows the radiologist to see things that he ordinarily wouldn't see absent the contrast material.

Q. And you say that this is a dangerous procedure.

A. It can be if the patient has an allergic reaction to the contrast medium.

Q. Mr. Eckerson, did Ms. DeMarco realize the dangers involved in this procedure?

A. I don't think so.

Q. And why do you say that?

A. Well, the radiologist never explained it to her.

Q. And who was the radiologist on March 17 of last year when Ms. DeMarco underwent this examination?

A. Dr. Philip Masterson.

Q. How do you know that Dr. Masterson did not explain the procedure to Ms. DeMarco?

A. Well, he gave me the informed consent form and told me to get her signature on it.

Q. And what is an informed consent form?

A. It's a form that explains the dangers of the procedure and tells the patient what alternatives are available.

Q. And did you get her signature?

A. Yes.

Q. Did she ask you what the form was for?

A. Yes.

Q. And did you tell her?

A. I never got the chance.

Q. Why not?

A. Dr. Masterson came into the room and told her it was just for insurance purposes.

Q. Is that standard procedure?

A. That depends.

Q. What does it depend on?

A. Well, it depends on the radiologist.

Q. What does the policy and procedure manual say?

A. Oh, the procedure manual is clear as a bell. It says the radiologist is required to explain the dangers of the procedure to the patient and to get her signature.

Q. How often did Dr. Masterson violate this explicit procedure?

BY MS. GOULD:

A. I object. Mr. Eckerson has not been present every time Dr. Masterson has performed his job in the Radiology Department. Therefore, he is not qualified to answer that question.

BY MR. MATTHEWS:

Q. How many times have you observed Dr. Masterson violating this procedure?

A. Every time I've worked with him.

Q. Mr. Eckerson, are there any procedures that should be followed to help prevent an allergic reaction to a contrast material?

A. Well, you really should ask patients if they have any allergies.

Q. On the day in question, did Dr. Masterson ask Ms. DeMarco about her allergies?

A. No.

Q. Do you remember why he did not ask her about her allergies?

A. I guess he thought we didn't have the time.

Q. Would the patient's chart include this information.

A. Yes.

(Deposition Exhibit 3 marked for identification)

Q. Mr. Eckerson, I'd like you to look at the document that I've marked Exhibit 3 and tell me what it is.

A. It's a copy of Ms. DeMarco's chart.

Q. And what does it say about her allergies?

A. It just says that she answered "yes" when she was asked about her allergies.

Q. Is there any other information on her chart about her allergies?

A. No.

Q. Is that unusual?

A. No, not really.

Q. Why not?

A. Sometimes the patient doesn't know exactly what she's allergic to, and sometimes the admitting nurse doesn't ask or gets busy with something else, things like that.

Q. I see. Now, to your knowledge, did Dr. Masterson check Ms. DeMarco's chart?

A. No, he didn't.

Q. You're certain?

A. Yes.

Q. How can you be so certain?

A. I asked him if he wanted to see the chart, and he said no.

Q. Why was that?

A. Well, like I said before, he thought we didn't have the time for petty details.

Q. Were those his words?

A. Which words?

Q. You said that Dr. Masterson didn't think you had time for "petty details." Did he use the words "petty details?"

A. Yes. That was one of his favorite sayings.

Q. Now, since Ms. DeMarco's chart indicated a long history of allergies, would the IVP have been canceled?

A. Not necessarily.

Q. Why not?

A. There are a few relatively new contrast materials that could be substituted for the one that we usually use.

Q. Such as?

A. Well, let's see, there's Iopamidol and Iohexol.

Q. Why would these be preferable?

A. The risk of anaphylactic shock is much lower if you use them.

Q. Just what is anaphylactic shock?

A. That's what happened to Ms. DeMarco.

BY MS. GOULD:

A. I object. The witness is not in a position to say exactly what happened to Ms. DeMarco.

BY MR. MATTHEWS:

Q. Mr. Eckerson, could you rephrase your answer without referring to Ms. DeMarco?

A. I've forgotten the question.

Q. What is anaphylactic shock?

A. That's the medical term for an allergic reaction.

Q. And is it life-threatening?

A. It can be, yes.

Q. If the risk of shock is much less with these materials, why didn't Dr. Masterson use them?

A. He told me that he thought they were much too expensive.

Q. Are there any other precautions that can be taken to lessen the risks that go along with an IVP?

A. Yes. You're supposed to have some intravenous epinephrine nearby and ready to go just in case.

Q. And what is intravenous epinephrine?

A. It's sort of like an antidote.

Q. And was that antidote available?

A. Not exactly.

Q. Would you explain what you mean by that?

A. We had some in the hospital, but we didn't have it in the Radiology Department.

Q. Was Dr. Masterson aware of this?

A. Yes.

Q. How can you be so certain?

A. Because I told him so.

Q. And how did he react?

A. Well, he got really angry. You see we were really swamped that day and I think he just didn't want to take the time.

Q. And what did you do?

A. Well, I told him again that we really shouldn't perform the test without the epinephrine.

Q. What did he do then?

A. Well, he told me he was running the department and to mind my own business.

Q. What did you say to that?

A. I told him it was my business.

Q. How did he react?

A. He told me to go to pharmacy and get the epinephrine.

Q. And did you?

A. Yes.

Q. What transpired next?

A. Apparently, Dr. Masterson went ahead with the test after I left. When I got back, the crash cart was already there. Ms. DeMarco had apparently suffered cardiac arrest.

Q. Is it standard procedure to begin such a test without the antidote present.

A. Absolutely not.

Q. You're certain of this?

A. Yes I am. I was so shook up I double-checked the manual about fifty times. Without the epinephrine you're not supposed to do anything.

Q. Yet, Dr. Masterson went ahead with the test?

BY MS. GOULD:

A. I object. Mr. Eckerson was not present in the room when the alleged test took place. He cannot possibly know whether Dr. Masterson administered the test.

BY MR. MATTHEWS:

Q. Mr. Eckerson, what is hospital policy at HGH when something like this event occurs?

A. You're supposed to fill out an incident report.

Q. And was one filled out in this case?

A. Not to my knowledge.

Q. Do you know why not?

A. Dr. Masterson said it wasn't necessary.

Q. Is that standard procedure?

A. No, like I said, the manual says to fill out an incident report.

BY MR. MATTHEWS:

A. I have no further questions.

BY MS. GOULD:

Q. Just for the record, Mr. Eckerson, you were not actually present in the X-Ray Department when Ms. DeMarco suffered her trauma, is that correct?

A. No, it's not correct.

Q. It's not correct? How so?

A. It's called the Radiology Department, not the X-Ray Department.

Q. Very well, then. You were not present in the Radiology Department when Ms. DeMarco suffered her trauma.

A. Yes. Like I said, I'd been sent to pharmacy.

Q. So, you really don't know what happened in your absence?

A. No. I only know that when I came back to the department the crash cart was already there.

Q. Mr. Eckerson, do you know in fact that an incident report was never filed.

A. No. I only know that Dr. Masterson told me that it wasn't necessary to fill out an incident report in this case.

Q. How often have you seen that happen?

A. See what happen?

Q. How often have you witnessed events that you thought needed an incident report when none was filed?

A. Practically every day.

Q. Mr. Eckerson, if Ms. DeMarco's heart attack had not resulted from an allergic reaction to the contrast medium, but had resulted from natural causes, would an incident report be required?

A. No. An incident report is required only when someone has made a mistake.

Q. Mr. Eckerson, are you still employed at HGH?

A. No.

Q. Why not?

A. I left the hospital about six months ago.

Q. Why was that?

A. I decided I couldn't take the pressure.

Q. Pressure like the day Ms. DeMarco suffered her alleged allergic reaction?

A. I guess so.

Q. Isn't it possible that you were the one who made the mistake on the day that Ms. DeMarco suffered her trauma?

A. I don't see how.

Q. Well, you just said that you couldn't take the kind of pressure you said you were under that day in the Radiology Department.

A. I didn't say that I couldn't take the pressure on that particular day.

Q. Admit it Mr. Eckerson, you cracked under pressure that day and decided that you, and not Dr. Masterson, a well-trained and highly respected radiologist, knew what was best for the patient.

BY MR. MATTHEWS:

A. I object. You're badgering the witness. Move on with the examination.

BY MS. GOULD:

Q. Mr. Eckerson, between the radiologist and the radiologic technologist, who is presumed by the medical profession to know what's best for the patient?

A. The radiologist, I guess, but . . .

Q. That's all. I have no further questions for this witness.

APPENDIX B

Computer Software and Service Vendors

APPLICATION	VENDOR
Accounting	Quicken INTUIT 66 Willow Place Menlo Park, CA 94025-3687 (415) 322-2800
Calendar	SIDEKICK PLUS and SIDEKICK Borland International 4585 Scotts Valley Drive Scotts Valley, CA 95066 (408) 438-8400
Corporate/Secretary of State/UCC	Information America 600 West Peachtree Street, NW Atlanta, GA 30308 (800) 235-4008
Document Generator	AutoLaw Corporation 12969 Calle de Las Rosas San Diego, CA 92129 (619) 484-3813
Document Summary Database Management	ATLIS Legal Information Service 6011 Executive Boulevard Rockville, MD 20852 (800) 638-6595
Full-Text Retrieval	Discovery-ZX Data Dynamics Corporation 310 S. Nina, Suite 5 Mesa, AZ 85202 (602) 497-1082

APPLICATION	VENDOR
	CAT-LINKS, Inc. 2100 North Broadway Suite 320 Santa Ana, CA 92705
Information Management Public Record Searches	Prentice Hall Legal & Financial Services 15 Columbus Circle New York, NY 10023 (800) 330-0431
Legal Research	LEXIS/NEXIS Mead Data Central 9393 Springboro Pike Dayton, OH 45401 (800) 227-9597
	WESTLAW West Publishing Company 50 West Kellogg Blvd. P.O. Box 64526 St. Paul, MN 55164-0526 (800) 937-8529
Litigation Support	Aspen Litigation Support 1600 Research Boulevard Rockville, MD 20850 (800) 545-2327
	The Litidex Company One Park Ten Place Suite 200 Houston, TX 77084
	American Legal Systems 475 Park Avenue South New York, NY 10016
Litigation Support Document Imaging	Techlaw Systems, Inc. 14500 Avion Parkway Chantilly, VA 22021 (800) 832-4529
Timekeeping/Billing	TimeSlips III TimeSlips Corporation 239 Western Avenue Essex, MA 01929 (508) 768-6100
Word Processing	WordPerfect Corporation 1555 N. Technology Way Orem, UT 84057 (801) 225-5000 FAX (801) 222-4477

APPENDIX C

The Trial Process

The Lermentov Case

The Lermentov case, which served as the commentary case in chapter 15 on the paralegal's role during the trial, will also serve as the nucleus for examples used in this appendix. Recall that in the Lermentov case your client, a certified public accountant named Mikhail Lermentov, was injured in a fire while he was conducting an audit at the laboratories and main offices of Billicheck-Kendall Pharmaceuticals, Inc. The company attempted to deny liability for Lermentov's injuries by claiming that all maintenance and security work done in their building is performed by two independent companies, Sergi Selinkov Security, Inc. and the Kolata Maintenance Corporation. Your attorney has attempted to settle the case but the defendants have not cooperated with these attempts. Consequently, the time for the trial has arrived.

C–1 PRELIMINARY STEPS IN THE TRIAL

Although most cases are settled or dismissed before reaching the trial stage, you must proceed on the assumption that eventually the case will reach trial. This means making a preliminary determination of whether a jury trial or a trial by a judge alone will be in the best interests of your client. If you are going to face a jury, one of the first steps in the trial will be to select the jurors. This selection process must be carried on with great care because the jurors will play a key role in the success or failure of your case.

Decisions Regarding Jury Trials

The Seventh Amendment to the United States Constitution guarantees the right to a trial by jury in certain types of civil cases. The amendment states, "In Suits at common law, where the value in controversy shall exceed twenty dollars, the right of trial by jury shall be preserved, and no fact tried by a jury, shall be otherwise re-examined in any Court of the United States, than according to the rules of common law." The amendment clearly preserves the right to a jury trial in cases involving common law for those litigants who wish to take advantage of that right. It does not, however, give the litigants a right to a jury trial in cases tried in equity. This is why, for instance, jury trials are not allowed in divorce proceedings, in disputes involving custody rights, or in other equitable cases.

Requesting a Jury Trial. The fact that the Constitution guarantees the right to a jury trial does not prevent the courts from making the request for such a trial the responsibility of the litigants.

For example, Rule 38(b) of the Federal Rules of Civil Procedure requires the litigants to demand a trial by jury. Such a demand must be made in writing at any time after the lawsuit has begun, but not later than ten days ɑfter the last pleading in the case has been filed. If such a demand is not made by either party, the right has been voluntarily surrendered by the parties. This means that the trial will be conducted before a judge. In such a trial the judge acts as both the finder of fact and the determiner of law. In a jury trial the jury plays the role of fact finder.

Factors in Choosing a Judge or a Jury Trial. Several factors should be considered by your attorney as he or she attempts to decide whether it would be in the best interests of the client to try the case before a judge or before a jury. The first factor to consider is the complexity of the case. If the case involves legal issues and concepts that may be difficult for the lay person to grasp, your attorney may prefer to present the case before a judge. The same might be true if the facts in the case are extremely complicated. Another factor to consider is available time. In general, the attorney can be relatively certain that a trial before a judge will take less time than a jury trial. This is because in a trial before a judge there is no need to select the members of the jury and no need to explain the law or the legal process to the judge, since he or she will already be well-versed in both.

Another factor to consider is the nature of the client. If the case is a personal injury case involving a client who has been disfigured or otherwise permanently disabled, the attorney representing the plaintiff would probably want to ask for a jury trial. In the Lermentov case, for example, your attorney would most likely decide to demand a trial by jury. Since the plaintiff has been badly burned through absolutely no fault of his own, your attorney would want to rely on eliciting the sympathy of the jury. In contrast, attorneys who represent large, impersonal corporate defendants, like Billicheck-Kendall in the commentary, would prefer to have a judge decide the case. Naturally, any party requesting a jury trial will have that request fulfilled since, as noted earlier, trial by jury is a constitutional right.

Even the location of the trial can be a factor in the decision to demand a jury trial. If your client is a local community member, and the opposition is someone from out of town, your attorney may elect to demand a jury trial. In the Lermentov case, for example, the plaintiff is a locally prominent CPA who was born and raised in the town of Red Forest, Alabama, while the defendant is a large corporation that was formed in Delaware. This would seem to indicate that your attorney would prefer a jury trial. However, she might also consider the fact that Billicheck-Kendall is the largest employer in town and is therefore an integral part of the local economy. Knowledge of the importance of Billicheck-Kendall to the economic health of Red Forest might cause her to reconsider the advisability of demanding a jury trial.

The Jury Selection Process

All cases involving a jury begin with the process of selecting or seating the jury. The jury members will be selected from a jury pool that has been gathered from among the local citizenry. Most jury pools are taken from the ranks of registered voters. Once a jury pool has been assembled at the courthouse, members of the pool will be asked to fill out preliminary information forms, copies of which will be given to the attorneys in the case. These forms will be used as part of the jury selection process. In federal court a civil trial uses twelve jurors. However, the parties are allowed to stipulate that fewer than twelve jurors will hear the case. Many state courts will require only eight jurors for a civil trial. Most states also allow parties to stipulate that fewer than eight jurors will hear their case. The federal court and most state courts also allow for the use of alternate jurors.

The Voir Dire Process.   Literally, "voir dire" means "to speak the truth." In trial practice, **voir dire** is the process by which the jurors are questioned to determine any bias that they might have that would affect their ability to be fair and impartial in the case. For example, in the Lermentov case your attorney would want to determine if any potential jurors are related to or are friends of the officers and employees of Billicheck-Kendall, Sergi Selinkov Securities, Inc., or the Kolata Maintenance Corporation. She might also want to know if any of the potential jurors has any financial interest in the outcome of the trial. Such information would indicate bias on the part of the juror and would be grounds for a challenge. Each side in the suit has an unlimited number of these challenges for cause.

Peremptory Challenges.   Each side also has a limited number of peremptory challenges. The federal court and some states allow only three such challenges, while other states allow as many as four. Additional peremptory challenges are allowed when alternate jurors are to be chosen. However, the number of peremptory challenges is always limited. This limit is imposed because an attorney making a peremptory challenge does not have to give a reason for the challenge. He or she simply exercises the peremptory challenge, and the juror is dismissed. The objective of the peremptory challenge is to allow attorneys an opportunity to dismiss jurors for certain "intangible" reasons that cannot be logically explained to the court. For instance, your attorney may feel that there is a certain "air of hostility" about a certain juror, or she might feel that the "chemistry" is not right between them. Such an instinctive reaction, though genuine enough to cause concern, would be difficult to explain to the court. For these instinctive situations the law has provided the peremptory challenge.

C-2 OPENING STATEMENTS

As the trial begins the first step will involve opening statements. The objectives and scope of these opening statements are not as precise and definitive as one might expect in a profession that prides itself on both precision and definiteness. Still, the opening statement is one of the most important steps, if not the most important step, in a jury trial. Consequently, a skillful attorney will know that he or she should keep the opening statement brief, use ordinary language in the statement, make the statement interesting, and use appropriate body language in delivering that statement.

Definition and Limitations

Each side in a jury trial is allowed time to make an opening statement. An opening statement presents facts to the jury and introduces the evidence that the attorney intends to use to prove those facts. A general rule of trial procedure states that attorneys are not permitted to argue their cases during opening statements. The exact meaning of this rule is not clear. Consequently, the judge has an enormous amount of discretion in what the attorneys can and cannot say during opening statements. Some judges are strict in adhering to the general guideline that attorneys cannot argue their cases in the opening statement, while others are more lenient, allowing attorneys to introduce points that another judge would almost certainly label as "argument." This means that, to be successful in an opening statement, an attorney must have an understanding of just how much "argument" a particular judge will allow. Such an understanding comes from experience and from a willingness to ask questions about the processes when the attorney is unfamiliar with a court and its judges.

Importance of the Opening Statement

The imprecise nature of the opening statement is made even more critical because of its importance. Some legal scholars argue that the opening statement is the most important step in a trial.

voir dire
The process by which jurors are questioned to determine any bias that they might have that would affect their ability to be fair and impartial in the case.

These scholars have several rather convincing reasons for placing such importance on the opening statement. First, since the opening statement occurs so early in the trial, the jurors are very attentive. This attentiveness heightens their awareness of what is being said and done during the opening stages. As the trial progresses, and they become more comfortable and secure in the courtroom, their attentiveness lessens. Also, although jurors are counseled to remain as objective as possible, they are, nevertheless, human beings who have a natural tendency to "pick sides" in any adversarial contest. After all, when they watch a television show or a movie they know whose side they are supposed to be on. When they attend a sports event, people are quick to pick sides.

The jurors carry this tendency to choose sides with them into the courtroom, and as early as the end of the opening statements may have unconsciously decided who is the "good guy" and who is the "bad guy." This places a heavy burden on the attorney who has been labeled the "bad guy" and gives an edge to the one who has been labeled the "good guy." The advantage given to the "good guy" has been termed by some scholars as the "halo effect" and by others as the "white hat syndrome." Basically, the halo effect or the white hat syndrome means that everything said by the "good guy" and every piece of testimony and evidence that is introduced in support of the "good guy's" argument is interpreted favorably, while everything damaging to that side's case is somehow rationalized or explained away. Of course, this does not mean that a juror will never change his or her mind. It just means that attorneys who have been labeled "bad guys" have a much more difficult time getting jurors to believe them.

Characteristics of a Good Opening Statement

Since so much of the success of a jury trial seems to depend upon the opening statement, an attorney should take great care in fashioning it. A good opening statement should be brief, interesting, understandable, sincere, and tactful.

Delivering a Brief Opening Statement.   Setting an absolute maximum length of time for an opening statement beyond which an attorney should never wander is difficult. Similarly, it is difficult to set a minimum length of time. It is, however, safe to say that an attorney should rarely, if ever, pass up the opportunity to make an opening statement, unless both parties waive that right. Waiving the opening statement, or even postponing it, gives an unnecessary psychological advantage to the other party. The opening statement should be long enough to capture the attention and imagination of the jury, but not so long that it puts them to sleep.

Most opening statements can be limited to thirty to forty-five minutes. Occasionally, when the facts are extremely complex, more time will be needed. Conversely, when the facts are simple, less time will be needed.

Delivering an Interesting Opening Statement.   At the beginning of this section, we noted that the jury's attention level is very high at the opening of the trial. The good attorney will take advantage of this interest level by delivering an interesting, even captivating, opening statement. This can be done by reducing the opening statement to a narrative. The opening statement involves facts, and nothing conveys facts in a more interesting or convincing fashion than a story. Cold, antiseptic facts, figures, and statistics should be avoided in favor of conveying a sense of the people and the action involved in the case. For instance, in presenting the case of Mr. Lermentov to the jury, your attorney might begin by stating that, "On the morning of March 4, 1991, Mr. Mikhail Lermentov awoke and prepared for a routine day conducting an audit at the offices of Billicheck-Kendall here in downtown Red Forest. At that time he had no idea that this day would be one of the worst of his entire life." From this point on, your attorney would follow the events of that day much as if she were telling a story. Such an opening statement is much more likely to capture the attention and sympathy of the jurors than one limited to a long procession of facts.

Delivering an Understandable Opening Statement.   Your attorney will be more likely to gain the interest and sympathy of the jury members if he or she avoids legal jargon and speaks the language of the jurors. Opening statements that are full of legal terms and unintelligible Latin phrases are guaranteed to alienate jury members, who may already view all attorneys with a certain degree of distrust if not downright hostility. If your attorney, for example, buries the Lermentov opening statement in references to *respondeat superior, vicarious liability, piercing the corporate veil,* and *alter egos,* she may bury her case along with it. In addition, depending upon the opinion of the judge in the case, the use of such terms may be considered arguing the case. Your attorney will do better to speak in ordinary, everyday language.

Delivering a Sympathetic Opening Statement.   An attorney must always remember that he or she is the client's advocate. This means that the jury expects the attorney to be on the client's side. To make the opening statement as convincing and sympathetic as possible the attorney must show the jury that he or she believes in the righteousness of the client's cause. If the jury members doubt the attorney's dedication to vindicating the client's rights they will have little faith in anything that he or she says on behalf of that client. For these reasons an attorney should immediately identify himself or herself with the client's cause. The jury will be much more convinced by the attorney who says, "We will prove that our case against the defendant is as solid as a rock," than one who says,"Don't believe everything the other side has to say about the plaintiff."

Delivering a Tactful Opening Statement. As noted above, the attorney should be brief, interesting, understandable, sympathetic, and sincere in the opening statement. However, this can go for naught if jurors are intimidated by the presence and actions of the attorney. For this reason, the delivery of the opening statement should be as tactful as possible. Attorneys should not be overly emotional, too loud, or excessively boastful in the opening statement. Rather, they should be soft-spoken, even-tempered, and genuine. It is also important for the attorney to keep his or her distance from the jury. Climbing on top of jurors may make a powerfully dramatic scene in a movie or television show, but in real life it invades the space of the jurors, intimidates them, and destroys their concentration on what the attorney is saying.

C–3 THE PRESENTATION OF EVIDENCE

As we saw in chapter 15, Trial Techniques, the paralegal is instrumental in preparing witnesses for trial. During the presentation of evidence this preparation pays off. The presentation of evidence can be divided into two stages: the case in chief and the rebuttal. During the case in chief both sides present the testimony and evidence that will hopefully convince the jury of the validity of their case. The plaintiff presents his or her evidence by calling witnesses to testify and placing those witnesses under direct examination. The defendant then has the right to conduct a cross examination of each witness. The roles are then reversed. The defendant places his or her witnesses on the stand for direct examination. The plaintiff then has the opportunity to engage in cross examination.

The Plaintiff's Case in Chief

If the plaintiff's attorney feels that certain facts in the case are uncontested because they were admitted to in response to a request for admissions, were a part of the defendant's answer, or were admitted in some other pleading or discovery device, then those facts may be read into the record. This generally occurs before the plaintiff calls the first witness.

Direct Examination by the Plaintiff. The plaintiff's attorney calls each of the witnesses who will provide facts to verify the validity of the plaintiff's version of the case. The plaintiff's attorney subjects each of those witnesses to direct examination. This is a question-and-answer period conducted under oath and recorded by the court stenographer. In general, the plaintiff's attorney may not ask his or her own witnesses leading questions. A leading question is one containing the answer. For example, your attorney could not call Mr. Lermentov to the witness stand and ask him, "Isn't it true that the storeroom next to the room where you conducted the audit for Billicheck-Kendall contained combustible material?" Such a question would be considered leading and would not be permitted.

Leading Questions by the Plaintiff. There is an exception to the rule that prohibits asking leading questions. When an attorney is faced with an adverse or hostile witness, he or she is permitted to ask leading questions. For example, in the Lermentov case, your attorney has elected to call several adverse witnesses including Yuri Vilnius, CEO of Sergi Selinkov; Julius Vilnius, CEO of Billicheck-Kendall; Kay Vilnius, treasurer of Billicheck-Kendall; Albert Vilnius, CEO of Kolata Maintenance and vice-president of Billicheck-Kendall; and Vytautas Vilnius, treasurer of Kolata Maintenance and vice president of Billicheck-Kendall. Each of these witnesses is also an adverse party and could, therefore, be the legitimate target of leading questions by Lermentov's attorney. For instance, it would be permitted for Lermentov's attorney to ask Julius Vilnius the following question: "Isn't it true that the storeroom next to the room where the audit was conducted contained combustible chemicals?"

Rules Regarding the Plaintiff's Direct Examination. The process of asking precisely the right questions during a direct examination session is not as easy as it may appear. Preparing in advance is essential. All friendly witnesses should be properly and thoroughly prepared before the day of the trial. They should meet with the attorney and discuss the questions that will be asked, the answers that the witness intends to give, and the probable questions to expect on cross examination. An attorney should never ask a question that he or she does not already know the answer to. The time for exploratory questions is during the discovery process, not at trial. An attorney also needs to know when to stop asking questions. Once the attorney has elicited the facts that he or she wants, questioning should stop. Continuing questions after that point can be very damaging.

Cross Examination by the Defendant. When the plaintiff's attorney has completed the direct examination of each witness, the defendant's attorney has the opportunity to engage in cross examination. In federal court and in most states the scope of cross examination is limited to facts covered in direct examination. If the defendant's attorney wants to explore new territory with a witness, he or she will have to call the witness during the defendant's direct examination session. The objective of cross examination is to discredit the witness, to cast doubt on the accuracy of the witness's testimony, or to show that the witness is somehow biased in favor of the plaintiff. One way the defendant can do this is to show that the testimony delivered at trial by the witness contradicts the testimony presented during the discovery process. Another way is to use leading questions that require simple "yes" or "no" answers from the witness, thus limiting his or her ability to elaborate on those answers.

Redirect Examination by the Plaintiff. When the defendant has completed the cross examination of a witness, the plaintiff's attorney has the opportunity to redirect questions to that witness. The objective of this part of the trial process is to allow the plaintiff the chance to reestablish the credibility of his or her witnesses and to clear up any factual disputes raised on cross examination. To make redirect examination as efficient as possible, the plaintiff's attorney is limited to those matters addressed by the defendant's counsel during the cross examination period.

The Defendant's Case in Chief

Once the plaintiff has completed his or her case in chief, the roles are switched, and the defendant has the same opportunity. The defendant's efforts are directed at discrediting the case that was presented by the plaintiff. The objective is to demonstrate that the plaintiff's version of the facts is not supported by the evidence. In addition, if the defendant raised any affirmative defenses, now is the time to present evidence that demonstrates the validity of these defenses.

Direct Examination by the Defendant. The defendant's attorney calls his or her witnesses and subjects them to direct examination. This is the same type of question-and-answer period that was conducted by the plaintiff. As was the case with the plaintiff's attorney, the defendant's counsel may not ask his or her own witnesses leading questions. For example, the defendant's attorney could not call Lon Anderson, an employee of both Sergi Selinkov and Kolata Maintenance, to the witness stand and ask him, "Isn't it true that Sergi Selinkov and Kolata Maintenance management decisions were made separately from any and all management decisions made for Billicheck-Kendall?" Such a question would be considered leading and would not be permitted.

Leading Questions by the Defendant. As is the case with the plaintiff's counsel, when the defendant's attorney is faced with an adverse or hostile witness he or she is permitted to ask leading questions. For example, in the Lermentov case, if the defense attorney has elected to call Mr. Lermentov to testify, he would be the legitimate target of leading questions by Billicheck-Kendall's attorney. For instance, it would be permitted for Billicheck-Kendall's attorney to ask Mr. Lermentov the following question: "Isn't it true that you knew of the risk imposed by the combustible chemicals located in the storeroom next to your office?"

Rules Regarding the Defendant's Direct Examination. The same rules governing the plaintiff's strategy on direct examination also apply to the defendant's plan for direct examination. Thus, the defendant should prepare in advance by meeting with friendly witnesses before trial. The defendant's attorney should never ask a question that he or she does not already know the answer to, and he or she should develop the discipline to know when to stop asking questions.

Cross Examination by the Plaintiff. When the defendant's attorney has completed the direct examination of each witness, the plaintiff's attorney has the opportunity to engage in cross examination. The scope of cross examination allowed to the plaintiff is limited to facts covered in direct examination. Like the defendant, the plaintiff wants to discredit the plaintiff's witnesses, to cast doubt on the accuracy of their testimony, or to show that the witnesses are somehow biased in favor of the defendant.

Redirect Examination by the Defendant. When the plaintiff has completed the cross examination of a witness, the defendant's attorney has a chance to redirect questions to that witness. This step allows the defendant the same chance that the plaintiff had to reestablish the credibility of his or her witnesses and to clear up any factual disputes raised on cross examination.

The Presentation of Rebuttal Evidence

After each side has had the opportunity to see the entire case in chief presented by the other party, both have the chance to present rebuttal evidence. Rebuttal evidence, or evidence in rebuttal, is designed to discredit the other side's evidence and to reestablish the credibility of the side presenting the rebuttal. To make the rebuttal as efficient and as fair as possible, the scope of rebuttal is limited to the evidence presented during the case in chief. No new evidence is to be presented during the rebuttal. When the plaintiff has completed his or her rebuttal, the defendant has the same chance to call rebuttal witnesses. Some states use the term *surebuttal* to describe the defendant's rebuttal. Others use the phrase *evidence in rejoinder* or *rejoinder evidence*. Regardless of the terms used to describe it, the defendant's rebuttal is limited to the rebuttal evidence put forth by the plaintiff.

C–4   CLOSING ARGUMENTS

As the trial begins to wind down one of the final steps involves the closing arguments. The objective and scope of closing arguments are more precise and definitive than they are for the opening statement. The evidence has already been presented, so it is clear that the closing arguments must refer to that evidence and must attempt to convince the jury that the attorney's interpretation of that evidence is the correct one.

Definition and Limitations

Each side in a jury trial is allowed time at the end of the presentation of evidence to make a closing argument. The closing argument will help jurors review the evidence that the attorneys introduced during the trial. Unlike the procedure followed during the opening statements, which prevents the attorneys from arguing their case, during the closing arguments attorneys are permitted to do their best to persuade jurors of the validity of their case. Moreover, they are also permitted to attack the presentation of the other side's evidence.

The Strategy of the Closing Argument

During closing arguments each attorney will explain his or her theory of the case and will demonstrate how the evidence presented at trial supports that theory. Each attorney will also do his or her best to destroy the jury's belief in the credibility of the other side's witnesses. Destroying the credibility of the opponent's witnesses can be accomplished in a number of ways. First the attorney may demonstrate that the witness has contradicted himself or herself on the stand. The attorney may also point out discrepancies between the witness's testimony in a deposition or interrogatories and his or her testimony during the actual trial. It may also be demonstrated that the witness lacks credibility because of bias or because of the inability of the witness to really know the facts that he or she testified to.

Characteristics of a Good Closing Argument

As noted earlier, the jury has a heightened awareness of the trial process at the beginning of the trial. The same is true, though to a lesser degree, at the end of the trial. This fact, plus the fact that this is the attorney's last chance to reach the jury, makes the closing argument very important. Since so much of the success of a jury trial depends upon the closing argument, an attorney should take great care in fashioning it. It is critical to know the characteristics of a good closing argument. To be effective, a closing argument must be well-planned and persuasive.

Delivering a Well-Planned Closing Argument. Planning is important because the closing statement must organize a mass of evidence and testimony into a coherent pattern that is understandable to the jury. The attorney begins the closing argument with his or her theory of the case and then moves to an explanation of the burden of proof and the evidence that strengthens his or her theory. The attorney will also attempt to point out weaknesses in the evidence the other side has presented. As noted above, the attorney will also try to discredit the witnesses that his or her adversary has relied upon.

Delivering a Persuasive Closing Argument. The closing argument must also be persuasive. Persuasiveness is often difficult to manufacture, so it is extremely helpful if the attorney is convinced of the righteousness of his or her client's cause. If jury members doubt the attorney's dedication to vindicating the rights of the client, they will have little faith in anything that he or she says on behalf of that client. For these reasons, in the closing argument, as in the opening statement, an attorney should identify himself or herself with the client's cause. In the Lermentov case, for instance, the jury will be much more easily convinced by your attorney if she concludes her argument by saying, "We have proven that the officers and directors of Billicheck-Kendall attempted to hide behind the facade of Sergi Selinkov and Kolata Maintenance in a feeble attempt to escape their legal obligation to protect all those who used their offices," than if she were to say, "The defendant's attorney did not prove that Sergi Selinkov and Kolata Maintenance were not the alter egos of the defendants."

C–5 JURY DELIBERATIONS

The responsibility of giving the jury instructions belongs to the judge. Once instructions have been given to the jury members, they retire to consider the case and to decide on a verdict. Once a verdict has been rendered, either party may request that jury members be polled. Jury members may also be required to answer interrogatories to determine if their verdict is in line with the answers to those interrogatories.

Jury Instructions

In both federal and state courts, the judge has the responsibility of delivering jury instructions. These instructions include an explanation of the law, the burden of proof, the weight that should be given to the evidence, the process to be followed during the deliberations, and the verdicts that can be rendered. Usually, such instructions are given to the jury after the closing arguments, immediately before the deliberation process begins. However, the judge may instruct the jury on some things, such as the law relating to the procedure at trial, the duties and the functions of the jury, the law that pertains to the case, and the use of evidence, before the trial begins and whenever needed during the actual course of the trial. Also, although the responsibility of final jury instructions belongs to the judge, the attorneys have, at the close of evidence, the opportunity to file a written request with the judge to deliver the instructions in a particular way. Before closing arguments the judge will inform the attorneys how he or she will instruct the jury. After closing arguments, the judge delivers the jury instructions. Before the jury retires to consider its verdict, the attorneys may, out of the hearing of the jury members, object to the instructions. The objection must specifically explain the grounds for the objection.

Rendering a Verdict

Once instructions have been given to the jury members, they retire to consider their verdict. Once a verdict has been rendered, either party may request that jury members be polled. Jury members may also be required to answer interrogatories to determine if their verdict is in line with the answers to those interrogatories.

Jury Deliberations.   Once the jury is behind closed doors it will consider the evidence in light of the instructions given by the judge and will attempt to arrive at a verdict. If the jurors are confused about some point or unsure of the law, they can ask for clarification from the judge. The jury can also see any of the evidence presented at trial. In federal court in a civil case a unanimous verdict is required, unless the parties have agreed on some number less than a majority. In many state courts, a three-fourths majority will be sufficient for the rendering of a verdict in a civil case. Once a verdict has been reached it is placed in writing, and the jurors return to the courtroom, where the verdict is read aloud.

Polling the Jury.   After the verdict has been read, either party may request that jury members be polled. Polling the jurors involves asking each juror if the verdict announced was the verdict that he or she rendered. As long as the required number of jurors answer that the verdict announced is the verdict that they agreed to, there is no problem and the jury is dismissed. For example, suppose in the Lermentov case eight jurors were involved in the deliberations. Suppose further that three-fourths of those jurors were required for the rendering of a verdict. If six of the eight answer during the polling process that they agreed with the verdict, the jury members are discharged. If, however, fewer than six concur with the verdict, then the jurors are sent back to continue their deliberations.

Interrogatories and the Jury.   Prior to closing arguments, either side in the case can ask that the jury be required to answer interrogatories as part of the deliberation process. The purpose of the interrogatories is to ensure that the jury really understood the determinative issues of law and fact in the case. The party making such a request must also submit written copies of these interrogatories to the judge and to the opposing attorney. If the judge approves the interrogatories, they are submitted to the jurors prior to their deliberations. During jury instructions, the judge explains the use of the interrogatories to the jurors. They are then required to answer them in writing and return the written answers with their verdict. As long as the answers are consistent with the verdict, the verdict will stand. Should even a single answer be inconsistent with the verdict, the judge may order the jury to conduct further deliberations. In some situations, the judge may even elect to order a new trial.

C–6   TRIAL AND POST-TRIAL MOTIONS

Before the trial has ended, the parties have the chance to end it by filing a motion for a directed verdict. After the jury has rendered its verdict, and the court has entered its judgment, a dissatisfied party has the opportunity to file a motion for a judgment notwithstanding the verdict and a motion for a new trial.

Motion for a Directed Verdict

The purpose of the motion for a directed verdict is to halt a trial that, from a careful consideration of the facts and the law, has an outcome that the court decides is inevitable. A motion for a directed verdict asks the court to direct the jury to render a verdict in favor of the party who has asked for the motion. It may be made by a party after the opposing side's opening statement, at the close of the opposing party's presentation of evidence, or at the close of all evidence. A party who has made the motion does not lose his or her opportunity to present evidence in the event that the court denies the motion. Nor does a party give up the right to a jury trial by making such a motion.

The court will grant a motion for a directed verdict if, after looking at the facts in a light as favorable as possible for the other party, and after applying the law to these facts, it decides that reasonable people could come to only one conclusion in light of the evidence, and that conclusion is favorable to the party who raised the motion. The judge is not required to obtain the assent of the jury to grant a motion for a directed verdict.

Motion for a Judgment Notwithstanding the Verdict

A motion for a judgment notwithstanding the verdict can be made by a party dissatisfied with the verdict rendered by the jury. Such a motion must be made within the time limits set by the rules. In federal court, the time limit is ten days after the court has made a judgment entry. Some states have longer time periods. Ohio, for example, allows fourteen days after the entry of the judgment. A dissatisfied party also has the chance to make such a motion if the jury was unable to reach a verdict and was, as a result, dismissed. In order for the judge to grant such a motion, he or she would have to be convinced that a group of reasonable people could not have rendered the verdict that the jury did in fact render and that such a verdict is clearly incorrect as a matter of law. If the motion for a directed verdict is granted, the other party has the opportunity to appeal that ruling or to file a motion for a new trial. If the motion is denied, the moving party also has the opportunity to appeal or to ask for a new trial. The motion for a judgment notwithstanding the verdict is also known as a motion for a judgment N.O.V. or a motion for a J.N.O.V. These abbreviations come from the Latin phrase *non obstante veredicto*, which means "notwithstanding the verdict."

Motion for a New Trial

A party who is dissatisfied with some aspect of the trial may move for a new trial. As is the case with the motion for a judgment notwithstanding the verdict, the motion for a new trial must be made within the time limits set by the rules. In federal court, the time limit is ten days after the court has made a judgment entry. Some states have longer time periods. Ohio, for example, allows fourteen days after the entry of the judgment. The motion for a new trial can also be joined to a motion for a judgment notwithstanding the verdict or may be presented as an alternative motion.

A motion for a new trial can be brought on the following grounds: (a) the verdict was contrary to law; (b) the verdict was totally defective; (c) irregularity in the court procedure; (d) excessive or insufficient damage award; (e) jury misconduct; (f) misconduct of a party; or (g) newly discovered evidence. For instance, in the Lermentov case, your attorney may discover that one of the jurors was offered a job at Billicheck-Kendall if a verdict was rendered in favor of the defendants. Such a discovery would constitute misconduct on the part of a juror and a party and would, therefore, be grounds for granting a new trial.

GLOSSARY

affidavit A written statement that certain facts are true or are believed to be true, made under oath.

affirm Action by an appellate court upholding a lower court decision.

affirmative defense A fact or circumstance alleged by a defendant in an answer, which if proven would defeat the plaintiff's claim, even if the plaintiff proves all of the contentions of his claim.

agent for service of process Individual designated by a corporation who is authorized to be served with a lawsuit.

allegations Contentions stated in a pleading.

amicus curiae brief A brief that is voluntarily filed by an attorney who is not a part of the case but who has been granted permission to present some legal argument before the court.

answer Pleading filed by a defendant in a lawsuit that challenges the contentions or allegations in the complaint.

appeal A request for a higher court to review a lower court's decision.

appellant A person bringing an appeal.

appellant's brief Brief of the person bringing an appeal.

appellate jurisdiction The power or authority of a court to review a trial court's actions.

appellee The person who opposes an appeal.

appellee's brief Brief of the person who opposes an appeal.

arbitration An out-of-court process for resolving disputes between individuals in which a neutral party hears both sides of the dispute and then makes a decision.

arbitrator A neutral, third party who acts as a judge in an arbitration hearing.

attachment A court order that property be seized and remain under the control of the court until the case is resolved; usually required if the court is exercising quasi in rem jurisdiction.

attorney-client privilege A privilege preventing the forced disclosure of written or oral communications between an attorney and a client or prospective client.

authorization A signed statement authorizing someone (such as a doctor or employer) to give the attorney information that otherwise might be treated as confidential.

Bates numbering A system for placing a number on a document by machine.

brief A written document in which an attorney discusses and analyzes legal issues in relationship to the facts of a case; can be prepared or filed in connection with a trial or an appeal.

broad production　A document production in which all documents even remotely relevant are produced, even those not directly requested.

canons of ethics　A code of conduct for legal professionals.

capacity　The legal right to sue or be sued.

caption　The part of a pleading or motion identifying the court, the parties, the nature of the document, and the docket number.

case on point　A case that has been decided in your jurisdiction and that involves both facts and legal principles that are so similar to the facts and principles in the present case that the attorney feels the court will be bound to follow the court's ruling in that earlier case.

cast of characters　A roster of all key players in a case, which may be drawn from witness interviews, documents, depositions, exhibits, and pleadings.

cause of action　Facts supporting a legally recognized right to relief from a court.

certificate of mailing　Statement attached to a pleading or motion indicating that a copy of the document has been mailed to certain identified parties or their attorneys; a method of proving that papers have been served, used when the party to be served has already appeared in the action.

chronological deposition summary　The organization of deposition testimony according to a particular time sequence.

chronology　A list of what happened, when it happened, where it happened, and who was involved in a case.

cite check　The process of determining the validity of cases cited in the brief.

civil laws　Laws dealing with private disputes between parties.

civil litigation　The process of resolving private disputes through the court system.

civil procedure　The area of law that regulates the method of resolving civil disputes in the courts.

claim statute　A type of law that requires that a written notice describing a claim be presented to the defendant before a lawsuit can be filed.

class action　An action maintained by or against one or more individuals on their own behalf and on behalf of numerous others in the same situation.

client's medical history and medical condition　A section of the settlement brochure that sets out the injuries suffered by the client and any future medical prognosis.

client's personal history　A listing of the client's family information, education, employment record, and church, professional, and civic organization memberships in a settlement brochure.

compensatory damages　Damages intended to compensate or reimburse a party for the actual loss sustained; most common measure of damages in a civil case.

complaint　The initial document filed in a lawsuit; states the factual basis for the claim.

compound request　A request for admission that asks a party to admit to two or more facts in one statement.

compulsory counterclaim　In federal practice, a claim by a defendant against the plaintiff arising out of facts alleged in a complaint; it must be asserted by the defendant or is barred.

compulsory joinder　The required association of multiple parties as plaintiffs or defendants in a lawsuit; occurs when the court cannot render relief without the presence of all the parties.

concurrent jurisdiction　The type of jurisdiction existing when more than one court has the authority to hear a type of case; can exist between federal and state courts or between two or more different state courts.

confidentiality agreement An agreement that prevents discovery of confidential information or trade secrets.

conflict of interest A law firm's loyalty to one client competing with loyalty to another client or potential client; usually arises when a firm is asked to sue a party who it currently represents or previously represented in another case.

consent decree An outline of the details of the settlement agreed upon by the parties.

consideration The exchange of values in a contract.

contingent fee An attorney's fee based on a percentage of whatever recovery is obtained.

contribution Concept that requires joint defendants to reimburse one another, in an equitable manner, for any judgment assessed against them, even though each defendant might be liable to the plaintiff for the entire amount of the judgment.

costs Out-of-pocket expenses incurred in pursuing a case in litigation; includes such items as filing fees and costs of service.

count In some complaints the parts stating the various causes of action; each cause of action is stated in a separate count; sometimes referred to as a cause of action instead of a count.

counterclaim In federal practice, a claim asserted by a defendant against the plaintiff; part of the answer.

court reporter An individual present at deposition to place the deponent under oath and take a word-for-word account of the proceeding and, if required, produce a written copy of the deposition.

courts of appeal Intermediate courts that primarily review the actions of lower courts.

criminal law The laws dealing with acts that are offenses against society as a whole; includes such acts as murder, robbery, and drunk driving.

criminal procedure The procedures and rules that apply when an individual is accused of committing a crime.

cross-appeal An appeal filed by the appellee based on a different legal rationale than the appeal filed by the appellant.

cross-claim In federal practice, a claim for relief made by one defendant against another defendant.

curriculum vitae A list of an expert's professional credentials, including each educational and professional credential, and a summary of publications and research projects.

damages The amount of money spent by a client because of injuries and all wages lost because of the injuries.

declaration A statement under penalty of perjury that certain facts are true or believed to be true.

declaratory relief A court order defining or explaining the rights and obligations of parties under some contract.

deemed admitted The rule stating that any request for admissions that is not denied is deemed to be admitted.

default The failure of a party, usually a defendant, to appear in an action.

defendant The party in a lawsuit who is being sued.

demand for inspection A demand for access to inspect a property that is relevant to the case, served upon all parties in the litigation even if it is directed only to the party who has custody of the property at issue.

demeanor The appearance of a person; an important factor in weighing the testimony of that person.

demurrer A pleading used in some state jurisdictions that challenges the legal sufficiency of the complaint.

deponent A party or non-party witness who is questioned during a deposition.

deposition The oral or written testimony of a party or witness given under oath outside a courtroom.

deposition summary A written record that reduces many hours of testimony to a few concisely drawn, easily read, and quickly understood pages.

deposition upon written questions A discovery tool that requires the deponent to orally answer written questions in the presence of a court reporter.

discovery The legal process by which the parties to a lawsuit search for facts relevant to a particular case.

discovery conference A conference of the parties to a case with the court in which they discuss the discovery process.

diversity of citizenship A basis for federal court jurisdiction; occurs when plaintiffs and defendants are not citizens of the same state.

docket number A number assigned to a lawsuit by the court; each pleading or document filed in the action must bear this number.

document index An index of documents produced in a case.

document production log A log used to track the production of documents, including the source of the document, the file in which the document is located, and whether the document is to be produced or excluded on the basis of privilege or work product.

documents Such diverse items as photographs, graphs, computer printouts, calendars, and accounting records.

duplicative A request for production of information that has already been requested.

en camera A private viewing by the judge to determine the validity of the objection based on privileged information or work product.

engrossed Restating the interrogatory to be answered.

entry of default Action by a court clerk noting that the defendant has failed to file a proper response to the complaint.

equitable relief Remedy provided by a court other than money damages.

evaluation of the claim A recap of the perceived value of a claim.

evidence log A document attached to an item of physical evidence recording the chain of possession of that piece of evidence.

ex parte Refers to motions or hearings where the moving party is not required to give prior formal notice to opposing parties.

exclusive jurisdiction The sole authority of *one* type of court to hear a case; often refers to the sole authority of federal courts to hear certain kinds of cases.

exemplary damages Another term for punitive damages; damages intended to punish the defendant for some extreme conduct rather than to compensate the plaintiff for the actual loss.

expert witness An individual with special education, experience, and expertise, who is hired to explain the technical aspects of a case to a judge or jury and who is allowed to express his expert opinion.

fictitiously named defendants Defendants in a lawsuit who are not identified by their correct names; usually refers to the practice in some state courts of including several "Does" as defendants to provide for discovery of additional defendants after the statute of limitations has run.

filed Depositing with the court a document that is related to a lawsuit.

flat fee A legal fee based on a fixed sum rather than on an hourly rate or on a percentage of a recovery.

form books Books containing sample forms for legal professionals to follow in preparing pleadings and other documents.

general appearance Taking part in a court proceeding by filing a pleading or motion, except for the limited purpose of objecting to the jurisdiction of the court.

general denial A type of answer in which all of the allegations of the complaint are denied.

general jurisdiction Authority to hear any kind of case except those brought in federal court.

general release A release granting full and final settlement, including all possible claims against all possible persons who might be liable for the plaintiff's injuries.

good cause Sufficient cause for a court to order a physical and mental examination in a case.

guardian ad litem An individual appointed by the court to represent the interests of a minor who is a party to a lawsuit.

higher courts Courts of appeal.

hourly billing A legal fee based on a fixed amount for each hour the law firm spends on the case.

in controversy A requirement that the condition to be examined in a physical or mental examination must be at the heart of the dispute in the case.

in rem jurisdiction The authority of a court to hear a case based on the fact that property that is the subject of a lawsuit is located within the state in which that court is situated.

indemnification A concept allowing one defendant, who has paid a judgment, to seek reimbursement from another defendant.

indispensable party A party who must be joined in a lawsuit in order for the court to be able to render a fair and complete judgment in the case.

injunction An order requiring a party to stop doing something.

interpleader A type of lawsuit in which the court is requested to determine ownership to certain property that is being claimed by several parties; the action is filed by one holding the property even though that person has no ownership interest in the property and is filed to protect the holder from delivering the property to the wrong party or parties.

interrogatories Written questions submitted by one party in a lawsuit to another party in that suit, which must be answered in writing and under oath.

intervenor brief A brief that is voluntarily filed by an attorney who is not a part of the case but who has been granted permission to present some legal argument before the court.

judgment The relief awarded by a court after a final determination of the rights and obligations of the parties before the court.

judgment creditor The party seeking to execute on the judgment.

judgment debtor The party who must pay the judgment.

judgment notwithstanding the verdict An order made by a judge, usually in response to a motion by a party, in cases where there is evidence to support only one verdict, but the jury fails to return that verdict.

judicial admission An admission that is placed into evidence and that can be presented to the court at the time of the trial.

jurisdiction The power or authority of a court to hear a particular case.

jury instructions An explanation of the legal principles that the jury must apply to the facts of a case in reaching the verdict, and the procedures that the jury must follow as they attempt to reach a verdict.

jury profile A narrative description of the characteristics of the ideal jury that you would like to assemble in the case.

laches An equitable principle, similar to a statute of limitations, that prevents lawsuits from being maintained after a delay of time, where the defendant would be unfairly prejudiced because of the delay.

leading question A question that suggests the answer.

legal error An error in the way the law is interpreted or applied to a situation.

limited jurisdiction Authority to hear only certain kinds of cases.

limited production A document production in which only those documents requested are produced.

local rules of court Rules that are adopted by individual courts and apply only in those courts.

long-arm statute A statute allowing states to exercise jurisdiction over nonresident defendants.

lower court Another term for a trial court.

mediation A form of settlement that uses a third person to help the parties resolve their differences.

mediator The individual in mediation who helps the parties come to an agreement regarding their differences.

medical diary A document in which the client keeps track of medical treatment, daily health complaints, type and amount of medication, mileage to physicians' offices, and other related medical expenses.

memorandum of points and authorities A legal argument in the form of a discussion or analysis of the law that applies to the case.

mock deposition A deposition rehearsal to prepare the client for the actual deposition.

mock jury A group of independent individuals chosen to reflect the probable makeup of the actual jury.

mock trial A practice trial prior to the date of the actual trial.

motion A request for an order from the court, usually dealing with a pending case.

motion for a directed verdict A motion made during a jury trial, requesting that the judge tell the jury how they should decide the case.

motion for a judgment notwithstanding the verdict A motion asking the court to have the verdict and its judgment set aside because the court is convinced that a group of reasonable individuals would not have reached such a verdict and that the jury's decision is wrong as a matter of law.

motion for a more definite statement A motion made in response to a complaint in which the defendant challenges the clarity or specificity of the complaint.

motion for a new trial A motion made after a trial requesting that the judge set aside the verdict or judgment and grant a new trial to the parties.

motion for a protective order A motion made during discovery asking the court to limit a discovery request.

motion for a summary judgment A motion requesting that judgment be entered immediately because there are no disputed factual issues in the case.

motion for change of venue A request from a party that the court transfer the case to a proper court.

motion for compulsory examination A motion asking the court to order a requested physical or mental examination.

motion for enlargement of time A motion requesting additional time for an appeal, including the reasons that the additional time is needed and the number of additional days required.

motion for judgment on the pleadings   A motion claiming that the allegations in the pleadings are such that no controversial issues remain and that judgment can be entered for only one party.

motion for relief from a judgment or order   A request of the court by one party to set aside any judgment, order, or proceeding.

motion in limine   A motion or request made of the court, usually at the start of a trial and outside the presence of the jury.

motion to amend   A request by one party to the court to allow a change in the content of a pleading.

motion to compel   A request by one party to the court for an order requiring the other side to comply with a discovery request.

motion to dismiss   A request that the court dismiss or strike the case.

motion to quash service of summons   A request that the court declare that the service of the complaint and summons is invalid, either because the court lacks jurisdiction over the defendant or because of some procedural problem with the service itself.

motion to quash the return of the service   Made by a defendant who claims he was improperly served with the summons and complaint.

motion to strike   A request made to the court to delete part or all of a pleading; can also refer to a request made during trial to delete testimony.

motion to tax costs   A motion made after trial challenging the costs of suit that are claimed by the prevailing party.

moving party   The party making a motion.

mutual release   The process of each party relinquishing its claims against the other party.

non obstante veredicto   Notwithstanding the verdict.

non-produce   Documents that are not produced to a party initiating a request for production of documents because they are not responsive to the request.

non-responsive documents   Documents that are not responsive to a request for production of documents and thus do not have to be produced to the party initiating the request for production.

notice   A formal, written notification to the person to be examined and to the other parties.

notice of appeal   The only document required for the filing of an appeal, which lists the party or parties taking the appeal, the judgment, the order or the portion of the judgment appealed (including the caption of the case in the trial court), and the court to which an appeal is taken.

notice of hearing on motion   The part of a written motion that describes the nature of the motion being made and tells when and where a hearing on the motion will occur.

notice of intent to take deposition upon written questions   Notice of the intent to take a deposition by written questions, listing the name and address of the person who must answer the question and the name of the officer before whom the deposition is to be taken; if the deponent is a non-party, a subpoena must be served.

notice of intent to take oral deposition   A notice of an intent to take the deposition of a party or witness, which includes the date, time, and place of the deposition, the name of the attorney taking the deposition, and the name and address of the person whose deposition is to be taken.

notice of intent to take oral deposition by non-stenographic means   A notice sent to an opposing counsel of an intent to take a deposition post-judgment by use of only a dictating machine or a tape recorder, with no court reporter present.

notice of removal   A document presented to the court in a case where concurrent jurisdiction exists between state and federal court, stating that the defendant is exercising his right to transfer the case from the state court to a federal district court.

open stipulation   An agreement between parties or their attorneys that a defendant need not answer a complaint within the time directed by law and need not answer until specifically notified by plaintiff to do so.

oral argument   The presentation of the basis for the appeal before the court of appeals.

oral deposition   A deposition at which the deponent is actually present to answer an attorney's questions aloud.

order   A ruling from the court, usually after a motion.

order shortening time   A ruling from the court, often in connection with motions, allowing a moving party to give less notice of a hearing on a motion than is required by statute.

original jurisdiction   The authority of a court to first hear or try the case.

overbroad   A discovery request seeking much more information than the other party needs or could ever use.

page-line deposition summary   A summary covering the deposition testimony in the order in which it occurred in the deposition itself.

partial release   The relinquishment of some claims and the retention of others by a party.

pendent jurisdiction   Authority of the federal courts to hear a matter normally within the jurisdiction of state courts; exists where that matter is combined with a claim that is within the authority of the federal courts.

permissive counterclaim   A claim by a defendant against a plaintiff that is allowed, but not required, to be asserted in a lawsuit; it need not arise out of the same circumstances described in the complaint.

permissive joinder   A concept allowing multiple parties to be joined in one lawsuit as plaintiffs or defendants as long as there is some common question of fact or law.

personal jurisdiction   The power or authority of the court to make a ruling affecting the parties before the court.

personal service   Notice of a lawsuit or other proceeding, which is given to a party by personally delivering a copy of the papers to that party.

petition   An initial document or pleading filed in court requesting some relief; in some jurisdictions the term is used instead of complaint.

petition for certiorari   A request for a rehearing before the United States Supreme Court.

petition for rehearing   A request that a higher court's decision be reviewed.

petition for writ of certiorari   A document filed in the Supreme Court requesting that the court grant a hearing in the case.

physical or mental examination   The examination of a party in a lawsuit to determine factual information about the physical or mental condition of that party.

plaintiff   The party who files a lawsuit.

pleadings   Documents filed in a lawsuit describing the claims and defenses of the parties.

post-judgment deposition   A deposition that can be taken after judgment, with only a dictating machine or a tape recorder, with no court reporter present.

post-judgment interrogatories   Written questions that the judgment debtor must answer in writing about his or her assets.

post-trial garnishment   A separate, but ancillary, lawsuit, filed in the court that rendered the judgment, to permit the judgment creditor to collect on a judgment.

prayer The part of a complaint in which the relief is requested; sometimes known as the "wherefore" clause or demand.

preliminary injunction A court order made prior to final judgment in the case, directing that a party take some action or refrain from taking some action until the trial in the case takes place.

primary source Books that contain the actual law, i.e., case reporters, codes, constitution.

privilege against self-incrimination A privilege that prevents a person in a criminal case from being a witness against himself.

privilege log A log listing all documents identified as being protected from discovery under either the attorney-client privilege or the work-product privilege.

privileged documents Documents that are protected from production because of attorney-client privilege.

procedural law Laws containing the methods used to enforce our rights or to obtain redress for the violation of our rights.

proof of service Written verification that papers have been delivered to a party, detailing when, where, and how the papers were delivered.

proof of service by mail Verification that a pleading, motion, or other document has been served by mailing a copy of the document to another party or attorney; sometimes referred to as a certificate of mailing.

protective order An order protecting disclosure of confidential material or trade secrets from production.

punitive damages Damages assessed to punish the defendant for some type of extremely offensive conduct; also known as exemplary damages.

qualified denial A type of answer denying all of the allegations of the complaint except those that are specifically admitted.

quasi in rem jurisdiction Authority of a court to hear a case based on the fact that the defendant owns property that is located within the state, even though that property is not the subject of the lawsuit, but is willing to satisfy a judgment from that property.

quiet title An order clarifying ownership of real property.

quiet title action A type of lawsuit in which the court is asked to determine ownership to real property.

real party in interest The person who is entitled to the relief sought in a complaint; usually the plaintiff, but in some cases the real party in interest is represented by another in a lawsuit.

record The original papers filed with the court.

redact The process of deleting irrelevant or privileged information on a document before copying the document for production to the party initiating the request for production of documents.

redacted page A page on which information on a document is deleted before copying the document for production to the party initiating the request for production of documents.

release A signed statement authorizing someone to give confidential information to an attorney.

reply In federal practice, the written response to a counterclaim.

representation letter A letter from an attorney to a new client establishing the ground rules of the litigation, including fees, billing rates, retainer, and work to be performed by the law firm.

request for a physical or mental examination A request for a party to submit to a physical or mental examination to determine the extent of the physical or mental injuries claimed by that party.

request for admission A request filed by one party in a lawsuit asking the second party in the lawsuit to admit to the truthfulness of some fact or opinion.

request for documents A request by one party in a lawsuit to the other party in that suit to allow the first party access to documents that are relevant to the subject matter of the suit.

request for the production of documents and entry upon land for inspection A request for the inspection or duplication of documents or other materials that are relevant to the subject matter of the litigation, including a request for permission to enter land for inspection purposes.

rescission An order rescinding or voiding a contract.

responsive documents Documents that are responsive to a request for production of documents and must be produced to the party initiating the request for production.

restitution An order to return money or property, usually paid in connection with a contract that was subsequently rescinded.

retainer agreement An agreement between an attorney and client setting forth the fee arrangement.

reverse Action by appellate court overturning a lower court decision.

reverse and remand Action by appellate court overturning a lower court decision and sending it back to the trial court for retrial.

rules of professional conduct Rules regulating ethical standards for legal professionals; see canons of ethics.

secondary source Books that explain or describe the law.

service of process Delivering a copy of the summons and complaint in a lawsuit to the defendant in a method prescribed by law.

settlement An agreement or contract between disputing parties in which differences are resolved.

settlement agreement A contract between two or more parties to settle a case; it involves the voluntary, mutual assent of the parties and the give-and-take element of consideration; the agreement must be legal and must be made by parties with the capacity to contract.

settlement brochure A multiple page portfolio that seeks to compile all information relevant to settlement negotiations.

settlement letter A detailed account of the information needed to determine the benefit of settling a case.

settlement summary A summary of all essential information outlining the benefits of settling the case at an early stage in the litigation.

shadow jury A secret jury selected by the law firm or the outside consulting firm to attend the trial and report on its impression of the trial witnesses, exhibits, and attorneys.

special appearance An appearance in a lawsuit for a limited purpose, often for the sole purpose of questioning the court's jurisdiction.

specific denial A type of answer in which the defendant specifically replies to each of the contentions alleged in the complaint.

specific performance An order requiring a party to perform a contract.

statement of the facts A narrative of all facts involved in the case.

statement of the settlement A recap of the settlement the client believes is reasonable.

statute of limitations A time limit in which to initiate a lawsuit or be barred from doing so.

stay   The act of halting or suspending a proceeding by order of a court.

stipulation enlarging time   An agreement between parties or their attorneys extending the time for filing or serving some document.

stipulation to amend the complaint   Written agreement among all parties allowing the plaintiff to make certain changes in the complaint.

subject matter jurisdiction   The authority that a court has to hear a particular type of case.

subpoena   An official document issued by the clerk of court commanding a person to be present for deposition or trial.

subpoena duces tecum   A subpoena listing documents that the non-party witness must produce at his or her deposition.

subscription   The signature at the end of a pleading.

substantive law   The area of law that creates, defines, or explains our rights.

summons   A document issued by the court explaining that the defendant has been sued and that he has a certain time limit in which to respond; a copy of the summons is served on the defendant along with the complaint.

supersedeas bond   A promise, supported by a form of surety, to secure suspension of a judgment and delay execution upon the judgment, pending the outcome of the appeal.

supreme court   A court of last resort.

surety   An individual or company that agrees to pay to the appellee the amount of any damages sustained due to the delay caused by the appeal if the appellant loses the appeal.

telephone deposition   A deposition during which the deponent and the attorney defending the deposition are present in one location and the attorney taking the deposition is in another location asking the questions by telephone; the deponent's answers are recorded by a court reporter who could be at either location.

temporary restraining order   A court order requiring that a party take some action or refrain from certain conduct, usually issued by the court without a formal hearing at the beginning of a lawsuit upon the application of one party; it remains in effect only until a hearing can be scheduled, and at that time may be replaced with a preliminary injunction.

third-party complaint   In federal practice, a claim asserted by a defendant in a lawsuit against a party not named in the original complaint; the claim must be related to the circumstances described in the original complaint.

third-party garnishee   A person or a company that is holding assets belonging to a judgment debtor.

tickler system   A calendaring system.

topical deposition summary   A deposition summary that organizes the testimony into specific subject areas.

transcript   The official daily record of the court proceedings; the verbatim copy of a deposition.

trial   A court hearing where the parties present their evidence to a judge or jury, who decide the case.

trial box   A box consisting of all supplies needed during the trial.

trial brief   A legal brief explaining the legal issues involved in the case and the law that demonstrates the validity of the position the attorney has taken in relation to those issues.

trial court   A court where the parties to a lawsuit file their pleadings and present evidence to a judge or jury.

trial notebook   A binder that contains, in complete or summary form, everything necessary to prosecute or defend a case.

trust account A special bank account maintained by attorneys into which they deposit all money belonging to their clients or other parties.

unduly burdensome An objection to answering a set of interrogatories because of such factors as an excessive amount of time required to answer, excessive expenses involved in finding the answer to the interrogatories, a request for information for which there is no compelling need, placing a burden on the responding party that outweighs the benefit gained by the requesting party, and disclosure of information that has already been disclosed in other discovery requests.

venue The proper geographical area in which to maintain an action.

verification A statement under penalty of perjury that the contents of a document are true to the best of the knowledge of the person verifying; sometimes attached to pleadings and responses to discovery requests.

voir dire The process by which jurors are questioned to determine any bias that they might have that would affect their ability to be fair and impartial in the case.

warehouse approach The type of document production in which both relevant and irrelevant documents are produced without any type of organization.

with prejudice A stipulated dismissal by which the claim cannot be brought to court again at any time in the future.

vithout prejudice A stipulated dismissal by which the lawsuit can be brought at another time in any court that has the jurisdiction to hear the case.

work product privilege A privilege preventing the opposing party in a lawsuit from using the discovery process to obtain letters, memos, documents, records, and other tangible items that have been produced in anticipation of litigation or that have been prepared for the trial itself.

writ of execution A document issued by a court that allows a party to seize and sell property and use the proceeds to satisfy the judgment.

INDEX

NOTE: Italicized entries refer to non-text material. Italicized entries following the word "defined" refer to definitions placed in the margins of the pages referred.